AF553885

Information Services

Information Services

Dr. Vineet Gupta

Mahaveer & Sons

(Publishers & Distributors)

New Delhi–110002

Edition 2017
© Reserved
ISBN-978-81-8377-106-1

MAHAVEER & SONS
3072/28, First Floor, Gola Market, Darya Ganj,
New Delhi–110002

PRINTED IN INDIA

Published by Mahaveer & Sons, Publisher & Distributors,
H-2/16 Ansari Road Near Shiv Mandir, Daryaganj,
New Delhi-110002. Prinited at Himanshu Printers, Delhi.

Preface

This book is devoted to the information technology and information services. With the development of science and technology and invention of new technical devices like computer, distances of two countries have been reduced in seconds and minutes. A number of national and multinational agencies are running in different countries and providing quick information services. This book ranges from the whole spectrum of the new information technologies and their relevance to the whole of information services, induding such things as library services, records management and archives etc. Furthermore this book is too much concentrated on the individual who operate these services: the 'information progressional' for want a better term. The term 'information services' has been tried to defined as that it refers to all of those activities which are traditionally grouped into defined function within an organization and assign titles such as 'library', 'information department' archive etc.

This book is arranged in such way that it begins and ends with applications, with the technology sandwiched in the middle. The introductory chapter of this book deals the purposes and main objectives of this book. Second chapter examines the nature of information services. Third, fourth and fifth chapter are concentrated on the technology–divided into three components, hardware, software and telecommunications. Chapter seven discusses the role, importance and benifits of information technology in the field of information services. In chapter eight the fouls falls upon the discussion of legal security and conservation implications of information technology. The scope of ninth chapter is widened. It is concerned with the introduction and use of Information Technology in more general terms. Chapter tenth has examined role of information professionals in future. Further education and training, the effect of information technology on the organization and transmission systems and multimedia are discussed with examples in the subsequent chapter of this book.

Contents

1
Introduction

There are many books dealing with information technology in its various guises. There are a smaller number giving general introductions to IT for information managers, and others which deal with particular aspects of IT for information services: microcomputing for libraries, online searching, etc.

This book takes a different slant from the others. In it, we try to consider the whole spectrum of the new information technologies (a daunting prospect in itself) and their relevance to the whole of information services, including such things as library services, records management and archives, etc. Indeed, we go beyond this, in considering an expanded role for information services in introducing and operating the new technologies on an organization-wide basis.

Furthermore, we will very much concentrate on the individuals who operate these services: the 'information professionals', for want of a better term. This involves an examination, not just of the future role for such people in the IT age, although this is important, but equally what they have to contribute towards information/handling in a wider context, beyond the traditional limits of 'library/information work'. The integration of, and synergy between, information services in their traditional role, and on a broader canvas, will be a major theme of the book. We will also examine the continuing relevance of the skills of the information professions and show their continuing, indeed enhanced, relevance in an IT environment.

We hope that this book will serve several purposes. First, it should serve as an introduction to the whole area of information technology as it relates to information professionals, and to the activities of information services. Second, it should prove useful as a sourcebook, since we have included a large number of references to enable the reader to follow up any particular point. (Apart from anything else, this will give access to the details which we have not been able to include, if this book is to be of reasonable length.) In choosing the references, we have tried to include as much recent material as possible, i.e. from 1987 onwards, and also to present 'classic' older material. Despite the rate of technical advance, many general principles remain unchanged, and are too often forgotten, and we have tried to bring this point out clearly.

Although we have not, for reasons of space, been able to deal with any topic in very great detail, we have given concrete examples wherever possible, either as a description in the test, or as a reference. This, we hope, will anchor flights of fancy in concrete reality.

We have deliberately emphasized applications rather than technologies *per se,* and have tried to present as broad a picture as possible, providing only that there is some relevance to information services.

We believe that only by considering the whole picture of developments, trends, and applications in the new information technology, and emphasizing in particular areas of integration, convergence, and overlap, will the true significance of technological advance be fully appreciated. We have, therefore, tried to set particular technologies into context: both the context of the rest of IT, and also the context of likely application areas.

In view of the criticism which are now being publicly expressed concerning the value gained from the introduction of information technology in business, commerce and government, we will take some time to look at what pay-off may realistically be expected from IT within information services. This does not mean a detailed analysis of benefits to be gained in particular cases, which could have only local value; rather we will consider such ideas as value-added services, the information-rich environment and the trend towards information resource management; we believe that it is this sort of area that the true pay-off from IT application will be found.

It is often considered that the new information technologies will exert a dehumanizing effect on their users, forcing everyone into a mould suitable for the machine. Experience suggests that this is not necessarily the case, and that a humanistic 'user-centred' approach to IT application is not merely more pleasant, but much more effective. Such an approach is particularly appropriate to information service operations, and information professionals are well suited to promote it within their organizations as a whole. This will be another major theme of the book.

We have arranged the book so that it begins and ends with applications, with the technology sandwiched in the middle; an appropriate enough metaphor for our approach to the subject. After an initial examination of the nature of information services in Chapter 2, Chapters 3-6 are devoted to technology; divided into three components of hardware, software and telecommunications, but emphasizing areas of integration and overlap. Chapter 7 considers, from a viewpoint of general principle rather than detail, the impact of IT on information services, and its significance and benefits. In Chapter 9, the scope is widened, to look at the introduction and use of IT in more general terms, emphasizing the user-centred approach. Although entirely relevant to information services, this is of wider applicability. Chapter 10 changes the focus somewhat, to look at the role of information professionals in the future. Other chapters examine some of the consequences of IT: legal aspects, education and training, etc.

In short, we hope that readers of this book will gain a better appreciation of what IT can and cannot offer in the provision of information services; what the real benefits are likely to be; and what role information professionals, and their skills, can play in the future. Not least, we hope to convey an enthusiasm (tempered with reality) for the new technologies, and for the ways in which they can, if used properly, improve information provision.

2
Information Services

This book is concerned with information technology and information services. Our first task was to decide upon the relevant technologies and the 'information services' to which we would be referring; it transpired that the former was by far the easier of the two. How one defines information services depends entirely on one's viewpoint. Proponents of the information society, and the disciples of the philosophy that end users will ultimately take care of all their own information needs themselves, would include all office workers, teachers, business and management consultants and consequently regard all their activities as information services. Others like ourselves, assume that it refers to all of those activities which are traditionally grouped into defined functions within an organization, and assigned titles such as 'library', information department', 'archive' etc.

To attempt to define too narrowly the activities that are encompassed by information services is, perhaps, counter-productive and may be we should take instead as our yardstick the dictionary definition of information: informing, telling, things told. Knowledge, items of knowledge, news. However, this takes us no further forward in deciding upon the extent of our coverage; for the sake of simplicity, and so that we can limit the scope of our comments so that they can be of real value and applicability, we have decided to be pragmatic and adopt the more conventional idea of information services. We appreciate that this will exclude many groups who function in an information capacity, but we believe that there is a definite trend towards a blurring of the boundaries between information specialists and those who would not normally regard themselves as part of any information profession - a subject to which we will be returning in later chapters.

In an attempt to bring order into this seemingly nebulous and ill-defined world of information services, one can categorize services as R & D commercial, corporate, library services, archives etc. It is an artificial classification to a great degree since the way in which information units operate, and the type of information that they provide, is also heavily influenced by corporate philosophy, organizational structure, the personalities of management, and the information workers themselves. But in all cases, the common requirement is that hey provide accurate and relevant information in the appropriate format and at the right time. In other words - they are *managers* of information. Another approach is to differentiate between medical, scientific and technical, sales and marketing, and general business information services. Again, all provide the same type of service; the reference sources may vary and the emphasis be slightly different but they perform similar functions.

In essence there are two parts to any information services— the responsive and the pro-active - which interact to varying degrees depending upon the nature of the customers of the service. The responsive side deals with specific enquires as they happen, and for commercial organizations with specific product questions they are generally predictable and repetitive. One is usually working in specific subject areas and many responses can be standardized. The need is for comprehensive and up-to-date information on products, one's own and ones competitors, and on the particular subject areas; in essence one is expected to be an expert in the field. The service may cover standards and patents, specialist literature, news, perhaps even product complaints and customer relations. In most instances, the response needs to be immediate, and accurate, but one can be pro-active and ensure that systems are developed to aid the information professional in that task and provide the necessary information as and when required.

To take a more specific case, in the medical information department of a pharmaceutical company one has a variety of customers: members of the public, the medical and allied professions. Apart from the technical side, there are ethical and legal constraints upon how one deals with such enquiries. For example, all enquiries from patients concerning therapy must be referred to their doctor and one must not advertise a prescription product direct to a patient; all medical information given out to doctors and pharmacists must be covered by the terms of the product licence; advice on treatment which is not covered by the product licence must be made with reference to published literature; and information on doses and adverse drug reactions are needed on the spot. Nearly all of these eventualities can be covered by maintaining suitable databases i.e. by being pro-active.

In more general terms, information services which are responsible for any product enquiry or complaint service must have access to relevant and accurate information immediately. Failure to react appropriately can have serious legal and, in turn, financial consequences for the company.

Sales and marketing information is usually for internal consumption only and covers sales data and competitor intelligence. Strictly speaking, it is not of instant importance but accuracy and the facility for manipulating data so that the most advantageous course of action can be taken in both the short and long term is vital.

At a higher level, information services provide support to those responsible for corporate policy and strategic decisions. Interestingly, longer-term strategies tend to be based on information which is short term in nature and constantly changing e.g. market developments, competitor activities. News articles give an indication of how the world sees an industry or company, specialist publications provide the company with information on their industry sector, and sales and market share data form the basis of projections and models. Data has to be supplied on a continuing basis to cover these eventualities, and on request when a crisis looms and instant decisions have to be made. Inaccurate or late information is at best useless and at worst disastrous for the company concerned, possibly threatening its very existence. In general, commercial information is random, uncontrolled, unpredictable and could be found anywhere. It is often disjointed and usually of short-term relevance.

In contrast, scientific and medical information tends to be systematic, well organized with recognized sources of information. It is scrutinized and verified by peer review and has a longer term impact upon an organization. In the scientific and research field, having full and accurate information is of importance in the longer term. A company carrying out research into a new device or pharmaceutical product will at some stage need to check that it is not already covered by a patent, and whether or not another company is close to launching the same or similar product. Failure to identify existing patents and locate information in technical and medical journals may result in the company investing large amounts of money in pointless research and development. Comprehensive searching of data sources is required not just on a one off but on a continuing basis.

So far we have talked about 'information services', but libraries are at least as important, if not more so, since they provide many of the basic sources upon which other information services rely. The assumption that libraries are solely repositories of books is no longer a valid one. They do indeed perform an important function in that they are an easy and convenient means of accessing published literature. But more and more they are extending their service to information provision. Public libraries are now offering business information services on a commercial basis to companies, and libraries within organizations overlap, with or are part of, wider information activities. Unlike the specialist units offering commercial and product support, many libraries cover a wide range of subject areas. Since it is not feasible to maintain a comprehensive collection on all topics, in many cases they provide access to information through online systems and by acting as a referral service.

Apart from acquiring published literature and data, many organizations generate vast quantities of documentation. Much of it is of short-term importance e.g. general correspondence, office administration, but there remains a core which can form a valuable source of information for future work. It poses problems in terms of the volume of material that has to be handled, and the amount of storage space that it occupies. The function of archive and records management may be part of administration or of information services, or it may exist as a unit on its own. The nature of the stored material varies: pictures, text, chemical structures, data, newspaper articles, sounds, film, and is dependent upon the activity of the organization. So a system may have to be adopted which can handle all forms of material as well being capable of identifying relevant material, and giving quick and easy access to it. There may be legal obligations on retaining documents for specified periods of time for example data from clinical trials, research information for establishing patent priority, details of complaints in cases of product liability.

Information services as a whole, must be able to find relevant and supporting documents and data, and to verify, substantiate and put that information into context. Procedures must enable the user to obtain, record, handle, input data and records in a consistent and standardized way. Information technology impinges upon all of these: information retrieval, information processing, information presentation, and storage of information which can be in the form of bibliographic references, full text, sales data, corporate intelligence, customer and client information, voice, still and moving pictures. We mentioned earlier that information professionals must be managers of information but, as will be demonstrated throughout this book, they must also be managers of technology.

3
Information Technology

In Chapters 4, 5 and 6 we will give an outline of the most important new information technologies affecting information services. We make no attempt to give in-depth technical descriptions, for two reasons. First, there are already many excellent detailed discussions available, and it would be pointless to duplicate them. Second, it is of strictly limited value to go into great technical detail in a book, when the pace of change in the area is so great that anything which is written becomes rapidly outdated in detail. We shall instead concentrate on important principles and general trends, with the aim of giving the reader an adequate appreciation of the nature of the technology to be able to see its significance for information services, and for information professionals. In particular, these chapters are intended as a background and basis for the rest of the book, which deals with the applications, and implications, of technology. We hope that these chapters are sufficiently well-balanced in their coverage of the whole of the new technologies to be sufficient in themselves for an understanding of the material in the rest of this book. Also, they should give a good basis for further reading on the latest developments in IT. A substantial list of references is given, to lead the reader further into subjects which we have been able to treat only in outline.

Although we have endeavoured to give a well-balanced coverage of all relevant topics, we have given particular attention to aspects of primary importance to information services (for example information retrieval systems). We have also tried to identify topics of particular significance for the future (for example, parallel processing architectures), and given them particular emphasis.

We have, purely for convenience, structured this material into the familiar three categories of hardware, software, and telecommunications, and have provided reference lists at the end of each chapter. We are aware that this will be regarded by some as a rather outmoded distinction, but we consider that it still has some value in organizing this type of material. Nonetheless, we have tried to emphasize the interrelations and interconnections between them, which are becoming of increasing importance, and (Sometimes) a source of confusion. Indeed, one of our main themes is the convergence and integration of both technologies and their applications. This implies essentially that the same function may be fulfilled in entirely different ways.

Convergence and integration

For a simple example of this, think of a computer graphics system, such as would be used in chemical molecular modelling systems, or in computer-aided design systems in engineering. A system of this sort will need to display a picture of an object such as a molecule or a plan of a building, on the graphics terminal, and allow the user to rotate the picture, to view it from different angles. This may be done in one of three ways: by software, using a program on the controlling computer for the purpose; by hardware, where the instructions are literally wired into the terminal; or by 'firmware', software instructions permanently encoded into the terminal local intelligence. The same basic result is achieved in each case.

Consider the need to search a computerized database. In the early 1970s, this would have been done inhouse, by a batch search process. Later in that decade, with advances in telecommunications and software, external on-line searching would be more usual. In the 1980s, with improved processing power and cheaper magnetic storage, an interactive inhouse system would be considered. In the late 1980s, with the availability of optical storage media, and powerful microcomputers, the CD-ROM (compact disc - read only memory) solution could be appropriate. Again, the same result is being achieved by different combinations of technology.

Consider also the three types of software system of primary importance to information services: database management, text retrieval, and library automation. Initially, these were very different animals, doing different jobs in their different ways. However, increasingly, there has been a great overlap. Database systems now often include powerful text handling capabilities. Library systems are including more and more retrieval capability, perhaps in the form of catalogue query routines. Text retrieval systems are expanding their capabilities in several directions, to overlap with both of the others; by coping better with numerical information, for example, and by sprouting library automation offshoots. The result is that there is no longer a sharp distinction between the three types of system.

On the hardware level, there was a time when three types of computer (mainframe, mini, and micro) were clearly and obviously distinguishable. No longer: the development of categories such as 'supermini' and 'supermicro' initially confused the situation, while the ability to link machines together in telecommunications networks has introduced a further level of complexity.

Another aspect of convergence is seen in the way in which the introduction of new technology, initially thought of as enabling an existing function to be carried out more efficiently, tends to lead to entirely new ways of working. A word-processing system, for example, may be introduced as a straightforward replacement for typewriting, i.e. a better way of producing a typescript document. However, new possibilities soon present themselves: the output may be sent: to a typesetter, perhaps via a desktop publishing package, thus cutting out a stage of the publishing process; or electronic mail may be used to distribute the document, avoiding the need for paper copies; etc.

We can also see integrative and synergistic effects within the development of the new technologies themselves. In particular, advances in microprocessor technology lead to the incorporation of 'local intelligence' in other types of equipment: computer-controlled multiplexers, improving the effectiveness of network operation; intelligent' matrix printers, allowing, very versatile output for a low cost; etc.

These simple examples illustrate a general point; that it

is unwise, even if possible to try to visualize solutions to user requirements in terms of one clearly defined aspect of the new technologies. There is almost certainly a range of technical solutions, constantly changing as the technologies develop and overlap from which the 'best' may be selected by an appropriate combination components. This will be a theme to which we will return frequently.

There are surprisingly few books covering the whole field of information technology. One of the best, summarizing a lot of material clearly in a short space is that of is a little longer and more detailed. The text edited by is also very readable, though it has no coverage of teclecommunications. Jenny Rowley's book (1988) is a useful basic introduction from a library viewpoint, while the volume edited by gives a thorough overview of the whole area, oriented towards applications in information management.

4
Computer Hardware

Introduction

In this section we will review the general principles of the operation of present day computer hardware, and identify some trends and developments of importance to information specialists. After a brief historical overview of developments, we will look in turn at processing (including a survey of future developments, and parallel architectures in particular), storage, and input/output devices.

There are many excellent sources available which describe computer hardware in more detail than we will attempt; we list only a small selection of them, which we consider particularly useful. The book buy is the best single source from a library perspective. For a UK/European perspective, the books by are readable introductions, while that by is a little more advanced and detailed is an excellent standard textbook, while there are many American college texts providing introductory level material.

We have unashamedly taken many liberties of oversimplification, in trying to bring out the most significant points, and we recommend the sources listed for a fuller treatment, and for more illustrative examples than we have space for here.

In terms of balance, we will give considerable attention to peripherals (storage devices and input/output (I/O technology) compared with processing hardware. This reflects both the significance of peripherals (particularly for interactive input and output) for user acceptance of computer systems, and also their increasing importance in cost terms. I/O and storage peripherals account for over 50% of the hardware costs of a typical microcomputer system of the late 1980s, whereas the processing unit costs amount to less than 25%.

Development of Computer Systems

Although it is often thought that the programmable computer has a history of only a few decades, its antecedents are to be found much further back in time.

Machines to aid people in day-to-day numerical computations have been around for a very long time indeed; the abacus for example. Similarly, the idea of mechanical control of a series of actions, the forerunner of program control, was known to Muslim scientists of the medieval world, and transferred to Europe by the fourteenth century; here, it is was applied first in clock making, with cathedral clocks varying their tunes according to the hour. By the eighteenth century, program control was being used in the manufacture of life-like 'automata'; dolls which could, for example, draw pictures, or play musical instruments; One example, still working in can write any chosen sequence of up to forty letters, under the control of pegs in its back.

Mechanical calculating machines also have a long history. Leonardo da Vinci made drawings of such a machine, but never constructed a working versin. The first operating calculator was built by Blaise Pascal, the French mathematician, who in 1642, at the age of 19, produced a gear-driven Pascal, the French mathematician, who in 1642, at the age of 19, produced a gear-driven adding machine to assist in calculation in his father's tax office. Calculators were improved on over the next two centuries, though only capable of carrying out a single function.

Something like the modern idea of program control was first introduced industrially in the weaving process, during the eighteenth century, and loom control was brought to a new level of sophistication by Joseph-marie Jacquard in 1805. His machines used a sequence of punched cards to control the threads of the weaving process; substituting a different set of cards altered the weaving pattern, allowing the rapid production of very different complex patterns in the woven cloth. To weave a portrait of own face, for example, required 25000 cards. Whereas the control in earlier machines resided in the machinery itself, in the loom the control instructions were entirely separate; in the set of punched cards.

These machines were, of course, designed to carry out a single function - the weaving loom could not do anything but weave - although the program control enabled easy variation within that function. It was not until the middle of the nineteenth century that the idea of a general-purpose computing machine evolved in the work of Charles Babage. His major contribution was the realization that, rather than designing machines to carry out a very small number of carefully predefined operations, it should be possible to design a machine which could carry out an infinite number of possible sequences of operations. The actual operations required in any particular application would be specified by the programming of the machine. This concept of stored program control provides the basis for all modern computes. Babage also introduced many other modern concepts, for example the idea of separate storage and arithmetic units in a computer, and the input of programs and data on punched cards. He set out to construct a machine which could calculate, for example, tide-tables, life-expectation statistics, or astronomical data; the formula for calculation, and the numerical data to be used, being specified on a stack of punched cards. The actual calculation would be performed by mechanical gears, driven by steam power. Unfortunately, the engineering technology of Babage's time was insufficiently developed to enable him to implement his designs successfully. Although he constructed a 'Difference Engine' to demonstrate the feasibility of his ideas (an early example of prototyping), his fully-blown 'Analytical Engine', which would have needed 50000 moving parts, was never completed. Its remnants are to be seen in the Science Museum in London, UK. If it had worked, it would undoubtedly have qualified as the first true computer, and his co-worker Ada, Lady Lovelace, as the first programmer; she prepared complex mathematical procedures to be used on the machine, but which could never be tested. Her name is perpetuated in the widely-used Ada programming language.

Meanwhile, a contemporary of Babbage, and also an Englishman, had been laying another of the foundations of the digital computer, although its significance was not, of course, realized at the time. George 'Boole, a self-taught schoolteacher from Lincolnshire, UK, developed a mathematical theory, showing how some quite complex logical problems could be expressed in symbols, manipulated, and solved, providing that everything in the problem could be expressed in terms of variables having only two states regarded at the time as an interesting topic in pure mathematics, was to find practical application a hundred years later, with the development of electronic devices.

Babage's ideas were not followed up, indeed were largely forgotten in subsequent decades. Machine handling of information, albeit without the program control aspect, became widespread around the turn of the century, particularly in the form of single-purpose calculating machines, and electrical punched card equipment. The latter was used for accountancy, tabulation, the handling of statistics, and a variety of other tasks, each performed by a single-purpose machine, using punched cards to store and sort information. The pioneer of punched-card systems was the American engineer Herman Hollerith, whose first conspicuous success was the mechanization of the analysis of the 1890 US census results. Subsequent enthusiastic adoption of punched-card technology in the business world led to the growth of company into an organization which eventually became IBM. Developments in punched-card systems up to 1930 resulted in highly-sophisticated data-processing systems, including the ability to handle textual, as well as numerical, information. The main drawbacks were speed limitations, inevitable in any electromechanical equipment, and the fact that decks of cards had to be carried between the single-purpose machines. (One of the authors actually used a punch-card system for information retrieval in a major research organization in the early 1970s, and can remember such a system still in use in a UK pharmaceutical company at the end of the decade; an example of how slowly this technology was ousted by the computer.)

Renewed interests in the stored-program concept, with its

implications for the feasibility of a general-purpose computing machine emerged in the 1930s. Alan Turing, a UK mathematician, established the principle that one simple machine could solve *any* logical problem, provided only that there was a clear sequence of steps to be followed; an 'algorithm'. Two years later, in 1938, Claude Shannon, a US technologist, showed how Boolean logic could be emulated mechanically, by the use of binary devices (i.e. those with only two possible states). Although no one realized it in 1938, the foundations of computing science were all in place. Turing had shown that the computer would be generally applicable and Shannon had told the world how it could be built'.

The impetus of the Second World War led to the development of the first true computers. Priority is difficult to assign, but it appears that Konard Zuse's machines, using second-hand mechanical telephone relays to perform logic and arithmetic, have a strong claim as the first operational general-purpose computers with program control; they were used in the design of aircraft. This claim has also been made for the UK Colossus machines: designed for code-breaking, they used valves, rather than relays, and consequently were much faster than Zuse's equipment. Small program changes could be entered by switch control but anything major required a physical rewiring.

In the USA, constructed the ABC (Atanosoft-Berry Computer) machine between 1939 and 1942. A special-purpose machine for solving simultaneous equations, with logic circuits using over 200 valves, the ABC was very influential on the design of later digital computers. In 1944 the IBM Mark I automatic computer was constructed using relays: only about a hundred times faster than a human operator with a calculator, it was said to sound 'like a convention of crickets' in operation. It was succeeded by the first really large electronic computer, completed shortly after the end of the war: using 19000 valves, it weighed 30 tons and was 100 ft long. This was ENIAC (Electronic Numerical Integrator and Computer), designed, like the Mark I, for calculation of artillery ballistic tables.

The developers of ENIAC, Mauchly an eckert, later designed and built UNIVAC (Universal Automatic Computer), the first commercial computer, and the forerunner of the first recognizable 'generation' of digital computers.

Computer Generations

The development of computer systems is generally described in terms of 'generations', with present-day machines being of the fourth generation. We will briefly outline developments in these terms, with a tabular summary given in Table 4.1.

First Generation

These were the large and clumsy machines produced during the late 1940s and most of the 1950s, almost all using vacuum tubes, requiring large amounts of power for their operation, and generating a great deal of heat. These machines were very unreliable, had primitive input and output facilities (punch cards, paper tape, etc.), and allowed only low-level language programming in machine code or perhaps Assembler (see Chapter 5). They were used almost exclusively for mathematical calculations and were restricted to a small community of specialist users.

Second Generation

In these machines, produced from the late 1950s, solid-state devices, particularly transistors, replaced vacuum tubes, resulting in smaller, more reliable, and much more powerful systems. Input/output and storage peripherals were improved, and the ability to transfer data between computers over telephone lines was introduced. The first high-level programming languages, such as Fortran, became available (see Chapter 5). Computes were still, on the whole, reserved for scientific and mathematical applications.

Third Generation

Third generation computers, which began to appear during the mid-1960s, were characterized by the use of 'integrated circuits', to replace conventional transistors; this again resulted in a decrease in size, and increase in speed and capacity. Disc storage was introduced on a large scale for holding data and input and output was further improved.

Table 4.1 Computer Generations

Generation:	1	2	3	4	5
Date	1940s-1950s	1950s-1960s	1960s-1970s	1970s-1980s	1990s
Typical memory size (Mbytes)	0.001	0.01-0.05	0.1-1	1-10	10-100
Typical processing speeds (MIPS)	0.01	0.05-0.5	1-5	5-50	1000-1000000
Languages	Machine code	Assembler	High-level	Integrated software	Natural language
Processing hardware	Valves	Transistors	Integrated circuits	VLSI	ULSI

A wide variety of high-level programming languages became available. Interactive computing appeared for the first time, supported by sophisticated systems software, such as time-sharing operating systems, and by the interactive terminal or visual display unit (VDU). Remote access to computer systems *via* telecommunications links became routine. Computer design became much less of a craft, with the introduction of whole families of compute systems, sharing a common architecture; the widely-used IBM System/360 series, the classic third generation computer, is a good example.

These factors led to a more widespread use of computes for both scientific and commercial purposes; although the mystique of the machine and its acolytes remained.

Fourth Generation

Generally taken as beginning in the early 1970s, the fourth generation of computes has resulted from the development of large-scale integration in semiconductor circuitry, resulting in an intensification of the trend towards more power in a smaller package. One result has been the diversification of computing away from the large mainframe computer, with the introduction of the minicomputer during the 1970s and the microcomputer during the next decade. Telecommunications links and networking have also had a great impact during the 1980s. These developments have brought computer power to an immensely wider community of users, and under local control. Although peripheral devices and software systems have improved to meet the new requirements, they in no way match the advances in raw processing power.

Fifth Generation

'Fifth generation' is a convenient shorthand term for the type of computer systems at present under development. These are characterized by such features as: novel architectures, giving vast processing power; enormous storage capacities; input and output largely by 'naturally language' speech; intelligent software systems; etc. We will discuss the ideas of the fifth generation later.

Development of Computing in Information Services

It slowly became apparent that large numbers of non-numerical operations were required, even in strictly mathematical calculations, and that computes represented a means for the efficient manipulation of 'symbols' in general, rather than just numbers. The electronic digital computer is therefore best regarded as a general-purpose symbol manipulator. From a relatively early date, the potential of the computer to deal with the sort of problems encountered in libraries and information services was recognized. The first applications of computers to library automation occurred in the USA in the late 1950s, and in the UK in the early 1960s. At about the same time, database producers, such as Chemical Abstracts Service, the National Library of Medicine, and the Institute for Scientific Information, embarked on extensive mechanization programmes, paving the way for on-line retrieval systems. Computer application to specialized forms of information processing, such as chemical structure handling, soon followed.

Library automation became widespread during the 1970s, fuelled by the increased capacities and capabilities of computer systems, including minicomputers directly under library control. The introduction of the microcomputer further extended this process, making local computing power available to all libraries and information centres.

Rapidity of Development

One of the hardest things to appreciate about the development of information technology in general, and of computer systems in particular, is the rapidity of developments. There are numerous anecdotal exemplifications of this. One says that if the motor car industry had experienced the same rate of improvement since 1945, then a Rolls Royce would, by the late 1980s, would travel three million miles on a gallon of petrol; for good measure, if more luggage space were required, the engine could be miniaturized so that nine would fit on a pin head.

Other indicators of the rapidity of change (again given for general effect, rather than absolute accuracy) are:

1. The time taken to multiply together pairs of ten digit numbers:
   Human with pencil and paper - 5 minutes for one pair
   IBM Mark I (1944) - 5 seconds for one pair
   ENIAC (1947) - 500 pairs in a second
   CRAY-1 supercomputer (1980) - 240 million pairs of 16 digit numbers in a second.
   This increase in processing speed is largely due to the use of faster switches (relays, valves, transistors....).
2. The size of (imaginary) computer equivalent in power to the human brain:
   1950 London
   1960 Royal Albert Hall
   1970 Double-decker bus
   1980 Saloon car
   1990 Television set
   The size reduction is due to change to semiconductor circuits, and then to an increasing degree of integration.
3. The cost (US dollars) of hardware required to store a 350 word document:

	Main memory	*Backup storage*
1950	1000 000	not available
1960	30 000	5000
1970	5000	1000
1975	1000	100
1980	100	6
1983	30	1
1985	3	0.1
1990	0.5	0.01

4. The cost of processing power in MIPS:

	1965	*1986*
Large business computer	9 000 000	600 000
Supercomputer	200 000	2500

Computer Processing

All computer memories, excluding only a very few of the earliest, have been based on physical elements which can exist in just one of two states: such an element corresponds to one *bit* of information. Binary symbols are used because electronic devices can store and process them rapidly and cheaply; voltages, charges, or currents may be either present or not. The basis of every digital computer, is, therefore, a processor consisting of a large number of electric circuits which manipulate electric currents and voltages. More specifically it is circuits such as *transistors,* switches of electric current, either allowing current to pass or block it. The term 'digital' is used to distinguish computers which handle discrete pieces of information, from 'analogue' computers which deal with continuous data. The latter are reserved for special tasks, especially for simulation, and will not be mentioned further.

The great majority of present-day computer processing is based upon silicon semiconductor technology, namely the ability to place many thousands of electronic components within a limited area of silicon, which has been 'doped' with carefully controlled amounts of other elements. Current research is now considering the use of memories based upon gallium arsenide, a compound with properties very similar to silicion, and devices based upon superconductivity or nonlinear refractive behaviour ('optical computers'). All of these are expected to allow significantly faster processing rates than silicon-based devices, but for the moment silicon is ubiquitous.

Semiconductor devices within the computer processor perform specific simple operations, such as addition or comparison. Very many of these, each performing their own specific function, are integrated together, into circuits on chips of silicon. This integration is the key to modern computer power; there are several degree of integration, as advances in chip design and miniaturization has allowed many more circuits to be included on a single chip:

small scale integration	SSI	tens of circuits
medium scale integration	MSI	hundreds
large scale integration	LSI	thousands
very large scale integration	VLSI	hundreds of thousands
ultra large scale integration	ULSI	millions

The current state of the technology allows VLSI to be used routinely in computer manufacture. Although it is possible to put all the functions of a small computer on a single chip, virtually all 'serious' computers consists of a number of individual chips, each with its own function, and combined closely together. A readable account of chip manufacture is given by Stevens (1986).

Information Representation and Manipulation

The physical devices have changed greatly, but principles of information representation and manipulation within digital computers have remained essentially the same. They are based on the manipulation of binary digits (or 'bits'), i.e. 0s and 1s.

The size of a computer can be described by the number of bits which its memory contains, but for most purposes larger units of storage are used to characterize machines. Generally these are, a *byte* which normally consists of 8 bits, and is sufficient to represent one character, and a *word* which can be of length 8, 16, or 32 bits, and which is the smallest unit of storage to which most of the computer's instructions can be applied. Memories are usually described as being of a size measured in kilobytes (kbytes) or megabytes (Mbytes).

Machines are therefore commonly described as 8-. 16-, or 32-bit word length (or 64 bit in the case of some super-computers). A larger word size allows room for storing larger numbers, giving scope for more instructions, and a larger range of associated information. In general, therefore, a lager word size implies a faster and more powerful computer, able to handle a larger amount of data, and to run more powerful software computer, able to handle a larger amount of data, and to run more powerful software systems. Microcomputers, for example, passed during the 1980s from the original 8-bit machines, such as the original Apples and Sinclairs, through the 16-bit computers typified by the IBM PC, to 32-bit systems.

Word length, then, gives a rough indication of the power of a computer. Another common way of expressing power is the time taken for the computer to execute one million instructions, measured in seconds; the speed of a computer system, or the microchip around which it is based, is often quoted in MIPS (million instructions per second) Unfortunately this can be a highly misleading figure, since it is very dependent on exactly what the instructions are, and may bear little relation to the system's observed speed in running 'real-life' software: not for nothing is this measure cynically defined as 'meaningless indicator of processor speed'.

The sets, or patterns, of bits which make up bytes and words are used to represent all information within a computer, whether program instructions or data items. The exact method of representation will vary from one machine type to another, particularly with respect to instruction formats. An 8-bit byte can accommodate 256 different bit patterns, and so is sufficient to allow for most of the characters which could be required to be printed, e.g. upper and lower case letters A-Z, together with the numbers 0-9 and a range of punctuation symbols, with allowance for non-printing characters such as end-of-line. The set of bit patterns corresponding to a set of characters is called a *character code:* standard codes are ASCII and EBCDIC.

Numbers are normally represented by one or more computer words. In the case of integers, the set of 8, 16, or 32 bits (according to the computer's word length) is treated as a binary integer (i.e. encoded in the notation of binary arithmetic). A real number is represented by dividing a word into two components, these being a simple decimal number (the mantissa) together with the power to which it must be raised (the exponent).

Computer architecture

A schematic diagram of a digital computer is shown below.

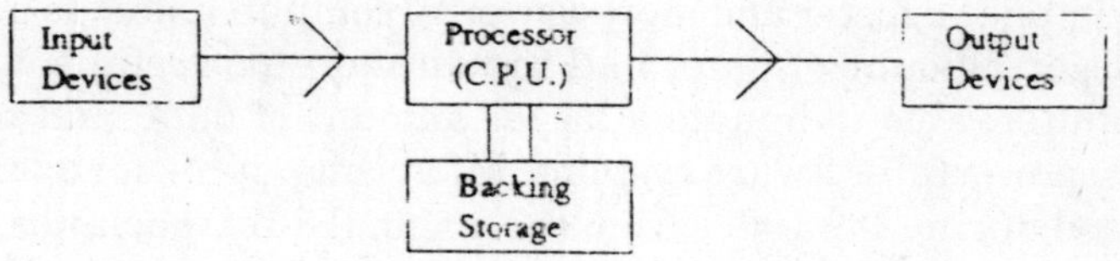

Diagram:

This is termed the 'von Neumann' architecture, a leader in computer development in the 1940s and 1950s. Its main feature is the central, single, processor, which accepts data from an input device, or from backing storage, performs some operation on it, and returns it to storage, or to an output device. This process is entirely, and necessarily, *serial* in nature, with one thing remorselessly following another. This type of machine is entirely general purpose, capable of running any program specified by its software.

This fundamental architecture has remained largely unchanged over the last three decades. Alternative computer architecture are now under consideration as part of 'fifth generation' computer research and will be discussed later.

Central Processing Unit

The Central Processing Unit (CPU) comprises three components: the control unit, the arithmetic unit, and the main store. All of these are composed of microelectronic devices, virtually always based, as we have seen, on silicon semiconductor technology. The main store is by far the largest component of the CPU, and is divided up into individual computer words, each of which may be accessed individually by its address.

The arithmetic unit contains a set of registers or accumulators, individual words of very high-speed storage into which words from the main store are copied, prior to instructions being applied to them. Attached to the registers is the circuitry which carries out the few hundreds of basic operations available to the computer. In essence, when an individual instruction needs to be carried out on some word in the main store, that word is copied into a register, the appropriate circuitry activated, and the register's contents copied back to the main store location.

The control unit extracts program instructions one at a time in the required sequence from their locations in the main store, decodes them, and issues instructions to the main store to access the required word, and to the arithmetic unit to activate the required instruction circuitry. A typical instruction word will be in three parts, these being:

* the code of the instruction which is to be executed.
* the identity of the register which is to be used.
* the address of the word in the main store which is to be processed.

Information is passed between the processor elements and the peripherals by a high-speed data channel, known as a 'bus'.

Types of Computer

Division of computers into clear-cut categories is increasingly difficult, since the boundaries are constantly shifting, and hybrid types of machine being introduced. There was a time, perhaps up to 1980, when the three main categories of system - mainframe, mini, and micro - were clearly distinguishable, on grounds of speed, memory size, storage capacity, etc. The increasing power in small chips, and the consequent ability to package raw computing power in very different ways, has led to an increasingly diverse and overlapping set of solutions to computer requirements. It has become largely, though not entirety, meaningless to attempt to give computer systems a single label, which makes their nature and use clear. As a general rule, the only reliable distinguishing features are price and function.

At the lower end of the spectrum, the *microcomputer*, or *personal computer* was introduced in the late 1970's, as a single-user, stand-alone 8-bit machine, of strictly limited capability. Since, then, this type of machine has greatly increased in power in its ability to run 'serious' software, and in the readiness with which it can be networked. There is still a reasonable distinction to be made between *home* and *business* micros, largely on grounds of price, memory size, and features such as integral hard-disc, now standard in all 'serious' business machines. Compatibility with the IBM business micro range is also generally regarded as essential, so as to take advantage of the vast range of IBM business software. The home/business distinction has been somewhat clouded during the late 1980s, by the arrival of very cheap machines, principally from Amstrad, which are able to fulfil many business needs. Micros may also have some degree of portability: the distinction is usually drawn between *desktop* (i.e. immovable), *laudable* (with considerable effort), and *laptop* (i.e. genuinely portable). In general, the more portable machines sacrifice power and functionality, and quality of display screen and keyboard, in return for their offer of greater flexibility of operation. The genuine 'handled' computer is still quite a way off. The problems of this degree of reduction in size are more associated with the display screen and keyboard than with anything to do with processing, in the longer term.

At the top of the microcomputer category is the *supermicro:* generally built around a powerful 32-bit processor, these are very fast machines, which are included in the micro definition because they are intended for a single user, or single purpose.

Microcomputers are very much thought of as an individual's machine - the 'personal' computer idea - even though they are increasingly being networked together, to form departmental, or organizational, systems.

Also associated with the microcomputer, is the *workstation* concept. This is a much-abused term, which can mean many things to different people. It usually refers to a machine with local processing power, which is able to communicate with the outside world, most usually as part of a network. Communicating workstations, with access to centrally stored data which is processed locally, are an alternative to multiuser systems, where all users access and process data on a single powerful central computer.

We may also mention here the *intelligent terminal.* This was a device intermediate between a 'dumb' computer terminal and a proper micro, in that it had some local storage and (usually very limited) processing capabilities. These terminals were often used, for example, for online searching, allowing uploading and downloading. From the mid-1980s, this sort of equipment was replaced by microcomputer workstations.

Minicomputers appeared in the 1970s, as the first alternative to the large central computing facility. They occupy an immediate role between mainframe and micro, and encompass systems ranging very widely in capabilities and cost, and fulfilling a variety of roles. Frequently they are dedicated to a single application - scientific computation and data analysis, and database handling are among the most common. They are also very frequently used as controlled in communications systems. They may be single-user machines, or the larger types can accommodate quite large multiuser systems. This however takes us to the *supermini* type of machine; large variants at the top of a range of minis, which compete with mainframes in their ability to undertake heavy processing tasks, and to run multiuser interactive systems.

Minicomputers are increasingly tending to appear in 'clusters' of several linked machines. This allows increased processing capabilities, towards the mainframe level, and a high degree of reliability, since if one machine is unavailable, the remainder of the cluster can take up the load.

Traditionally, minis have been under departmental, rather than central, control, and were instrumental in beginning the wider control of computing power, which was completed by the micro. The situation is now very open, with minis filling every role from personal machine, at the lower end of the range, to central multiuser resource, at the upper end.

Mainframes are the largest type of computer in general use, and are designed for 'heavy duty' computing: supporting large multiuser systems; accessing very large data files; carrying our large data-processing tasks; etc. They are typically the central computing resource for a large organization, although there is an increasing trend for them to be challenged in this role by clustered' systems of large minis. Conversely, there is a type of machine termed a *mini-mainframe* a mainframe computer, cut down in capabilities and cost, but still able to run all the systems and software of the mainframe range. This is an important consideration for a general data-processing operation.

We should also mention the *supercomputer*. This is the category which has perhaps changed more than any other, since it is defined as those machines which, at any time, are at the forefront of computer technology. The series is the best known example. They are the most powerful machines available at any time (and the most expensive) and are generally to be found in research institutes and other places where the applications always outstrip available computer power, and where intensive calculation is required; some scientific computation, weather forecasting, defence etc. Although it is unlikely that the most well-endowed information service would ever have access to such a machine, they are still of significance, since technological advances appearing in suprecomputers generally percolate down to humbler machines. Parallelism is a good example, applied in supercomputers for over a decade before its appearance in more mundane surroundings.

Besides these basic types, there are also machines designed for a specific purpose, such as *array processors* (for numerical computation) and *database machines* (for specific types of information retrieval), although these are generally derivations of one of the main categories.

With the exception of small micro systems, and some special purpose machines, it is now the rule for computers to be designed as part of a series with the same overall architecture. This has many advantages for the user, in that new machines can be purchased which will be compatible with the existing system, and also that one machine may be replaced by a large one, without the need to replace either system or application software: 'upward compatibility. Given the costs of software, this is a very important consideration.

Current Trends and Future Developments in Computer Processing Hardware

Although there have been great changes in the power, construction, size, and appearance, of digital computer systems since their introduction in the 1940s, the basic (von Neumann) architecture has remained largely unchanged. In this section, we will look at some future prospects for computer processing hardware (storage and input/output technologies being considered in other sections). First, we consider some relatively minor changes, of scale and of construction, which are nonetheless very significant for users. Then, the Japanese 'fifth generation' concept, which has greatly influenced views of the future, and the consequent projects undertaken in the USA, UK, and Continental Europe are described. The main focus of the section is on 'parallel architecture', the most important novel hardware concept for the near future. Finally, some more long-term possibilities are considered.

One clear trend is towards a diversification of physical form, and changes of scale, in IT equipment. The general trend has been for the size of computer system to decrease, with miniaturization of components. This is now allowing the production of genuinely useful 'hand-held' or 'pocket' computers, such as the PSION organizer, used for example in libraries for stock checking, in health services, in large shops, and (most notoriously) by drug smugglers, to maintain lists of contacts. The same sort of microcomponents are appearing in the new generation of 'intelligent' office systems such as photocopiers and fascimile machines, see Dingman, (1986).

Within the confines of the architecture, there have been a number of discrete advances in hardware technology, corresponding to the various 'generations' of computer, the most recent being the adoption of large-scale integration of semiconductor circuitry. A number of less dramatic, but nonetheless significant, incremental improvements have been made recently, and others are in the offing, promising advantages in performance.

One example is RISC (reduced instruction set computer) technology, introduced in microcomputers during 1986, and since then adopted in IBM's personal computer range and likely to be widely used in the workstations of the 1990s. This involves the use of a smaller than usual instruction set, which can be accessed more rapidly (each instruction requiring only one cycle), with consequent improvement in performance; an example of the importance of efficient 'firmware'.

An often discussed possibility is the replacement of silicon in integrated circuits by some other semiconductor material, which would increase processing speed. Gallium arsenide, the leading contender, has been under investigation for some years, and is sometimes cynically said to be 'always the technology of tomorrow'; it is more difficult to manufacture components with this material than with silicon, and components are consequently more expensive, but its use confers considerable speed advantages. It may well be used in those parts of the processor unit where speed is of the essence, for example high-speed memory, see Meindl, (1987).

Fifth Generation Computers

In 1981, the Japanese government announced the setting up of the Fifth Generation Project, a collaborative project involving Japanese academic and industrial researchers in designing and implementing by 1990 a prototype knowledge-processing system. This would incorporate a novel (parallel) computer architecture, with distributed processing, a massive storage capacity and intelligent, knowledge-based software, an important component of the scheme. By the late 1980s, the aim had evolved into the implementation, by the mid-1990s, of system with immensely rapid processing, communicating with their users by speech in natural language, and accessing massive databases with intelligent, deductive software. This project is being undertaken by the Japanese Institute for New Generation Computer Technology, in the ICOT programme, see Bishop, (1986).

To achieve this aim will require quite revolutionary advances in processing speeds, resulting from highly parallel architectures and the use of very large scale integration (VLSI) semiconductor, technology, as well as peripheral devices for input and output by speech, and storage devices to cope with the enormous quantities of data, including pictures and images, envisaged. Similar advances in software design, enabling natural language understanding and question answering, and an entirely new form of genuinely intelligent software, will also be needed.

The feasibility of producing fifth generation computers, as proposed, is very much in doubt, but the sheer scale and potential significance, of the project led many other nations to set up their own fifth generation projects, to counter what they feared to be a Japanese thrust for world economic domination towards the end of this century. In the USA, the MCC and Darpa projects were an immediate response, and several heavily-funded long-term projects followed, studying a range of fifth generation system components, while the EEC devoted 900 million to the ESPRIT research programme in Europe. In the UK, the government funded the Project, but provided only a limited degree of support to its successors.

Although on a smaller scale than projects elsewhere, the UK Alvey project typifies the response to the challenge of the fifth generation. The main areas supported by Alvey were five crucial components (termed 'enabling technologies') of fifth generation systems:

* The use of very large scale integration (VLSI) techniques for seminconductor chip design and manufacture.
* Novel architecture, this being basically the use of highly parallel computing systems.
* The application of software engineering techniques to the design and implementation of large software systems.
* Human-computer interface (HCI) studies, to provide more sophisticated methods of interaction between computers and their users.

* Intelligent knowledge-based systems (IKBS) for inferential and deductive processing from knowledge encoded explicitly within computer systems.

We shall mention the software design and HCI issues later, and will look at the question of intelligent software in more detail. Of the remaining areas, VLSI is plainly going to continue the trend of ever increasing computer power in small packages, at least until some ultimate limit of performance is reached, and an alternative form of switching mechanism to conventional semiconductors is adopted.

The other topic, parallel architectures, is of such direct relevance to the use of computers in information services that we shall look at it in more detail now.

Parallel Processing Hardware

The processing in current computers typically involves a sequential, or serial, processing of operations, with each instruction being applied to a single data item. Although this computer architecture has proved to be remarkably flexible, there is now considerable interest in the use of alternative architecture, in which instructions, data, or both, can be processed in parallel. At least in part this interest has arisen from the fact that it will not be possible to substantially increase current processing rates on conventional processors owing to physical constraints such as the time it takes for electrons to move around a computer memory: thus further increases in performance can only come about if several processes can be carried out simultaneously.

The idea of parallel computation is not entirely new. A simple example of parallelism is provided by 'database machines', such as the ICL Content Addressable File Store (CAFS), which permit the searching of several data tracks from a disc in parallel. A limited degree of parallelism has been built into a number of experimental machines and supercomputers (under such names as 'pipelining, 'dataflow', 'vector processing' and 'array processing'), and is now becoming available for standard machines in the form of add-on hardware devices such as array processors. Future developments are likely to involve computers specifically designed for parallel operation. Such highly parallel systems seem to be particularly well suited to many information retrieval problems, where a series of relatively simple search-and-compare operations need to be applied to very large numbers of data records.

To make sense of the various types of parallel processing hardware available, it is useful to categorize it according to whether more than one instruction, and more than one record, can be treated simultaneously:

SISD (single instruction, single data)
MISD (multiple instruction, single data)
SIMD (single instruction, multiple data)
MIMD (multiple instruction, multiple data)

The 'conventional' computer is of the serial SISD type; taking one piece of data and doing one operation on it, then either getting another piece of data, or doing another operation on the original. The MISD configuration does not appear to be a feasible, or useful, option. The new parallel processing architectures therefore fall into the SIMD and MIMD categories.

SIMD machines perform a single operation on numerous data items simultaneously, e.g. looking for a string of characters within a larger string.. Examples of their use within information service provision are the chemical structure searching system of CAS Online (in which connection tables for substructure searching are passed out to a set of minicomputers, working in parallel) and CLSI's library automation hardware, which uses up to thirty 32-bit microprocessors working in parallel within a single machine. One important class of SIMD machines, with potential application to information retrieval, arc known as 'distributed array processors': ICL's Distributed Array Processor' (DAP) has been used for document retrieval experiments. Another example is ICL'S Content Addressable File store (CAFS), which combines devices for the retrieval of information from disc storage with parallel processing of material received. CAFS is gaining quite wide usage, particularly as a means of speeding up retrieval from relational databases.

Another is the US 'connection machine', used at MIT for artificial intelligence experiments, which includes 64000 individual processors.

MIMD machines perform numerous operations on numerous data items simultaneously, and require a linked network of independent processors, which can communicate with one another. This is the type of parallelism with the most exciting long-term prospects, in that the flexibility of the many processing units each operating independently to maximum effect offers the potential of many-fold increases in power. They also offer great reliability, since if one processor fails its work can be shared among the others. An important example is the 'transputer', from the UK Inmos company, a 32-bit RISC microprocessor, specifically designed for connection in parallel, in communicating networks.

Transputer chips can be used in several ways. They may be built into modules, which can be plugged into conventional mini- or microcomputers during 1987 and 1988 several micro-computer manufacturers, including announced 'add-on' boards using a single transputer. Alternatively, they can be used to construct whole machines, which would rival conventional supercomputers in power.

Among its many other applications, the transputer seems highly suitable for information retrieval purpose, since a transputer network can share the work of searching a file of items among its constituent processors. As each item is found to match or not, another is sent to that processor, so that the whole network works to its full potential. In practice, transputers can be connected together in various configurations (chains, rings, stars, trees, etc.), and the appropriate choice of configuration determines how closely the maximum linear increase in speed, as more processors are to the network, can be approached, see Cringean *et al* (1988). Yet another form of parallel computing device is the 'neural network'; known since the 1960s, the concept, has gained wide interest in the late 1980s, because of its compatibility with parallel hardware.

It has to be appreciated that all parallel hardware requires specially-written, or modified, software to take advantage of its features. Algorithms have to be devised to take advantage of the way in which the hardware operates, very different from the serial approach. Interestingly, this involves a rediscovery of the methods for dividing up large problems which were employed in the time before the digital computer, when large problems were solved by people working with mechanical calculators. Conventional programming languages can be modified to run on parallel processing systems, or entirely novel ones may be created: Inmos, for example, has developed the Ocean programming language for transputer systems. It is not therefore a trivial matter to change to a parallel processing system, or to 'add on' a component of parallelism: as with most other hardware advances, the software aspects are crucial.

There seems little doubt that parallel hardware, in one form or another, will play a major role in the information handling systems of the 1990s. Research indicates that these systems will certainly be able to process 'conventional' retrieval applications very rapidly. Beyond this, it is generally agreed that any attempt to produce software systems with a degree of intelligence - question answering systems, for example or software able to process natural language - will need the processing power only obtainable from highly parallel hardware.

Long-term Prospects

There are a number of entirely novel forms of computer processing hardware at various stages of research. All are based on new physical forms of switching devices, replacing semiconductors, and hence giving faster processing. The basic problem with semiconductor technology is that the only way of significantly increasing performance is to reduce the distance which the electrical signals must travel between the components. However, as the electronic circuits are miniaturized, and packed closer together, the heat output increases to unacceptable levels. Packing techniques, in any case, are already approaching the molecular level, so that improvements in this direction will shortly be halted.

The new concepts include devices involving *superconductivity*. These allow the current flow to be maintained almost indefinitely, thus avoiding the heating problem. This concept received a great boost from the discovery of high-temperature superconductors in the late 1980s. Prior to that, the idea of computer processors working in tanks of liquid helium, to give the ultra-low temperatures believed necessary for superconductivity, was being taken quite seriously in some quarters.

Most of the longer-term prospects involve processing units which get away entirely from electronic circuitry, using other materials which can change state, and thus represent binary digits.

Optical computers involve units which use the presence and absence of light for information representation, and hence are limited only by the speed of light; a 10 000-fold increase in speed over electronic systems was believed possible. A working optical computer was demonstrated at the 1986 computer fair, using laser generated light instead of electron flow, and optically bi-stable crystals instead of microcircuitry. Other research has involved hybrid integrated circuits, using a combination of silicon, gallium arsenide, and fibre optics.

Optical computers are particularly appropriate for parallel processing, since several light beams may be transmitted along the same path without interference.

Organic or biological computers would use some large organic molecule or a macromolecule, such as a protein, which could exist in two states; the most likely mechanism would be a conformational change between two different three-dimensional arrangements of isomers. This concept is still at the earliest stages of development.

These technologies, exciting though they appear, are not likely to have much impact on 'standard' computer systems, of the type used by information services, at least until the turn of the century. Overall, they hold out the prospect of essentially limitless, and cheap, processing power. The problem, as now, will be to produce software systems capable of making effective use of this power and putting it to good use.

Computer Storage

Computer systems include two types of digital information storage; *internal* storage, within the CPU, and *backing* storage, on external devices such as discs or tapes. A variety of different technologies are available for implementing both types of storage, and these may be evaluated according to a number of criteria, such as speed of operation, capacity, cost, reliability, the degree to which individual storage elements are readily accessible, etc. Improvements in storage capacity have been very marked in recent years, and further improvements are in prospect.

More detailed accounts of computer storage technologies are given in general texts.

Internal Storage

Internal storage within the CPU is also known as *main, primary,* or (for historical reasons) *core* storage. It is used to hold those instructions and data required at any moment while a program is running, which must be available essentially instantaneously. Silicon semiconductor chips are almost invariably used at present for internal storage; these are categorized as either RAM (random access memory) or ROM (read only memory) chips. ROMs are used for data which is never altered, e.g. a computer's operating instructions, while RAM is used for 'ephemeral' data and instructions used in the execution of a program.

Internal storage capacity is measured in bits or bytes, and multiples thereof. The size of the individual chips comprising the internal memory has rapidly increased; from the 4-byte chip of the early 1970s, via 16 kbyte and 64-kbyte chips, to the current standard 256-kbyte chips, with research into 1 Mbyte and 4 Mbyte chips well advanced.

Backing Storage

Backing storage, also termed *external* storage, is used to hold programs and data which are read into internal storage when required. By far the most common form now, as for the last thirty years, in *magnetic* storage media, either *tapes* or *discs.* Other forms of magnetic storage, including magnetic *drums,* no longer have any significant usage, while other technologies, such as magnetic *bubble memories,* have been devised but never gained wide use.

With both magnetic tapes and discs, data is recorded onto a plastic surface, coated with a varnish containing an oxide which can be magnetized in one of two directions; each magnetization representing one bit of data. Data is written and read by read write heads (RWHs), small electromagnetics, close to the surface, which can also erase and overwrite data. (The closeness of the RWHs to the disc surface is graphically shown by their flight being likened to a jumbo jet attempting to fly along a busy main street at a height of three metres, without hitting anything. It is for this reason that discs must be kept in clean conditions: particles of fine dust, or even smoke , are larger than the head-surface gap.) Reading is effected by allowing the magnetized material to induce a current in the RWH, while writing occurs when currents in the RWHs are used to magnetize particles on the surface.

Magnetic tapes are very commonly used for storing large amounts of information to which rapid access is not necessary, particularly for archival data, back-ups etc. Hundreds or thousands of feet long, and holding thousands of characters/in, tapes are a cheap means of storing large volumes of data (typically > 100 Mbytes). Data is stored on a tape in blocks of a few hundred bytes, and is read or written one block at a time. Access is generally slow, since the tape must be read serially (i.e. end-to-end) to find the required element of data. Small cassette tapes, of relatively low capacity, are used with microcomputers.

Magnetic discs are the most widely used form of backing storage, and are suitable for holding information required relatively rapidly, e.g. data for a running program. In the type of disc drive used in larger computer systems, data is recorded on the flat surfaces of a stack of circular discs revolving on a common spindle. There is usually one RWH for each side of each disc, and the set of RWHs can move radially across the surface of the discs to pick out individual data tracks, the data being written to disc concentrically. Accessing an individual block of data involves both a *seek time,* the time taken to move across the surface of the disc to the appropriate track, and a *latency time,* the time taken for the required block to come under the RWHs. The seek time is by far the greater of these, typically 0.01s. This is very slow, by comparison with computer processing speeds, and disc seek times are one of the main limiting factors in the speed of operation of computer systems, especially of retrieval systems with information stored on disc.

Disc capacities have increased greatly, from original values of about 30 Mbytes to present units with capacities of 1 Gbyte (one thousand million bytes). There has been no comparable increase in speed of data access, because of the limitations of rapidity with which the mechanical components of the RWHs can operate.

There is a great variety of types of disc, and a corresponding variation in storage capacity. Smaller computer systems use single discs, rather than packs, such as the hard disc units for microcomputer systems (typically 10 Mbytes to 60 Mbytes); these are sealed units, including both the disc and its RWHs, giving protection from dirt in the environment. '*Floppy discs* are widely used with microcomputers; compact (generally 5.25 in or increasingly 3.5 in 'microfloppies'), cheap and convenient for transfer of programs and data,. Not truly random access devices, they are limited in storage capacity (typically 3 kbytes to 1 Mbytes), with relatively slow access times, and less convenient than a hard disc in day-to-day use. They comprise a disc of mylar plastic, coated with the magnetic oxide material, encased in a flexible plastic jacket, with an opening for the single RWH. Continuing improvements in magnetic storage are likely to result from new magnetic materials particularly the film media and more advanced design of read/write heads.

A new development in technology of potentially very great importance is *optical disc storage*. Digital data is burnt into the surface of a plastic disc coated with a low melting point metal, e.g. tellurium, by a laser beam, the presence or absence of a hole corresponding to one bit. Information is read by another laser, coupled to a mirror system to detect the presence or absence of the microscopic holes.

There are three kinds of optical disc. The most common is 'read only', for which a master disc is prepared, and replicate discs produced cheaply; this type of disc can only be used for distributing information. 'Write once read many (WORM)' discs allow users to write their own information, but once written it cannot be altered. 'Erasable' or 'multiple write' discs are under development, allowing the data-carrying holes to be physically removed, and information thereby erased.

Optical disc technology gives very high capacity storage at low cost, and in a form allowing rapid access (but slower than magnetic discs). A single 12 in disc can already hold about 1 Gbyte at a very low cost, and further improvements can be expected. The actual capacity is crucially dependent on what is stored, and how: for example, whether images of pages or digitized text.

Optical discs are likely to play an important role in computer storage, office automation etc. in the future. Publishers are particularly looking at the CD-ROM (compact disc - read only memory), a small disc holding about 600 Mbytes (roughly equivalent to one thousand full floppy discs, or over a quarter of a million typed A4 pages, or the contents of a 6 ft wide floor to ceiling bookcase - choose your own analogy), as a mechanism for database updating and electronic publishing. By the late 1980s, databases such as were available on CD-ROM, together with a variety of encyclopedias, dictionaries, and similar reference tools. The final status of optical publishing is not entirely clear, though some niche is assumed, see Hendley (1987).

Other likely applications of optical disc technology, in its WORM form, are; a compact and cheap alternative to magnetic tape storage for archiving machine-readable information; an alternative to microforms for archiving 'images'; a cheap alternative to magnetic discs for data storage on microcomputers, see Grigsby (1987).

A newer development is 'compact disc-interactive (CD-I), which allows discs to contain a digitized mixture of media forms: text, 'still' images and graphics, and sound, with video sequences at a later stage. These would be produced in the player, under microprocessor control, giving great scope for so-called 'edutainment' products, combining education with entertainment. If, for example, the user wanted to find out about whales, the CD-I system could produce descriptive text (printed on a screen or spoken, maps of distribution, photographs, video sequences, and sound recordings of whale song).

A combination of magnetic and optical technologies, magneto-optical recording with lasers used to read, write and erase data on this magnetic film, is under development. This may offer the economic advantages of optical storage, with the performance and erasibility of magnetic media. It is certain that both these forms of storage will be of significance for the foreseeable future.

Computer Input and Output Devices

The nature of the devices by which information is put, into, and received from, computer systems can greatly affect the acceptability of these systems to their users. This is basically dependent on convenience of use for the task in hand, (particularly for input devices), and on general quality of results (particularly for output devices).

It is worth noting that, as with most developments in computer hardware, the provision of software to make effective use of input and output devices has generally lagged well behind advances in hardware.

Input Devices

Input devices are, of course, of importance to all computer systems, and do not, on the whole, receive the attention that their importance justifies. They are described in detail elsewhere.

The most common input mechanism is still the familiar QWERTY *keyboard*. This dates from the Victorian typewriter layout, the four straight rows of keys being adapted to suit the mechanical system used. The QWERTY design was actually chosen to slow the typist down, so as to avoid jamming in rapid use; the keys being laid out so as to increase the difficulty of typing English text. Amazingly, this deliberately 'user-hostile' design has survived for over one hundred years, long after the rationale for its use had disappeared.

The depression of a key on a computer keyboard closes a circuit, causing the appropriate character to be inserted in memory, and displayed on the screen. There is therefore no need for any particular pattern of keys. The QWERTY keyboard has been retained, with a few minor ergonomic improvements, because of the vast expenditure in retraining which would be required, if it were significantly altered. One radically new keyboard, designed to assist rather than hinder its user, has been produced by Maltron and is available both in the USA and Europe; this has keys arranged in separate groups for left and right hands, and for fingers and thumbs. The keyboard itself is shaped and contoured so as to match the natural movements of hands and fingers. Although the Maltron keyboard has undoubted advantages, the intertia factor posed by legions of QWERTY-trained typists will ensure that its acceptance into routine use will proceed slowly, if at all.

Pointing devices have increased in popularity in the last few years; all of these are used to indicate a point on a screen, e.g. to make a selection from a menu. Obviously these devices will work only with appropriate interactive computer software, and they cannot be used to enter even the smallest amount of text directly. The most widely used are the *mouse,* the *light pen,* and the *touch screen.*

The mouse, so-called apparently because the early version had two buttons (eyes) and an attached wire (tail), is moved around on the desk, or other flat surface, thereby moving a cursor on the screen, by transmission of the movements of a freely-turning ball under the mouse. The user presses buttons on the top of the mouse to indicate that they want to perform a certain operation associated with the area under the cursor on the screen. Mice are very widely used in microcomputer systems, in conjunction with WIMP (windows, icons, mice, pointers) software interfaces, of the kind pioneered by Apple with the microcomputer. Windows, in this context, are independently controlled parts of the screen, displaying different information, for example text drawn from different files, while icons are pictorial representations of commands; a wastepaper basket for deletion, filing cabinet for storage, etc. Obviously, some device is needed to indicate which part of the screen, e.g. which icon is required, a mouse, or some kind of pointing device.

One of the more widely-used pointing devices is the *light pen,* which is used to indicate points on the screen directly, by touching it. The pen has a tubular body, with a lead to the computer at one end, and the light censor at the other. Light pens differ greatly in their capabilities and sensitivities. The more sophisticated sort are used in chemical information systems, to draw in molecular structures as well as select items from menus.

Graphics tablets are devices used, particularly in the earlier years of interactive computing, in conjunction with mice and light pens; they are not common today, now that light pens can be used directly on the screen, and mice run free on the desk. Similar devices are used to accept limited handwritten input, using a grid system on the tablet or pad to assist recognition. This has only proved practical for very standardized input, such as the filling in of forms with limited resonse.

Touch screens, as their name implies, are interactive screens on which the user indicates the desired spot by touching it with a finger, pencil, or whatever; there is no need for special pointing devices. The screen has a sensitive grid, generally of infra-red beams, so that the point of contact is detected by the breaking of the gird. They are, as may be imagined, not very sensitive in assessing an exact position, and the system can only be used for such things as menu selection. Touch screens have been used, without great success in personal computer systems. Their main value is in public information systems, offering the completely inexperienced user an easy way of choosing from a simple menu system.

Voice Input is a technology which has received much attention, since it holds out the promise of a completely 'natural' way of communicating with computer systems, especially if combined with voice output from the system, which we shall consider later. Of the two, voice recognition for input is by far the more difficult problem.

The difficulties arise from the simple fact that people say the same thing in different ways. This is of course most obvious when there are two different speakers, with different speech characteristics and patterns compounded by regional accents etc. Even for one person, however, the voice may change markedly according to mood, state of health, and even time of day; noticeable to human listeners, who can easily compensate to understand what is being said, this poses great problems for a machine. It is therefore much easier to develop *speaker dependent* systems; trained to recognize a single person, or small number of people, than their *speaker independent* equivalents, which must attempt to understand everyone. It is also much easier to construct systems able to understand *isolated words* than systems to cope with *connected speech,* where the syntax of the string of words must be analysed in some way to comprehend its meaning.

This leads to a four-way categorization of voice input systems, which is useful in setting this technology in context.

Speaker dependent / isolated word systems are the simplest sort, and account for most voice recognition systems in practical use in the late 1980s. These generally recognize the voice patterns of only one person, and then only if words are spoken singly and clearly, with definite gaps left between them. The user must 'train' the system, by speaking, several times, each word which the system will subsequently recognize, thus building up the system's closed vocabulary. Most recognition systems have been limited to vocabularies of between 50 and 500 words, but this limitation began to be overcome from the mid-1980; the Kurzweil Voice System 3000 can recognize 1000 words, while the IBM Tangora system has a vocabulary of 5000. This has to be compared with the 50 000 word vocabulary of the average educated adult, and the 100 000-plus vocabularies of professional and scientific disciplines; on the other hand, particular applications, such as database access, need a much smaller set of terms.

This type of simple system is widely used in industrial settings, where it is useful for the hands to be kept free, for issuing simple commands from a preset list. It is also perfectly acceptable for simple database queries, for example travel information services. A project to evaluate a system of this sort for online searching has been described by Philip *et al.* (1988). Voice input can be used for all system commands, since they come from a very restricted set, but search terms, which can of course vary enormously in a general database, may have to be spelled or entered at the keyboard.

Speaker dependent/connected speech systems allow one, and only one user, to speak sentences into the machine, again after training. The vocabularies which can be used are small (typically only about 50 things can be said), and the grammar must be kept simple. The user is therefore constrained to use a very stilted form of speech.

Speaker independent/isolated word systems are available, but are limited to very small vocabularies (typically just 'yes', 'no', the numbers one to nine, and a few other appropriate words), as a trade-off for their ability to recognize these words as spoken by any person. They have limited applications where a very large number of people need to access a computer system, using a several limited vocabulary; perhaps simple enquiry systems.

Speaker independent/connected speech systems are the ultimate goal, since they would allow access by any user, speaking in reasonably normal language, to the system. The difficulties associated with the technology mean that it is not likely that systems of this sort will be available much before the turn of the century.

Voice input can be implemented in a variety of ways, from complete hardware systems, through peripheral devices attached to minis or macros, to plug-in chips and circuit boards; or software packages to run on standard hardware. Thought needs to be given as to how the user will address the machine; many systems require the wearing of a headset, unpopular at best, and entirely off-putting to casual users. A lot of thought will have to be given to human factors and the human-computer interface in particular, if voice input systems are to be happily accepted by users.

There are many potential applications for voice input. One is the easy automatic creation of text in word-processing or office automation systems; the 'typewriter that types when spoken to'. The Kurzweil Voice Writer, developed in the late 1980s, goes some way towards this, with a total vocabulary of between 7500 and 20 000 words, and allowing a degree of speaker independence. Accessing databases by spoken query is another often-quoted possibility.

In general voice input may be expected to work best, in conjunction with voice output, for applications where there is a formally structured human-computer interface, and where users are constrained to communicate using a clearly defined artificial language. Although systems can recognize 'keywords' from within longer phrases, this can be quite tricky, if not dangerous, to apply. A travel enquiry system could be trained to recognize place names, but it would also have to know that 'To London, please' meant the same as 'To London', but that 'Anywhere but London' was quite different. Similarly, a voice-controlled database system, which looked for commands such as PRINT in the user's spoken instructions could identify 'print', 'print all these', or 'hurry up and print something', as all requiring printing to be done, but what would it make of 'I don't want you to print this lot'? (There are numerous, possibly apocryphal, stories of voice systems which could not deal adequately with negative commands, usually with disastrous consequences.) The prospect of indulging in idle chit-chat with computer systems, with no restriction on what is said, will have to await major advances in intelligent software for natural language processing.

Barcodes, incorporating information in a pattern of stripes, produced and read by special equipment, were originally used as a means of identification and checking in US freight trains. The information is represented by black and white bars in some logical pattern, according to whichever of the more than 40 different coding systems is being used. The codes are read by a mean of white, or infrared, light shone at the code and moved across the bars. The reflected light is packed up by a detector within the reader, which emits a small current whenever light is reflected into it, from a white bar. The computer picks up the output voltage generated by this current. The system has a good deal of redundancy built into it, so that damaged codes can be read.

Barcodes are widely used by food retailers, and for industrial data-capture requirements. In the context of information services, they are widely-used in library issue systems, and are now beginning to be used for serial control with identifiers such as ISSNs printed as barcodes. As cheaper equipment becomes available, they are slowly gaining wider use for general data transfer, for example as a means of 'publishing' computer programs. The similar *'softstrip'* with information encoded as dot patterns, may be used for journal contents pages, or even full text of articles, see Lance (1987).

Optical Character recognition (OCR) is a relatively old technology, developed since 1960. It attained quite wide use during the 1970s, particularly in the USA, but rather faded from view during the next decade. It is widely used for reading information presented in a standardized typeface, particularly if that has been developed specifically for OCR; examples are bank cheque details, credit card vouchers, gas, electricity and telephone bills, and vehicle licensing documents. Improvements in this technology during the 1980s seem likely to greatly increase its utility, as a means of getting a lot of information into computer systems very quickly.

A typical OCR machine of the 1980s is about the size of a desktop copier; paper is fed in, and moves under a scanning head, which digitizes the scanned material. So far, so good. Now comes the tricky bit.

The essential point about OCR is that, unlike image storage, it does not just store a 'picture' of the input material, but converts it into fully computerized text. Of course OCR software may be applied to computer-stored images produced by scanning. In order to carry out this conversion, the system must recognize the characters in the text presented to it, and this is where the problems arise, due to the great variety of ways (fonts, typefaces, sizes, etc.) in which text appears. This has resulted in most OCR equipment being restricted to just one form of text, or at best one in each document scanned. OCR systems have also generally had great trouble in dealing with such things as footnotes and captions to illustrations, not to mention poor quality printing, greatly reducing the facility with which the equipment can deal with a wide range material. Nonetheless, a variety of equipment has been produced and used, the best known being the range of OCR machines, originally developed as readers for blind people. Some systems are preprogrammed to recognize a number of the more common typefaces, while others have to be trained each time. The extent of operator intervention in recognition also differs between systems. Despite the limitations of material which could be handled, and the high proportion of errors, OCR, with subsequent editing as necessary, has often been viewed as a reasonable alternative to keyboarding, for entering a large amount of material.

An interesting development, from the mid-1980s, has been the development of 'intelligent character recognition (ICR)' systems, see Jones (1988), the best known examples coming. For example, is able to 'learn' about the fonts with which it will deal, and to cope with 'real-life' texts, including mixed type faces and a mix of text and graphics, in a much more robust and sensible manner than previous OCR equipment. If the promise of this 'intelligent' approach holds good, then OCR will give the opportunity for entering a great deal more material into computerized form.

Early OCR machine were peripherals to mainframe computers, but now they work either with macros or minis; some, such as the Kurzweil machines, use their own special hardware.

Some progress is also being made with *handwritten character recognition,* again using intelligent software, as an alternative to typing at a keyboard. As with voice recognition, the systems have to be 'trained' to deal with each user. It is not clear just how useful this technology will actually prove to be, even if technically successful.

Image Processing technology has advanced to the point where devices are now available for routine scanning and storage of printed pages, graphics etc., which can then be retrieved and displayed when required. The important difference between this technique and OCR is that the material entered can only be stored as pure graphic images, and displayed as they were entered. If it is the image of a printed document, for example, the individual words are not accessible, as would be the case with OCR.

Image scanning systems comprise the scanning device itself, with some means of placing the items to be scanned in the correct position; either a baseplate on which the items are positioned or, increasingly common, a feeding mechanism like a photocopier. Scanning a piece of paper generally takes a few seconds, and almost anything with reasonable black and white contrast can be scanned successfully; text, hand-written messages, diagrams, photographs, etc. The image is then stored as a bit pattern in computer memory. Of course, there is little point in successfully scanning and storing images if they cannot be put to use; the development of software for handling image data, and for integrating it with text, is an important area of development at the moment. As was noted above, stored images of text may be converted to fully computer-readable form by OCR software.

The most significant future prospects for input devices are an increasing availability of alternatives to the keyboard, particularly voice input for commands, and a wide use of optical character recognition and image processing for handling large volumes of information, especially in office automation applications.

Output Devices

Considering the importance of output devices, and the quality of the results, for user acceptance of IT systems, surprisingly little in the way of comparative material has been published on them specifically. They have been described in the context of input and output together and of computer peripherals generally as well as in general texts discusses a range of output devices in the specific context of office automation; the issues raised are, in fact, of wider relevance.

The range of output devices has developed greatly since the early days of computers, which relied on equipment taken from existing data processing systems; cathode ray tubes, adapted typewriters, etc. By the 1960s, the impact line printer was dominant, and the unpleasant form of printing from these old systems is still many people's idea of 'computer output'. During that decade, however, the introduction of interactive computing lead to that other symbol of IT, the display screen. During the 1970s and 1980s, the spread of 'small' computer systems lead to a wider variety of output devices, particularly character printers, while at the other end of the scale high quality laser printers were developed. As with all other IT equipment, reliability and flexibility has been much improved by the replacement of mechanical parts with electronic controls.

Output devices can conveniently be divided into *interactive,* which handle both input and output, and *archival,* which produce a permanent record, but have no input facilities, and hence cannot be used for interaction. The one type of interactive device which gave an archival record, the *teletype*, was once very widely-used, but is now rarely seen.

The most familiar computer output device is, of course, the visual display unit (VDU), based on the cathode-ray *display screen.* The technology is essentially the same as in the domestic television set, with symbols displayed by directing beams of electrons into a photosensitive screen; in fact the screens used for videotex and teletext information services are virtually unmodified TV sets. Most VDUs, however have much better resolution that this. Screens are increasingly using the technique of *bit-mapping,* whereby the output to the screen is directly controlled by main memory, each bit corresponding to a black or white point on the screen, rather than being sent down a data link. This leads to faster updating, and hence better handling of graphics.

Most current VDU screens are very limited in their ability to display the equivalent of a printed document. The size of the screen will only allow for the display of about one-third of an A4 page, while the resolution of most VDUs is inadequate. Larger screens, with higher resolution, are becoming available, but it is highly debatable if even the best of them is as acceptable as a printed page.

Devices of this kind have improved markedly in facilities, quality, and price in recent years. *Graphics display,* based on either faster or calligraphic systems, is now commonly available, whether on unsophisticated microcomputer displays, or on high-quality graphics terminals. Colour is equally widely available. The remarkable displays possible with colour graphics are well illustrated (in every sense of the word by Deken (1983), and the technical details fully described by Foley and van dam (1983).

There are two forms of graphics display currently is use. *Vector,* or *calligraphic,* displays construct their pictures by drawing lines on the screen; they give very high-quality representations, though usually with restricted colour options, and are mainly used in expensive terminals for interactive graphics applications (such as molecular modelling and computer-aided design), where the picture must be redrawn rapidly. *Faster* graphics displays work by filling in specified areas of the screen; the higher the resolution, i.e. the more points which can be addressed, the better the quality of the picture. The great majority of graphics displays now use this technology, since it is relatively cheap to implement, and can deal with a wide variety of colours. With continuing improvements in the speed with which the display can be 'refreshed', i.e. updated and changed, it seems likely that faster graphics systems will largely replace the vector alternative, except perhaps for some specialized applications.

There has of course been a great deal of controversy about the ergonomic, and health and safety, aspects of the use of VDUs and this is discussed further in the section on human factors in Chapter 9. The general view seems to be that, provided the equipment is properly installed and maintained, in a sensible environment, any problems which arise are much more likely to be due to the nature of the work than the VDU itself.

Alternatives of CRT displays have made little progress towards widespread acceptance, because of the problems of attaining adequate resolution, and a bright enough display to be read in natural light, at an acceptable cost, some devices began to appear in the mid-1980s based on technologies such as light-emitting diodes (LEDs), liquid crystal displays (LCDs), plasma gas discharge units, and electroluminescene. Some are based on a large array of small elements, assembled to form the symbols on the screen; an example is the use of liquid crystal technology in the display units of portable microcomputers. Others use a single large-area display, with symbols individually controlled; for example the plasma panels used in large flat-panel displays in banks and retail settings. These offer the prospects, ultimately, both of very small portable 'book-like' displays, and of large 'desktop' screens. However, the challenge to designers to develop a display of sufficient size, resolution, and acceptability (in terms of eyestrain etc.) to be a real alternative to paper for sustained reading, or rapid scanning, is still considerable.

Turning to the 'archival', non-interactive devices, computer printers, of which there are a great variety available, are the principle means of producing 'permanent' computer output. There are three ways in which they can be categorized:

1. *Impact* (in which the characters are formed by a part of the device physically striking a ribbon, or similar medium) and *non-impact* (where some non-contact process is used). The most important practical consequences is that impact printers are noisy, but can produce multiple copies, albeit by the messy expedient of carbon paper, or similar. Non-impact printers are quiet, but restricted to single copies.
   Examples of impact printers are line printers, daisywheels, and dot matrix devices; non-impact devices include laser printers, ink-jets, and thermal transfer devices.
2. *'Shaped Character'*, or 'formed' or 'full' character (which have predefined character sets, physically present in the device, as with the characters in a typewriter), and other kinds (which generate characters as needed). Formed character printers usually give higher quality, but are slower, and entirely, inflexible, i.e. the character set cannot be changed without physically changing the device.
   Shaped character devices include line and daisywheel printers; the other category includes laser devices, matrix printer, ink-jets, and thermal transfer printers.
3. 'Character', or 'serial' printers, 'line' printers, or 'page' printers (according to how much information is printed at one instruction from the computer).
   Laser printers and similar devices are page printers; everything else is character, except (obviously and tautologically) for line printers.

We will now briefly consider these various kinds in turn.

Line-printers, the workhorses of the input device family, have been widely used for many years in large computer installations. Designed for the rapid printing of large amounts of information, they are noisy, inflexible, and generally limited to low-quality output. There are a number of distinct types (belt, band, drum, train, and chain), which differ according to the means adopted to bring their preformed characters under the bank of hammers which prints a line across the paper. Despite their disadvantages, line printers have retained a place in larger computer installations, where robustness and speed are of the essence. Indeed, a new generation of line printers (slower, quieter, and with somewhat improved quality) was developed to meet the needs of office automation (so much for the paperless office).

Serial Printers, printing one character at a time, are very commonly used. Most widespread are the *impact printers,* in which the print-head actually strikes a ribbon; all are to some extent irritatingly noisy. The two main kinds are the *daisywheel,* and similar *thimble,* printer, and the *dot-matrix* device.

Daisaywheels, which resemble electronic typewriters with characters mounted on spokes around the wheel, provide good quality ('letter quality') output, but are slow (typically between 10 and 50 character/s), relatively expensive, and inflexible. They cannot cope with graphics or colour, and the only way to alter the character set, or typeface, is to physically change the daisywheel.

The matrix printer, the most widely-used type during the 1980s, has a print-head consisting of a vertical column of pins, which are pushed forward in appropriate combinations to form the characters as patterns of dots. The number of pins in these devices has steadily increased from an original eight, giving truly dreadful output, through 18 to 24, with a consequent improvement to 'near letter quality' (NLQ) printing. 'Multi-mode' printers can trade-off speed against quality, by making several passes over the paper, improving quality by filling in the character shape more fully, or alternatively by using only some of the pins to increase speed. There is usually a choice of standard modes: high-speed/data-processing quality; medium speed/draft quality; low sped/NLQ.

Matrix printers are highly versatile, being able to construct characters as required, either under the control of a ROM cartridge in the printer itself or of a software package. Poor-quality graphics can also be produced, and limited colour included, although only by using ribbons with differently coloured inks. They have the advantages over the daisywheels of relative cheapness, quietness (though they are still noisy) and speed (up to 500 character/s, albeit with poor quality output). The multi-mode printers of this type, with microprocessor control, developed during the 1980s, are able to provide a 'one printer' solution, for all types of output, if very high quality is not an issue.

Non-impact serial printers have the great advantage of silent operation, and are improving in reliability and quality: they include *ink-jet* and *ink-dot* printers (particularly suitable for colour graphics), *electrostatic* printers (used on facsimile machines etc.), and *thermal transfer* printers (likely to be widely used with small computer systems because of low cost, versatility, and portability).

Ink-jet and ink-dot (or ink-drop) devices, which spray coloured ink into paper with the droplets controlled electrostatically to form characters ,were developed during the 1960s, but did not become generally available until the late 1970s, and have always been plagued with problems of reliability and relatively high cost. During the 1980s, a new range of smaller ink-jet printers appeared, with these problems apparently largely overcome. The latest variant of this technology is the *bubble-jet* printer.

Of the printer types which form characters by some thermal or electrostatic means, none had found wide use until the mid-1980s, because of their restriction to special paper. A new type of thermal transfer printer, using a thermal transfer ribbon to transfer spots of dye to ordinary paper, has many advantages, when very high quality is less important than its genuine portability, owing to a low power requirement enabling battery operation and to small size, and silent operation.

Page printers, which essentially print a whole page at one command, are generally accepted as the best available general purpose computer printers (albeit at a relatively high cost), and are rapidly gaining a very wide use. These are usually always *laser printers,* although other technologies such as *ion deposition* or *magnetic head* are used. The principle of operation is essentially that of the photocopier, and all employ a number of equivalent steps. These include: preparing the printing surface (usually a drum); writing the image to be printed into the surface; developing the image with a toner; transferring the image to paper, and fixing it with heat, pressure, or similar; and cleaning the printing surface so that the cycle can be repeated.

In the laser printer, the most widely used type, a photoconducting drum, acting as an insulator in the absence of light, has a layer of positive charges, dissipated when illuminated by a lesser beam. This beam is modulated by the digitized image, leaving positively charged dots. Negatively charged toner is spread over the drum, sticking to the positively charged areas, so developing the image, which is then transferred to paper. In the ion deposition printer, an electrostatic image is formed on an aluminium drum with a dielectric surface, by means of an ionic gun cartridge; a charged toner develops the image, which is transferred to paper by pressure. Having fewer mechanical parts than laser printers, ion deposition devices should be more reliable (though, in truth, reliability, is not usually a problem with any page printer). In the magnetic head printer the drum is coated with a magnetic layer on which the image is built up by a recording head. The image is developed with a magnetic toner, and fixed on paper by heat or pressure.

All page printers have the advantages of fast (in excess of 100 A4 pages/min. of large units silent operation, producing high quality output, and unmatched versatility, combining text (in any size or typeface), graphics etc. Colour is not yet, however, commercially available. These printers are increasingly being used for electronic, or desktop, publishing.

Of course, the versatility of page printers is only made possible by the use of appropriate software ('device drivers'), generally provided by the manufacturers, and for more sophisticated applications, such as desktop publishing specialist software is required. It is the quality of this software, as much as the capabilities of the device, which determines the look of the final product.

Graph plotters, in their two forms of *drum* and *flatbed,* both of which, use direct contact between pen and paper to produce their output, have until recently been the only means of obtaining hard copy of graphics. In the 1980s, two contrasting developments in plotter technology became evident. At the top end of the price range, new kinds of high-quality colour plotters, for example electrostatic devices, were being devised for specific tasks, particularly in computer-aided design. At the other extreme, the increasing use of colour graphics in microcomputer systems led to the widespread use of cheap colour plotters, of the flatbed type.

There is not, however, the same distinction between printers (text) and plotters (pictures) that there once was. A trend observable from the mid-1980s is for specialist plotting equipment to be replaced by general purpose printers, which can cope with graphics: lasers, in-jets, and multi-mode matrix devices. It seems likely that this trend will continue, leaving plotters for special purposes, e.g. for very high-quality graphics, or extensive use of colour.

There is still a lack of printers and plotters to reproduce high-quality colour graphics screens: device are therefore available to plug into terminals or micro-computers to produce a *photograph* of the screen. *Video recordings* can be similarly produced: as well as reproducing graphics displays, they can be valuable for training purposes.

Production of *voice output* from computers have been a subject of research for many years, and began to find a widespread practical application during the 1980s. The problem is an easier one than that of using speech recognition for input. Machine-generated speech, in fact, predates the digital computer, since 'speaking clocks on telephone services were introduced in the 1930s, with recorded words joined together as needed. The first speech output from computer systems was developed during the 1960s, with samples of speech, stored in digital form, output by a synthesizer. Although recognizable, such speech sounded highly artificial and unnatural, since each word or phrase was spoken in exactly the same way, and with the same inflection, regardless of context. More recent variations of this technique are much improve, although the result is still unmistakably 'machine speak'; a common reaction is that it sounds as though the synthesizer has a cold.

Research and development, dating form the 1970s has investigated genuine 'speech synthesis', using one of four techniques:

waveform encoding, based on generation of waveforms which

match mathematical models of the frequencies of human speech patterns:
analysis / synthesis, generating output speech which sounds as much as possible like input;
synthesis by rule, combining phonemes, the basic building blocks of speech, according to rules;
synthesis from concept, with computer responses generated from algorithmic means, rather than from anything stored.

Waveform encoding at present produces the most 'natural' sounding speech, and is widely used in voice response systems, voice massaging, etc.; analysis/synthesis and synthesis by rule still tend to sound 'artificial' although they may have their own advantages. For example, synthesis by rule is particularly appropriate for applications in which computerized text is converted into speech, for example in the reading of printed text for blind people. Synthesis from concept is not as yet developed into a practical technology.

Recent developments in speech synthesis have resulted in commercial systems suitable for issuing simple messages, instructions and warnings, and in voice massaging systems. They will probably be of most value when used in conjunction with voice input as we have noted earlier. Speech output by itself is also of value in systems for converting written text to speech, using optical character recognition as input perhaps as readers for blind people, see Jones (1988).

Voice output will most probably be used in conjunction with other forms of computer output, particularly visual display, since large amounts of information are more readily assimilated by eye rather than by ear. A project implementing voice interfaces for online searching will use various combinations of output by voice and on the screen. One possibility is to use the screen to show a full reference, a library catalogue entry, for example, with a 'voice over' summary. In general, voice output will probably be reserved for warnings, summaries, interruptions, etc. except fork cases when only voice is available, for example in telephone enquiry systems. As we noted earlier, a carefully designed human-computer interface will be essential, if voice systems are to be accepted by users, and fulfil their true potential.

Other forms of sound output, apart from voice, have been implemented experimentally; with a synthesizer attached to the machine, and appropriate software, the range of noises which can be produced are limited only by the designer's imagination. Sadly, many examples are of little more value than the immensely irritating 'sleep' with which unsuppressed systems often greet their users. Some of the more interesting examples attempt to use sound to match some attribute of the information being handled. Musical notes are generated in some cases, with pitch and duration varied in line with variations in data being processed. Others, integrated with the WIMP style in line with variations in data being processed. Others, integrated with the WIMP style of interface, produce 'thuds' as a file is selected, with 'heaviness' proportional of file size, and supposedly satisfying 'crasnes' as the wastepaper basket icon is selected for deletion., Satisfactory use of this type of sound output awaits the design of a genuinely user-oriented interface.

In conclusion, future prospects for output devices will probably include: higher quality, and higher resolution, display screens, including very larger and very small sizes; more widespread use of laser, and similar page printers; greater availability of cheap and versatile dot-matrix and thermal transfer printers; a greater role for voice output, in conjunction with voice input, in systems with a restricted range of commands and responses. In more advanced computer systems, the idea of 'artificial realities', with interaction by voice and gesture, highly advanced displays, and various touch devices, can be visualized, but their relevance for information services is not yet clear.

Conclusions

We have tried to give an account, in outline for the most part, of the development and present state of computer hardware, drawing attention to important trends and to particularly significant technologies.

From the point of view of the application of IT in information services, as with many other application areas, it is clear that the capabilities of processing hardware have greatly outstripped the abilities of available software to make use of it. Similarly, deficiencies in computer systems for information services are more often due to the quality of the input/output peripherals, or of the design of the user interface, than to any limitations of processing or storage capacities. It is therefore rather ironic that, as we have seen, the major trends in IT development suggest greatly expanded processing and storage capacities, at ever-decreasing cost. While this obviously presents new opportunities, most obviously in the size of databases which can be stored and searched locally, it places still more intensive demands on the already inadequate software and interface aspects.

Some solutions to this problem will clearly come from other hardware developments; for example the availability of improved input/output devices, such as high quality display screens;.and the trend towards 'intelligent' interfaces of all kinds, from versatile printers to conversational voice interfaces: and the availability of processing hardware especially geared towards information handling applications, such as.

5

Computer Software

Introduction

It is worth re-emphasizing what we said in Chapter 3; that we are not attempting to deal with this large, important and complex area in any degree of detai!. Rather, we will give an overview, setting those aspects of computer software of greatest importance for information services into their context in the bigger picture. We will also identify, and point out the significance of, a number of new trends in software of particular relevance.

This section opens with an overview of software concepts generally, then moves on to those types of software with most direct impact on information services: information retrieval, in its various manifestations including archiving and records management, software for library housekeeping, expert systems, and administrative and office software systems.

Perhaps surprisingly, there are very many fewer textbooks and review articles dealing with the general are of 'software' than for 'hardware', Naturally, software is covered in general computing sources, although it is not usually given the space which its importance merits, when compared with hardware, and there are many sources of further reading on specific topics, which are noted in the appropriate place below.

General Software Concepts

Software is a generic term covering the concepts, procedures and instructions which cause computer systems to do useful things. Software consists of abstract ideas, of which the physical form (symbols in a printout, electronic or magnetic records in processing or storage etc.) is immaterial. Usually, software is thought of in terms of *programs*, discrete units of software which cause the computer to carry out a particular task, and or *systems or packages;* integrated collections of programs. The distinction between these three terms is rather loose, however, and they are almost interconvertable in common usage.

The importance of software cannot be over-estimated, since it is software which applies the power of the computer to the users problems. Software is therefore much closer conceptually to user requirements than is hardware, and most users will require, and possess, a more detailed understanding of software than of hardware. It has been clear for some some years now that the rapid increase in the capabilities of database machines, and some kinds of parallel processing. Nonetheless, it is primarily to developments in software and in human factors that we must look, for improvements to systems which will maximize the actual, as opposed to potential, value of the ever more powerful hardware systems which will become available.

Computer systems has not been matched by corresponding increases in availability and quality of software: this lack is now a major impediment to increased use of, and value derived from, computer systems.

Software may conveniently, if over-simplistically, be divided into two categories: *systems software,* programs designed to control the execution of other programs and to utilize hardware effectively, and *applications software,* programs to solve users' problems. We will consider these two aspects of software separately below. It is, however, important to realize that both kinds of software share essentially the same nature.

The basics of Software

Software design is usually spoken of as involving two important abstract concepts: algorithms and data structures. For information retrieval purposes, there is a third important concept: file structures.

Algorithms, crudely stated, are procedures, or, recipes, for computation defines algorithms loosely as 'problem-solving methods suitable for implementation as computer programs', making the important distinction between the algorithm (the method itself) and its implementation in the form of a specific program. Algorithms are, perhaps, most commonly, thought of as mathematical procedures, but are just as relevant to non-numerical, text procedures: sorting searching, pattern matching, parsing, etc.

To appreciate the nature of algorithms a little better, we will take the simple example of sorting a list of items; it does not matter whether they are numbers, letters, names, or anything else, so long as there is a clear order into which they are to be sorted. This is a clear definition of the problem, i.e. what is to be done, and it could be made clearer and more formal. However it does not tell us how it is to be done; i.e. the algorithm which is to be used.

One way of sorting a list, speaking loosely and informally is to first find the smallest clement of the list, and put it in the first position; then find the second, and put that in second position; and so on, for as many items as are in the list. This is the so-called *selection* sort algorithm. Another way of achieving the same result would be to look at the first two elements of the list, and exchange them if they are not already in the correct order; then to consider the items in positions two and three; and so on, to the end of the list. Then the whole procedure would be repeated, again and again, until the situation where no exchange was made going through the whole list, which would then be sorted. This is the *bublesort* algorithm, and is quite different in nature from selection sort. Sorting is a very important practical problem in computer science, as well as an inviting topic for testing new algorithms, and many different algorithms are available. The important points to note are that they provide different ways of achieving the same end, but are not by any means entirely equivalent: some are much more efficient than others; some are more suited to one type of situation than another (for example, some sorting algorithms are very fast when the list is nearly sorted already); some are more easily implemented in practice, etc. The choice of algorithm is often crucial to the performance of a software system. Points out that careful implementation may improve the performance of software by, say, five or ten times, but correct choice of algorithm can easily have, a thousand-fold effect.

Data structures, or information structures, are intimately connected with algorithms, since they describe the way in which collections of items of information are organized in computer memory during processing they are therefore created by, and for, the associated algorithm. Data structures have forms such as lists (in which the items may be linked together in various ways), tables, arrays (of two or more dimensions) and trees (collections of these comprising 'forests).

File structures describe the way in which large numbers of records are stored in a computer's backing store. They generally relate to the intellectual organization of information, i.e. the way in which it is conceptually accessed by software, rather than the physical storage is made by the computer's system software. Examples of file structures include sequential files (the simplest, with one record simply following another), random access files (for rapid access to any record), and a variety of forms of indexed structures, including the inverted files generally used in bibliographic retrieval systems, indexed sequential (ISAM) files, and tree structures, such as the b-trees commonly used in database systems.

Once a software procedure is understood and specified in terms of these abstract concepts, it is coded into a form which the computer can use, by manes of a *programming language.* We should say that it is not generally necessary for a user of software systems to have any real appreciation of the algorithms, data structures, and file structures used in the software, to apply it effectively. However, anyone wanting an understanding at more than a superficial level of software systems will need to gain at least a general appreciation of these ideas. For anyone involved in the evaluation and selection of software, some knowledge of this area is highly desirable in sorting out the really significant factors in technical specifications, and in debunking sales type.

Programming Languages

Programming languages are the means by which instructions for the procedures to be performed are expressed to computer systems. The variety of languages have steadily increased as computer systems have developed, and this variety shows little signs of increasing. An excellent basic introduction is the paper by Tesler (1984); more detail, in a readable form, will be found in the book by Wilson and Clark (1988).

In general, the trend has been to make languages more powerful, easier to understand and to use, and generally more accessible to people other than computer specialists. As languages have become better matched to their users, they have made less efficient use of machine resources; although a cause of concern to computer professionals in years gone by, this has always been more than counterbalanced by improvements in processing power. The advantages of 'higher-level' languages in allowing the rapid production of comprehensible software have more than outweighed any loss in performance. This worry is still voiced, however, in connection with 'very high-level' languages.

Ultimately, a computer can only operate on instructions in *machine code* (binary), and very early computer systems were indeed programmed directly in this way. The most basic machine instructions have still to be encoded into computers by their manufacturers in this form. Since machine code is intimately associated with basic machine operations, this code must be different for each type of processor gives a machine code program for the addition of all the odd numbers in a list, which would run on a Motorola 68000 microprocessor, and is reproduced below (we have to take his word for the correctness of it!).

```
00100100   01011111
00100010   01011111
00110010   00011111
01001110   11111010   0000000   00001110
00001000   00101001   0000000   00000000   00000000   00000001
01100111   00000010
11010100   01010001
01010100   01001001
01010001   11001001
00111110   10000010
01001110   11010010
```

Assembly language, was developed as a more convenient and memonic form of machine code. Like machine code, each assembly language is suitable for only one make of computer, and, again like machine code, there is a close correspondence between instructions in this language and the operations performed in the machine's circuitry. The code is converted to machine language with a virtually one-to-one translation of instructions, giving highly efficient code, making the most of the processor's resources. The Motorola 68000 assembly language routine for the summation of odd numbers is given below.

```
SUMODDS    MOVE.L.     (A7)+.A2.
           MOVE.L.     (A7)+.A1
           MOVE.W.     (A7)+D2
           CLR.W.      D2
           JMP         COUNT
LOOP       BTST        0. (A1)
           BEQ.S.      NEXT
           ADD.W.      (A1). D2
NEXT       ADDQ.W.     #2.A1
COUNT      DBF         D1.LOOP
           MOVE.W.     D2.-(A7)
           JMP         (A2)
```

This is obviously somewhat more comprehensible than its machine code equivalent. One has the feeling that, given sufficient effort, one could actually make out what it does. There is still the direct link with hardware in the specification of the machines internal registers (A1 etc.), *but* there are also recognizable programming features, such as labels (LOOP etc.).

As an example of the machine-specific nature of assembly language programming, an example of PLAN, the now obsolete assembly language used in the ICL 1900 series of computers, is given below (for a different algorithm):

```
        STOZ   0
        LDX    5    1(1)
CORK    LDX    6    MODF+3
        BZE    4    CLUNK
        SLL    5    6
        SRL    5    18
        BXGE   5    '5', EEK
        ADN    1    5
        BRN         CORK
EEK     ADN    6    1
        ADN    1    5
        BRN         CORK
CLUNK   ADS    6    PRODNO
```

There is some similarity in the structure of the language to the Motorola example (statement labels, branching instructions, arithmetic, etc.), but the instructions are entirely different.

Assembly language was used very widely during the 1950s and 1960s, and is still used today for specialized applications, particularly where speed of operation is important, and especially when the constraints of the limited power of microcomputers dictate the use of the most efficient code possible. It has been a constant source of amazement to one of the authors, who had to use an assembler for a programming amazement to one of the authors, who had to use an assembler project, and changed to a high-level language with immense relief, that many micro-computer hobbyists actually choose to use assembler language, to bring them closer to the workings of the machine.

High-level languages, developed during the 1950s, get away from the need, seen in both machine code and assembly language, to specify instructions so as to take explicit account of the way in which the machine is working; there is much more of a split between hardware and software. They are sometimes termed 'third generation' languages, by analogy with hardware generations. Theroretically, a program written in one of these languages should run on any machine, but in practice there are subtle (sometimes not so subtle) differences between 'dialects'; thus one speaks of 'DEC Fortran', of 'IBM Basic'. High-level languages have to be converted to machine code by a program termed a 'compiler', and are (on the whole) considerably easier to program, and to understand, than assembly language. Several hundred such languages were known to be in use in the late 1980s, but a small subset of these accounts for most programs, certainly those in routine commercial use.

Still the most widely-used of the high-level languages are three old favourites: Fortran (devised for scientific and mathematical work); Cobol (for commercial data processing) and Basic (an interactive language, originally for time-sharing minicomputer systems, which gained immensely wide popularity with the advent of the microcomputer): these three together were the major languages in almost 70% of sites surveyed by the UK National Computing Centre in 1987 (NCC 1987).

Of more recently developed languages, one of particular significance is Pascal, widely used for teaching, tough not so widely in the 'real world'. It was designed to reflect the need for a clear and 'structured' language, which would encourage good programming practice, and result in easily understood and modifiable programs; an indication that the main problems were no longer associated with making good use of machine resources (becoming ever cheaper), but much more to do with developing software which would be robust and easily modified (becoming ever more expensive). Two other widely-used languages of this generation are Ada (adopted for defence purposes in the USA, and hence heavily 'pushed' throughout the West) and C, a highly structured language, with some low-level assembler-like features for efficiency.

Special purpose languages also abound, such as Snobol (text processing), Lisp (artificial intelligence), and APL (array and matrix manipulation).

These high-level languages made the computer accessible to a new breed of programmer who was not necessarily a mathematician or computer scientist, and to scientists, engineers, and other professionals, who were sufficiently motivated to learn the art. They were, and are, suitable for the end user, as such a person would be understood in the information services sense.

To give an illustration of the diversity of languages, Basic, Pascal, Cobol and Lisp versions of the odd numbers summation, taken from Tesler (1984), are presented in turn below, for a set of just four numbers (23, 34, 7, 9).

Basic program

```
100     DIM T (100)
200     READ N
300     FOR I = 1 TO N
400     READ T(I)
500     NEXT I
600     GOSUB 1100
700     PRINT S
800     GOTO 2000
900     DATA 4
1000    DATA 23, 34, 7, 9
1100    REM MAKE S THE SUM OF THE ODD ELEMENTS IN ARRAY
        T
```

```
1200    LET S = O
1300    FOR I=1 TO N
1400    IF NOT ODD(T(I)) THEN GOTO 1600
1500    LET S=S + T(I)
1600    NEXT I
1700    RETURN
2000    END
```

Pascal Program

```
Programme Sum odd Numbers:
  type Term Index = 1..100
       Term Array = array [Term Index] of integer:
var my Terms: Term Array
function Sum Odds (n: Term Index : terms: Term Arrray): integer:
var i: Term Index
       sum:integer
begin
       sum:=0:
       for i:=1 to n do
       if Odd 9 terms [i]) then
       sum: = sum + terms[i]:
Sum Odds: = sum:
end:
begin
my Terms[1]: = 23 my Terms [2]: = 34:my Terms [3] : = 7:my Terms [4]
= 9:
Written (sum Odds (4. my Terms)
end.
```

Cobol Program (excerpt)

```
       Data Division.
       working Storage Section.
01 Numeric-Variables Usage is Computational.
02     Terms Picture 9999 Occurs 100 Times Indexed by 1.
02     N Picture 999.
02     Sum Picture 999999.
02     Half-Term Picture 9999.
02     RMDR Picture 9.
```

Procedure Division

```
Example.
       Move 23 to Terms(1).
       Move 34 to Terms(2).
```

```
        Move 7 to Terms(3).
        Move 9 to Terms(4).
        Move 4 to N.
Perform Sum-Odds.
Sum-Odds.
        Move 0 to Sum.
Perform Consider-one term varying 1 from 1 by 1 until 1>N.
Consider-one-term.
        Divide 2 into terms(1) Giving Half-term Remainder RMDR.
        If RMDR is Equal to 1;. Add Terms(1) to Sum.
```

Lisp program

```
(DEFUN SUMODDS)
        (LAMBDA (TERMS)
                (COND
                (NULL TERMS)0)
                ((ODD (CAR TERMS)) (PLUS (CAR TERMS)
(SUMODDS (CDR TERMS))))
                (T (SUMODS (CDR TERMS)))))
(SUMODDS (23 34 7 9))
(SUMODDS (23 34 7 9))
        = (PLUS 23 (SUMODDS (34 7 9)))
        = (PLUS 23 (SUMODDS (7 9)00
        = (PLUS 23 (PLUS 7 (PLUS 9 (SUMODDS'( )))))
        = (PLUS 23 (PLUS 7 (PLUS 9 0)))
        = (PLUS 23 (PLUS 7 9))
        = (PLUS 23 16)
        =39
```

To someone who has no knowledge of computer programming, these routines will be simply perplexing. For someone who has experience with programming a high-level language, but does not know the particular one exemplified, there will be some recognition of programming constructs (loops, subroutines, if statements, etc.), and some appreciation of the characteristics of the language; the 'English-like' nature of Cobol, for example, an why cynics believe that Lisp is an acronym for 'Lots of Irritating Spurious Parentheses'. However, only someone trained in use of the language can fully comprehend it, so as to be able, for example, to modify it. Languages of this sort are a great improvement on machine code and assembly language, in terms of comprehensibility and programmer productivity (generally considered to be about seven-fold greater with a third-generation language). They cannot be said by any means to open up the computer to the great mass of people who could take advantage of it.

This does not mean of course that one must be a programmer to *make use* of programs. On the contrary, most people use programs and packages with no need even to know in what language it is written; we, for example, have little interest in the languages used in the word-processing systems being used to write the text of this book, and it would not help us in any way to know what these are. On the other hand, this means that end users are entirely at the mercy of professional programmers in the quality of the product provided, and that they have no opportunity themselves to alter the operation of the system to suit themselves, nor to make even the smallest extension or improvement. This is the root cause of the 'software backlog' which we shall discuss later.

Most recent are the so-called 'fourth-generation' (4GL) or 'very high-level' languages. It is difficult to give any precise definition of exactly what constitutes a fourth-generation language, since the term is used rather loosely by suppliers. They are generally provided as part of integrated applications systems, such as database management systems, and allow users to program their own applications very easily; for this reason, they are sometimes termed 'applications generators'. They are also termed 'non-procedural' languages, by comparison with 'procedural' high level languages of the sort described above. Whereas a procedural language requires the programmer to specify the steps needed to achieve the desired result, thus telling the computer not merely what to do, but how to do it, with a non-procedural language the user specifies the output required, but need not know anything about the details of the data manipulation necessary to achieve it.

Fourth-generation languages are certainly convenient to use, but this convenience is paid for in an inefficient use of processing resources; with the increase in cheap processing power, this is not the problem that it would have been a few years ago. There are also strict limits on the flexibility of use of 4GLs; they are designed to do particular things, such as access information in an associated database, and cannot go beyond this. Nonetheless, their use in increasing, since they allow much more rapid development of new options than would be possible with a conventional programming language. Some of these languages are designed to be tools for end users, who are able to make *ad hoc* database enquiries, design, new output formats, etc.; others are primarily for the use of system developers. Some are purely adjuncts to a single database management system; examples are the Natural language with the ADABAS database, and the AF applications generation to the S1032 DBMS . Others are complete in themselves, and generally include their own database system. In the NCC's 1987 survey, 4GLs were used by about half the sites (NCC 1987).

'Fifth-generation' languages are under development, associated with the concept of the fifth-generation computer. Aimed at making all the computer's facilities available to the user in virtually normal language, and based on artificial intelligence ideas, they require enormous processing power. This prospect leads us to consider expert and intelligent software.

Expert and Intelligent Software

This is an area which has received a great deal of publicity, since the term 'expert system' was first coined, in the late 1970s. We will try to give an overview of the whole area here, in preparation for discussion of applications in information services in later sections.

Intelligent and expert systems are notoriously hard to define. The British Computer Society's Specialist Group on Expert Systems has proposed the definition:

An expert system is regarded as the embodiment within a computer of a knowledge-based component. From an expert skill, in such a form that the system can offer intelligent advice or take an intelligent decision about a processing function. A desirable additional characteristic, which many would consider fundamental, is the capability of the system, on demand, to justify its own line of reasoning in a manner directly intelligible to the enquirer. The style adopted to attain these characteristics is rule-based programming. Richard Forsythe (1984b) offers the alternative definition that an expert is 'a piece of software which causes TV producers to lose all sense of proportion'; an indication of the media hype which surrounded these systems in the early 1980s. He also suggests a list of 'distinctive features' as being more useful than any definition. These denote an expert system as:

* limited to a specific domain of expertise;
* able to reason with uncertain data;
* able to explain itself in sensible way;
* delivering advice as output;
* designed to grow incrementally;
* having a clear separation of knowledge and inference mechanism;
* typically (not necessarily) rule-based.

Over the last decade, it has become increasingly difficult to assign systems with absolute clarity as 'expert' or 'intelligent', not least because of the enthusiasm with which software marketers apply the terms to the most unlikely cases. The term 'intelligent knowledge based system' (IKBS) is increasingly being used, to denote a rather broader range of capabilities than the original 'expert system'. As a rule of thumb, we can regard a system as intelligent if it encodes knowledge in some explicit and recognizable form, if it provides some sort of advice based on that knowledge (rather than just a calculation, for example), and if it can explain its operation to its users in their own terms.

There are essentially five components of an intelligent system, though they will not all be present in every system so described:

* a knowledge base
* an inference engine
* a knowledge acquisition system
* a user interface
* links with other systems

The *knowledge base* is the heart of any intelligent system, as it is here that its 'expertise' is stored. There are a variety of means for knowledge representation. *Rules* are very often used, and indeed were at one time considered synonymous with expert systems, as in the BCS definition above: hence the commonly-used term 'rule-based' system. Other representations are used in some systems, such as *frames, scripts, decision trees, and semantic nets.*

An example of a rule in the medical diagnosis expert system is:

IF It is not known whether the organism was able to grow aerobically

AND The site of the culture is blood.

OR The lab has attempted to grow the organism energetically
AND The organism was able to grow anaerobically
THEN There is evidence that the aerobicity of the organism is focal (50%) or anaerobic (20%).

Note that it includes both, uncertain information and a probabilistic result.

This is transferred into the Lisp language used as:

```
premise:    (SNAD (NOTKNOWN CNTXT AIRGROW)
            (SOR (SAME CNTXT SITE BLOOD)
            (SAME CNTXT ANTRY)
            (SAME CNTXT ANGROW)
action:     (CONCLUDE* CNTXT AIR TALLY' ((Focal
            500)(ANAEROBIC 200)))
```

A further example of rule-based knowledge representation comes from the X-CON system for computer configuration:

IF: The most current active context is assigning a power supply
And an SBI module of any type has been put in a cabinet
And the position it occupies in the cabinet is known
And there is space in that cabinet for a power supply
And there is an available power supply
THEN: Put the power supply in the cabinet in the available space.

This has to be supported by a database of component specifications, and a set of templates which allow the system to determine relative positions, free space, etc.

The *inference engine* is the software which enables the knowledge base to be processed, so as to reach conclusions, give advice, etc., in any particular case. Essentially this involves either reasoning from the given data to form a hypothesis ('forward chaining') or working back wards from a hypothesis to be proved or disproved ('backward chaining'). Many IKBSs use a mixture of approaches for inferencing. Some are able to deal explicitly with inexact or uncertain information, and some carry out statistical analyses of the probabilities of their results.

The importance of the *knowledge acquisition procedure* is sometimes underestimated. In the great majority of systems, certainly in all the early expert systems, the knowledge was extracted and synthesized by a system designer, coded in the appropriate formalism, for example IF... THEN rules, and entered into the system. This is the task of the new profession of 'knowledge engineer', and is an immensely time-consuming task for systems of any degree of complexity. A lot of attention has been given to the possibility of 'machine learning'; that is to say, allowing the system to form its own knowledge base automatically, from sets of information and examples of cases presented to it. This is till a largely unsolved problem.

The *user interface* is of crucial importance, a fact only realized relatively late on in the development of intelligent software. Explanation is of great importance, since users will have little confidence (or, more dangerously, too much confidence) in 'black box' systems, which simply produce answers with no justification. The style of interface is also of particular significance, since, if users are to make use of intelligent systems as routine aids, they must be simple and pleasant to use.

Links with other systems are increasingly important. Early expert systems were entirely self-contained, and did not communicate with the world outside. There is now a general realization that IKBSs must be able to interact with other software: to draw information from a DBMS, for example, or to interact with a spreadsheet model. This is one aspect of the general process of the integration of intelligent systems with the wider information processing environment, which we will discuss later.

Expert and intelligent systems may be implemented in a various ways. There are special programming languages available, such as Prolog and Poplog, for this purpose; Lisp is also often used. Some high-performance workstations support 'knowledge engineering environments', such as KEE, ART, and Knowledge craft, which usually include several languages and knowledge representations and a powerful user interface. These are often referred to generally as 'Lisp machines', since they are especially adapted to use this language, and are particularly suitable for development work. It is, however, perfectly possible to use a 'conventional' programming language, such as Pascal or C, for expert systems work, and some of the best established systems are implemented in this way. Often, expert system: 'shells' are used: these are packages, often for standard microcomputers, which offer a particular form of knowledge representation and inference, and allow the user to develop small systems very rapidly. Examples are Xi, Crystal, and Savoir. Opinions are divided as to the merits of shells, with their convenience having to be balanced against restricted power and flexibility.

Experience is showing that expert systems are most appropriate used for limited and well-defined topics, with well-understood areas of knowledge. They are mainly valuable for diagnostic and advisory tasks: fault-finding in equipment, diagnosis of disease, interpreting the results of laboratory tests, advising on analytical laboratory procedures, providing legal and financial advice, etc.

Results in broader areas, requiring a lot of 'real-world' knowledge and 'common sense' have been disappointing, because of the sheer enormity or encoding all the relevant information into the system. It has also been found difficult to make a rule-based system perform on a par with a genuine human expert; they are really 'competent' rather than 'expert' systems. Human experts, after all, do not generally proceed by rules, but by a form of pattern recognition, drawing on their experience to recognize similar situations long-standing critics of the claims of 'artificial intelligence', discuss these points thoroughly. The failure to provide the kind of fully automated high-quality machine translation software, promised for so long but finally given up in favour of less ambitious, but more practical, translation aid is another example of the failure to deliver 'true' artificial intelligence.

The references cited above describe the 'classic' examples of expert systems: for chemical structure elucidation, for medical diagnosis, Prospector, of analysing geological data, for planning chemical synthesis, etc. Two particularly interesting examples show up clearly the points noted above. One example is the X-CON system (formerly R1). exemplified above, and used by DEC to assist their engineers in configuring Vax computer systems, ensuring that all necessary components are supplied. A second is the translation into rule-based systems of the labyrinthine complexities of the UK nationality and social security legislation, allowing inferences on their application to particular cases to be drawn (and identifying a number of self-contradictions in the legislation as a by-product). These are both clearly very well-defined and self-contained topics, where the knowledge base is completely known; however they are of sufficient complexity and difficulty as to make the intelligent system approach genuinely worthwhile.

The number of such 'ideal' cases for expert system application is probably quite restricted. Beyond these, expert systems are best thought of as 'competent' systems, valuable in the absence of a human expert, and as an assistant to the human expert, to whom they can act as a 'memory aid', utilizing their capability for entirely objective analysis of all information to hand. Certainly they are to be regarded as a tool, analogous to other forms of software, rather than cloaked with the 'thinking machine' mystique from the wilder shores of artificial intelligence. As we noted earlier, they will certainly be of greatest value when fully integrated with other software systems.

We will consider specific roles for expert systems within information services in later sections; they include intelligent interfaces to retrieval systems and aids to technical processes such as cataloguing and classification. We might also note that it has been suggested that information professionals would be well suited to carry out knowledge engineering tasks, because of their appreciation of knowledge representation techniques. One of the more depressing aspects of the development of intelligent systems is the frequency with which the artificial intelligence community seems to reinvest concepts such as the thesaurus.

Although expert systems *per se* seem to have a rather limited applicability, the more general concept of 'intelligent' or 'knowledge based' systems has wider promise. These ideas can be applied to any sort of program or package, enabling it to display more 'sensible' behaviour, as an aid to its users. An example is the intelligent database, which would have a knowledge of the information contained, and of the requirements of its users, and possibly some limited understanding of natural language. Such a database would then be able to answer rather vaguely-phrased questions from users with no knowledge of the internal structure of the data or the mechanics of the system.

This may well lead to what has been termed the 'intuitive' software interface, one which adapts to the needs of its user, and when in doubt does something sensible. This can be seen as the continuation of a line of improved interfaces, starting with command-driven systems, though menus, and WIMP systems.

Systems Software

Systems software is generally supplied by hardware manufacturers, or may be written by the staff of large computer installations. In includes operating systems (discussed later), assemblers, compilers, and interpreters (to convert programming languages into machine code), programs for controlling input and output devices, copying data between storage media etc., and utilities for sorting, merging, and editing files, controlling program libraries etc.

Operating systems are programs whose purpose is to enable users' software resources. This includes the control and allocation of processing power, storage space, input and output devices etc., maintaining security, handling files and so on. Operating systems generally have a hierarchical arrangement, so that at each level the details of what goes on at lower levels can be ignored. Operating systems have tended to grow more complex, to deal with timesharing, networking, greater requirements for user-friendliness etc. although micro operating systems must of necessity be relatively unsophisticated.

Most users will have little say over choice of operating system, certainly in the case of minicomputers and mainframes. Here there will be a very limited choice, or no choice, at all, of operating systems provided by the computer manufacturer, and specific to that range of machines: VMS for the DEC range of Vax computers, for example, or ICL's VME.

There is one important exception, and that is Unix. This operating system is of particular significance, sine it is available, albeit with local 'dialects', across as wide range of computers, including some workstations and microcomputers. This makes things much easier when software systems are to be transferred between different machines. Unix is a powerful system, with facilities which make it suitable for library/information applications, see Unix (1986). CLSI for example decided during 1988 to base their range of library automation software on Unix, rather than on the proprietary systems used formerly, in order to maintain flexibility in choice of hardware, as well s to take advantage of Unix-based facilities such as electronic mail.

Another exception, though not so widely used, is the Pick operating system, again available on many different types of equipment. Pick includes relatively advanced user features, such as databases (relational database, data dictionary, enquiry language, etc.) and file handling, and supports an unusually wide range of application generators. It is therefore likely to be particularly useful in a library/information context. It has for example been used as a basis for several integrated library systems, since it offers particularly good integration of system modules, and very easy transfer of software to new equipment.

For microcomputers the situation is much simpler, since there is not the same situation of each type of computer having its own operating system. The early 8-bit machines almost invariably used the CP/M system, while the more recent 16-bit micros generally support some variant of DOS, following the IBM *de facto* standard. Unix is also available for some microcomputers, generally those at the more powerful end of the spectrum. The newer PS/2 range of IBM personal computers have their own operating system, OS/2, which is likely to assume the same significance as DOS, in giving a *de fcto* standard. OS/2 has a number of advanced features, to take advantage of the increasing power of the microcomputer.

The WIMP (Windows Icons Mice Pointers) style of operating system, with the screen divided into distinct 'windows', for simultaneous display of different items of information, and commands implemented by 'icons', graphical representations such as pictures of floppy discs, filling cabinets, and wastepaper baskets (trash cans) to denote file selection, storage and deletion respectively, selected by a pointing device such as a mouse, is an alternative to the highly unfriendly style of earlier micro systems software, see Gibb (1987). Pioneered on the Apple Macintosh, this has become available for a wider variety of microcomputers and workstations, with the 'Windows' software now a standard 'insulator' between the user (particularly the inexperienced user) and the DOS style of operating system.

The sophistication of operating systems is, in general, increasing. Not only are operating systems for all kinds of computers acquiring improved interfaces, particularly with the use of windows, icons, etc., following Apple, but a wider range of features of direct usefulness to the user are also becoming available. Interactive 'operating environments' are increasingly providing their own utility software, including such things as word processing, graphics, and database routines.

Operating systems are also increasingly being used as a means of integrating separate pieces of applications software, as an alternative to the monolithic 'integrated package'. This has been shown for library applications with. This could be taken further by the adoption of hypertext concepts, to provide 'software maps', showing the function and interrelation of available software, see Dubois (1989).

Most users will have little need to appreciate the intricacies of their operating system. If there is a choice to be made as to which system to choose, factors which must be considered are the ease of use of the operating system, and any restrictions it places upon choice of software, particularly for microcomputers. Since most information professionals will regard the operating system as nothing more than the means of running their applications software, this last point is crucial. Depending upon how it is written, there may be considerable difficulties in transferring applications software between different operating systems.

Applications Software

Applications software comprises the procedures and instructions which enable computer systems to do what the user requires. This is what most users think of as software: databases; word processing, etc.

In this section, we will outline some of the factors and trends affecting applications software in general, before considering the sorts of software of particular relevance to information services in the next section.

It is as well to clear up one point of terminology at the outset. Pieces of applications software may be variously described as *programs, packages, or systems*. Generally these terms, in this order, denote an increasing size and complexity, but there is no clear-cut distinction.

Types of applications software

By 'types of software', we do not mean its purpose; financial calculation, graphics, modelling, information retrieval, etc., but its more general characteristics, applicable to any software, whatever its function.

Up to the early 1960s, there would not have been much to be said along these lines. The only general points which could have been made about software would be the programming language in which it was written, and the computer system on which it would operate. The situation now is considerably more complicated, due to the every-increasing power of hardware, and sophistication of software.

Much of the complication has resulted from the increase in the extent of *interactive,* as opposed to batch processing, software, and of *time-sharing* and *networking.* These have given software developers many more options in the way in which software operates. Another major factor, unknown before about 1970, is the trend towards *integration* of software, which will be discussed below.

A further important influence on the software scene has been the microcomputer, which has created entirely new demands and offered new opportunities. The rise of a *de facto* standard, in the form of the IBM PC, has provided an enormous market, and stimulated the development of business software in particular with its novel graphic interface, has stimulated an entirely new generation of software products, based on the WIMP style of software interface discussed in the previous section.

Microcomputer software has been criticized for repeating the errors, and reproducing the problems, of mainframe systems of the 1960s, and there is much truth in this. Some microcomputer software can most charitably be described as 'cheap and cheerful', but, on the other hand, some micro packages have unique features not available in larger systems. It is often the case that ideas are first encapsulated in micro software, only appearing later in mini or mainframe versions. Comments on micro-computer software of relevance to information services are given.

It is increasingly common for software systems to be offered on a variety of hardware; sometimes all the way from micros to mainframes. This is very valuable for upward compatibility, when the user wants to increase the scale of operations, by using a more powerful computer, without having to change the software. It is important to assess exactly what is being offered in the micro versions in such cases; sometimes they will be essentially the same as their bigger siblings, sometimes they will offer somewhat reduced capability (fewer records, smaller field sizes, etc.), and sometimes important features may be lacking altogether.

Compatability (or lack of it)

The *computing environment* in which the software operates is a crucial master, and it is only too easy to be misled as to the chances of running a particular piece of software on one's own equipment. The programming language used, as we noted above, is of little or no consequence, and users will generally not be aware of what it is, providing only that the computer and operating system being used support the language, which is generally the case with all 'respectable' commercial software.

The sort of factors which must be taken into account include:

* type of computer;
* amount of memory and disc storage required;
* any special hardware, e.g., graphics displays, mice;
* operating system;
* other systems software required, e.g. graphics libraries;
* whether networking is supported.

The problem of transferability of software between different environments has come very much to the fore with the wide adoption of the IBM PC as the industry standard microcomputer, and many 'clones', of varying degrees of compatability. The safe, or cynical, viewpoint is to say that one should not accept that software will run on one's own system until it has been seen to do so.

Integration

'Integrated software' is perhaps most commonly thought of as a microcomputer business package, generally including spreadsheet, database, graphics, and word processing. There are, however, numerous examples in mainframe and mini-computer software (for example, some library automation systems).

The benefits of integration to the user, in terms of convenience and ease of use, need not be spelled out, but there is a drawback. It is more often than not the case that each element of an integrated package is inferior to a program dedicated to the same purpose, or that an integrated package is based around one really high-quality component, with the remainder being mediocre.

Integration does not necessarily imply a single monolithic package, from a single supplier. Increasingly there is a trend towards *modular* software, with the components acquired as needed, which may be a more, convenient way for users to acquire just what they need at each stage. This may be taken a stage further, with components from different suppliers linked together, avoiding the problem of 'integrated mediocrity' mentioned above. Given an example of the integration of divers resources and systems into a network, offering true integration from the user viewpoint. This linking may be achieved in various ways, at the level of the applications programs, or by the operating system. It may be more realistic to think in terms of 'inter software compatability', based on the *de facto* standard of popular operating systems and interfaces, rather than true integration, see Dubois (1989).

Software Design and Documentation

The process by which software is designed and constructed has changed markedly since about the mid-1970s, and it is worth outlining some of the reasons for this, and their consequences.

This must be seen against the background of an increasingly recognized fact of IT life: the 'software backlog'. As hardware capabilities have increased, and costs have fallen, so it has become increasingly impossible to produce software to take advantage of these improvements. This backlog can be seen in two manifestations. In any organization which provides its own software for its users, either by writing it inhouse, or by customization and adoption of commercial software, there is almost always a waiting list of work to be done, often amounting to many man years of effort. More generally, anyone considering the raw power of present-day computer systems, and then investigating exactly what can be done with them, using available software, is forced to the conclusion that things are not right; the power is not being properly used.

The methods by which computer software is produced have changed considerably in recent years, inspired by the emergence of the new discipline of 'software engineering' (a term first coined in 1968), which has encouraged improvements in programming practice, such as structured, or modular, programming.

The traditional pattern was for a systems analyst to

undertake a detailed analysis of user needs, resulting in an elaborate specification for the software, which would then be coded into a programming language. This process is increasingly perceived as being inadequate, and resulting in development backlogs, software which does not meet user needs, and poorly understood and maintained software. One solution is seen as increased availability of 'off-the-shelf' packaged software, so that the user can simply be handed an appropriate package to meet (more or less) the requirements of the moment. Another is the use of fourth-generation languages, application generators and flexible integrated software to produce 'prototypes' of programs to meet user needs; such prototypes cannot only be produced very readily from scratch, but can be quickly modified to suit changing requirements, and customised for slightly differing needs. These solutions will only meet fairly standard requirements, but they are meeting with some success in the 'information centres' of larger organizations.

The *documentation* of software systems, and support for their users, has been a major problem, and appears to be getting worse as microcomputers programs proliferate (the cynic may believe this to be the cause of the plethora of 'How to' books on the use of micro packages). All too often, documentation both for the user and for the system administrator and maintainer is treated as an afterthought, with obvious results. Not infrequently, users have to write documentation for their own use, virtually from scratch. Coleman and Pratt (1986) describe the various kinds of documentation required for any major piece of software, and make suggestions for ensuring its adequacy.

There is a trend towards 'automatic' documentation, or 'self-documentation', provided by application generators and fourth-generation languages. This if so undoubted value to system designers and maintainers, but is of strictly limited use to the average user; concerned only with the technical details of the software, rather than the user's perception of its workings, it is written in the most extreme computerese, hardly surprising considering its author.

One possible solution, for the user, lies in reducing dependence on printed documentation by improving the user interface (on-line help, icons and graphics interaction etc.), and perhaps by the use of expert systems. Quality of assistance available to the user is a primary point to be considered in evaluating software. We will return to the question of documentation of systems in Chapter 9.

Selecting and Acquiring Software

There are four principal alternatives for acquiring software:

* 'off-the-shelf' software package;
* 'turnkeys package - hardware and software;
* write your own program;
* have custom-made programs written for you.

Until the early 1970s, the great majority of software were written, either inhouse or by a software supplies, for a specific application, with little standardization. Since then, there has been an increasing tendency for software systems to be produced as 'packages', generally by a specialist software house to serve the purposes of many users with the same, or at least similar, requirements, rather than for programs to be written on-demand for a particular application. This usually results in high-quality software being available at a realistic price, at the cost of the lack of tailoring to a particular requirement. This may be significant, if the result is that the users' work patterns must be made to fit the software, rather than the other way round, and if customization by the supplier is either impossible or very costly. There are well-attested stories of relatively minor alterations to standard software costing far more than the original price of the package.

Each of these four approaches to software acquisition noted above has its own set of advantages and disadvantages. We will briefly outline these here, and further exemplify them in the later section on library housekeeping software. There is also the potential for acquiring 'free', or almost free, software from the public domain, *via* bulletin boards etc. This is not generally to be recommended, because of the risk of computer viruses, in addition to the problems of interconnected, and possibly flawed, software.

The first two, standardized, approaches, off-the-shelf and turnkey, will generally have advantages of cost. The turnkey approach, with hardware and software supplied, and probably maintained from a single source, has the great advantage of simplicity. It can be applied on all levels, from the small micro-based application to a very large library automation system, and is likely to be a popular approach whenever the user organization is unwilling, or unable, to devote time or resources to technical aspects. Using standard software, as noted earlier, brings the advantages of accessibility of new development, and the opportunity to be part of a large user group, with the potential for mutual assistance and for bringing pressure on suppliers.

The second two, 'customized', approaches have the obvious advantage that, in theory the customers get exactly what is required for their particular circumstances; the compute fits the users, and not the other way round. In practice, of course, things are not this easy; the customized option is often more expensive, and if the 'DIY' approach is chosen, then inhouse expertise is required. There is also the danger that customized systems may not be maintained and upgraded as well as standard software systems, although there is the converse point that users will not be bothered by frequent upgrades and improvements, which may not be wanted. These points must be set against the undeniable value of genuinely customized computer systems, under the complete control of their users, with built-in flexibility, and able to be integrated together in a way usually impossible for standard software.

There is a shifting balance between these two philosophies of software acquisition. During the late 1970s and early 1980s., the balance swung heavily in favour of buying in standard packages. More recently, there has been something of a movement the other way, fuelled in part by the increased power of the software tools, such as database systems, available to the builders of customized systems. Also there has been a recognition that for those computer systems crucial to the basic objectives of an organization, it may be foolish to restrict oneself to using exactly what everyone else uses. The decision must depend on the particular local circumstances; descriptions of the sort of considerations which will apply have been given by organizations who chose the inhouse route for its advantages of integration, flexibility, and local control; from a major chemical/biological databank system to a microcomputer-based library acquisitions routine. Conversely, there are also accounts given by those who have moved from inhouse development to packaged for turnkey system: for example in library automation systems.

The increasing availability of packages means that users must be able to evaluate software for their needs; not an easy task since several options are usually available and the situation (in terms of software features, machines supported etc.) changes rapidly. It is important to realize that each piece of software has its own indefinable 'feel', and users must try to identify the software (and supplier) which feels right for their way of working. There is no substitute for seeing software working in a similar environment to one's own.

There are many approaches to the evaluation of information systems and products, software packages included. These range from simple informal procedures, to fully formalized and rigorous evaluation strategies. Give an example of the latter, in the context of defence systems software. The question of software evaluation for and by information services will be discussed in more detail later.

Software for information services

In this section, we give an overview of the kinds of applications software of most direct relevance to information services. This includes four major categories:

* software for information retrieval (internal and external),
* for library housekeeping,
* expert systems software,
* administrative and 'office' software.

We will, of necessity, only outline the most significant points, and emphasize important trends and developments.

Information Retrieval Software

Information retrieval is often seen as the core activity of all information services, and this type of software is therefore of particular importance.

A distinction is often made between *internal* and *external* information retrieval. In the former case, the information is stored and searched locally, on the organization's own computer systems; in the latter, it is stored on a central computer system, which may be accessed by many user organizations. Sine the mid-1970s, external retrieval has, in practice, meant on-line searching; interactive retrieval with access via a telecommunications network.

There has been a continually changing balance in the perceived merits of internal and external retrieval, with changing advantages of convenience and cost. During the 1960s and early 1970s, many large organizations held acquired computerized data-bases, for example bibliographic abstracting and indexing services, on magnetic tape, and searched them as a batch process on inhouse computer systems. The advent of interactive on-line searching led to a move away from internal information processing, and towards reliance on external searching. During the 1980s, the trend has to some extent reversed, with more powerful computer processing, and cheaper storage, particularly in the form of optical media, such as CD-ROM. This in turn is likely to be countered by the improvements in network technology, allowing increasingly reliable, and cheap, access to large remotely-held information stores. This changing balance point is typical of the effects of advancing technology. Developments in IT cause a reassessment of the relative merits of alternative approaches, and an ever-changing mix of techniques. It is certain that both internal and external retrieval will feature in information services in the future.

There are two main types of software relevant to information retrieval: *database management systems* (DBMSs) and *text retrieval systems*. In the past these have been entirely separate concepts, although there is increasingly a tendency for them to overlap, as each adds features generally associated with the other. We also note that many *library automation* packages are also adding genuine information retrieval capabilities. This is another clear example of the convergence of technologies, which has been one of our themes throughout this book.

We will consider information retrieval systems under several section headings, always remembering that these are not watertight divisions, and convergence and overlap is an important factor. In the first two sections, we will cover database management systems and text retrieval systems, followed by shorter sections on videotex and on graphic and image searching systems. Then follows a section on some newer techniques for dealing with computerized text handling, which we categorize as 'browsing, navigating, and hypertext'. Finally, we consider some research and development in information retrieval, and try to assess where this may lead.

Database Management Systems

Database management systems (DBMS), date from the mid-1960s, when the increasing use of the computer in a variety of commercial, technical, and educational environments made it desirable to move beyond the simple 'flat file' structure for storing and retrieving information, and when the advent of magnetic disc storage and increased processing power provided the enabling technologies. A database, in this sense, comprises an organized collection of related sets of data, which may be treated as a single unit from the point of view of the user (or the computer program operating on behalf of the user). A DBMS is the system which manages this sort of database, allowing access by many uses, while maintaining the integrity and reliability of the data.

DBMSs are of great importance in data processing, and are a complex subject. In this section, we will try to give an informal appreciation of the aspects and attributes of these systems of most relevance to the information professional. There is a large amount of published material on the topic. Among the most readable introductions are the book which uses library examples throughout, the article by and the book by give comparisons of the DBMS and free text approaches.

DBMSs are best suited to handling *structured* data, whether numerical, factual, codes, short items of text, or whatever. Databases are therefore constructed of *fields,* generally quite short: a good example is a library catalogue, where each record has fields for author, title, data of publication, ISBN, etc. Most DBMSs have some facilities for dealing especially well with numeric data; performing calculations, simple statistics, etc. Retrieval is a matter of straight forward selection on data values in the relevant fields, ensuring 100% recall and precision. This structure, among other advantages allows for convenient and rapid updating. DBMSs are increasingly described as *relational* (or 'relational-like', 'quasi-relational', 'with relational features', and similar). This is one of the most over-hyped concepts in IT, and needs to be kept firmly in context. In short, and informally, a DBMS may be described as relational, to the extent that it allows the interrelating of data elements in answering complex queries. There is a formalism, introduced and based on the mathematics of sets and their relationships, which defines accurately, the extent to which a database is 'truly' relational; needless to say, this is largely ignored by the writers of software advertisements. Genuinely relational databases allow great flexibility in the treatment of the information in them, essentially by allowing the users to form their own 'views' of the database; explains this in detail, and with a clarity unusual for most writings on this subject. However, this power is bought at the price of the computer resources needed to run the database system. For many (perhaps most) applications, the power of a fully relational system is not needed and amounts to the use of sledgehammer to crack a nut; the 'relational' label, even if accurate, is note therefore necessarily a good thing.

A DBMS, in general, provides a *flexible framework* for applications, which are then developed as required by the system's users, or by a software house which uses the DBMS as the core of an application package.

DBMSs provide a range of options for input (from a batch file, on interactively, usually by a form on the screen), for editing and updating and for general house-keeping' (e.g. reducing wasted disc space). Output is also usually very flexible, offering either standard reports and summaries or *ad hoc* answers to enquiries, and allowing users to specify their own output requirements. There are also often links with other software system, such as spreadsheet and word processing packages, allowing data to be conveniently passed between them.

All DBMSs have some query language, to allow users to get information, out; many have more than, one. In general, the query language is specific to the database, with all the obvious consequences for the user who must access a variety of systems. There are, however, some trends towards standardization; the Structured Query Language (SQL), for example, is supported by an increasing number of DBMSs.

In general, DBMS query languages come into the fourth-generation language category; that is to say that they are 'non-procedural', freeing the user from any need to appreciate the detailed workings of the system, and designed to allow rapid generation of new applications, for example a new report format. For the most part these are 'formal' languages with a clearly, indeed rigidly, defined command syntax. In the SQL query language, this search would take a form such as:

```
Select Title
    From Catalogued-Book
    Where Author = "Austen J"
```

In QUEL, the querry language of the Ingres database, the same query could be represented as:

```
Range of cb is Catalogued-Book
Retrieve (cb.Title) Where cb.Author = "Austen J"
```

In QRS, the query language of the MDBS III micro-computer database system, the querry would be:

```
List Title
    For Author = "Austen J"
    Thru catalogue-list
```

Formal query languages such as these have a clear similarity in their nature, although the details of the syntax are of course different.

There are alternatives to this style and query language. The most common are graphical query languages, and of these the best known is Query-By-Example (QBE). This is gaining acceptance as a *de facto* standard, and is for example, provided as an alternative to SQL as the interface to IBM's standard database systems. QBE essentially provides a 'form to fill in', so that the query is built up and viewed, in terms of the search parameters and required output. For example a search in a library catalogue DBMS for books by the author Jones published since 1986, outputting the title and ISBN, could take the form:

Book Record	ISBN	First Author	Title	Year	Publisher
	p.xxx	JONES	p.xxx	>1996	

Though at firs sight simple, this graphical approach is similar to the more formal languages in that the user must have some knowledge of how the database system operates, if complex queries accessing multiple datasets are to be constructed.

Another graphical query language is Cupid (casual user

pictorial interface device), which uses symbols to represent the components of a query (attribute name, constant, logical operation, etc.), with the user choosing the relevant components and building a 'picture' of the query. This type of query language fits in very well with the WIMP style of interface, and will undoubtedly increased in popularity. It is best used with the hardware increasingly found on workstations; a large screen and a plethora of pointing devices. They point the way to still more advanced database interfaces, such as Foral-LP, SDMS, and LID discussed, which aim at removing entirely the need for the user to have any knowledge of database structure, still less of command syntax and which replace keyboard entry by an entirely visual 'pointing' style of searching. Systems of this sort, like databases with natural language interfaces, are still at an experimental stage, and it is not clear whether they will have any real usefulness in a practical situation.

Most DBMSs also have a 'database manipulation language' (DML), designed for the writing of programs to manipulate or process the information in some way, e.g. for the preparation of a particular form of report, rather than for direct enquiry by the user. Often it is possible for DML routine and commands to be included within programs written in 'conventional' programming languages, and *vice versa* the DML of the S1032 database system, for example, can call;, or be called by, programs gives an example of the user of the DML of the Knowledgeman micro DBMS:

```
clear
        at 3,30 output "Books by J. Austen"
        at 6,20 output "Title"
        at 6,55 output "Number"
        at 6,70 output "classmark"
        let line = 8
obtain record from Catalogued-Book where Author = "Ausaten J"
while set (Catalogued-Book) = false do
        at line, 10 output Catalogued-Book. Title
        at line, 55 output Catalogued-Book, Isbn
        at line, 70 output Catalogued-Book, Classmark
        let line = line + 1
obtain next record from Catalogued-Book where Author = "Austen J"
endwhile
```

DBMS may be thought of loosely as a complex set of interrelated file structures. Users, and application programs, do not need to know anything about how the data is actually stored, but they do need to know about the *nature* of the data and its *interrelation-ships*. This leads to the requirement for 'data modelling' in any database system. Construction of any database system requires a careful definition of data elements, and their interrelations. These are expressed in a 'data definition language', and in the more complex systems by a 'data dictionary', somewhat akin to a conventional thesaurus. The logical structure of the data differs between systems, the most common types being hierarchical, network, and relational. This structure will not be apparent to the user, except that the simpler non-relational systems may be easier to use, and faster in operation, but may be incapable of answering directly some types of query, not specifically considered when the system was constructed. A truly relational system should confer complete flexibility, in that if a query can be posed sensibly, i.e. if it is a 'real' question in terms of the data within the system, it should be answered.

We must not forget, or underestimate, the simplest kind of database program, the 'electronic filing system'. This may actually be preferable for the operation of relatively simple databases, on account of its ease of construction and maintenance, and simplicity of use.

It will be clear from what we have said above that database management systems are most appropriately used for information which has a high degree of structure. Nonetheless there are numerous examples of DBMSs being used for what is, by anyone's standards, textual information, although usually with some degree of structure gives a good account of the issues involved, in the context of the use of the Oracle DBMS with text information. Serials management system is based on dBase III, for example, while several other examples are given in the book.

Furthermore, a number of DBMS products are now expanding into the text retrieval area, providing the sorts of text searching facilities noted below.

Text Retrieval Systems

Text retrieval systems, by contrast to database

management systems, are best adapted to handling large volumes of unstructured text. Retrieval systems of this sort, after a decade of relative obscurity during which they were devoted to largely unsung bibliographic applications, are now gaining much use in a variety of application areas. In addition to traditional library/information applications, they are being applied to such situations as medical, legal and financial records, governmental, office and personnel administration, and in engineering and laboratory work. Interesting examples have been given of leg, and financial, applications. The increased automation of text handling functions in the office environment, and in records management, has played a major part in increasing the visibility of text retrieval systems. Again, we will only attempt to outline the major aspects of these systems, which are well described by other writers. A large number of text retrieval systems are described in outline in the directory edited by Robert Kimberley (1988).

The most significant distinction between text retrieval and database systems lies in the structure of the information with which they deal. Whereas DBMS records, as we have seen, have a clearly defined field structure, text retrieval systems must rely on the looser structure of sentence, paragraph, section, etc. with a record generally equivalent to a document. In the extreme case of a true full-text system, a document could be the complete contents of an encyclopedia! This looser structure gives greater flexibility in the way in which information can be accepted and processed, but necessitates rather different retrieval features. Dealing with the complexities, idiosyncrasies, ambiguities, and incompleteness of text, retrieval is far from the simple matching of the DBMS (Tenopir, 1985; Blair, 1986). Text retrieval systems can be applied in one of two ways: finding a record within a file (somewhat analogous to DBMS retrieval) and finding a 'place' within a record (a uniquely 'text' concept).

Most text retrieval systems support the following sorts of search facilities, appropriate for the particular needs of text queries:

* string matching
* stemming, truncation, and partial match
* word and phrase matching.

* Boolean (AND, OR, NOT) combinations
* proximity search
* limiting by field (sentence, paragraph, etc.)
* controlled vocabularies and thesauri
* stop word lists
* phonetic matching
* production of printed indexes

Increasingly, they are handling numeric data better than in the past, by allowing range searching for example, tending to promote the overlap in function between these systems and DBMSs.

In common with DBMSs, text retrieval systems support input either interactively or as a batch process, provide editing facilities, and allow for output defined by the user. There is not generally such a range of possible output options, no facilities for producing reports and summaries. In general, text retrieval systems offer a rather fixed set of applications, by contrast to the 'framework' offered by the typical DBMS. This is changing with some of the more recent systems, such as Trip, which are to be regarded as 'text processing engines', which may be adapted by the users for their own particular needs. On some occasions, users have written their own shell around a text retrieval package, to provide facilities not provided directly Elspeth Scott, for example, (1987) describes a menu-driven shell for Stairs, to provide improved input, editing, and output facilities.

Text retrieval systems do not generally have such a range of possibilities for query language as do DBMSs, being restricted in most cases to a command-driven or menu-driven 'formal' style or query. For example, the Stairs package has a set of commands, such as SEARCH (text search), SELECT (field matching and range search), BROWSE (to look at retrieved records), SORT, PRINT, etc.

Like DBMSs, text trivial systems were originally conceived to work with magnetic disc storage. A new development is their adaption for optical storage media, and particularly CD-ROM, when the retrieval software is provided with the text database on the optical disc.

Text retrieval systems are most familiar to many information professionals as the command languages for commercial on-line retrieval systems. In many cases these are essentially the same as the retrieval system in its standard 'packaged' form; the DataStar system, for example, uses the BRS/Search text retrieval system. There has been considerable criticism of the host system operators for maintaining rather old-style software, without attempting to introduce more recent developments for example, complains that online systems are inefficient, over-expensive, and hostile to end users. While there are clearly many constraints on the hosts, trying to satisfy a large and dispersed group of users, with very different requirements and levels of expertise and often lacking access to any hardware other than a dumb terminal, it is undeniably true that most online searching systems tend to have a rather dated feel to them. Most advances can be expected to come in the form of front-end software, on the searcher's microcomputer, assisting with database selection, query formulation etc.

Text retrieval is of increasing importance for records management and archival applications. Generally, standard systems are used; examples of the use of Cairs, Stairs, status, and Basis, as well as micro DBMS packages such as dBase III and Delta. Some specially configured packages are now appearing, such as the Tindoc variant of the Tinman retrieval system, to cater for requirements such as file tracking, and retention information. A related application is museum documentation; again standard packages are commonly used and again specialist systems, such as Muscat are available. A good international overrun of museum documentation systems is given in the volume edited.

Office automation is another area in which text retrieval is gaining in importance, as the need is realized for efficient and flexible access to the mass of material in machine-readable form. A number of the standard text trivial packages are being used in this way, as the papers in the volume edited by demonstrates: that by is a good example.

Full text retrieval, from full-length documents in electronic form, without reliance on any form of indexing, is of increasing importance, with the large amounts of text in computerized form in office automation and electronic publishing systems. This type of retrieval system also has an important role in searching databases on CD-ROM. The features needed are somewhat different from conventional information retrieval, the efficient identification of words and phrases within very large amounts of text being only the start. 'Data tagging', the identification of particular items within the text, and the automatic generation of abstracts and summaries, are ideas beginning to be introduced into operational systems. Research is now aimed at providing ways of browsing within full text and 'navigating' around it in the same way that one would do within a printed document, and we will discuss this in a later section.

We have already noted several aspects of the increasing overlap between text retrieval systems and DBMS packages. There is also an increasing overlap between text retrieval systems and library automation packages. The latter have always, of necessity, had retrieval features (indeed they may well be regarded as a series of linked databases), but are now greatly increasing the scope in this respect. Many library systems are now adding 'online public access catalogues' (OPACs), retrieval systems of very varied levels of sophistication. Some are components of integrated library automation systems, such as OCLC, GEAC, or ALS, while others use text retrieval packages, such as Cairs or BRS/Search. CD-ROM may also be an appropriate medium for a microcomputer-based OPAC, see Akeroyd (1988).

On the whole the design of these systems, particularly in allowing subject access by keyword for the inexperienced user, is improving. They are very 'visible' programs since they are the most prominent example of information retrieval in most library systems, and the first example of an information retrieval system for many library users.

This is an example of library housekeeping systems 'branching out' into information retrieval. Conversely, several information retrieval systems, such as providing library automation modules, as we shall discuss further in the library housekeeping section.

Videotext Systems

First we must clear up a question of terminology. Videotex is a fairly generally used term, referring to information services delivered to a large and dispersed group of users, and displayed on modified television sets, or computer terminals. There are two principal kinds.

Broadcast videotex is transmitted widely, typically piggy-backing onto existing television signals, as in the UK systems; it is restricted to a few hundreds of pages of information, selected by the viewer by a push-button device. The information provided typically deals with rapidly updated factual material:

* weather forecasts
* travel news
* financial affairs
* sports results

This type of service is also known as *teletext* (not to be confused with *telefax,* described in the telecommunications section). Although it may be useful, broadcast videotex cannot realistically be described as an information retrieval system.

By contrast, *interactive* videotex, as its name implies, allows two-way communication of information between user and source (for example, to specify a search term), and also allows for much larger databases to be made accessible. This type of videotex is also termed *viewdata,* and can realistically be regarded as a genuine information retrieval system.

Indeed, in some ways, it seems like the ideal, since its emphases have always been on the following points:

* simplicity
* ease of use
* user-friendly environment
* interactive capabilities
* easy to learn procedures
* low-cost central computer resources
* low-cost terminals (micros or adapted TV sets)
* inexpensive standard software
* colour always available
* low-cost, simple graphics
* based on proven technology
* extensions to electronic mail and other services

The essence of viewdata systems is the provision of simple menu-driven access to pages of information, which in turn lead on to other pages. The menu systems are generally tree-structured, although most systems allow simple keyword access. It appears to be, and in many ways is, the ideal information system for the inexpert and occasional user although to be effective a viewdata system must be carefully designed.

Yet, despite all these advantages, viewdata has never really attained the success predicted for it. Only in France, where it received a great deal of government backing, has it achieved any degree of domestic acceptance. In the UK, with the unfortunately abortive start to the Prestel service, in the rest of Europe, and in the USA, the take up of public and domestic viewdata services has been universally disappointing.

Greater success has come to the development of private view data services, particularly those with a genuinely interactive component, for example travel reservation systems, and systems for financial services (such as the UK stock Exchange's Topic system) and for retailing. Viewdata systems have also been installed for internal information systems within organizations, generally for management and administrative information, taking advantage of simplicity of use to appeal to those who might otherwise be loath to use computerized information systems. Viewdata systems can also be used to provide information to a user community, not particularly computer-oriented, and scattered across a wide area; one typical example is a service for Canadian farmers.

There seems to be considerable potential for the use of videotex in libraries and information services, see Yeates (1986), but this does not seem to have been realized to any large extent. Most examples are for internal management information, or for public access to limited databases of local information and facilities (Hicks, 1986; Marshal, 1986).

The strengths of viewdata (its very simple menu-based indexing structure and its use of simple page displays) are at the same time its weakness. There seems to be a general agreement that videotex will only achieve wider use if it can be integrated with other computer systems and technologies, for example by using a viewdata system as a gateway to other resources: retrieval systems, mail, etc. It is also possible to augment a viewdata system with more elaborate searching facilities has demonstrated.

Regarded in this way, as a simple and basic system, providing a gateway to other facilities as required, viewdata is likely to increase in importance.

Graphic and Image Retrieval and 'Composite Documents'

We have so far considered retrieval systems which deal with text, numbers, codes, etc. We must now briefly refer to systems which deal rather with graphical and image representations. Needless to say, these systems rely on appropriate hardware for dealing with graphics information - display screens, printers and plotters, graphics input devices etc.

Undoubtedly the best known form of graphical information retrieval is that incorporated in chemical structure searching systems. Chemical substances are usually represented as structure diagrams, because of the vagaries of chemical nomenclature, and these may be stored within a database in the form of a connection table, in which the atoms and bonds are explicitly represented Graphical searching software allows the user to draw in the structure, or part of a structure, which is required, using a pointing device such as a light pen or mouse. This is translated by the searching software into an appropriate search formulation, and the results are expressed to the user as structure diagrams on the VDU screen.

This type of software allows the user to express a query, and see the results, in a much clearer and simpler form than would be possible with the use of text, i.e. chemical nomenclature. Nor does the user need to be aware of the internal data representation or search logic being used by the system. There are some similarities with the more advanced DBMS interfaces discussed above; in both cases the information being handled (data fields and chemical structures) are more amenable to a formal and algorithmic treatment than is the 'messier' area of text.

Handling of 'pure' images within databases generally involves searching of a text database linked to a file of displayable graphic images. Future advances will certainly include direct searching of graphic data elements, by some kind of image matching, as in the example given by Petrie of the searching of a database of trade marks.

A particularly important aspect is the integration within a single document, or database record, of different types of information from different sources: text, data, spreadsheets, graphics, etc. Usually these are combined together at the document preparation stage, perhaps improved in presentation by desktop publishing techniques, and stored in a retrieval system. 'Composite' documents of this sort usually have to be generated using different types of software package; which requires a degree of integration, or at least compatibility, between software products. The integration of different data types is, in practice, fraught with difficulty, as is seen for example, in the combination and integration of text with financial data and with graphical representation of chemical structures. Integrative software, such as the Framework package may provide a solution in some cases.

Browsing, navigating and hypertext

Browsing is a rather ill-defined, but highly important concept. We will take it as referring, in general, to any sort of informal or unstructured access to information. In particular, it implies a 'semi-directed scanning', with some aim, albeit loosely defined, in view, or a process of 'getting an overview' of the contents of a document, set of documents, or other information source. It is a particularly important form of information handling, since it is known to be associated strongly with the creative and innovative use of information. Browsing facilities also make information sources much more accessible to casual and inexperienced users.

For the most part, computerized retrieval systems do not support browsing very well, to the extent that one distinguished librarian declared that the idea of browsing in computer systems was 'shear lunacy'. Increasingly, however, research and development is providing software to allow browsing in various ways, and in many different kinds of information.

Very few commercial retrieval systems allow browsing in any real sense; although many contain a BROWSE option, this usually only amounts to examination of an alphabetized list, or examination of a list of retrieved references. An exception is the retrieval package, described as a 'browsing and navigating' system. This allows users to find their way around the database, following a preset data structure, which must be carefully defined at the outset. It is particularly well suited for 'factual' databases.

A quite different approach to browsing is statistical in nature, allowing the user to select similar items is statistical in nature, allowing the user to select similar items to a starting point, by assessing the number of terms in common. This avoids the need for a formal query formulation, which may be very difficult with the vague starting points typical of browsing, and also makes the command syntax much simpler. The same methods can be used to partition a database into clusters of related items. The best developed approaches of this type have been pioneered at initially for chemical structure databases, and this software has been implemented in a real world setting at Pfizer Central Research. The Sisre microcomputer database system has similar features. The Sire microcomputer database system has similar features, based on the experimental work.

A very different approach to browsing is that who use artificial intelligence techniques to allow the user to browse within a single document, rapidly getting an idea of its content. Browsing within electronic documents was also a problem tackled by the BLEND electronic journal project.

This brings us rather neatly to *hypertext.* It is most unfortunate that this term begins with 'hype', since this is many people's impression of the nature of what is, in fact, emerging as a genuinely useful technology. We will give a rough outline of the topic here, hoping to avoid some of the overblown claims made for systems of this sort; useful references are while gives an annotated bibliography.

Hypertext basically involves *non-sequential* reading and writing users are able to link concepts together directly, creating 'trails' of associations between ideas, either within a single document or across documents. The links are essentially the same as those used in printed documents:

* cross-references
* citations
* footnotes
* annotations
* index terms
* definitions

but now invoked within an interactive computer system. The links may be hierarchical, leading the user to material at ever increasing degrees of detail, or lateral, in some form of cross-reference, see Brown (1988). The term *hypermedia* is used when this linking scheme is applied to a system containing more than just computerized text; graphics, video, voice, etc.

Hypertext is not really a new idea. The original idea arguable datas from hypothetical 'memex' system, which was able to make linkages between any two pieces of information within it. The first working hypertext systems were devised in the 1960s by Doug Engelbert with the NLS system, and Ted Nelson, with the Xanadu and Fress systems. First coined the term 'hypertext}, envisaging all the world's scientific literature being linked together in one massive hypertext structure. Interest in hypertext has reached what can only be described as frantic proportions during the 1980s, with the coupling of relatively old concepts with the newly available graphics interfaces on workstations, and on micro-computers such as the Apple Macintosh. Commercial hypertext products such as Apple's Hypercard, Owl's Guide and Exrox Notecards have appeared during the late 1980s (Goodman, 1987; Halas *et al.,* 1987; Franklin, 1988b; Kinnell, 1988). These make use of the pointing devices to indicate the required links (for example, by pointing at a term in the text if a definition is required), and of the windowing features to show different parts of the document.

Hypertext is a particularly useful way of making available computerized material which has a good deal of internal structure, such as an instruction manual, where there will be a good deal of cross-referencing. The documentation of computer systems is one obvious application area. Legal texts are another: whilst reading some part of the text, the reader may find it useful to jump to the text of a relevant statute, a report of a cited case, a definition of a legal term, etc., considers possible uses for hypertext in a library context. Hypertext concepts may also be usefully included within operating system interfaces, to provide 'maps' showing available software with an indication of what it will do, and how to go about using it.

There are also exciting possibilities for the use of hypertext in the design of educational packages; gives examples of the experimental Intermedia hypertext system being used in this way for English literature and cell biology. The extension to *hyperemedia* offers the potential for much more elaborate multimedia 'edutainment' packages, taking advantage of improved storage and output hardware. The design of such products involves very specific skills.

This, however, brings us to a major problem with hypertext; the sheer intellectual effort required to produce a usable product. Five Wilson's work (1988) with legal texts has shown that the task can be automated to some extent, for example by setting up automatic links to citations, which can be recognized by their formal expression in the text. Nonetheless, the task in general remains formidable. There are also still a number of unsolved problems with hypertext, particularly the difficulties for users to become disorientated within a document. And, of course, there is a good deal of straightforward cynicism, as a counterbalance to the hype; the main claim of hypertext, it has been said, is that it makes computers work almost as well as books. Yankelovich *et al.* (1985) give a detailed comparison of print-on-paper with hypertext-on-disc, and conclude that the book is still to be preferred; they concede that *hypermedia* has undeniable advantages, however. A comparison of books and hypermedia for the specific hope of coaching leads to the same conclusion.

Most hypertext systems are created basically for reading; that is to say that the purpose is to guide a reader through a structured document. It may also have considerable application as a tool for cooperative writing, allowing comments and amendments to be added in, and linked together.

As with a number of the other technologies which we have discussed, hypertext will reach its full potential when it is fully integrated with other aspects of IT; Karen Smith (1988), for example, foresees a link between a hypertext system and online retrieval, while describe a hypertext system (Guide) acting as a front end to an information retrieval package (Prism). Hypertext is also commonly regarded as an ideal tool for controlling image databases held on optical storage media. Once the hype disperses, hyptertext and hypermedia will no doubt still be here.

New Developments in Information Retrieval

We have already noted some of the newer developments in retrieval systems, which began to become available to users during the late 1980s. These include the WIMP style of interface, browsing facilities, and front ends for external online searching.

We now examine two main strands of research and development, both of which have been under way for over a decade, and which seem likely to have a major impact on retrieval systems in the near future. We denote these as the statistical and knowledge-based approaches.

The statistical approach to information retrieval has been under investigation for the last two decades. The area has been well reviewed in books, and the references given below are a rather selective set of more recent and leading papers, with no pretence of being comprehensive.

The statistical approach involves the use of algorithms which enable the computer to carry out automatically several steps usually requiring intellectual input from indexer and/or searcher. Four procedures common to most implementations of this approach are:

1. automatic indexing
2. automatic query analysis and search generation
3. best match searching
4. relevance feedback

Automatic indexing methods are used to generate indexing terms from the computer readable text of a full document, or of a title, abstract etc. There are several methods available, but most involve the removal of common and insignificant words (and, the, etc.), followed by 'conflation', the balancing of variant forms of the same word, by for example, removing different endings; more sophisticated methods can be used to bring related terms together. Weighting may then be applied, to reflect the importance of each term, based on the frequency of its occurrence in the document, compared with its occurrence in the database as a whole. The same methods can be used to extract search terms from a query, which may be a set of terms, a sentence, discursive paragraph, etc.

The problems of Boolean searching, i.e. the use of logical operators such as AND, OR, NOT, are well known: unfamiliarity for the novice searcher or end user and difficulty of query formulation in some cases (for example, ill-defined or very complex questions) even for the expert searcher. They can be overcome by a best-match search procedure, which finds documents having as many terms in common with the query as possible. Various weighting procedures, to reflect the perceived importance of the concepts, can be used. The user is then presented with a list of documents, ranked in order of probable relevance.

The user may indicate to the system which of the retrieved documents are in fact relevant. A new search can then be automatically set up, by comparing the indexing terms in the relevant and irrelevant documents, and assigning appropriate weights to the search terms; the 'relevance weighting procedure.

Statistical procedures may also be used to divide text files into clusters of documents, each cluster containing related material. This may offer a directly usable method of browsing, or may help to increase the efficiency of other searching procedures.

These ideas, which should lead to much easier access to text retrieval systems, and perhaps to better retrieval performance in some cases at least, have been very slow to gain acceptance in real-life systems, despite the enthusiastic support of experts. As we noted in an earlier section, some of these facilities are becoming available in systems to support browsing in text databases. Examples are the Instruct systems. Relevance feedback has also been sued successfully in a museum documentation system and in an experimental from-end system for the Datastar online service.

A quite different approach to improving computerized information retrieval is that of the knowledge-based information system also referred to as 'intelligent' or 'expert' retrieval systems), statistically-based systems, having been under development since about 1980. A number of different types of system are included within the scope of these terms; again, after much research, they are beginning to gain practical use.

It is rather stretching the normal meaning of the term to describe as intelligent some of the systems now beginning to appear in operational settings. Some provide an automatic behind the scenes vocabulary control, by a so-called 'hidden' thesaurus. Others allow, with varying degrees of tolerance, natural language queries, while some research aims at allowing systems to assess the user's existing knowledge, and indeed to anticipate information needs, and to formulate unexpressed questions. An intelligent retrieval system can best be thought of as one which will always do something sensible for its user.

The use of expert systems as intelligent interfaces to complex retrieval systems has been considered by many researchers, and small-scale practical examples have been demonstrated. Intelligent assistance for the online searcher has been a topic for very active research. These are systems, which go beyond helping with the mechanics of system usage (logging on etc.), accepting that the major problem for most users of whatever level of expertise is the choice of database and formulation of search strategy.

Perhaps the most interesting product in this area is Tome Searcher, which acts as intelligent interface for online searching of databases of electronics and computer science, having a knowledge base derived from the Inspect thesaurus. Tome analyses a user's query, selects appropriate thesaurus terms, and constructs Boolean search statements. The same software could be adapted for any database in any subject area, given the necessary intellectual effort for construction of the knowledge base. Indeed the Tome software is derived from the Plexus system, a referral system for horticulture. Another expert system for online access is, using a knowledge base constructed from the Mesh thesaurus to search the Medline database for information relating to cancer. This system also uses rather unusual hardware in the form of a touch screen, to allow users to select the required terms without needing to sue a keyboard. A third system of this sort is 13R, an intelligent interface devised by and his team, which is intended to help the user formulate queries and carry out retrieval by choice of several strategies; again a thesaurus is used to provide the 'domain specific' subject knowledge. This system is intended to adapt its behaviour to the needs of different users.

This sort of system points the way towards the concept of the intelligent database, a goal of fifth-generation computer research. There is also the prospect that conventional document retrieval systems will be supplemented by knowledge bases, in which agreed consensus knowledge will be explicitly stored; one example of this is the Hepatitis Knowledge Base.

We have described these two approaches, statistical and knowledge based, as though they were entirely and necessarily separate; and indeed this is how they have developed. However, the effect of convergence and integration may be also be seen here. It is particularly interesting to note that in a comparative evaluation of the Instruct statistical searching system and the Plexus expert system, the best results were obtained when the two were used in combination, submitting the profile of terms generated by Plexus to the Instruct best match procedure. There is surely a pointer for the future here.

Software for Library Housekeeping

The term 'library housekeeping' or, else, 'library automation' can be sued to cover a number of functions. It is taken here to mean primarily four 'core' functions:

- cataloguing
- acquisitions
- serials control
- circulation control

Other relevant aspects, such as information retrieval (which may be subsumed as 'enquiries' in the cataloguing function), communications (for access to remote data bases, transmission, of interlibrary loans etc.), and administrative and budgeting tasks, are dealt with elsewhere in this book.

The most useful sources for further details of library housekeeping systems are the books have useful description of microcomputer applications in this area. Gives a buyer's guide to library automation systems, covering a relatively small number of systems in considerable detail, give brief details for a larger range of systems. A series of books gives very detailed description of the operation of single (large library systems, including GEAC.

Library automation was one of the earliest applications of the computer to library/information work, beginning in the 1960s with 'home made' systems on the mainframe computers of the parent organization. A major expansion took place in the 1970s, with increasing availability of computer power, including minicomputers under the control of the library, co-operative automation schemes, and commercial packaged software and turn-key systems, including both hardware and software. These trends continued in the 1980s, fuelled by the introduction of the microcomputer, with associated software, bringing the possibility of automation to the smallest library.

In general terms, there are six kinds of software which may be used for library automation: integrated packages, modular packages, function specific programs, variants of information retrieval software, general business software, and

DIY customized systems. We will look at each of these separately.

1. *Integrated Packages*—Here, all the functions are present in a single monolithic system, which would certainly include the four core aspects, and probably others. An example is the microcomputer version of Bookshelf. Use of a package of this sort provides a simple 'total solution', 'neat and convenient', but at the cost of any degree of flexibility, since the library using such a package must adapt all its procedures to fit in. There is also, inevitably, a high initial cost. Turn-key packages, where the hardware is provided along with the software by the same supplier, is a still fuller form of integration.

2. *Modular Packages*—This sort of software comprises a set of modules, each dealing with one aspect of the total task, e.g. cataloguing and acquisitions. Coming from the same supplier, the modules fit together, giving the advantages of a fully integrated package. They have the advantage that the user can choose the modules as required, thus building up a system slowly, spreading the cost, and avoiding the need to pay for unwanted facilities. The user can retain flexibility by replacing a module by more suitable software from another supplier if required. This approach has proved very popular, and most integrated packages, and turnkey systems, are of this sort. Examples are GEAC, CLSI, and ALS (for large computer systems), and Micro library and Calm (for microcomputers).

3. *Function Specific Programs*—These are pieces of software which fulfil one specific task. It is of course possible to construct a total system by buying a number of these programs from different suppliers, but there would then be considerable problems, since information could not be exchanged easily between them; there might also be problems of compatibility of hardware or operating system. They are often used to meet a specific need, e.g. to do a job which is not done satisfactorily by one's existing system. For example, a special library might have an existing retrieval system which performed quite adequately for cataloguing and circulation, and would look for software for acquisitions or serials. Also, there are some functions which have not been well catered for, in the past, by integrated systems, such as communications, and specific programs may be chosen for these purposes. Examples are buy (for acquisitions), Bibliolend (for circulation); PC-SMS (for serials control), and

AIM (for inter-library loan administration).

4. *Variants of Information Retrieval Software*—A number of information retrieval packages may be used for library housekeeping, using their normal facilities. A few have spawned offshoots dedicated to library automation, obviously having much in common with their parents. Use of this sort, of software, though it may be lacking in some features by comparison with 'true' library software, is a very popular option with special libraries, because of the ability to integrate fully the library and information systems. Examples are TINLIB, In magic-Biblio, and Cairs Library Management System.

5. *General Business Software*—Most libraries have access to software of this sort, e.g. DBMSs, spreadsheets, word processing packages, etc. While it would be possible, with ingenuity and perseverance, to construct some kind of library housekeeping package using these alone, the results are not likely to be fully satisfactory. However, this sort of software can be useful for providing specific functions, in an unsophisticated way (for example, a DBMS can be used for cataloguing), and this could be useful if a 'proper' piece of software were not available. Examples are given, among others, of the use of dBase II for the administration of a reserve library collection and by of the use of a spreadsheet to allocate shelf space. It is also very useful if these standard packages can be linked to the library software, for example to read issue statistics into a spreadsheet, or borrows' names into a word processing package. Some of the larger integrated housekeeping systems include these sort of software within them.

6. *DIY*—This almost certainly means programming a package such as a DBMS, rather than writing from scratch in a programming language. It obviously offers the maximum extent of 'tailoring' of a housekeeping system to the needs of a library, but is very demanding of staff time and expertise. Very few libraries could contemplate writing any substantial part of a housekeeping system for themselves, but it may be a useful expedient for 'plugging a gap', 'customizing' the user view of the system, or integrating separate pieces of software; cases where a modest effort can make a big difference to the effectiveness of a system.

Once the general strategy for choice of software, from

among those mentioned above, has been made, there are several considerations remaining, which must be taken into account in choosing between deferent systems of the same kind. These considerations are described in detail in the earlier section on software evaluation. It is important to realize that systems which provide much the same functions may nonetheless have their own 'personality', often reflecting their origins, e.g. as ordering/ acquisitions or information retrieval systems.

Recent trends in library housekeeping systems include an increasing range of software, most commonly as modular integrated packages. Existing packages are converging to a large extent, as each package acquires features and facilities originally lacking. There is increasing overlap between originally diverse types of software. For example, as we noted in an earlier section, several library automation packages are now incorporating powerful text retrieval capabilities, an opposite move to the growth of library automation offshoots from information retrieval software.

Much software now runs on a range of machines, from microcomputers upwards; the ability to upgrade to a more powerful computer without changing the software being an important consideration. This has promoted the increasing standardization on operating systems such as Unix and Pick, which was noted earlier. Networking for library automation systems on minis and micros is another growing trend.

Expert and Intelligent Software

We have discussed the nature of expert and intelligent software systems in an earlier section, noting that these are of most use in limited and self-contained areas, for diagnostic or advisory purposes, and that they will act as an assistant to the human expert, or as a 'competent' substitute, in the absence of human expertise.

We now look at the specific applications for this kind of software in information services. We have already considered, in an earlier section, the application on which most effort has been-expended: intelligent interfaces to retrieval systems. In this section, we will look at other applications, noting regretfully that, on the whole there has been a lot of speculation and little action.

The major application areas seem to be in the so-called 'technical processes': cataloguing, classification, indexing, etc. These are tasks calling for background knowledge and training, but essentially routine in nature, an expert system aid could speed up the process by automating some aspects of the task, as well as helping in quality control. It is an open question as to whether it is possible, or desirable, to entirely automate these procedures via intelligent systems.

Cataloguing is a clearly suitable topic for an expert system, since there is a clear, hopefully unambiguous, and self-contained set of rules, to be applied consistently to all the material to be input, notes several research projects in this area, generally aiming at producing a 'cataloguer's assistant', rather than full automation and also review progress. Classification has also been the subject of research.

Indexing is also a prime target for intelligent machine assistance, especially in the case of a large indexing operation, where large teams of indexers must conform to standard procedures. The National Library of Medicine has developed a system, to act as assistant to trained indexers on the Medline database. Automatic abstracting, a goal of information science research over three decades, is a more elusive concept, although again research is underway; it may be that some of the intelligent browsing systems referred to an earlier section may point the way to an ability to automatically detect the 'main point' of a text. Collection development is another area of development.

Assistance to users is another obvious potential application area for expert systems. The kind of 'text' animation' systems, referred to earlier, which have been used to encode complex legislation could certainly be applied to the rather simpler task of guiding users to make best use of an information service. As suggests, it could be worthwhile for information services to build simple systems of this sort for themselves, to answer the most popular types of enquiry. This use of expert systems could ensure that users get the best possible level of assistance, even in the absence of the appropriate human expert.

Naturally, the pervasive nature of the concept of 'intelligent' software implies that the most effective resources will result from an integration of expert system concepts with other hardware and software techniques. One interesting examples is the Bibilofile system, which combines hypertext and expert system software with voice output, providing a verbal description of, and guide through, a library catalogue, ultimately recommending material on the basis of the user's responses.

Information services may also become involved with the 'expert support system', to be discussed in the next section. This is one means of integrating the ideas of intelligent software into the management information service function.

Expert and intelligent systems certainly have a role to play in the information services of the next decade, though perhaps not so great a role as their most enthusiastic proponents might suggest. They will be most effective when combined with other hardware and software advances, when restricted to manageable fields of application, and when used primarily as an adjunct to the skills of the information professional.

Administrative and Office Software

Developments in new technology affect the administrative procedures of libraries and information services as much as their specifically professional functions. These developments are those associated with the 'electronic office', since information service administration has much in common with general office work. The main influences have been the widespread use of standard microcomputers (the IBM PC and its clones), with the consequent spread of packaged software for business purposes, and a variety of improved communications links, both within the organization and without discusses this whole area in detail, and useful material is also given.

Certainly the most familiar of these office systems is word processing, now increasingly denoted as 'text processing' in view of the improved functionality of the systems available. As well as its obvious usefulness in all aspects of information service operation, text processing can act as the single most important integrator for all information management functions. This leads on to document preparation, with integration of text and graphics, which in turn points the way to full desktop publishing (DTP), with packages such as Pagemaker. Libraries and information units, like other departments within an organization, have the opportunity to do a great deal in the way of preparing high-quality documents of various sorts from their own, relatively modest, resources. A great deal has been written on DTP, of which some useful sources are the books gives a snappy series of recommendations the articles are useful. A specifically library/information context is given.

It is clear that many organizations have suffered a great deal of wasted time and resources, as their staff wrestle rather amateurishly with complex DTP products. Regardless of the availability of hardware and software, high-quality document preparation requires training, experience, and practice. The need for skilled design is as great with the desktop varieties of publishing as with the traditional kind rather than just good text preparation, is felt to be needed, then it should be left to a small number of staff to build up proficiency, rather than letting everyone have a try. However, excellent results can often be obtained much more straightforwardly from a good word-processing package, and this will be sufficient for many purposes, without the need to go to DTP as such.

The other three major components of the business software portfolio are databases, spreadsheets, and graphics.

The value of a suitable database system for a wide variety of administrative tasks (simple indexes, personnel records, inventories etc.) needs no emphasis; such packages have a place even within a library/information unit which may have much more sophisticated retrieval tools to hand gives an example, the provision of a database of local company information. These packages can usefully be combined with other standard business software; examples are given.

Of the other forms of business software, spreadsheets, the earliest and most widely used form of business software, except for word processing, are valuable for a variety of financial calculation and budgetary purposes. Presentation graphics software is not only useful for presenting data in reports etc. in a more assimilable form, but can be used to produce signs, logos, promotional material etc.

It is also worth mentioning the plethora of business software which generally comes under the heading of 'utility', either as separate (usually very cheap) programs, of components of larger systems. These vary from programs to deal with computer-related problems (e.g. saving space on disc), through routines to make other software more usable (e.g. pop-up windows), to useful items in their own right, e.g. mailing list software. Some are substantial and valuable pieces of software, including planning and diary aids, and 'ideas processors'.

Just as important, of course, as software features in modern office technology is communications capability; this encompasses communications software (part of an integrated package or a separate item), electronic mail in its various forms, networks, fax etc. These are considered in the sections of this book dealing with telecommunications.

The increasing attention being given to electronic archiving and records management is worthy of note, with so much material in electronic form, the most appropriate means of storing it long term (in digital or image form) and of retrieving it when required are being actively studied. The problems are not merely technical (concerned with the economic and conservation aspects of using the new storage media such as optical discs, and the most appropriate retrieval software), but involve organizational policy and legal considerations.

The relative merits of specialized, or customized, programs with regard to standard, integrated packages are discussed as avidly in this area as anywhere else. IT is probably fair to say that integrated packages probably serve the administrative needs of information services quite well, while modular software will help to overcome any significant; disadvantages.

Use of new technology for administrative tasks reaches a fuller state of development in office automation and decision support systems. The term 'office automation' coves a wide variety of types of system, of very disparate degrees of sophistication. One may generalize by saying that any true office automation system must provide a variety of business software tools (certainly all those mentioned above), together with a variety of internal and external communications links, in an integrated and convenient form, which matches the need of its users. Whatever else these office systems may be, they are certainly not, as yet, 'paperless'. There are, in fact, very few cases of genuine integrated office automation systems so far, most implementations having been *ad hoc* and piecemeal. It goes without saying that it is highly unlikely that any library information service would itself adopt a full office automation system, but rather would have to use the one chosen for the organization as a whole. One important trend of special relevance to information services, as was noted above, is the increasing realization that office automation systems require a true text retrieval capability, if maximum advantage is to be gained from the large volume of computerized material generated.

Decision support systems have developed from the spreadsheet, perhaps in combination with a database, as a primarily financial management tool, though now with rather broader objectives. They aim to extract relevant information, present it in an acceptable form, and support analysis, modelling, and 'what if questioning. A new trend is to introduce expert system concepts, to provide an 'expert support system', making the data available in an intuitively sensible manner to users without computer system knowledge. Increasingly, systems are tending to be geared towards collaborative and group decision making.

Conclusions

We have shown something of the vast range of software of relevance to information services, while making the points that it constantly lags behind the increasing power of hardware, that it is often unsuited to the users' real needs ('as user-friendly as a cornered rat', as one commentator colourfully put it), and that incompatibility and lack of standards remain a major problem. We have tried to show some of the trend, which should help to overcome these problems: increasing intelligence and 'intuition' in software; greater availability of modular packages; improvements in integrative power of operating systems; etc. Software is also appearing which can take greater advantage of hardware features such as powerful workstations with large high-resolution screens. It is also worth noting that a number of novel software products make clear and direct use of 'library information' concepts: knowledge-based systems incorporating thesauri, for example, and browsing software. We will return to this point in Chapter 7.

6
Telecommunications

Introduction

'Those whom the Gods wish to destroy they fill with an uncontrollable urge to connect their computers to a telephone line'.

In this way David Hewson introduced his article on the state of the telephone network in the UK, see Hewson (1986). For 'computer' one might just as well substitute the name of any piece of information technology for the subject of telecommunications is unique in its ability to generate a feeling of impending doom in its users. Apart from the vagaries of communications networks themselves, the fact that it is one of the most jargon-ridden areas of IT does little to inspire users with confidence. This is unfortunate, since telecommunications has become an essential part of information provision and it is an area where its correct application can improve the standard of service offered to customers of an information service in terms of speed and timeliness.

The many forms of communications (telex, teletex, fax etc.) and office automation (word processors, electronic typewriters, microcomputers) are undergoing a logical and physical convergence so that it is now possible to carry out many of the everyday functions of business and office life from one terminal. The gradual implementation so ISDN (Integrated Services Digital Network) ion which there is no demarcation between voice and data transmission facilities is hastening this convergence. Some appreciation of current trends in this area is therefore essential if one is to make the most cost effective use of what is available. An added complication is that telecommunications, once regarded as a 'natural' monopoly, is now undergoing deregulation in many countries. Thus the customer has an increasingly wide range of choice in suppliers of equipment, carrier, and network services — something that he or she may find confusing rather than a advantage. Not only does the customer have to keep up with technological advances, but he also has to assess the relative merits and demerits (including costs, services provided, backup and support) of one supplier over another.

Telecommunications is a complex subject and in this chapter we will touch only upon those areas which directly impinge upon business and information services.

For more detailed discussions of the topic and technical background, the reader is referred to Black (1983), Knox (1985), Langley (1986) and Lane (1987a and 1987b). We will first of all describe some of the basic concepts and terms used in telecommunications, then go on to discuss the types of networks that are in common use, take a look at the systems that are collectively known as electronic mail, and finally review how all these technologies combine and interact an electronic publishing and document delivery.

Basic Concepts

Telecommunications may be defined as a system of the conveyance, through various forms of energy, of:

* speech, music and other sounds,
* visual images,
* signals serving for the importation of any matter otherwise than in the form of sounds or visual images,
* signals serving for the actuation or control of machinery or apparatus (Telecommunications Act 1984).

A telecommunications network at its simplest may be regarded as comprising an arrangement of *transmission paths* and *switching centres* through which *signals* are conveyed by the *transmission medium.* Before information can be transmitted, it must first be converted into signals which are capable of being carried by the network. The signal is represented by the variation of some property of the carrier with respect to time.

In the conventional voice telephone system, the changes in air pressure at the microphone are represented by a corresponding variation in electrical voltage. This continuous variable wave is an example of an *analogue* signal. In contrast, communications between computer systems involve the transmission of data represented by discrete pulses of fixed amplitude representing 0 or 1 i.e. they transmit *digital* signals. Until very recently the two modes of communication were because of their very nature handled in different ways and on separate networks, but with the gradual replacement of analogue lines with digital networks on an international scale the differentiation will eventually be unnecessary.

A number of terms are used when describing the performance of a telecommunications channel and the transmission of data. The *bandwidth* indicates the range of frequencies which can be carried by the channel, and is expressed in hertz, kilohertz or megahertz. For example twisted pairs of wires have a bandwidth of 500 kHz whereas optical fibres have a bandwidth of up to 60 MHz. The greater the bandwidth the faster the change from one state of signal to another i.e. from 1 to 0 and *vice versa,* can be detected. Thus in practice, the greater the bandwidth of a transmission medium the faster the data can be transmitted along it.

The noise of a channel is a measure of the degree with which messages are interrupted by unwanted signals. Noise can be generated by the telephone exchange and by the interaction between different types of exchanges that coexist on most public networks; electrical devices form outside the network; electronic devices within the network introducing distortion and losses.

The *capacity* is a measure of the maximum rate at which signals can be transmitted without error and depends on both bandwidth and noise.

The *baud rate* is a measure of line speed. The term *bits per second or bps* is also used and although technically they are not the same, for most practical purposes their values are identical. Speeds commonly used for online searching are 300 and 1200 baud, the quality of the communications line being the rate limiting factor. On most conventional voice networks 2400 baud is usually the maximum attainable speed without noise and corruption of data becoming a serious problem. Split speeds e.g. 1200/75 are employed by some systems such as the view- data service; the first number refers to the speed at which data is received and the second at which it is transmitted. Although access to online databases is often by way of dedicated digital data networks such as British Telecom's PSS (packet switch stream), where higher speeds can be reached, the connection between the user and the network is often along conventional voice networks. For users wanting to transmit and receive information at greater speeds, high-speed data lines can be leased.

Synchronous Transmission is where data is transmitted in a continuous stream from one computer to another. The computers must be in step i.e. synchronized with each other throughout the transmission and its is generally used for transmitting large volumes of data at high speed. With *asynchronous transmission* the information is set character by character, the start and finish of the character being marked by *start* and stop bits. When at rest the signal between two computers is kept at a low frequency. As soon as a key is pressed on the keyboard, the signal changes from low to high frequency for one bit duration before the signals making up the character are sent. This is the *start bit* and its purpose is to make sure that the receiving computer knows when to start reading the signals as a character.; The *stop bits* (one or two) are low frequency signals which are sent so that the start bit is easily recognizable. One stop bit is most commonly used; two stop bits are normally only used with mechanical teletype machines. All database systems accused by way of public networks use asynchronous transmission.

Word length, sometimes referred to as 'data bits', is the number of bits that make up a character. For example telex uses a 5-bit code called the *baudot* code. The ASCII (American Standard Code for information Interchange) code is the most commonly used for data transmission. It is a 7-bit code with one parity bit for error checking. The eighth parity bit may be used in some protocols for extra character sets or graphics.

Whether or not a line can carry signals in both directions

is an important parameter of protocols. A *duplex* line can carry information in both directions in contrast to a *simplex* line on which data can travel in only one direction. *Half duplex* systems allow information to flow in either direction but not at the same time: *full duplex* systems can handle information flow in both directions simultaneously.

Multiplexing is a technique whereby a single physical link may be shared by several signals by the allocation of different frequency ranges to each user (*frequency division multiplexing)* or different time slots (*time division multiplexing)* With the newer optical fibre networks a third form now as *wave division multiplexing* (WDM) where the different signals travel along the fibre at different wavelengths is being developed. The task is carried out by *multi; plexers,* also known as 'muxes', which in the past have been differentiated into analogue multiplexers and digital multiplexers. One consequence of the digitalization of networks that is occurring worldwide is that such a delineation of function is no longer necessary, and we are now seeing a new generation of integrated muxes which can cope with all types of data flowing through, for example, an office telephone branch system.

Protocols are rules governing the initiation and maintenance of data flow. Telecommunications standards are agreed internationally, the main coordinating organizations being the ISO (International Standards Organization) and the CCITT (Comite Consultatif International de Telegraphy et telephony). An appreciation of the compatibility, or possible incompatibility, of different protocols is important when interconnecting dissimilar types of equipment and networks. At the simplest level there are the protocols used in the transfer of data from a personal computer to a printer, or between terminals on a local area network. At a higher level, local area networks can be run using a variety of protocols which can give rise to difficulties when linking several networks either inhouse or across public networks. But the information professional is most likely to have to deal with online access protocols and to ensure that communication parameters e.g. baud rate, data bits, parity, stop bits are set up correctly on their terminal.

Transmission Media

Transmission media vary widely in physical form, speed and capacity. Depending on the bandwidth and type of cable, *repeaters* and needed every 2-55 km to compensate for the loss of signal strength in the sections between repeaters.

The conventional voice telephone network - in the UK the PSTN or Public Switched Telephone Network - uses *twisted pairs* of copper wires. Twisted pairs are susceptible to electrical disturbance, and interference and transmission rates are comparatively slow, making them incapable of carrying large volumes of information at high speeds.

Coaxial cable is essentially the same as that used for TV cables. Coaxial cables can support higher transmission rates than twisted pairs and are less susceptible to noise. They are often used in local area networks (LANs).

Optical fibres are small diameter glass fibres contained in a plastic cover. The centre or core which carries the signal is of slightly denser glass. The difference in refractive index of the core and surrounding glass guides the light along the core. The information is transmitted either as pulses of light (digital) or as light varying in brightness (analogue). Transmission speeds on optical fibres are far greater than on any of the other forms of physical media but the switches controlling the routing of signals are still electronic and prevent the media's full potential being realized. Under development are optical switches which work on wave division multiplexcing techniques. Con-commitment with research into improving the hardware are the development of new international standards such as SONET, the synchronous optical network standards which, it is hoped, will assist in the realization of the full potential of optical networks.

Optical fibres have a greater capacity than cables yet occupy less space, are unaffected by interference from machinery, and have lower maintenance costs being less vulnerable to corrosion and damage. Overall costs are now coming down so they are being increasingly used in LANs as well as in national and international networks. British Telecom is currently replacing the existing copper wire lines of the UK network with optical fibres as part of its programme to digitize the UK telecommunications network. The network provided by British

Telecom's competitor, Mercury Communications, is entirely made up of optical fibres.

Microwave (broad band radio of 18 or 23 GHz) is used for point-to-point transmissions along paths through the air referred to as 'line of sight'. It is most useful in mountainous or inhospitable areas where it may be the only possible means of telecommunication, and for high volume traffic over short distances. It can be difficult, though, to obtain licences for 'lines' in some areas such as central Lonson where the frequencies are already heavily oversubscribed.

Communication satellites, although associated in most peoples minds with the transmission of television, are generally used for long distance links and for the transmission of large volumes of data at high speeds. There are a variety or services and projects under way which involve the use of satellite channels in document delivery services and video conferencing. The best known is Apollo, article procurement with online local ordering, sponsored by the ESA and CEC, and in which the British Library Document Supply Centre (BLDSC) is participating. Satellites are also extensively used by the electronic publishing industry, see Bushford (1988). International newspapers and periodicals are able to extend their markets by locating their printing plants in countries far from head office. Transportation costs are reduced and the technology enables the publisher to work with shorter deadlines, and production can be delayed to incorporate the very latest news.

The use of new media such as optical fibres and satellite channels allows the rapid transmission of large amounts of data. It means that services such as high resolution and high-speed fascimile, and video conferencing, which necessitate the sending of large volumes of data over broadband networks of high capacity are now technically feasible and economically viable.

Transmission of digital (computer) information

Although networks capable of carrying data in digital form are becoming more common, if a conventional voice network is to be used at any stage for computer data, the computer's digital signals must be converted into analogue form before transmission: the analogue signal is converted back into digital form at the receiving end. This process is carried out at both ends of the line by a device called a modem (modulator/ demodulator). The telephone networks of several countries are gradually being digitalized (see below), so that they can carry both voice and data without any initial modification to the signals. Once digital networks are universal, modems will be sobsolete but, as this is likely to take many years, it seems that we will be using them for quite some time to come.

Despite the strict regulations and controls imposed upon the manufacture and operation of modems choosing the most appropriate mode is not straightforward; especially if one has to accommodate an international range of services and systems. Different frequencies, assigned by the CCITT, are used to transmit and receive data at different frequencies, assigned by the CCITT, are used to transmit and receive data at different speeds. In Europe, one must have a modem which uses these frequencies. The USA has its own frequencies defined. If one wishes to access a US system, such as a bulletin board, direct rather than going by way of data networks from Europe, or *vice versa*, it is not a simple matter of installing a modem that can be switched between Bell and CCITT tones; some equipment generates tone that are similar to those employed by the PTTs in the control and operation of exchanges and can cause severe disruption to the networks. In the UK all equipment that is attached to the public network must be approved by BABT, the British Approvals Board for Telecommunications. The legal consequences of attaching non-approved equipment is discussed, in Chapter 8.

The interface between the terminal and the modem has been standardized as the RS232 standard, a *serial* interface which sends data bit by bit down a single line. It is made up of 25 pins and wires which, in addition to data, carry signals for controlling and maintaining the flow of that data. A detailed description of the functions of each pin is given. Although the standard lists 25 pins, only nine (numbers 1-8, and 20) are essential for most everyday data communications activities such as linking up to online hosts. A few manufacturers have therefore modified the configuration of the interface for use with their own equipment. An example is the DB-9, a nine pin connection which incorporates pin numbers 2-8, 20 and 22, and which is used with IBM PC/AT machines. To compound the confusion IBM has reverted to the

25 pin connector for their range of PS 2 personal computers. Macintosh personal computers also have 'partially' standardized interfaces; the earlier machines had a DB-9 connector but an RS422, rather than RS232, port - another serial communications standard but set by the EIA (Electronic Industries Association). The more recent Mac XL, however, has a DB-25 while the Macs Plus, SE and II have a circular connector called a mini DIN-8.

It is not surprising that users become confused; we have taken the interface between terminal and modem as a particular example of how variations in standards can occur, but it is not uncommon. It can arise with any form of information technology despite international standardization, and it is happening to some degree with OSI (see below). An organization possessing equipment from different manufacturers - even different models from the same manufacturer - may have difficulties when attempting to interconnect machines, or exchange plugs and cables; this is in addition to any logical incompatibility that may exist due to the installation of different software, protocols etc.

The most basic form of modem is the *acoustic coupler,* a device with two cups and into which the telephone handset is placed once the remote computer has been dialled. They are relatively inexpensive but susceptible to interference from noisy surroundings, and can only transmit and receive reliably at speeds of 300 baud.

There are other modems which can be integrated into a telephone set or standalone and they vary in degree of sophistication and price. At the lower end of the market are single speed manual dial-up models. The user has to dial up the telephone number and make the connection to the host computer by pressing the appropriate button on the modem as soon as the host has responded. Modems capable of operating at different speeds are more expensive but offer the user greater flexibility and choice of services.

Autodial modems, if used in conjunction with the appropriate software, allow the user to program into the system the telephone numbers of services or computers which are accessed on a regular basis; once it has been set up, the number is dialled automatically by the modem by pressing a button on the modem or *via* a keystroke from the terminal; In addition the user can program the system to transmit NUAs (network user address), IDs, passwords etc., at the appropriate points in the log-on procedure. This relieves the user of the burden of typing in long log-in sequences, an error prone process at the best of times. It is not recommended, though, if the terminal is 'publicly' available and access to the remote system is to be restricted either for security reasons or on economic grounds; some end users find the temptation to try out everything that is available irresistible and, oblivious to the true cost of online services, can run up large bills without realizing it.

Some modems are what are called 'intelligent' being able to recognize the speed at which the receive computer is working and adjust their transmission speed accordingly; they usually have error detection and correction capability as well. It one does autodial and intelligent modems, the type of communications package installed on the computer is critical if one wishes to take full advantage of all the features. These modems have a programming language of their own, and the communications software must use that language. The first intelligent modems with programmable functions were produced by a US company called Hayes. Today there are several manufacturers of similar machines which operate in a similar manner and adhere, to a greater or lesser degree, to what has become known as the Hayes standard. These are referred to as Hayes compatible machines but, as always, total compatibility is not guaranteed and the only way to be certain that equipment will work under a given set of circumstances is to actually try it out.

The modems that we have described so far are external to the computer, but gaining in popularity are the modem cards which can be slotted into the back of the micro-computer. The advantage of this arrangement is that there is less equipment and wiring cluttering up the desk.

A word of warning. One should beware of over sophisticated set-ups and ensure that there is always some easy means of checking what is going on. A case in point is the library that found itself presented with a telephone bill substantially greater than it had expected, after the installation of a new online communications system on a PC. It transpired that when a user logged off from a database and dropped the communications line, a bug in the system caused the computer to automatically radial the host and reconnect.

Data Networks

For users of online databases and those who transfer large volumes of data over long distances, networks dedicated to data transmission e.g. British Telecom's PSS, France Telecom's Transpac, offer a more reliable and cheaper means of transmission than the public switched telephone network. Data is transmitted from one country's packet switch system to another's through IPSS - international packet switch stream. Data networks are specifically designed to carry data and enable information to be transmitted at high speed and without corruption from the noise that is so often associated with voice networks. The user is connected to the network *via* a PAD (Packet Assembler/Disassembler) which packages the data into blocks and assigns address information before sending it through the network to its destination. A system of multi; plexing called time division multiplexing or TDM (see above) is used so that several subscribers can use one channel simultaneously.

The link between the user and the PAD is commonly made *via* conventional voice network, so noise can still interrupt, corrupt and even terminate transmissions. One way of avoiding such interference, which at best is irritating and at worst can make one want to drive a sledgehammer through the screen, is to have a PAD installed on one's premises and lease a data line direct to the nearest data network node. Alternatively, there are services such as British Telecom's Multistrean. These offer several facilities including VPAD which allows videotexts terminals to access non-videotex hosts *via* PSS, TPAD - a system used by major credit card companies for online card and transaction verification and EPAD. EPAD software, which can be installed on the user's terminal or intelligent modem, carries out error detection and correction on all transmissions between the asynchronous terminal and the PAD at the data network.

In most countries, charges for using the public networks have two components: one based on the length of time connected to the network and the other on the volume of data sent. Tariffs vary from country to country as does the split between time and data charges. This lack of unity in tariff structure makes it very difficult for international users to monitor expenditure and plan future budgets, but for Europe at least is is hoped that along with deregulation, implementation of ISDN and the removal of trade barriers, there will also be a harmonization of the tariff structures.

Integrated Services Digital Network (ISDN)

The discrimination between voice and data traffic is gradually being eroded as more reliable and faster transmission media are introduced, and new standards and protocols are developed to handle the multiformity of information that is now generated for transmission. The potential impact and role of optical fibres and satellite communications has already been touched upon, but an essential part of this revolution in telecommunications is Integrated Services Digital Network (ISDN).

International standards have been agreed for a totally digital communications network, capable of carrying voice, data and images. The basic ISDN service operates at 144 kb/s divided into two 64 kb/s channels for carrying data and one 16 kb/s channel for data control, known as the 2B + D system. Each country's PTT has assigned its own level of priority to ISDN so the rate of implementation will not be consistent worldwide. It will be many years before telecommunications is totally digital and hybrid networks will probably remain with us into the next century. A few PTTs started to introduce ISDN services before all the standards were finalized; for example British Telecom's IDA (Integrated Digital Access) offers an 80 kb/s service at present (64 + 16 kb/s) but there are plant to start upgrading the network in 1989.

The line speed of the basic ISDN service is still considerably slower than that required by some users so the CCITT is considering a broadband ISDN, or B-ISDN, that would add three digital video channels of 45 mb/s each. In the meantime, faster leased lines are available from most PTTs. British Telecom's Kilostream offers synchronous speeds of up to 64 kb/s similar to IDA, and Megastream speeds of up to 8 Mb/s. Megastream is particularly suitable for video conferencing, CAD/CAM applications and large corporate networks.

For the majority of people, the most obvious manifestation of a digital network is the generation by the telephone set of tones, instead of a series of clicks, when a telephone number is entered. Data information services such as Financial Times Business Information's City Line, which provides the latest share prices on the UK stock market, have put the new multi frequency tone sets to good use. Once connected to the service, information on a particular stock is retrieved by keying in a pre-assigned three digit code. The tones from the telephone set activate the remote system to play back the recorded information associated with that code. On a more practical note, software used with autodial modems usually have two options for dialling; pulse dialling for standard voice networks and tone dialling for digital lines. Users must remembers to change the settings from pulse to tone dialling if the local telephone network is digitized, otherwise the exchange will fail to recognize the signals and the communications system will not work.

Value Added Networks/Value added Data Services (VANs/ VADS)

VANs are services provided by commercial organizations using lines provided by the common carriers e.g. British Telecom and Mercury. The companies operating the VANs offer extra facilities such as electronic mail, videotex, teleconferencing or home banking. International VANs are useful for organizations with offices in several countries and who need to communicate with each other on a regular and speedy basis. In the UK, the preferred term is VADS (Value Added Data Service). The Department of Trade and Industry (DTI) set up the committee in 1986 to promote awareness of VADS and to encourage their use in industry. It is a joint effort between the DTI and industry, the industry sponsors being British Telecom, Istel, INS, IBM and Fastrak.

VADS can be grouped into three areas,:

1. Communication:
   * managed data network services (MDNS)
   * electronic mail
   * messaging
   * videoconferencing
   * text and image
2. Information:
   * electronic publishing
   * database access
3. Transaction:
   * ticket reservation
   * teleshopping
   * home banking
   * linked automatic teller machines
   * EFTPOS
   * EDI

Many information professionals will come across some of the services offered by Istel, a major player in computer-integrated manufacturing and VADS. Over Istel's communications network called Infotrac runs Infosearch; this gives customers access to databases hosted by different suppliers through a single log-on procedure and simplified command structure, a facility that a large-number of end users of financial and commercial information find attractive.

Although to them it seems a revolutionary step forward in information retrieval, the provision of gateways which facilitate transparent connection to information located on multiple host computers is not new to information professionals. Several database hosts have offered access to other systems through their own network for several years. An example is ESA-IRS which has gateways to Profile, Textline, and Pergamon. What is novel is that the service has been specifically aimed at a group of people previously uncatered for, the so-called end user, by giving them a means of retrieving information without their having to learn several different log-on sequences and command languages. Such an innovative approach to the market has not been greeted with enthusiasm by all; many information workers see this as a threat to their position and standing within their organization, an idea upon which we will expand in later chapters. '

In addition to Infosearch, Istel runs electronic data interchange (EDI) services, an electronic messaging system called Comet, and a number of videotex-based systems for the retail sector.

With all VADS, there are overlaps where one type of service is used for several functions, and an organization may make use of several services provided by different VADS. VADS are typically used by groups of related companies, closed user groups, and industry specific sectors. The motor, travel and pharmaceutical industries are heavy users and in particular of EDI.

EDI is the direct transfer of invoices, orders, etc., between computers of trading companies. It enables the volume of transaction paperwork to be considerably reduced and savings to be made in time and costs. The US is still the world leader in use of EDI, but the UK is not far behind and well ahead of the rest of Europe in uptake and development. EDI growth in the UK has reached 35-40% per annum and it is predicted that it will play a central role in business leading up to 1992. Initially, the US and Europe used different operating standards for EDI, but have now agreed to adhere to EDIFACT (Electronic Data Interchange for Administration Commerce and Trade). Other areas are still causing difficulties though; suppliers often have their own stock codes and use different service providers. Pressure from industry groups who make extensive use of EDI have encouraged the adoption of common codes and some of the providers of VADS are looking at ways of linking their networks together, the most promising being X400 (see below).

Local Area Networks (LANs)

So far, we have dealt with data networks provided by the PTTs and third parties. We now take a more parochial view and look at local area networks or LANs. The popularity of local area networks is on the increase, many people seeing networked systems as a more flexible alternative to implementing a mini or mainframe computer systems. LANs are used to connect a number of different types of data equipment on a single site. They can consist of up to 500-1000 terminals but interconnection of small numbers of PCs are now commonplace.

Advantages are that resources such as printers, software, storage, processing power, and data can be shared. Disadvantages are that there may be a reduction in performance in terms of speed, the organization is more vulnerable to breakdowns, software that will permit multiuser access must be installed and there is the seemingly insurmountable problem of incompatibility of equipment from different manufacturers. Although many people tend to think solely in terms of linking PCs and printers, LANs can be used to extend access to devices such as fax and CD-ROM players or to video micrographic systems giving easy local access to central reference databases and document collections.

Installing a network is an attractive proposition, but putting it into practice and achieving one's goal is not as easy as some of the glossy sales brochures pretend are useful introductions to the subject,. But anyone contemplating such an exercise should seek expert advice. Apart from the technical aspects of installation, it is essential to ensure that not only are current needs met by the network, but also that it is flexible enough to accommodate growth in use and expansion of the organization.

As a network grows and the number of users increases, there eventually comes a point when its performance and speed of response degrades significantly. The point at which this occurs depends upon several factors, the major ones being the transmission media of the network, the mode of access, frequency and volume of data and the number of terminals attached to the network.

LANs can be run on twisted pairs of wires, coaxial cables and, now that costs have been reduced appreciably, optical fibres. The range of facilities and the network capabilities will vary according to the physical media connecting the terminals. Networks can be classified as *basebanb* or *broadband.* Base and networks use a single channel which limits its use to either voice or data transmission: broadband networks have a number of high frequency channels so that several types of message e.g. voice, images or data can be sent at once. By installing appropriate interfaces, individuals can access electronic mail, video, fax, telex, etc., from any desktop terminal attached to the network.

Another factor which affects the performance of a LAN is its topology or configuration. The three major topologies are the linear bus, ring and star. In a linear bus system all the stations are connected directly to a central cable or bus; the most well-known example is probably Ethernet. Access to the network is by CSMA/CD (carrier sense multiple access with collision detection) or by token passing. With CSMA/CD, the transmitting terminal listens to the channel to check whether there is already a signal on the line; if the line is in use the terminal waits until the channel is clear before sending the message. If a collision of data should occur, then it is detected by the system and the terminal waits for a random length of time before attempting to retransmit. With token passing the token - in essence an electronic key - travels from station to station. When a station needs to send a message it takes control of the token and only when the message has been delivered is the token freed for further use. A terminal can only send a message if it is in control of the token.

The advantages of a linear bus are that they are cheap to install requiring the least amount of cabling and terminals can be easily added along the length of the cable. The disadvantages are that the whole network goes down if the trunk cable fails at any point, cable failures are difficult to isolate and network performance decreases under heavy use.

In a ring system the terminals are connected to each other in a ring. Ring networks generally use token passing access methods. Cable breaks are easy to detect but, as with linear bus topologies, the whole network goes down if the cable fails at any point. They are also difficult to modify by adding extra stations.

In star systems, all the stations are connected directly to a central point, usually a file server. Signals travel from the server to the station along each station's individual cable. A polling access scheme is used whereby the file server checks with or polls each station to see if it is sending a signal. The server then handles signals as they come in and redirects them to the appropriate station. Advantages are:

* consistent network performance under heavy network use,
* no data collision,
* only individual workstations go down if the cable fails,
* it is easily modified.

Its main disadvantage is that it is expensive and cumbersome to install because each terminal requires its own cable. A star network is probably the most reliable type of network for users who rely heavily upon computer processing facilities; in addition to the security features inherent in its structure, several suppliers provide extra safeguards through disc mirroring. Disc mirroring keeps copies of the same data on two physical discs. If one disc fails the server switches to the mirrored disc. Disc duplexing takes the duplication a stage further and includes the discs drivers, controller boards etc. Such a system is more expensive than the simpler networks, but the extra expenditure is justified for users whose business could suffer in the event of a system failure, number of users and terminals attached to the network increase. One solution is to break the network into smaller sub-networks assigned to particular functions and to link them together by bridges. Explains:

> this technique works well because computer usage tends to follow human patterns, with people interchanging data and sharing resources much more frequently at a departmental, or work group level, than with the rest of the company.

One step on from LANs are wide area networks, or WANs, which interconnect offices and organizations scattered over wide areas using circuits provided by the common carriers or by VANs. An example is JANET, the joint academic network, which gives access to computers and services in academic institutions, electronic mail and PSS.

Open Systems Interconnection/OSI

We have already hinted that linking networks is not always straightforward because of the lack of common standards and protocols. The International standards Organization has attempted with partial success, to address the problem with open systems interconnection, known as OSI. OSI defines a set of standardized procedures for the exchange of information among terminal devices, computers etc., see Rolfe (1986) and consists of seven layers.

Level 1, the *physical* layer, specifies the hardware for basic communications even down to the plugs and sockets. It also covers the protocols for data transmission and how the data bits are to be sent and received.

Level 2, the *data link* layer, covers the assembly and transfer of blocks of data, and also error detection and correction.

Level 3, the *network* layer, deals with the routing and relay functions within the network.

Level 4, the *transport* layer, describes the communications protocols for reliable end-to-end exchanges. Various methods of multiplexing are included at this level.

Level 5, the *session* layer, outlines the data synchronization and hand-shaking protocols.,

Level 6, the *presentation* level, defines code structures and methods for data encryption and compression.

Level 7, the *application* layer, handles the interface with user applications and communications services e.g. file transfer, terminal support.

In principle, all systems which conform to the OSI specification should be able to interconnect, but there has been criticism that there are too many options within the specifications to achieve total compatibility between different manufacturers. Also, the rate of uptake has not been as high as had been hoped; the EEC has decided to take a firm stand on the issue and has issued a directive effective from 19 February 1988 that all public administration projects costing over 100000 ecu (European currency unit) must conform to OSI specifications. However, the move is unlikely to have any effect in the immediate future since many are obvious to the requirements.

Business Communications and Electronic Mail

We now look at the services which are provided on some of the networks described above, and form an important part of everyday, business communications. We use the term business communications in its broadest sense of information transfer between organizations at all levels; libraries and information departments are a part of those organizations and use several, if not all, of the means offered within office automation systems for sending and receiving data, documents etc. For an in-depth discussion of electronic mail the reader is referred to Vervest (1986) who has produced a comprehensive book on the topic.

Electronic mail is the transmission of messages or documents in electronic form. The original message may be on paper and converted into electronic form for transmission with a paper copy being regenerated at the receiving end, as is the case with facsimile (fax) transmission: alternatively the message can be sent memory to memory without the production of a paper intermediary, examples are communicating word processors, teletex. The term electronic mail is often assumed to refer to computer-based mailbox, systems but in practice encompasses diverse technologies such as fascimile transmission, telex and videotex). The trend is towards a convergence of technologies both in terms of the hardware used to access the systems, and in the provision of user transparent protocol conversions such as X400. Thus one can no longer consider any of the different forms of electronic mail in isolation. We do so here purely for the sake of convenience.

Telex

Telex was the first form of electronic messaging to be used on a large scale for business communications. It is often regarded as the backwater of IT and market research companies continue to predict its imminent demise and replacement by fax and computer based mailbox systems. There is evidence both for and against. In the USA Western Union found that its 1988 telex traffic was declining twice as fast as in 1987, most users preferring to use fax instead, on the other hand, has reported an increase in both the number of fax users, and in the number of telexes sent and received.

There are a number of drawbacks to telex. It uses the 5-bit baudot code to encode characters which are thereby limited to upper case letters, numbers and a few symbols. Information contained in a document has to be rekeyed, it cannot transmit graphics, and transmission is slow at 50 characters/s. The dedicated telex lines are separate from the rest of the telephone network and have to be leased separately. Despite the disadvantages, it remains as widely used as ever and in some parts of world is still the only reliable form of communication. Furthermore the clear legal status of orders and contracts sent by conventional telex will continue to be an important factor in its survival.

The introduction of more sophisticated machines incorporating VDUs, memory, and text editing facilities has also played a significant role in ensuring it retains a place in office automation. Messages can be prepared and stored in memory and sent to several addresses (multiaddress broadcast). Automatic dialling of prestored numbers and redial if the line is engaged are standard, and messages can be received and transmitted simultaneously. For the security conscious, some systems have a password facility so that only the intended recipient can retrieve the message. One does not even need to install a dedicated telex machine to send the receive telexes; there are now a wide choice of telex packages consisting of boards and software which can be installed on desktop microcomputers, but the user still has to rent a separate telex line. Alternatively, one can subscribe to one of the many electronic mail vendors who include telex in their services.

Fax/Facsimile Transmission

Fax is a means of converting an image into electronic signals which can be transmitted over a communications link and converted back into an image at the receiving end. The major advantage of fax is that it can transmit anything that can be put down on paper text, graphs, diagrams, handwriting, photographs, Chinese and Japanese script. No keying in of text is required and transmission is at a maximum of 9600 baud on the standard telephone network.

There are at least two million users of fax worldwide, with the Japanese making up a large proportion of users. The complexities of their Kanji alphabet has forced them to concentrate their efforts on the development of fax rather than on telex or character based transmission systems. The number of users in other countries is increasing steadily, so much so that fax has become as an important part of business life as telex. In the US mail order firms now accept purchase orders via fax and banks are permitting its use for cash transfer.

Fax works by scanning the document to be transmitted line by line and measuring the reflectivity at a number of points referred to as pels or pixels. High reflectivity equals white: low reflectivity equals black. Each line can be transmitted so that the signal is either a wave form (analogue terminals) or as a series of pulses (digital terminals). As a large proportion of the page of a document consists of white space, transmission can be speeded up by sending a code marking the location and extent of the white area instead of an individual signal for each point within that area. Some machines encode runs of identical pets within a line - known as white line skip or Modified Huffman coding: others have a facility for encoding blocks - referred to as white block skip or 'read' coding. A standardized form of white line skip is commonly used in group 3 machines but a standard for white block skip only exists for group 4. Some manufacturers have implemented a form of white block skip on group 3 machines, but in many instances the protocols are incompatible. Consequently, it is often only possible to use data compression techniques when machines at both the transmitting and the receiving ends are the same model.

Fax machines, or transceivers as they are sometimes

called, are classified into groups according to standards defined by the CCITT.

Group 1. Analogue terminals taking approximately six minutes to transmit an A4 page. Now considered to be obsolete.

Group 2. Analogue machines taking three minutes or less to transmit an A4 page. Some have white line skip.

Group 3. Although the standard does not specify whether they should be analogue or digital, nearly all are digital. Transmission times of less than a minute possible. Claims of transmission speeds of 15 seconds or less should be treated with caution since they can only be achieved if transmission speeds of 9600 bps are used, a feat not always possible with conventional telephone lines.

Group 4. The latest standard for digital machines for use on ISDN at a speed of 64 kbits/s. Transmission speeds of five seconds or less can be achieved, and white block skip, error detection and correction incorporated as standard.

Group 4 is to be subdivided into three classes. Class 1 machines are fascimile machines only; class 2 machines will in addition be able to receive teletex documents; class 3 will be able to generate and send as well as receive teletex. BLDSC offers group 3 fax transmission of articles as an option in its urgent action document delivery service. It is also participating in a project with University College London involving the use of group 4 fax to transmit documents via Megastream and the public IDA. Group 3 machine are the most widely used at present making up to 92% of installations in the UK, see the article in *Information Media and Technology* (1987). Group 4 are for use with digital networks, and so have a very small market at present being limited to private data networks or leased data lines.

As with telex, today's fax machines have a host of facilities and options which make using them that much easier and more economical. At the upper end of the market, the provision of memory lets the user scan and code documents and then store them. They can be transmitted later during the day, making use of off-peak cheap rate phone calls. A few of the more sophisticated transceivers are able to receive and transmit documents at same time, to broadcast a document to several addresses, and to offer password and ID facilities so that only authorized personnel can view confidential incoming documents.

The standard resolution for group 3 is 3.85 lines/ mm vertically, but the finer mode of 7.7 lines/mm is now more commonly used. Higher resolutions of 15.75 line/mm are optional on some machines but result in slower transmission times. For transmitting photographs, the machine must be able to encode scales of grey, the minimum number required for satisfactory reproduction being 16. These specialized machines also incorporate automatic error detection and correction. Colour fax first appeared as early as 1925 and were a composite of three separate facsimile transmissions of the same picture. Each component was produced using a different colour filter in the path of the scanner. No major improvements in the technology were made until recently when single transmission colour fax machines were introduced, the impetus coming from the newspaper industry which now regularly carries colour pictures in its publications.

The current vogue, though, is for fax cards which plug into the back of microcomputers, see Costello (1988). The first one gained approval in the UK in May 1987 and by the end of 1987 10 000 had been sold. It is estimated that the figure will have reached 400, 000 by the end of 1988. Add-on boards cost approximately the same as fax machines at the lower end of the market which in the UK is currently 900-1000, but the real cost of installing a fax board may be greater than this and depends on how it is to be used and what equipment the customer already has installed. Files created using word processing or spreadsheet packages can be faxed directly but if the PC is to be used for documents that already exist on paper the user has to invest in a scanner. A dot matrix is adequate for text output, but a laser printer is essential for graphics, drawings and high quality work. If one wants to process incoming files by, for example, transferring it into a word processing package, OCR software has to be installed.

Fax boards provide a greater degree of flexibility and increased efficiency than the conventional dedicated transceivers; they can be integrated into networks so that individuals have easy access to fax facilities whatever their physical location within the organization. But for users who perhaps have only one standalone PC, a major drawback of some of the earlier systems is that the PC cannot be used for any other work while it is operating as a fax. If it is inconvenient to have the machine occupied in this way for any period of time, then the purchaser must ensure that the package facilitates receipt and transmission of fax files in *background*.

Communicating Word Processors and Microcomputers

Some dedicated word processors and most microcomputers can be adapted for file transmission over telecommunications lines by the addition of appropriate software and hardware. Most packages used for accessing online databases are also capable of transferring files from one system to another. The advantages are that the transfer is memory to memory and no intermediate paper copy need be generated. However, successful transmission and receipt of the file is all too often dependent upon the systems at either end being identical. As well as having to ensure that the communications software and protocols are compatible, there is the problem of documents that have been formatted within one word processing package or spreadsheet being unreadable within another: the easiest solution in most cases is to convert the information into a standard unformatted ASCII file. It is this problem of incompatibility that teletex was intended to resolve.

Teletex

Teletex is not to be confused with teletext services such as Ceefax and Oracle (see below). It is an internationally agreed standard for communicating electronic typewriters and word processors. Documents are prepared on the machine and transmitted to the recipient over the public telephone network or PSS. The transmission and receipt is carried out in the background and is memory to memory so that local operations are not impeded. The teletex standard incorporates an international Latin based character set as well as some graphics characters. There are gateways between the teletex service and the telex and PSS networks, and an interface with group 4 fax is under development.

Teletex evolved from a series of studies carried out by the German government and a Swedish group in the 1970s, both of whom where investigating the future of telecommunications in their respective countries. It is widely used in some parts of

Europe but has been little used in the UK since its introduction in 1985. Originally seen as a revolution in office communications, see the article in *Index* (1983) for example, it has failed to achieve the same level of popularity as in Germany and Sweden. A document delivery project using teletex, called Hermes, and funded by the Department of Trade and Industry was planned but funding was withdrawn in December 1984. This was to have been an experiment to investigate the use of teletex for document ordering, document delivery and electronic mail.

Its failure to capture the UK and other markets has been attributed to the improvements that started to be made in other electronic mail services around the time of its launch. There was a general move instead towards known technologies such as fax and telex, and now the problems of incompatibility between different mailbox systems, a major objection to its use by many potential subscribers, are being overcome with the implementation of X400 services. In the light of current developments in the more familiar forms of electronic mail it is unlikely that potential users will be convinced of the need for teletex. British Telecom recently announced that it was going to close the UK links to the PSS and telex networks, known as Interstream 2 and Interstream 3 respectively, because growth in use of the service was insufficient to justify the costs of maintaining it. The UK telecommunications watchdog has taken up the case on behalf of UK users who have complained against the decision.

Videotex

The ITU and CCITT 1984 definition of videotex is:

An interactive service which, through appropriate access by standardized procedures allows users of videotex terminals to communicate with databases via telecommunications networks (OECD 1988).

It is a very broad definition and covers a multitude of sins, but over the years the term videotex has come to be associated with systems where the emphasis is on simplicity of use, information and transaction capability. For these reasons, it now plays a very important part in the provision of VADS.

Videotex, also referred to as view-data, displays information in a format which the incorporates colour and graphics. It is essentially a page based system in which the pages or screens are arranged hierarchically. The first services used series of menus as the sole means of accessing information, although the searcher could go direct to a page if its number was already known. A few systems now use a combination of menu access and a limited form of keyword indexing but, generally, sophisticated multicriteria search strategies are still not feasible. Videotex systems are therefore best suited to highly structured information which covers a narrowly defined subject area.

The first public videotex system to become available was the UK Prestel service in 1979. It was initially aimed at the domestic market, but it is the business world that has subsequently taken greatest advantage of videotex, see OECD (1988) a fact that is reflected in the large number of videotex based services offered by VADS. It has proved an ideal medium for order and transaction processing, the most famous example being Tops and the pharmaceutical industry has found it invaluable as a means of providing a user friendly form of data input for doctors involved in clinical trials and the monitoring of adverse drug reactions. Also in the UK, a home banking service has been introduced using the closed user group (CUG) facility, and the database producer ICC has reintroduced the videotex version of its company information service.

For some time after its launch, it seemed that videotex would never be more than a curiosity used only by a minority of special interest and industry group. Recently, though, it has undergone a revival, new applications have been found for it in the leisure industry, community informations, and education. In the UK the number of Prestel subscribers was 70, 000 in December 1986, the vast majority of these being in the business rather than the domestic market which was its original target audience. In France, on the other hand there are currently 3.5 million Minitel terminals most of which were distributed free of charge to telephone subscribes so that they could refer to an electronic form of their telephone directory instead of hard copy. Yet here again, the emphasis is shifting away from domestic and towards business users, and in particular financial services, a sector of the market increasing by around 75% compared with a 9% fall in use by the general public. While Europe as a whole will continue to lead the world in the development of videotex for public services, France is expected to continue to account for approximately 90% of terminals.

The original intention was that the videotex should be a means of bringing information by electronic means into homes using equipment that was already possessed by the occupants. Hence, it was devised to be accessed *via* a television set fitted with a low cost adaptor and telephone. Since then, the range of equipment that can be used for view-data has widened. Businesses where staff regularly use videotex for long periods have dedicated videotex terminals. Occasional users may opt for a personal computer and a communications package with a videotex option which may offer full compatibility or text only display; ordinary asynchronous software will not be decode videotext signals.

The UK Prestel Standard was the first videotex standard to be defined but has comparatively coarse mosaic graphics and a restricted number of colours and characters. The French Antiope standard is more sophisticated but incompatible with Prestel. As a compromise, an international videotex standard was laid down in September 1983 by the CEPT based on both the Prestel and French Antiope system. There still remain national variations in systems which means that those who wish to access them must ensure that they have the requisite software and hardware, or subscribe to a VADS which provides gateways and protocol conversion.

Teletext is the broadcast form of videotext and transmits information alongside television pictures using the unused part of the television signal. Examples in the UK are the Ceefax and Oracle information services. The 'pages' of information are viewed on a television set fitted with an adaptor, and selected via a series of menus and a simple electronic keypad. The database is transmitted screen by screen so there is often a lag time between selecting a page and its appearance on the television. In order to avoid long waiting times the number of pages sent is usually restricted to about 300, thus limiting the volume of data that can be comfortably supplied through this medium. It is generally used for public information such as weather forecasts, travel news, news headlines etc.

Computer Based Mailboxes

Computer based mailbox systems, or CBMS, are probably what most people think of when they hear the term electronic mail. These services were originally set up solely to provide 'mailboxes' or computer space in which messages could be left for individuals. A subscriber to the service is allocated an 'address' within the system into which other subscribers can deposit 'mail'. Although anyone who has that person's address can leave messages for them, the contents of the mailbox cannot be retrieved and read by anyone other than the authorized user. Retrieval and viewing of messages is controlled by a system of passwords, but the system is not foolproof and there have been several well publicized accounts of how mailboxes have been hacked or broken into.

The advantages of using CBMS are that one does not have a establish person to person contact in order to deliver the message as is the case with a telephone call, and it is much quicker, to send a message by electronic mail than by post. It does not guarantee, though, immediate retrieval of the message by the addressee. CBMS also offer the flexibility of being able to access or leave messages at any time and from any convenient location.

Some organizations employ electronic mail to transfer data which would normally be sent by post. Several authorities within the UK National Health Service transmit patient recourse, results of laboratory tests, and consultation reports, between hospitals and general practices using the services. Telecom Gold, Prestel Mailbox etc. (Harper, 1985; Gaunt, 1986; Cowie, 1985), and believe it to be a much quicker and ultimately cheaper way of sending the information than the standard postal route.

For communications with branch offices and subsidiaries across the world, many companies have inhouse electronic mail installed as part of their office automation system, or make use of VADS and MDNS. For communications with people outside the organization, there are commercial services such as Telecom Gold, Mercury Link 7500. In addition to the sending of simple messages most electronic mail vendors offer additional facilities such as telex, courier services, fax, gateways to databases, mailing list service. The costs of these services have several components and vary from vendor to vendor: there are usually signing on fees and minimal usage fees; charges for connect time; charges based on volume of information sent and on the time of day when the call was made; fees for storing and filling messages; and fees for extras such as mailing list services, gateways to databases.

Apart from certain industry specific applications, CBMS have not spread as quickly as had been anticipated. The lack of standardization between the different systems has been a problem and until recently it was impossible to transfer messages from one vendor to another. Nevertheless, there is evidence of growing interest in the application of CBMS to general business communications; an interest that is likely to increase all the more as conversion protocols such as X400 are introduced.

X400

A major problem with the vast array of electronic mail systems is that information cannot easily be passed from one system to another because of the different protocols adopted by each. Information can only be passed from telex to telex, fax to fax, or between subscribers of the same CBMS service. Teletex attempted to solve part of the problem by enabling suitably adapted word processors, electronic typewriters and telex to interchange information but as we have seen, it has not been universally implemented, and it does not address the issue of how to transfer messages from say Telecom Gold to Link 7500. Instead it is the X400 series of standards that is seen as the total solution.

X400 is a message handling system which will ultimately provide access to telex, facsimile, and electronic mail from a single terminal. At the time of writing only information transfer between different electronic mail services has been demonstrated but commercial services are already available. British Telecom having launched Gold 400 in the UK. As well as translating electronic mailbox messages so that they can be transferred from one vendor's system to another, it has been suggested as a means of interconnecting VADS.

Electronic Publishing and Document Delivery

These two important topics, formally regarded as entirely distinct, are now beginning to overlap, due largely to the changes wrought by improving network technology, Nonetheless, it will be simpler to consider them in turn.

Electronic Publishing

'Electronic publishing' is an umbrella term covering a variety of techniques and systems for the delivery of information in machine-readable form. It overlaps with a number of other topics, especially document delivery, and also computerized database production.

Electronic publishing is, in fact, a prime example of the convergence of technologies, since it relies on the integration of at least three technological components. First, computer printers of sufficiently high quality and flexibility to effectively replace conventional type-setting and graphical presentation are required assuming that one output from the publishing process is print-on-paper, as is usually the case); and are now available in the form of laser and ink jet printers. Second appropriate software is needed to compose computerized material, generated by word processing techniques, into typist form (thereby enhancing readability and reducing volume of pages by up to 40%), and to integrate text with graphics (either stored or computer-generated images). Third, reliable and economic telecommunications are required to gain maximum benefit from the flexibility of the electronic publishing process. Additionally, scanning devices or optical character recognition equipment may be used to capture information from existing documents for repackaging.

Electronic publishing may also be seen as the convergence of information technology, publishing skills, and information product design, see Gibbins (1984). The last allows repackaging for a variety of output formats, in both electronic and print forms. This may be particularly significant for database producers — for example, the commonwealth Agricultural Bureau uses computer type-setting to produce its abstract journals from its database. A new initiative is the 'knowledge warehouse', an 'active achieve' of electronic publications, which may be used for creating new products (customized databases etc.), as well as for storage and retrieval. The information will be stored on optical disc, with a computer-searchable index.

The Electronic Journal

The 'electronic journal' concept has been around for some time, but very few examples have been produced, and survived for any length of time.

One approach to the electronic journal is to provide a conventional printed product, with the text also available, often including added material, in electronic form, perhaps on a floppy disc. This is done, for example, in the *Tetrahedron* journal devoted to chemical computation, launched in 1988.

More adventurously, the electronic journal concept may imply a purely electronic product, distributed *via* a network. The most successful approach of this sort to date has been the project known as BLEND-LINC (Birmingham Loughborough Electronic Journal Development - Loughborough Information Network Community). Since 1980 this project has involved about fifty scientists with a common interest in 'computer human factors' in a practical investigation of various forms of electronic journal.

The components of BLEND have included: a referred papers journal; an unreferred 'poster papers' journal; a journal of software reviews; an abstract journal with reader annotation; teleconferencing; and electronic mail. A number of problems have been encountered and overcome, particularly involving the accessibility and reliability of equipment and telecommunications, and the need for novel software for using the electronic journal:

* submitting
* refereeing
* reading
* browsing
* annotating etc.

The British Library's Project Quarter is continuing work along the lines begun by BLEND. This three-year project, launched in 1986, aims at developing a single integrated information storage and communication system, combining computer networking with the storage, retrieval, and display of larger amounts of data, including text, graphics, moving and still pictures, and voice. This will involve the linking of electronic mail, computer conferencing, creation and searching of bibliographic databases, and electronic journal publishing. A main objective is the development of an electronic work station, for both data retrieval and display, and for communication. Where appropriate, Project Quarter will ling up with document delivery systems, such as Adonis and APOLLO. Unlike BLEND, it will involve academic users who are not directly concerned with computing in their day-to-day work.

Other electronic journals of the late 1980s are made available on online searching services: Learned Information's *Electronic Magazine,* dealing with the area of electronic information.

It is clear that the major problems for the electronic journal are those of user acceptance (particularly in as much as it may bring about changes in the structure of scientific communication), and economics (particularly complex, since the whole of the editorial, production, and distribution processes are affected) suggests that electronic publishing has found, and will find in the near future, greater success. In the USA than in Europe on account of two main factors: European professional workers are less computer-literate, and more resistant to change in general; and the IT European infrastructure, in terms of availability of terminals and PCs, effectiveness of networks, etc., is less well-developed. The general opinion seems to be that it will be a long time before any significant number of journals are published and distributed in a completely 'paperless' manner, but even so the increasing significance of electronic publishing should not be overlooked.

There is, of course, another sort of procedure, which is sometimes included under the heading of 'electronic publishing'. This is the so-called 'desktop publishing (DTP)', i.e. the preparation inhouse of printed products, starting from information in electronic form. Although DTP is not necessarily dependent upon telecommunications links, the ready transfer of information *via* networks greatly increases the potential for repackaging and customising of material for this kind of local publication.

Electronic Document Delivery

Electronic document delivery has a good deal of overlap with electronic publishing to the extent where it may be difficult to clearly distinguish the two topics. Like electronic publishing, document delivery is a good example of the convergence of technologies. Some means of archiving the document is required (paper, microfilm, optical disc); then the information has to be converted into electronic form before it can be transmitted via a communicatio ıs channel (PSTN, PSS, LANs, satellites); finally a copy of the original document, either in paper or electronic form, is generated at the receiving end.

Document Delivery Technologies

Essential to all forms of electronic document delivery are the telecommunications links. The development of more reliable and faster transmission media, especially satellite links, means that greater volumes of data can be transmitted at higher speeds, as we have emphasized earlier in this chapter. We now summarize the relevance of the technologies discussed above for document delivery applications.

Telex is not normally associated with document delivery, since it does not allow faithful reproduction of the original page. Nevertheless, in certain parts of the world, it may be the only means of transmitting rapidly the text of documents.

Fax allows the transmission of text, script, drawings, photographs, etc. *via* the telephone network. Anything which can be committed to paper can be sent via fax., which is therefore a very suitable medium for document delivery. Group machines are the most common type installed at present, and are used by the to supply copies of articles as part of the 'urgent action service'. BLDSC also recently started trials using Group 4 far to deliver documents to University College, London *via* Megastream and IDA.

In theory, word processors and microcomputers can send documents to each other *via* telephone lines, but the incompatibility problems mentioned above mean that this rarely happens in practice. Teletex has been mooted as a candidate for document delivery (see below) but, until it becomes universally accepted, it is likely to remain solely a means for business communication.

Video micrographics, an extension of CAR microfilm, are used by some organizations for document storage and retrieval. Images of documents are stored on microfilm - or, more recently, optical disc - and a computer provides the means of indexing the document for rapid retrieval. When an image has been retrieved, it is converted into digital form and transmitted to the user *via* a LAN. The user can display the image on a screen, print it out, or reprocess all or part of it for incorporation into another document.

Document Delivery Projects

A number of innovative electronic document delivery projects have been carried out in Europe, with some achieving a degree of practical success by the late 1980s, These have tended to have highly contrived acronyms, and when four projects were named after the Greek gods Hermes, Adonis, Artemis, and Apollo, Maurice Line assigned them the collective acronym of PANTHEON Public Access by New *Technology to Highly Elaborate Online Networks.*

Artemis (Automatic Retrieval of text from *Europe's Multinational Information System)* results from a report of the Commission of the European Communities (CEC): 'ARTEMIS: A system for documentation, digitalisation and teletransmission'. A number of pilot projects, exploring the technical and economic issues of electronic document delivery, were instigated as a result.

Project *Hermes* was funded by the UK Department of Trade and Industry, within its information technology programme. It was to have been a demonstration project carried out by the National Physical Laboratory and PIRA, using teletex for electronic mail, online requesting, and delivery of documents, and it was intended that optical discs would eventually be used as a storage medium for the documents. Alas, funding was withdrawn in December 1984.

*Adonis (*Article *D*elivery *O*ver *N*etwork *I*nformation *S*ystems) arose out of a study into how photocopying was affecting commercial publishers. In 1980, six European academic publishers formed a consortium, with the initial objective of storing the electronic form of journals on optical disc in a central archive. Copies of articles would then be transmitted on request *via* communication links. The scheme was shelved several times, but was relaunched, slightly modified, in 1987. Instead of being stored centrally, journals are supplied on CD-ROM to document supply centres such as BLDSC, which generate copies of articles in response to requests.

Apollo (Article *P*rocurement with *O*n-*L*ine *L*ocal *O*rdering) was originally conceived in 1981 by the Commission of the European Communities (CEC) and the European Space Agency (ESA). This project is specifically looking at the potential use of communications between satellites and ground stations for document delivery at very high speed. The first full practical demonstration was held at Boston Spa, UK in January 1987, and BLDSC intends to use Apollo for satellite delivery of documents to Western Europe.

Docdel was commissioned by the CEC in 1981. This wide-ranging project comprised ten full-scale experiments: three on document delivery, four on electronic publishing; one on the handling of graphics and extended character sets, and one on the role of invisible colleges.

The three document delivery experiments were:

* *Transdoc,* a comparison of optical discs and microfilm as storage media.
* German patents, with an online database and documents delivered via data networks, leased lines or videotex.
* *Eurodocdel,* European documents, searchable via videotex. Electronic mail was used to order the documents, which were then transmitted by post or fax.

Docdel 2 is intended to exploit the results of Docdel 1 and to broaden the scope of the experiments, and in particular to incorporate the use of satellite technology where feasible.

Quarter is a three-year project funded by the British Library, which commenced in 1986. Its aim, as described above, is to create a single integrated electronic storage and communication network system, which thus overlaps the areas of document delivery and electronic publishing. It is hoped that the project will become involved in Docdel 2 and Apollo.

viscount (viewdata and inter library systems communications network) is a UK project, launched in 1985, to develop an interlibrary communications network for interlending and bibliographical checking and processing. The system uses British Telecom's public networks, in conjunction with a private viewdata system used for electronic massaging.

Future Developments in Telecommunications

The three areas within the telecommunications industry

that are undergoing the most rapid and most radical changes are those of hardware, protocol conversion systems, and regulatory issues. The first two continue the theme that has run throughout this chapter on information technology; the convergence and integration of technologies and their applications. Up until the last year or so, anyone wishing to send a fax or a telex had no choice but to use a dedicated stand alone fax or telex machine; if one wanted to send a file or document created on a word processor, it had to be sent in a format and using protocols that could be understood by the receiving word processor; and if one intended to use an electronic mail service to send messages to a business colleague or acquaintance, both parties had to subscribe to the same service.

While many users of electronic systems still find themselves in this position, there are changes occurring in the type of both equipment and software that we install in our offices. As we have shown, the desk top personal computer is playing a central role in many of these developments with fax and telex boards become part of most office automation manufacturers' standard list of products. The personal computer, already used as a terminal to access online databases and electronic mailbox services, is becoming as important in telecommunications as in data processing.

Electronic mail vendors no longer concentrate on mailbox services, but offer gateways to telex, fax, videotex, and online databases to name just a few, and conversion protocols such as X400 are quickly being added to the list. These bureaux as they were once known have, in fact, become providers of value added and data services, services which have started to spread through the entire information community.

But it is the subject of deregulation that is causing the greatest upset in the telecommunications industry itself. The provision of telecommunications services has traditionally been regarded as a natural monopoly, an assumption that has been vigorously challenged over recent years. In the USA, the Consent Decree of 1st January 1984 resulted in AT and T, the sole provider of telephone lines and services in the USA, being divested of its regional operating companies. Long distance services and facilities remained with AT and T but local exchange services and facilities were assigned to the seven Bell Operating

Companies. In the UK, the 1984 Telecommunications Act empowered the Secretary of State for trade and industry to grant licences to operators other than British Telecom for the provision of public telephone lines and services. The UK now has a duopoly in which Mercury Communications is proving to be a worthy competition to British Telecom.

Deregulation also extends to the supply of telecommunications equipment. Ink Europe, the green paper Towards a Dynamic Economy (*COM 87-290)*, outlines proposals for the liberalization of the telecommunications industry throughout Europe by 1992. There has been debate, some of it heated, as to exactly how this is to be achieved and when, particularly as it has serious implications for those manufacturers who have until now had a captive market. But what effect will liberalization have on the customer?

We have already reaped the fruits of deregulation in the UK, with competition amongst manufacturers leading to a wider choice of better, more sophisticated and cheaper equipment. One wonders how long it would have taken telex, for example to evolve in a protected market from the old punch tape machines into the systems we see today. But although we will see a continued increase in the number of products coming onto the market in the short term, researchers believe that in the longer term technological developments will be more gradual and, as the market becomes saturated, there will be rationalization with many products - or even manufacturers failing to survive. Nevertheless, the rate of change over the next three to four years will be great enough to guarantee customers a more varied and interesting market, and that this section on telecommunications is out of date as soon as it reaches the book shelves.

7

Information Technology in Information Services

'My department is in possession of full knowledge of the details of the invention and [its] possible use is limited'.

In this chapter we will consider how information technology is actually used in, by, and for information services, looking at both the present situation and likely future trends. We will try to ascertain what is the real significance of the use of IT within information services; what are the benefits and the problems.

We will particularly try to answer the question as to what is the real payoff from IT applications. During the late 1980s there began to be voiced a very real disillusion as to the value of the great investment made in IT in business and commercial systems - we will consider whether there is any cause for a similar reaction to IT in information services.

Finally we will look at the continuing relevance, if any, of the 'traditional' skills and abilities of the information professional in the IT age, somewhat anticipating the fuller discussion in Chapter 10.

IT And The Changing Information Context

It would be too easy, to describe the applications of the new technologies within information services in terms of improvements to existing functions - information retrieval, document delivery, etc. - and just leave it at that. In fact, we will indeed look at things in rather this way in a later section, simply because that is a rather natural way to view things. But it is important to realize that one of the major effects of IT is to bring about great changes in the context and pattern of information transfer and communications in the broadest sense. We should first consider these factors, as a reminder that the most significant influence of IT will lie in the creation of entirely new services and the integration and overlapping of existing ones.

Illustrates some of the possible changes which may come about, due to the adoption of IT by the various components in the 'formal' information transfer system of the published literature. Figure 7.1 illustrates the 'traditional' system, with information passed between authors, publishers, database producers, online hosts, libraries, intermediaries (probably online searchers), and users. Figure 7.2 shows the effect of the generation of text in machine-readable form by the author, who is the enabled to use 'informal' electronic publishing techniques (electronic mail and bulletin board) to supply the material direct to its ultimate user, effectively removing all intermediate steps, and entirely removing the publisher from the scene. Figure 7.3, by contrast, shows the publisher using electronic and optical publishing techniques to bypass the database producer and the online host, in supplying database services directly. Figure 7.4 shows an altogether more complex situation, with new links being set up right along the publication chain, including the online host taking on the role of database producer, using machine-readable data from the primary publication stage, and user-friendly interfaces bypassing the intermediary. Figure 7.5 gives an indication of how the database producer could respond; taking on the roles of primary publisher, online host, and document delivery service, by using of electronic publishing technologies. Finally, Figure 7.6 indicates the ways in which library and information services (LIS) may themselves take on the roles of publisher, database producer, and online host, by appropriate application of the new technologies.

These ideas are indicative of the way in which information technology, and associated economic factors, allow for a breaking down of the barriers between the hitherto rigidly defined components of the communication chain, allowing the potential for a great variety of possible communication pathways.

Similarly, the new technologies have the potential to blur the distinction between formal and informal communication, for example by electronic publishing and networking. In an analogous way, the divisions between internal and external information will be lessened, by the user, for example, of CD-ROMs, common interfaces to internal and external databases, downloading from external databases, see Jameson (1987). This must be seen in conjunction with the much greater proportion of material becoming available in electronic form, either from the initial stage by text processing and electronic publishing, or at a later stage, by techniques such as image processing and optical character recognition.

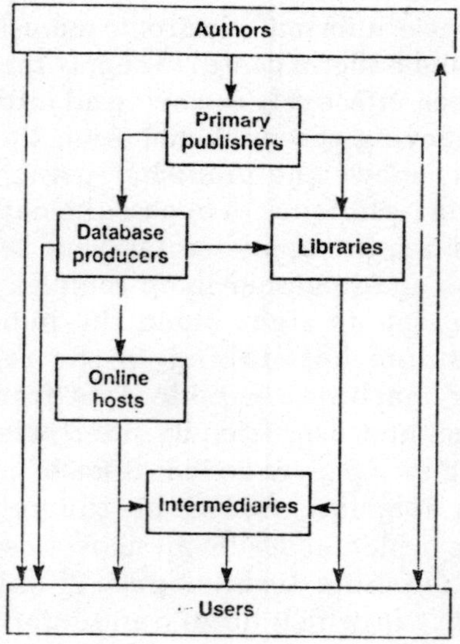

Fig. 7.1 'Traditional' information passing system

This, then, is the changing framework within which information services must operate, and this is the reason why the most significant results and benefits of information technology application will lie, not in the improvement of existing functions and services, but in the creation of new and integrated services. These services will be adapted to the new frameworks of communication, based on much wider access to information in electronic form, created and transmitted by a much more flexible, overlapping and changing set of pathways and networks than was possible before.

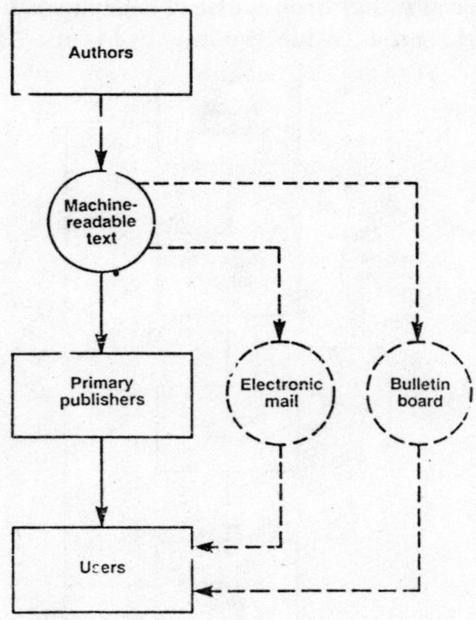

Figure 7.2 : Informal' electronic publishing techniques

The information service operators of the future will not find it profitable, or indeed possible, to draw neatly boxed diagrams of information pathways and sources labelled 'external', 'internal', 'published', 'unpublished', etc. Instead, the frameworks will have to be drawn up to suit the world view, in information terms, of each user, or user group, since the possibilities will be both more numerous and more fluid. An excellent pictorial representation of this sort of world view is the 'engineers' information sources', depicted by and shown in Figure 7.7.

Essentially, these frameworks will be showing the way in which the rich diversity of information sources and communication paths may be integrated in the most suitable way for their users.

Integration of information from diverse sources, and of different kinds, has been a major theme of this book. Information technology provides both the necessity for this, by supporting the creation and dissemination of the spectrum of information types, and also the solution in integrative software and interfaces. Another type of integration is also of relevance and importance.. This is represented, rather crudely, in Figure 7.8.

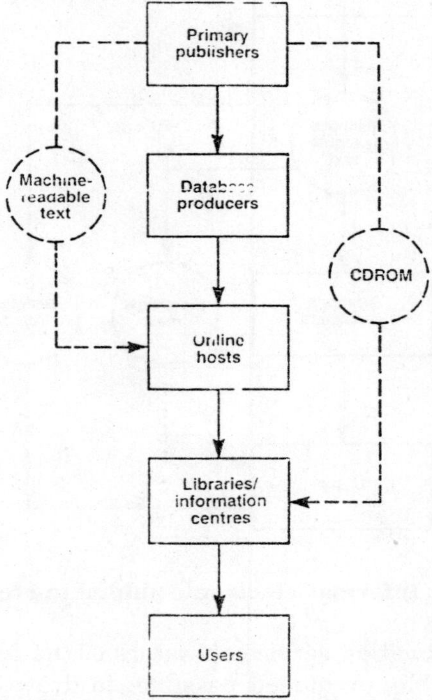

Figure 7.3 Publisher uses electronic and special publishing techniques to bypass the database producer and online host

This Shows a pyramidal representation of information, with data ('facts and figures') at the base, information (text-based) summaries, reports, etc.) at the next level, and knowledge (evaluated information) at the apex. In technological terms, these levels can be said to correspond loosely to database or text retrieval systems, systems integrating different types of information (text, graphics, etc.), and knowledge-based systems. Roughly speaking, ascending this pyramid corresponds to providing value added' information services, a topic to which we shall return. Integrating these levels of information provision will be a major challenge for information services.

Applications of IT

In this section, we will review some of the more important applications of information technology in information services. We will not discuss them in great detail, as they have, for the most part, been covered in the last chapter. We will try to bring out some of the most important factors of these applications, so as to lead into the later sections with the significance and benefits

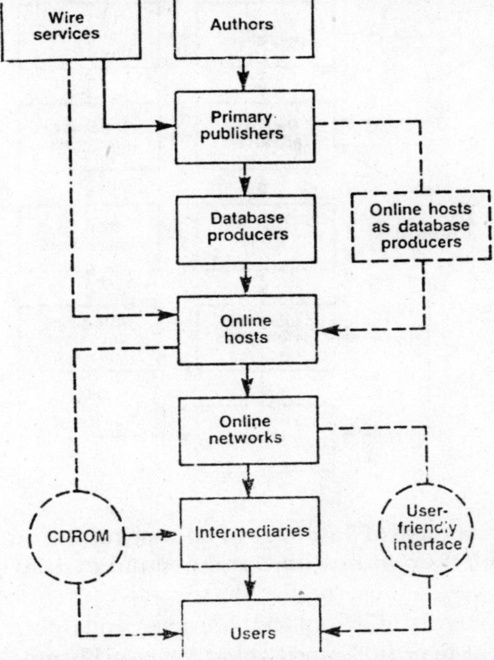

Figure 7.4 Online host takes on the role of database producer, using machine readable data from primary publication stage and user-friendly interfaces bypassing the intermediary

of IT application. We will also include all applications under four main headings of 'information retrieval', 'current awareness/ intelligence', 'delivery of material', and 'administration'. By combining together tasks and services normally considered separately, we hope to bring out more clearly some common factors. Of course, we must remember that there will be a degree of overlap between the four categories, which are by no means mutually exclusive.

The take-up information technology by libraries and information units has, on the whole, been slower than might have been expected, although there are considerable differences between sectors and organizational types.

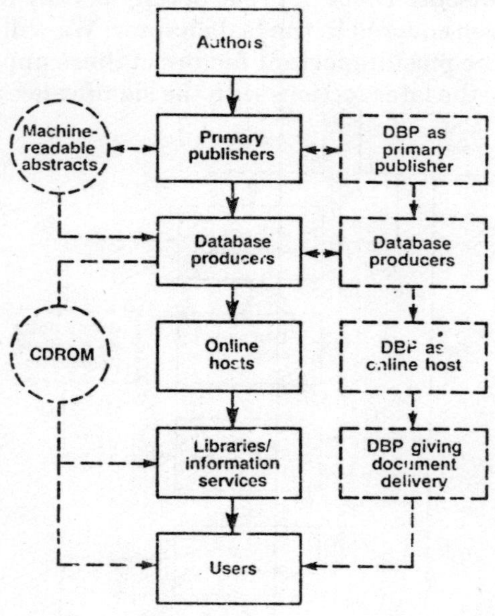

Figure 7.5 Response of database producer taking on the roles of primary publisher, online host and document delivery service

A 1987 survey of UK special libraries and information units indicated that over 90% used some form of IT, with 85% being computer users. Perhaps surprisingly, information retrieval and library housekeeping, generally regarded as the primary focus for computerization, had been adopted by only 53% and 49% respectively, while administrative applications were reported by 64%. Only 41% used fax transmission (although the proportion was increasing dramatically), and only 31% electronic mail.

Another 1987 UK survey, this time of public libraries, showed a roughly comparable level of adoption of IT. An estimated 60%, for example, were using computers for circulation control, although only 18% had all service points connected 41% for community information provision, and 50% for administration. Significantly, 60% indicated an intention to introduce or extend IT use during the next year.

IT awareness seems to be consistently increasing, and smaller units, in particular, are being affected by the increasing availability of genuine business computing at 'home computer prices'. It is unlikely that any information service will have remained untouched by IT at the beginning of the 1990s.

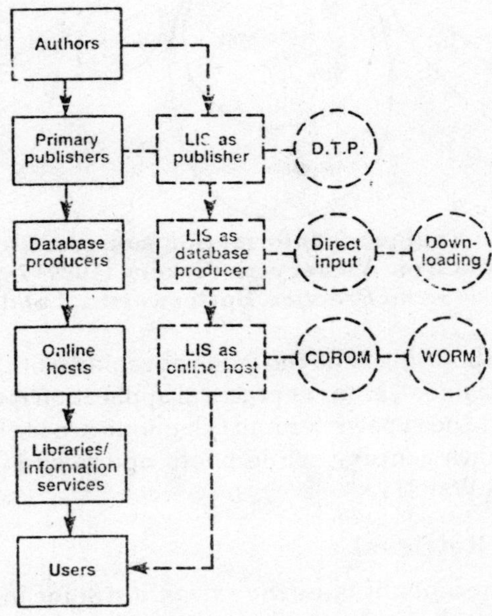

Figure 7.6 How library and information, services can take on the roles of publisher, database producer and online host

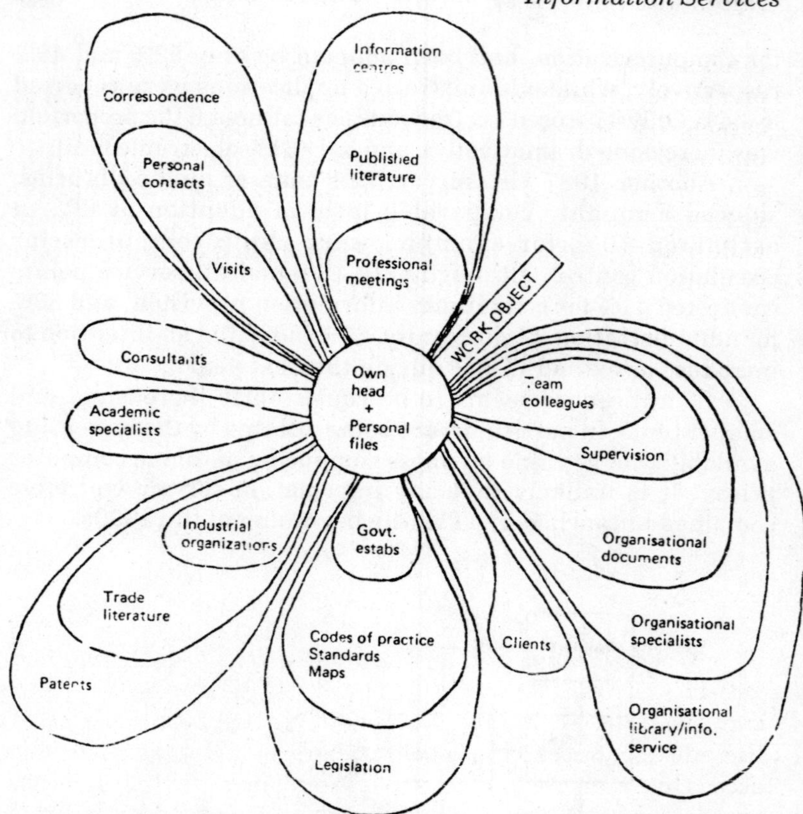

Figure 7.7 The Engineer's information sources. (Reproduced with permission from Vickery an Vickery (1987) *Information Science, in Theory and Practice*, Butterworths, London)

It is worth noting that the general rapidity of IT advance may be overestimated, as far as practical application is concerned. Points out that the typewriter and telephone are both products of the nineteenth century, while photocopiers and computers predate World War II.

Information Retrieval

This often thought of as the *raison d'etre* for information services, covers all database systems, dealing with all types of information, whether internal or external to the organization. This will include online searching of external information, inhouse access to external information bought in on electronic or optical media, inhouse databases of many kinds, library catalogues (local or dispersed), and retrieval systems integrated into such organizational systems as office automation, archives and records management, and management information systems. The software systems which may be employed cover a wide range: database management systems, text retrieval systems, videotex, and others.

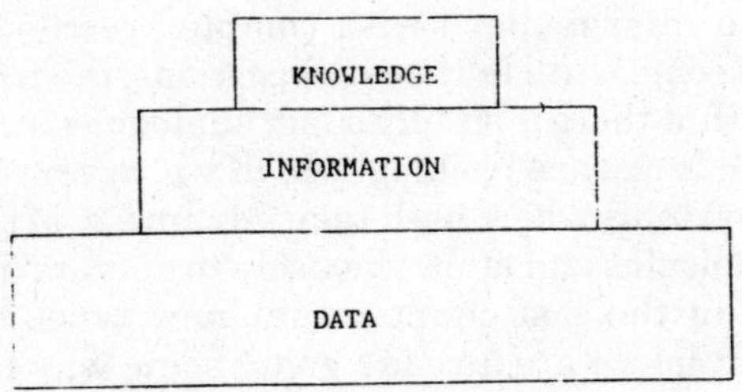

Figure 7.8 Pyramid integration

We may contrast this situation with that which applied to 'pre-IT'; retrieval being carried out by way of printed indexes, card files, etc. There are a number of major advantages, due to the advent of IT. For one thing, there is immediate and local access to a much wider range of material; online searching, for example, has expanded greatly from its modest beginnings in the early 1970s. It provides the small information service with access to a vastly greater number of external sources than could be acquired in printed form, and with many more potential access points. Higher quality searching is possible: for complex searches, involving.

Boolean combination of concepts; for precise searches, *via* full-text searching etc.; for searches requiring comprehensive recall, with the wider range of sources and access points available in electronic form; etc. Information sources are more up to date; most noticeably the business, financial, and news services updated as the information changes. It is also much simpler to provide genuine integration between internal and external sources, either by a common interface or by an actual integration of material Downloading of material from online sources is also of increasing importance. Fuller retrieval facilities can also be included in office and archive systems, leading to an commonality of information handling facilities throughout the organization. Finally, there are types of searching which can only be carried out with a computer system; chemical substructure searching is a good example.

Against this, it is sometimes said that there are negative aspects to the use of computerized retrieval systems. Two points often raised are the lack of browsing facilities, and the 'distrasting' of the end users from their own information, by the use of the intermediary with complex retrieval systems. While there is some truth in these suggestions, the true situation appears to be that there is simply a lag, analogous to, and largely caused by, the 'software backlog' which we referred to earlier, in providing systems which both take advantage of the power of the new technologies and allow the users to operate in a 'natural' way. We say in the last chapter that new types of retrieval system and interface are already going some way to overcome the two points mentioned. End-user searching of bibliographic database is gaining in popularity, despite the problems associated with Boolean logic, query formulation, etc. It is already much more re-established with factual and numeric databases.

A point which is more difficult to counter is the argument that information which does not get onto a computer database, and much never will despite the increasing amount available, will simply be ignored. This material falls into a number of categories: older rather than recent; literary rather than technical; discursive rather than factual; cultural rather than profit-oriented; alternative rather than mainstream; from the developing world rather than the developed; etc. 'Off-line and out of mind' is a dangerous, and undeniable, trend, and can only be countered by an awareness that the medium (*pace* Marshal McLuhan) is not the message in this context, and that it is the content, rather than the form, of information which really matters. We shall say more about this later.

It is interesting to observe an ever-changing set of balances in the application of IT. One such is the balance between the provision of access to the published literature externally and internally. 'Pre-IT' such access was internal; by purchase of printed indexes. The first IT applications were also internal; batch processing retrieval systems, run on the organization's own computers. Then came online searching, and the whole focus of interest shifted to external access; indeed some organizations even mounted their own information on external computer systems. More recently, with powerful microcomputers able to search quite large databases, and particularly with CD-ROM, the balance has swung back towards internal processing.

A similar balance can be seen with end-user searching *vis-a-vis* the use of the intermediary. Printed index searching was largely the domain of the end user, unless organizational policy decreed that it should be done by an information professional; certainly most end users felt that they could do it, if necessary. Online searching, and some complex inhouse retrieval systems, shifted the bulk of searching to the specialist intermediary. 'User-friendly' interfaces, and searching systems built with the inexpert user in mind, are beginning to move things the other way.

For information retrieval, at any rate, we can see that the application of the new technologies does not so much bring about an irreversible alteration in the way in which things are done, but changes an existing balance. This point is to be bourn in mind, amid all the hype about the latest style of retrieval system. It does not invalidate the overall effects of the adoption of IT, in providing better access to more material in electronic form, and in integrating a variety of applications.

Current Awareness/Intelligence

The provision of some form of 'alerting' service is an almost universal function of information services. This covers such things as 'current awareness' services based on newly published literature and news services, competitor intelligence, and what is sometimes termed 'scanning the environment', i.e. discerning trends of relevance to the users of the service.

Information technology has certainly made some impact on this area, largely by providing more rapid access to information which appears initially, or at least rapidly thereafter, in electronic form; chiefly news and business services of one kind or another. Online search services provide 'SDI profiles', with searches being run against each update of the database, and some organizations are integrating these directly into organizations are integrating these directly into organizational or personal databases.

However, it has to be admitted that IT has not made as much impact on the intelligence function as on other application areas. There are several clear reasons for this.

First, a lot of material only gets into electronic form some time after it first appears as print on paper; literature references in bibliographic databases are a good example. Immediacy is the essence of current awareness and therefore electronic current awareness is often regarded as a backup to more conventional scanning, to ensure that nothing significant has been missed.

Second, a lot of relevant material will not become available in retrievable electronic form at all. It may be 'informal' in nature (most of the really valuable intelligence is), and be gained in personal conversation, at conferences and meetings, etc. Or it may appear as part of very general material, or as isolated snippets, and may only make sense when put together by the 'prepared mind' of the user.

Third, electronic current awareness may simply not be acceptable to the users. This kind of informal information gathering is generally carried out in familiar and pleasant ways: reading a newspaper, scanning journals in an odd five minutes, discussing with colleagues, etc. IT systems, as available at present, are not an adequate substitute for this 'browsing' access to printed materials, and to informal networks, which is a powerful stimulus to innovative thinking. They may (perhaps) be so for the 'formal' style of current awareness, with an information officer mechanically scanning journals, according to a predefined list of terms and topics of interest.

Current awareness, then, is not well served by current IT products and services. The situation will only begin to change when more relevant material is available from the outset in electronic form, and when IT systems are used to support informal information exchange and networking.

Delivery of Material

This rather broad category covers such IT applications as library automation systems (for acquisitions, serials control, cataloguing, etc.), document delivery systems, and electronic and optical publishing. We might also include office automation and records management systems in the larger organization.

The most obvious result with these systems is that they can improve availability to 'formal' information, and can speed up access for the user: hence the enthusiastic adoption of automated housekeeping and delivery systems within libraries.

Rather more significant, in the longer term, however, is their impact on the whole communication and information transfer process, which we noted in the opening section of this chapter. It is these sorts of system which are primarily responsible for changing the structure of the 'traditional' publication process, and have the potential to alter the entire communications systems of science, business and commerce, etc. Whether this will in fact happen quickly, indeed whether it will happen at all, seems rather doubtful. Electronic publishing and in particular the concept of the 'electronic journal', has found a very slow acceptance. This is for a number of reasons, most of them economic of socio-cultural, rather than technical reasons.

Professional communication patterns have emerged slowly over a long period, and their operators and users are reluctant to abandon them, just because technology permits them to do so. To this we must add the undeniable, and irreproachable, reluctance of information users to abandon print-on-paper for the terminal screen, for anything other than factual look-up.

So, although electronic delivery systems have made a major impact on some information service operations, and are beginning to change the nature of those operations fundamentally, progress is likely to be rather slower than some might suggest. This is no excuse for ignoring the opportunities presented for increased flexibility and customization of services, and for entirely new types of service, in the new context of widespread electronic information transfer.

Administration

Under this heading, we include the applications of IT within the administration of information services, and also technologies for communications (for example electronic mail) and for presentation (for example desktop publishing and hypertext) which can help to improve services, or to create new ones.

Naturally, one function of IT as an administrative aid to improve efficiency, and to reduce the extent of uncreative routine work; this should be as possible within an information service operation as elsewhere. Similarly, it should be clear that the use of document preparation software, either a sophisticated text processor or a fully blown DTP system, can improve the look and acceptance of the products of information units , who are often in need of a boost to their image. Again, the use of electronic mail (e-mail) to accept queries and send search results to users can be botin a time-saver and a boost to the service's visible effectiveness. These are the clear benefits of IT application.

Of greater interest, perhaps, is the potential for improved or novel services. These are most likely to happen with the integration of technologies; the example, given earlier, of a combined hypertext/voice/expert system approach to an 'intelligent' library catalogue comes to mind. This combination of presentation and communication reaches a new peak in some of the products envisaged by educational technology, based on hypermedia, products of this sort, albeit less advanced, will find a home in information services.

Another form of integration comes to mind, in considering the use of IT in information service administration, and this is an integration of the communication services, of the organization as a whole. This could well be led by the information services, if they themselves are well adapted to this application of IT.

Significance and Benefits of IT

In this section, we will consider the benefits which accrue to information services in adopting the new technologies. We will use eight main headings, not in any order of importance: value-added services, user-centred services, information rich environment, integration within the organization, improved communications, enhancement of knowledge and expertise, legal obligations, and improved efficiency. We must again emphasize that these, like most concepts associated with IT, are interdependent, and it will become evident that there are considerable overlaps between them. We will not treat any of these exhaustively, but will control ourselves with outlining their nature and significance.

Value-added Services

The concept of 'value-added ' information services has been much discussed during the late 1980s, albeit with rather different meanings attached to the phrase. (Please note that this is not the same idea as 'value-added networks', discussed in Chapter 5). We take it to mean any service which offers something more than the straightforward facility to store and retrieve the information as given. This could mean such things as:

* information enrichment, by analysis, indexing, etc.;
* selection and evaluation of information;
* customization or tailoring for a particular group of users;
* integration with other systems;
* improved presentation of information;
* provision of better searching facilities.

These are by no means new aims; they were indeed the primary rational for the 'information analysis centres', which flourished during the 1960s.

The perceptive reader will have noted, that they are very much the advantages which carefully designed IT applications provide for information services, and which we have discussed in proceeding sections and chapters. Thus, although it is not correct to say that technology automatically provides value-added services, nor that such services cannot be provided in the absence of technology, it will generally be the case that the adoption of IT provides the basis from which value-added information services can be created. An excellent example is the Cambridge Crystallographic Data Centre, whose database is well-known for its careful evaluation of information (made possible by computer analysis) making it considerably more reliable than the primary literature. Another example is the enhanced value conference by reprocessing of down-loaded information for local requirements.

User-Centred Services

As we have seen, information technology has sometimes

been perceived as presenting an obstacle, or putting a barrier, between users and information; as, for example, in the need for intermediaries in online searching. This, we have tried to show, is a temporary swing of a balance. In the longer term, the new technologies give information providers and information services the ability to put information very directly (and literally) into the hands of the users; user interfaces for database searching, and CD-ROM databases, are recent examples. Further, IT systems have the flexibility to allow customization for the needs of the user group, and indeed the individual user. The relational database is a striking example, enabling different 'views' of the information store to be created flexibly as required and as appropriate.

A user-centred approach is the only effective defence against the impersonal monolithic system, often held up as a good reason for avoiding IT. We will return to this idea in Chapter 9.

Information-rich Environment

The phrase 'information-rich environment' is intended to sum up the situation which all information services should aspire to: their users being surrounded by the information they need and can use, in an appropriate and accessible form, without in any sense being swamped by it. This environment is particularly stimulating for innovation and creativity in the information users, perhaps one of the ultimate goals for any information service.

IT contributes to the creation of this environment in several ways:

* by giving access to a wide range of information sources;
* by improving ease and quality of retrieval;
* by providing high-quality presentation, appropriate to its use;
* by integrating formal and informal information channels;
* by creating 'lateral' information systems;
* by allowing a ready integration of information and data from different sources;
* by promoting personal communication through networking, e-mail, teleconferencing etc.

Again, we cannot say that IT applications alone will in any way bring about this state of affairs automatically; indeed, it is likely that printed material, and face-to-face communication, will play a big part in any environment which could realistically be called 'information rich'. However, it should be clear from the examples above that technology and electronic information transfer, will play a large part in the creation of such an environment.

Integration Within the Organization

A number of examples have been given earlier of the ways in which systems associated specifically with information services can permeate into the wider organization; text retrieval systems used in office automation or records management, for example. Not only is this valuable in its own right, but it can point the way to an organization-wide integration of information handling, which, in turn, allows the introduction of what is generally termed 'information resources management'; we will look further at this in Chapter 9. In other words, it allows the total information store of the organization, which has usually been built and maintained at great expense, to be made available to all who need it, and thereby maximize its usefulness.

This is plainly to the benefit of the organization as a whole; rather more self-centredly, there may be clear advantages to the information service and its staff, if they are recognized as having particular skills to offer to the organization-wide applications of information systems.

Improved Communications

Information professionals tend to think of IT applications as concerned with such things as databases, searching, cataloguing, document delivery, etc. While these are important, a wider perspective suggests that the major advantages of IT may come in the communications are. Plainly an information service has to be in the communication business, and implementation of IT can help improve the quality of its communications greatly. The means, and some obvious applications have already been mentioned: e-mail for dealing with users; delivery system for acquiring material; and so on. Illustrates this on his study of the use of electronic mail in academic libraries. But beyond this, information services have the opportunity to make use of the new communications technologies in novel ways.

Most importantly, there is the opportunity to become involved in lateral or informal communication networks. This can tend to redress the unfortunate balance which has seen information services overlay concerned with the formal and vertical communications systems, which may sometimes be of lesser importance to the needs of their users and organizations. It may also be appropriate for information services to take a leading role in the introduction and application of new communication systems (e-mail, teleconferencing, broad-band LAN, etc.) to the organization as a whole; another opportunity for increasing responsibility and influence.

Enhancement of Knowledge and Expertise

Too often information services have seen their role as purely handling information and data (although this itself is arguably a major step forward from just handling books and bibliographic references). Information technology now offers the means for an involvement in the next step, involvement in the handling of knowledge and expertise (one hesitates to say wisdom); see, for example, the top level of the pyramid shown in Figure 7.8.

This does not necessarily mean expert systems, although the creation of knowledge bases to preserve and make available the accumulated expertise of individuals and organizations may well be a particularly appropriate task for an information service. It may equally refer to the application of other 'knowledge handling' techniques, such as hypertext, collaborative writing, and, indeed, the process of information analysis and evaluation which has been a 'traditional' information service function.

Legal Obligations

The implementation of information technology systems has various legal, implications, which are discussed in a later chapter. On the more positive side, we should remember that IT can be of enormous help in enabling organizations to comply with legal and regulatory requirements.

Improved Efficiency

One of the often-quoted of IT is that it will 'increase efficiency'. Indeed there is every reason to believe, and experience has shown, that the appropriate use of new technology can indeed have this desirable effect in the operations of an information service.

This is best seen in the use of those IS systems which minimize uncreative and routine procedures: word processing and spreadsheet systems and other administrative software; library housekeeping routines; document delivery procedures; and perhaps some expert system applications.

The analysis becomes a little more difficult when considering IT in traditionally 'professional' tasks, such as database searching. It is undoubtedly true, for example, that online searching enables most queries to be answered much more rapidly than would be possible with a printed index. But this does not usually mean, as was commonly thought at the beginning of the 'online age', that the same number of searches would be done by a much reduced group of intermediaries. What has generally happened is that the availability and power of the online systems has generated a great expansion in the number of search requests, i.e. has identified an information need hitherto unexpressed, and has also generated new types of request. Online is, for example, particularly good at providing 'a few good references' and a more effective information service is thereby being provided, but without exactly the benefits of efficiency that might have been anticipated.

The same sort of problems are likely to occur whenever clear cut efficiency advantages are looked for, as a result of an IT implementation. In particular, cost savings are rarely demonstrable, and it is arguably unreasonable to look for them. This is because a realistic cost comparison can only be made when exactly the same procedure may be carried in two different ways, whose associated costs are to be compared. But the introduction of a new information technology system where there was none before, or the replacement of one IT system by another, of considerable greater capability, is not this sort of situation at all. By definition, as we have tried to emphasize throughout this book, the correct way to introduce IT is *not* to directly replace one procedure by its exact computerized equivalent. This is a recipe for misuse, and under use, of the system's capabilities. Rather, the introduction of a new system should be an occasion for a careful reevaluation of what is being done, and why, and an assessment of whether the power of the new system enables things to be done better. In most, if not all, cases, there will be advantages to be gained from a change in procedures, such that a straight cost comparison does not truly reflect the situation. Of coarse, money must come into any choice of new systems, but an oversimplified cost-benefit analysis does no-one any good. The true benefits of IT applications are better seen in the new services provided, and in the kind of criteria described above.

Problems of Information Technology Application

It would be foolish, as well as dishonest, to maintain that there are no problems associated with the introduction of information technology within information services. Although the whole message of this book is that IT, used sensibly and appropriately, brings great advantages to information services, there are a number of potential problems which should be clearly recognized. We outline below some of the most likely problems; this is by no means a list of everything which can go wrong (that would indeed be a long list), but we believe that the great majority of problems can be attributed to one or more of the failings listed below.

Probably the most common factor to be found associated with unfortunate experiences in the application of IT is inadequate planning. We will deal with the area of planning for the introduction of IT in detail in the following chapter. For the moment, we will note that the failure to fully involve the users of a system is perhaps the most common failing. Also, a failure to take the opportunity to look anew at the procedures and services to which the new systems are to be applied is a common failing; computerizing the *status quo* is a recipe for frustration.

A failure to appreciate, and to plan for, *continuous change* is also a probable indicator of trouble in store. The speed of technical development is such that the new system will be barely installed before it could be considered obsolete. If there is no clear idea of how and when upgrading will be carried out, then there is a danger that the new system will either essify, or (more probably) will be a continual state of flux, as new innovations are introduced before the old system could be used to real advantage.

There is also the problem of *unrealistic expectations,* on the part both of system developers and users (if these are different people). If the impression is given that the new system 'can be used by everyone without any training', 'won't have any limits on size of file; will enable all our searching to be done by one person'; means we can throw away all the old card records', etc., and then these expectations are not met, the result is all too predictable, disillusion and resentment and a determination never to be misled by a technocrat again. A lack of appreciation of the potential, and the limitations, of the new technology can lead to a see-sawing between unrealistic optimism and total negativity on the part of users (and even, sometimes, management).

This points to another cause of problems: *inadequate knowledge and appreciation of the new technologies* among information service staff, and consequent inability to deal effectively with IT specialists; whether staff from their own organizations, or systems suppliers.

Partly as a result of this last point, failure of an information service IT application can often be attributed to an *over - concentration on technical issues,* at the expense of user needs and information science principles. Most commonly this manifests itself in an overenthusiastic planning for storage capacities, retrieval speeds, type of interface, etc. before adequate consideration is given to what information is going to be stored in the system, and who is to use it.

Disappointment with IT systems in information services often stems from the fact that there is *not enough material of the right sort, available in electronic* form, *and that* document delivery services, are not adequate to meet the need. This may lead to particular frustration, for example if a computerized searching service identified interesting material, which the user is not able to obtain quickly, if at all. Or, points out, if there is a shortage of 'supporting' equipment such as microform readers and photocopiers, to back up an efficient retrieval service, this can also lead to frustration. This problem is largely economic and organizational in nature, rather than technical.

Indeed, all the points given above are mainly organizational rather than technical, and indeed it is our view that most problems in IT implementation result from this cause; we will consider this further in Chapter 8.

The most common technical problems can be simple stated. They are *poor quality software,* inadequate to take advantage of hardware capabilities, and the whole problem of *incompatible equipment and software,* and *lack of standards.* Both of these problems have been discussed in Chapter 4, and both are being slowly ameliorated, as noted there. However, it would be foolish to pretend that they are going to be rapidly overcome.

An Illuminating Comparison

In order to point out some of the factors involved in the success or failure of IT applications, which we have outlined above, we will look at two particular types of system, both described in an earlier chapter. These are graphical chemical structure searching systems, and office automation systems; specifically their retrieval components.

We certainly do not wish to suggest that one of these applications in a success and the other a failure; the situation is not so clear-cut as that. It may also be objected that we are really comparing chalk with chess, and there may be some truth in the accusation. Nonetheless, we believe that experience with these two applications does bring out rather well some general points.

Chemical structure searching systems really began in the 1960s, with batch searching based on various codes and notations; searching was a job for a specialist intermediary. During the 1970s, progress was made towards searching *via* graphical interfaces, making these systems accessible to the chemical community in general. During the 1980s, their use has increased dramatically, both as inhouse systems such as OSAC and PSIDOM on minis and micros, largely searched by end users, and as commercial online systems such as CAS online and DARC, largely operated by intermediaries but with an increasing amount of end-user access. Without doubt, they represent one of the main success stories of IT in information services.

Office automation systems have been available since the 1970s, with tremendous investment incurred. It is only relatively recently that the need for genuine text retrieval appears to have occurred to suppliers, with some honourable exceptions. Genuine integration of retrieval, for the majority of users, still seems a long way off, for example, see Hills (1987). Indeed the systems as a whole appear to fall well short of their expectations, as a respondent to expresses clearly:

> ....it hasn't taken off as fast as people would like to think, and where it has taken off there's probably a large number of people who are desperately, covering their tracks and saying wonderful things but where there's a big question mark, either in terms of its functionality, or its benefits, or its useability.....

It is not at all clear, in the general situation, what their needs actually are. There is no clear understanding of what material is to be searched, how (full-text, summary, keywords, etc.), or even why. The research in experimental information retrieval carried out over many years has found little application in operational referral systems, still less office automation. There has been very little involvement of information professionals in the design and operation of these systems, and what input has come appears to be too little and too late. The whole process appears to have been largely technology-led, with all too obvious results.

We would not wish this comparison to be pushed too far. However it does show the importance of a number of the factors noted above, in determining the success of IT application.

Information Skills and Information Technology

In considering the use made of IT by information services, it is important to consider the information professionals who are the staff of these services. What if anything, is their particular contribution to the successful application of new technology? Or are they, in effect, to retrain as computer people.

First, we do not want to minimize the necessity for information professionals to gain, and retain, a good appreciation of the new technologies and their application; that, in part, is what this book is all about. On the other hand, that is by no means all there is to it. Information people, in our opinion, have a great deal to contribute to the use of IT, most obviously within their own department, but also in a wider context.

There are basically three contributions which the information professional should be able, indeed uniquely able, to make; to put it another way, there is a combination of relevant skills involved in the practice of information science, which is not likely to be found elsewhere.

The first of these is essentially an attitude of mind, backed up by a corpus of expertise. IT is a concern with the nature of information *per se,* that is to say with the *content* of a database or document, and with its relevance to a particular use or user, rather than with its form - magnetic, optical, paper, or whatever. Information systems are thus to be seen as a means to an end, and the quality and appropriateness of information contained in them is of greater importance than their technical specifications. This is of particular benefit in ensuring that a proper *balance* is maintained in the provision of services including a variety of media: for example, in ensuring that printed handbooks, dictionaries etc., are available, to enable the best use to be made of computerized retrieval systems.

Second is the set of skills associated with the 'traditional' processes of subject analysis and description: classification, cataloguing, indexing, thesaurus construction, etc. It is remarkable to realize just how many of these techniques are appearing, under new names, in knowledge bases, data dictionaries, hypertext systems, etc. It is also interesting to note that, despite predictions to the contrary, controlled vocabularies retain their importance in computerized systems. Indeed, the thesaurus is at the heart of many expert systems, data dictionaries, etc., as was noted in Chapter 4. Regardless of hardware and software advances, advanced databases and knowledge-based systems will increasingly require detailed intellectual coding of knowledge, based systems will increasingly require detailed intellectual coding of knowledge, and the techniques required for this will be drawn, in large measure, from the corpus of library/information expertise.

Third is the set of attitudes and skills stemming from the intermediary role, often assumed by the information professional. Often regarded with some disdain, this role is, in fact, remarkably similar to that of providing a 'bridge' between users and the designers and operators of system, having a good appreciation of the concerns of both. This provides a good basis for a number of important functions associated with the introduction and use of IT. Again, because, of ignorance of what the information professional has to offer, these qualities are being, in essence, reinvested.

It seems clear that 'information skills' are by no means redundant in the IT age; that, on the contrary, they are of increasing relevance, and offer the promise of new roles for the information professional. We will return to this them in later chapters.

Conclusions

In this short chapter, we have tried to bring out some of the most important factors involved in the use of information technology within information services, so as to focus more closely some of the material presented in Chapters 3 and 4, and to act as an introduction to the succeeding chapters.

We have tried to show that the success of information technology applications is dependent upon the extent to which certain guiding principles of service provision are emphasized. Of these, the most important are the concepts of *value-added services,* of the *information rich environment,* and of *user-centred services.* The key advantages of information technology in achieving these aims are *flexibility* (allowing customization for user needs), and the potential for *integration* (or convergence or overlap) in constructing new services.

The particular set of skills possessed by staff of information services are of direct and continuing relevance with the increasing use of IT systems. In particular, the three key points are: concern with information content, rather than form; subject analysis skills; and ability to link between users and technology/ technologists. These abilities can best be used in integrating information services more fully into the organization's activities, so as to maximize use of its information resources.

8

Legal, Security and Conservation Implications of Information Technology

Introduction

For people involved in the provision of information services, the legal aspects of their work have, in the past, been mainly related to the laws of copyright. Today, the situation is not that straightforward. Copyright continues to be an important issue but, in addition to dealing with the photocopying of publications, it has been expanded to cover the practice of downloading data from online databases and the copying and writing of software. Furthermore, the widespread adoption of technology in libraries and information units has brought with it a host of other legal considerations with which the information professional has had to contend.

Most countries have introduced data protection laws which, for the most part, are concerned with computerized personal records. Information professionals responsible for the implementation and purchase of hardware and software will probably be involved in negotiations with vendors, and even though they may not be responsible directly for the drawing up and signing of contracts, they can, as the ultimate users of the system, provide valuable input at the discussion stage; and the majority will at some time have to sign an agreement with an online database provider. Telecommunications equipment must be approved by the appropriate regulatory body. Companies are increasingly dependent upon information technology, so system maintenance contracts have to be checked to see that suppliers provide appropriate support, and insurance policies reviewed on a regular basis to ensure that they give adequate cover in the event of a computer disaster. The new product liability laws cover a wide range of manufactured goods but apply equally to software packages, and then there are the legal questions regarding the acceptability and conservation of the electronic forms of documents.

To complicate matters laws relating to IT are, to a certain extent, in a state of flux with many having only recently been added to the statute books. Consequently, the 'fine print' is far from being writ in tablets of stone and awaits the clarification of court judgements. As if all that were not enough more and more organizations are adopting a broader, international approach to their business strategy which in turn means that information is probably going to be transmitted across national borders. It is no longer sufficient to be aware of the laws and regulations of the country in which one is working; variations in the legislature of other countries also have to be considered. Even member countries of the EEC have to be looked at individually, for while EEC directive give the broad brush strokes of legislation that is to be enacted, each member country is at liberty to fill in the fine details as it sees fit. Prime examples are data protection and product liability which will be discussed in more detail later.

From what we have said, information professionals who use IT extensively in their work cannot be blamed for wondering whether or not they ought to have a lawyer permanently at hand to protect their interests. It is indeed difficult to keep abreast of all rulings and amendments to legislation, but most of the major developments which impinge directly upon information work are reported in the computer and IT journals - there is even a publication dedicated solely to IT and the law called *Computer Law and Practice.* It is not our intention of offer expert advice on the subject but rather to indicate the areas of which the practitioner ought to be aware and when to proceed with caution. If in doubt, and in all instances where heavy investment is being made in terms of both money and time, appropriate legal advice should always be sought.

Copyright

Traditionally, copyright has been associated with the photocopying of documents and articles in paper form. Although this still forms the central core of most copyright laws, the widespread adoption of computes and online databases has resulted in legislation being extended to cover the copying of the electronic form of data, the production and copying of software, and computer generated works.

Downloading and Online Contracts

Anyone who has been responsible for introducing online databases into their organization will have had to sign an agreement with suppliers of databases. Part of these contracts is usually concerned with the practice of downloading. Downloading is the transfer of records from external databases into a local system, where they can be edited off-line for printing or incorporation into inhouse databases. Faster line speeds can be used for retrieving the information (the user is not limited to the speed of their printer) thus reducing telecommunications costs and connect time. Also, the information can be processed and enhanced before printing. More importantly, from the suppliers point of view, downloading gives the customer the opportunity to reuse the data, for example by generating multiple copies of SDIs, or by incorporating it into an inhouse database. Many database producers are worried that these practices result in decreased revenues; once the records are part of an inhouse system, the customer has no need to search the online databases for that information in response to similar enquiries in the future.

There are no general guidelines as to what is or is not permissible, as database vendors vary in what they consider to be legitimate downloading and copying. Contracts between database producer or host and the customer may specify the number of copies of printed output that can be made for SDI purposes: however, some suppliers adopt the opposite approach and allow unlimited copying - provided that the information is for internal use and not re-sold - believing it encourages their customers to make grater use of their services. A few go to the other extreme and prohibit entirely the copying of any part of the database onto machine-readable media and limit to one the number of end users to whom the data can be distributed.

The customer may have to sign a special agreement and pay extra fees if information is to be downloaded into an inhouse database; but some hosts actively encourage the practice by offering special formats and tagged fields which allow the customer to transfer the data into their own local system with the minimum of effort. From the customer's point of view, the situation can become more confused with hosts that provide access to a large number of databases; each database provider will have its own conditions which, if significantly different from the terms in the standard agreement, the host will have to add as an appendix to the main body of the contract.

Software

In the majority of countries, copyright law has been extended to cover the duplication of software. Copying software other than under the conditions laid down in the licence is illegal. For single use this commonly means that the purchaser of a package can install the program on a single machine for access by one user at a time; special licences have to be purchased for networks and multiuser systems.

Making copies of the purpose of backup is usually regarded as a legitimate form of copying; nonetheless, some software producers incorporate sophisticated methods of copy protection into their package which permit a once only installation procedure if it is being loaded onto a hard disc, but do not allow backup copies of the master disc to be made. Not surprisingly this has been the cause of quite considerable friction between purchasers and producers of software. If the master disc becomes damaged or the system has to be reinstalled, the customer has to wait for a replacement to be sent and may even be required to pay for the service. Meanwhile the customer's system remains unusable and business is halted. It is encouraging to see, though, that the number of software producers who employ elaborate copy protection on their discs is on the decrease; some have gone as far as to provide their existing customers with programs that remove copy protection from software already sold to them.

The reluctance of producers to change their policies is understandable, thought, as illegal copying of software is not as rare as one would like to believe. Many users of software do not look upon the duplication of programs for friends or colleagues at work as theft; they are ignorant of the fact that making unauthorized copies is a tort and a criminal offence, and that they can be used for damages if found guilty. It has been estimated that companies and their employees are collectively stealing more software than the professional criminals. FAST (Federation Against Software Theft), an organization which lobbies for more effective software protection legislation, and investigates suspected cases of piracy, is attempting to raise awareness of the impact of illicit copying on the software industry. It advises companies on ways of alerting their employees of the serious nature and consequences of such practices, and recommends procedures for eradicating piracy within the organization. To be really effective, though, directives stating the company's opposition to illegal copying must come from top management, and written guidelines and procedures made available to all employees involved in data processing.

No company has yet been taken to court for inhouse copying; many have instead opted for out of court settlements in an effort to avoid any adverse publicity that might ensue. 'Pirates' operating on a commercial scale have not been dealt with so leniently. IN 1988 the UK courts sent the first person to prison for copyright infringement, forgery and illegally importing software in the UK.

Possessing counterfeit or pirated software is as illegal as copying it for resale, so purchasers must be sure that the source of their programs is legitimate. Even if software is bought in good faith it can be confiscated if it is subsequently identified by the authorities as being a pirated copy. Buying packages from a recognized supplier and becoming a registered user has other benefits, including access to customer support services, opportunities to install upgrades at reduced prices, and rights under the product liability laws should personal injury occur as a result of a defect in the product.

Copyright also impinges upon the activities of the writers of programs as they have to ensure that their work does not infringe the copyright of an existing product. However, there is continuing debate is exactly what constitutes breach of copyright and how software should be treated under copyright law. In many countries software has been given the same status as literary works; in the UK this was confirmed by the 1985 amendment to the 1956 Copyright Act. The result has not been entirely satisfactory and the new Copyright, Designs and Patents Bill which is currently (1988) going through the UK Parliament has been criticized for failing to address the issue adequately.

Legislation in the USA favours protection for the logic - defined as the 'sequence, structure and organization' - behind the program or for its look or feel. In a recent case, courts in the USA found that Softklone's Mirror program infringed the copyright of DCA's Crosstalk because Mirror had copied the arrangement and design of Crosstalk's status screen. The US Copyright office has now ruled that when a software company copyrights a program, it automatically copyrights the graphics and textual displays produced by the program.

Computer Generated Works

Raises a question frequently overlooked in discussions on copyright: 'Does copyright subsist in a work which has been generated by a computer? The UK 1956 Copyright Act requires an author to exist before copyright in a literary, artistic or musical work can subsist. Again, the new UK legislation has failed to tackle the problem wholeheartedly. Those involved in drafting the Bill have merely stated the obvious i.e. that it is not a straightforward issue and that a general solution is not possible. Goes on to summarize the views that have been expressed on the subject and lists the three possible owners of copyright as being:

* the creator of the program which generates the work,
* the originator of the data upon which the computer operates to generate the work,
* the person responsible for running the computer to produce work, or,
* a combination of any of these.

The matter has been the subject of several court hearings and appeals, and the consensus of opinion at present is that if the computer is no more than a tool, and sufficient skill and labour has been exerted by the human creator, then copyright belongs to that person. Examples are a literary work using a word processor, the production of designs and drawings using CAD, and musical works generated with the aid of synthesizers.

In contrast, a directory that has been automatically printed from a database is regarded as *computer* generated and no copyright subsists in that directory, despite the fact that human effort was involved in periodically updating the database. The question of how works involving the intervention of expert systems are to be treated remains unresolved.

In the USA there is no requirement to show a direct human involvement, so computer generated works automatically qualify for protection under copyright law. One only has to prove *ownership* of copyright works. Simple though this may sound, it has merely shifted the emphasis of litigation away from copyright specifically and towards establishing proof of ownership.

Data Protection

Since the late 1960s there has been much deliberation over the repercussions of computerization on individuals rights and privacy. The main areas of concern have been first, that electronic data can be processed much more quickly than in paper form and more rapidly disseminated to a large number of parties; and second, that errors which may occur at any stage of the processing will be passed on and could cause harm or distress to the subject of that information. Data protection legislation is intended to safeguard individuals' rights and privacy with respect to the processing of personal information.

Information departments are frequently responsible for databases containing information on individuals: medical information departments in the pharmaceutical industry keep details of enquiries, product complaints, adverse drug reactions, clinical trial data etc.; many library and information units in all industries hold mailing lists of their customers and clients and libraries maintain records of borrowers and their loans. So, data protection is an issue which *directly* affects *all* information professionals, and in view of the serious consequences of failing to comply with data protection laws, we make no apologies for discussing the subject in some depth.

Different countries enact legislation in different ways and it was realized at an early stage that problems could arise if some countries' laws were not recognized by others as being sufficient. This in turn could result in the imposition of restrictions on the transfer of data across national boundaries. To forestall such an event, efforts were made to arrive at a consensus of opinion in respect of principles upon which all data protection laws should be based. The first of these were the 1980 OECD Guidelines Governing the Protection of Privacy and Transborder Flows of Personal Data. The second was the Council of Europe Convention for the Protection of Individuals with Regards to Automatic Processing of Personal Data, which outlines the eight data protection principles that form the basis of the European countries" legislation. The European Convention was opened for signature in January 1981 and, amongst, other things, allows ratifying countries to restrict the flow of personal information to countries that do not have acceptable data protection laws.

The eight data protection principles are:

1. Personal data is to be obtained and processed fairly and lawfully.
2. Personal data shall be held only for one or more specified and lawful purposes.
3. Personal data held for any purpose shall not be used or disclosed in any manner incompatible with that purpose.
4. Data shall be adequate, relevant and not excessive in relation to that purpose or purposes.
5. Personal data shall be accurate and where necessary kept up to date.
6. Personal data held for any purpose shall not be kept for longer than is necessary for that purpose or those purposes.
7. An individual shall be entitled.

(a) at reasonable intervals and without undue delay or expense,

(i) to be informed by any data user whether he holds personal data of which that individual is the subject, and

(ii) to access to any such data hold by a data user, and

(b) where appropriate to have any such data corrected or erased.

8. Appropriate security measurers shall be taken against unauthorized access to, or alteration, disclosure or destruction of, personal data and against accidental loss or destruction of personal data.

How the principles are enacted is left to individual countries. Consequently national data protection laws vary in the type of data covered, subject access provisions, and whether or not manual files are included. In general, though, for data to be covered by legislation it must be personal data; that is data relating to an identifiable living individual and not a fictitious person or a corporate body. The fact that an individual may be represented by a code or other information in the record does not mean that the data user, who is the controller of the information, is immune from the law. In the UK, if the user holds a list, in either electronic or paper form, which translates that code or information into an individual's name then the data is covered by the Act.

Although the European convention does allow for manual files to be covered, it is not mandatory and some countries have decided to exclude these from their own legislation. In the UK, the data must be in a form that can be processed by 'equipment operating automatically in response to instructions given for that purpose', see Data Protection Act (1984). Even though reference may be made in the computerized record to the fact that further information is available in manual files, the data user is not required to register or to give subject access to them. In contrast, France, Denmark and Norway have decided to allow employees access to manual files held on them by their employers. In Germany, changes are being made to the Federal Data Protection Law which will mean that all personal data held by companies, whether stored manually or on computer, will be subject to the regulations.

All libraries and information units that operate computerized systems, or any form of office automation, are affected by data protection. Systems likely to be covered include, loan records, personnel files, catalogues, and mailing lists. For a detailed discussion of the implications of the act for library and information management, the reader is referred to, and for a wider overview to.

Unlikely though it may seem, some fax and telex applications are covered by data protection. A few of the newer machines incorporate memory and processing capabilities, and add-on telex and fax boards for PCs are increasing in popularity. It is now possible to process a mailing list, automatically selecting recipients on the basis of some defined characteristic such as occupation, individual preference, professional status etc., for a 'mailshot' which can be distributed by fax or telex. Under these conditions, telex and fax operations are covered by data protection legislation.

Many people mistakenly believe that mailing lists are excluded from the UK Act. Mailing lists are exempt if the data is held: 'only for the purpose of distributing, or recording the distribution of, articles or information to the data subjects and consisting only of their names, addresses or other particulars necessary for effecting the distribution,' 'other particulars' being telex, fax, mailbox addresses. Even then, the exemption is only applicable if the data subject has been asked whether or not he or she objects to the data being held and he or she has not objected. Should the information contain an indication of the person's status, or some code which enables the data user to selectively mail a group of individuals, then the exemption is lost. In fact, most mailing lists do not comply with the requirements of the exemption.

Word processing, that is operations performed exclusively for preparing the text of documents, is generally exempt from data protection; but this does not apply to all work carried out on a word processor. Word processors have increased in sophistication and capabilities, especially those at the top end of the market, and many enable the user to search documents for phrases or names, to analyse and select data, and to merge the retrieved information with a document. Under these circumstances, the 'word processor' is behaving more like a 'data processor' and the purpose for which it is being used probably covered by data protection legislation.

There are exemptions to both registration and subject access provisions but many data users assume wrongly that their systems fall into one of the exempt categories —the exemption for mailing lists has already been mentioned. Far too many people, and that includes information workers, assume that data protection is for confidential documents such as medical or personnel records. They are not aware that by adding a person's name to a record in, say, an enquiry database they are holding personal data and must register the fact. The exemptions are narrowly defined and in practice rarely applicable. It is safer to assume that all systems must be registered. Even library catalogues and loan records are 'personal' as far as the law is concerned. During the committee stage of the UK Act an attempt was made to exempt them from registration. The amendment was rejected on the grounds that library records can be used to calculate royalty payments; therefore any errors or mistakes in the records could lead to loss of income for the author concerned.

Implications of data Protection for the Data user

Failure to observe data protection laws has serious consequences for anyone processing personal data. In the UK it is a criminal offence to process personal data without registering the purpose for which it is being held and processed; and it is not only the company but also its employees who are liable to prosecution if they knowingly or recklessly violate the laws.

Data protection places obligations upon the user of registered systems. Thus it is in every information professional's interest to acquaint themselves with their responsibilities under the act. All purposes for which the data is held must be registered and the data must not be used for purposes not registered. The size of the installation is immaterial as far as the law is concerned; a company which uses a small personal computer is liable in the same way as an organization running a mainframe system as has been demonstrated by a recent court case, involving a data user whose only processing power was a small microcomputer.

The data must be just sufficient to carry out the purposes and must be up to date and accurate, although the later does not apply to data gathered for research or archive purposes. Under subject access provisions an individual has the right to ask a data user whether or not the data user holds data about him or her (the data subject). The data user has to say whether or not he or she does hold such information and also to provide a copy of that data in an intelligible form. All codes that appear in the record must be defined but an explanation of scientific or medical terminology is not required. The only requirement is for the information to be in a format that can be understood by an independent expert in that field. It is the responsibility of the data subject and to find such an expert if necessary.

Should the data subject find that the information is inaccurate or incorrect, the data user must erase or correct the information on request. If the data subject has suffered harm or distress as a result of inaccuracies or loss of data, the subject may have a right to appropriate compensation.

The European convention allows individual countries to modify subject access provisions. Most notable in the UK are those that cover the detection and prevention of crime, collection of revenue and taxes, national security and medical records. Under German law, subject access can be denied if it would substantially prejudice the aims of the data user or the purpose of its activities regardless the need to protect the legitimate interests of the data subject.

Data protection can have a significant impact upon the international operations of organizations. They must comply with the domestic laws of all the countries in which they process data and may have to amend or set up new procedures. They may also have to contend with the imposition of controls on the transfer of data from one country to another - known as transborder data flow or TBDF, should one of the countries not have recognized data protection legislation. TBDF covers the movements of personal data in *machine readable form* across national borders by any one of a number of media e.g. cable, satellite, magnetic tape, disc, cards etc. It does not involve the transportation of computer printout or other paper documents containing personal data.

Last but not least, the eighth data protection principle states that data users must take reasonable precautions to ensure that personal data is accurate, and is not lost or disclosed to unauthorized people. The subject of data integrity, security and unauthorized access is covered below.

Data Integrity and Security

Precautions for ensuring data integrity and security should be part of normal procedures and routines, but there are an alarming number of organisations who fail to implement any form of data security or recovery plan. Apart from the fact that under data protection laws data subjects can sue for damages if they have suffered as a result of damage or loss to personal data, some companies are now so dependent upon computers that they cannot survive for more than a few days, or, in some cases, a few hours, in the event of a computer failure. It has been estimated that over 50% of UK organizations have no contingency plans to which they can refer in the event of a system failure. A similar survey in the USA revealed that 80%

of computer dependent companies who suffered a computer disaster went bankrupt within 18 months and 93% went out of business within five years. For systems that are so vital to an organization's very existence, one would expect the company to adopt a three pairs of braces two belts and spare pair of trouses approach to back-up and recovery; but, on the contrary, far too many data processors neglect even to take regular back-ups. Proper disaster recovery plans are a rarity.

The first step is to assess the risk and decide upon the level of protection that is appropriate for the type of data that is held. While precautions make sound business sense, one should beware of going to the other extreme and adopting procedures which are unnecessarily complex and expensive. The next step is to define the procedures to be followed but as McIntre (1988) points out, the solutions must be implemented, something that is not always easy to achieve; management has to appreciate the importance of security and give it their full support. McIntre lists eight requirements for successful implementation:

1. commitment to computer security from top management,
2. organizational structure where responsibility for an application is matched by the authority to ensure security measures are applied correctly,
3. training programme that explains the reasons for the measures,
4. recognition that in certain circumstances productivity may fall as a result of implementing security measures,
5. ensuring that the knowledge required to run an application is not vested in one single individual,
6. security responsibilities that are part of everyday work,
7. chosen security solutions are realistic,
8. the likely impact of the chosen solutions on people should be determined i.e. do not forget the human factor.

Taking regular backups is one part of data security, and most obvious, but it is the one most often taken for granted or even completely overlooked.

The commonest form of backup is the pair of crossed fingers... It is mostly used by people who know that computers never break down, who never accidentally delete the wrong files, and who don't run programs that do nasty things to discs.

He likens such an approach to 'a game of pass-the-parcel with a fizzing stick of dynamite inside -the only question is when and how much damage.' But as he goes onto explain, not all backup systems are reliable. Some do not perform an accurate backup and others may not restore the data onto another computer. Several different media are suitable for backing up data including floppy discs, magnetic tape, and boxes. Has described the relative merits of each one and some of the basic procedures that should be considered as part of everyday working practices.

Having an off-site copy of a backup is advisable in case of fire or theft, to avoid colleagues inadvertently using backup tapes and discs for other files, and as protection against the panic factor. All too often, files are restored in a state of emergency and panic, sometimes with disastrous results. Having an off-site copy guarantees that should the primary measures fail there will be an archive that can be used when people are in a calmer frame of mind, and less prone to mistakes.

Corruption or loss of data can be caused by a number of agencies: operator error, noise on telecommunications lines during transmission of files, power surges, and mains supply failure. The last two are not as common as manufacturers of mains filters and UPS (uninterruptible power supply) systems, would have us believe, but when it does occur it can wreak havoc with data and bring an organization's data processing activities to a halt. The problem can be circumvented by attaching mains filters, and constant voltage regulators or transformers. If a total power cut cannot be risked then a UPS, which provides power without interruption in the event of a total mains supply failure, should be installed.

Error-free file transfer over telecommunications lines can be achieved by using error detection/correction protocols, the most rudimentary method being the use of the parity bit. Before transmission, the transmitting computer counts the number of one bits that make up the character before transmission. If odd party is selected, the value of the parity bit is chosen so as to make the total odd: with even parity the value is chosen as to make the total even. This type of error checking does not allow for the transposition of bits, or for two errors which cancel each other out.

More reliable forms of error detection and correction involve the generation of checksums; the sending computer divides the data that is to be transmitted into blocks and carries out a calculation on each block. The result, known as the checksum, is transmitted with the block and the receiving computer carries out the same calculation. If the checksums are identical, it is assumed that the data has not been altered or corrupted end route: if they differ then retransmission is automatically requested. Another form of error checking is the check digit, a system used by banks and insurance companies. A digit is appended to, for example, a bank account number so that the total of all the digits is a multiple of ten. As with parity checking, it does not detect transposition of numbers, so the digits may be weighted according to their position within the string.

Operator error as a cause of data loss is an area of major concern, particularly in connection with desktop computers. The increase in power and sophistication of personal commuters over the past few years has resulted in their widespread use by employees at their own desks to store and process information. Because the user has access to all the functions of the operating system and is free to experiment, loss due to operator errors is a serious problem with PC bases systems. Users may type in an incorrect command format, and even the most experienced have been known to format their hard discs. Formatting a hard disc is not always a total disaster; most versions of DOS do not obliterate information on the hard disc during the process and the data can often be restored with the help of a utility program. However, a recovery should not be tried unless one is really sure of the correct procedures; should the attempt fail enough damage may have been done to ruin all further chances of retrieving the information, even by professional data recovery experts. Similarly, the DOS erase command does not remove the data from the disc; it merely marks the file as no longer required so that it does not appear on the directory. Only when it is overwritten with new data is it actually 'erased' from the disc.

It is possible to retrieve files not already overwritten by using an 'unerase' program, but this then raises the question of unauthorized access to sensitive data that is assumed to have been deleted. The only way to ensure the complete removal of confidential information from magnetic media is to overwrite the data with zeros or other characters. Again a utility program will do the job, but access to it should be restricted; once data has been overwritten in this way it is irretrievable. There is no second chance.

As was mentioned earlier, users of desktop computers have complete freedom to experiment. With an abundance of cheap utility programs and shareware on the market, many users are tempted to try out novel software which are sometimes unpredictable in their behaviour and effect. For example, improving hard disc performance by running a disc optimizer is a common practice but one that is fraught with danger. If power cuts and surges occur while the optimizer is working data may be lost, and some optimizers have been known to convert data into 'gobbledygook'.

Public domain software and shareware were once considered to be safe sources of useful, cheap programs but since the appearance of 'viruses' potential users have had to treat these programs with caution. Viruses are programs that have been written with the intention of disrupting the normal running of a program or computer, and they can infiltrate the system in such a way that they are extremely difficult to detect until they take effect.

Some appear to be little more than harmless pranks; one causes a little green dot to bounce around and edge of the screen a few minutes after the computer has been switched on. Others are far from benign and are written with the sole intention of destroying the user's data. This can happen in a single operation, but the more insidious viruses chip away at the data bit by bit. It may be several weeks before one realizes anything is amiss, and by them it is highly probable that all backups have been infected', along with other machines within the organization. Viruses can be passed from one machine to another by communications channels, so organizations working with networked systems are particularly vulnerable. Thus it is very important to be sure of the source of the programs one is about to use and a further incentive, if one was needed, not to use pirated copies.

In the USA, the situation has caused sufficient concern to make Congress consider introducing federal laws to deal with the problem. A new bill, if passed, will make it a federal crime to install a virus on a computer.

Unauthorized Access

Under the data Protection Act, users of computer systems and bureaux are legally obliged to take reasonable precautions to prevent unauthorized access to personal information. Unauthorized access to a company's computer system can prove to be very expensive. Consultants at UK's have estimated that 'high-tech' thieves steal between three and five billion US dollars annually in the US. It is believed that many companies who are victims of computer crimes silent, fearing that the publicity might adversely affect their business. Experts estimate that only 20%-30% of crimes are reported.

APSAIRD, the association of french insurers, has reported that French companies suffered at least 15,000 breaches of computer security in 1986, 70% having been committed by the companies own employees. A total of 700 million was lost, an increase of 15% on 1985. A total of 44% were the result of theft fraud or sabotage, 30% caused by accidents or breakdown; 24% by software or human error. Furthermore, out of 37 large European companies studied by UK consultants only one was found to be adequately secure. It has been suggested that the move towards greater standardization in computing and compliance with OSI will make life easier for the computer criminal on the basis that what works for one system will work for others. In essence, the initial barrier to a company's files i.e. communications, will be easier to breach and the system's security will be more dependent upon measures implemented inhouse.

Passwords and IDs are the first, the nearly always the most vulnerable, level of an organization's computer security system. Ensuring that passwords are changed regularly, particularly when staff leave, is essential but often forgotten; and the repeated exhortations of a advisers that they should not be obvious (spouses name, birthday etc.) or trivial seem to go unheeded (a colleague of one of the authors has commented on the astonishingly large number of files that he can access by entering passwords such as 'Fred'!) Neither should they be written on pieces of paper attached to the terminal. This is an are where continual monitoring and education of users who use the system is necessary.

Entry to the system can be made more difficult by employing physical devices such as keys and smart cards. The latter can be programmed with personal information and authorization codes, thereby restricting access to specific files or system functions but do have a disadvantage in that they can be stolen. For particularly sensitive data some form of encryption should be considered, but this is one area where it may be unwise to be too stringent as to who has access to or control over the decoding key. Employees have been known to leave organizations taking with them the essential decoding information and paralysing the data processing operations of their former employer.

Systems that are accessible from outside the building *via* a telecommunications link are of course susceptible to the attentions of hackers. A dialback system provides an extra level of protection to that afforded by passwords and keys. It does not immediately admit the password holder; instead the communications link is dropped, the system looks up the telephone number associated with the password that has been entered, and then rings that number thereby ensuring that the call was made from an authorized telephone number. A second password may be requested to conform identity. Auto-dial and auto-log on communications packages, convenient though they may be, should not be used in conjunction with systems that contain sensitive information.

As well as breaking into computer database, hackers can eavesdrop' on messages passing along telecommunications links and divert them to another telephone number. Pacific Bell, a public telephone service operator in the USA, recently drew up a list of hackers' activities that were concerning them: adding call charges to customers' bills; altering the day or date stored on the telephone exchange; stealing facsimile messages in transmission: redirecting calls to another number. So employing some of encryption for confidential data and a secure system of passwords and IDs is as important for electronic mail as for inhouse systems.

In the UK, there is no law against a person gaining unauthorized access to computer systems provided that no damage is caused and there is no attempt to defraud. It is not possible to steal information held on a computer because information is not property within the meaning of the 1968 Theft Act. In a much publicized case, two hackers succeeded in breaking into the. British Telecom attempted to prosecute under the Forgery and Counterfeit Act 1981 claiming that the hackers had made a 'false instrument' in order to gain unauthorized access to the system. The hackers were initially convicted but the ruling was onverturned on appeal. British Telecom in turn appealed to the House of Lords who decreed that what the hackers had done was tricery but not illegal as they had not caused any damage and not attempted to defraud anyone. More recently, West German authorities were forced to drop a case against a student who had broken into defence computers because the student's activities were not covered by any of their existing legislation.

In the USA the situation is somewhat different: computer-crime laws are on the statute books in 48 states. A former employee of a securities trading firm in currently awaiting trial on charges of harmful access to a computer - a felony in the state of Texas which carries a sentence of up to ten years in prison.

Maintenance and Insurance

If the worst should happen and data processing is brought to a halt because of fire, theft, hardware failure or sabotage, reinstatement of systems and data is likely to be costly in terms of time, money and manpower. Ensuring that adequate maintenance and support is available should be high on every computer users list of priorities. If an organization is heavily dependent upon its computer systems, a maintenance and support contract which guarantees repair or replacement within 24 hours is the very least it must consider. It is likely to be expensive, though, so the costs must be weighed against the likely effects of software or hardware failure on business and income. If an organization's circumstances do indeed warrant this form of cover, they should beware of clauses within the contract which could be used as a defence by the support company in the event that it fails to provide the service. If just a few minutes downtime could prove disastrous, there should be arrangements with other organizations or bureaux for duplicate processing facilities to be made available for essential work during emergencies.

Insurance policies must also be reviewed on a regular basis and modified to take into account changes in circumstances. Physical loss or damage to storage media and machines as a result of fire or flood are usually covered, but not the consequences of corruption of information. One should check that both accidental and deliberate erasure or corruption are included and the exact wording of the contract scrutinized. For example does it cover disasters resulting from operator error, logic bombs, and hackers and does it cover the cost of data reinstatement? The value of data itself and losses consequential to failure of data processing facilities .e.g loss of profitability and contracts, are not normally part of the standard contact, but may be included if the insurance company is satisfied with the customers backup and security provisions.

Contracts

We have already touched upon contracts in the context of online databases, maintenance and insurance; in this section we shall in addition be looking briefly at the subject of contracts and contractual liability with respect to information technology in general. It is a complex subject which we can only deal with here on a superficial level; readers wishing to read about it in more depth are referred to Edwards and Savage (1986), and Morgan and Stedman (1987). For most information professionals though, the only contracts that they ever have to concern themselves with are those made with online database suppliers and software licences.

The precise details of contracts with database suppliers vary considerably from vendor to vendor, so the customer is advised to study each contract very carefully. Apart from pricing structures and the standard clauses on the payment of charges and conditions of access, contracts between providers of online systems and their users are to a large degree concerned with copyright and the amount, if any, of copying and downloading of information that is permitted. There are also the ubiquitous exclusion clauses, and disclaimers appertaining to non-liability in the event of inaccuracy of data causing harm or financial loss.

Software licences are similar in principle in that they dictate how many copies the licensee may make (Copyright) and again attempt to limit the suppliers liability in the case of defects. The so-called shrink-wrapped licences where the purchaser does not know the limitations that have been placed upon the use of the program until he has bought the product, unwrapped it and found the licence agreement inside, are unenforceable under English law. However, the copyright provisions still apply as they subsist independently of contract.

Contracts of sale associated with hardware and bespoke systems are a potential minefield. Installing new equipment or commissioning a bespoke system to meet ones own particular needs will require a considerable amount of investment in time and money. Contracts detailing customer requirements, supply deadlines, testing procedures etc., are complex documents; this is one area where the customer must have all agreements checked by their own company's legal department so that all eventualities are taken into account. For example, the contract must define when ownership is transferred: is it on delivery of the goods, on payment or when they system has passed acceptance tests. Patent indemnity clauses are often forgotten but are nonetheless important. If a supplier sells goods which infringe the patent of a third party, then the owner of the patent can obtain an injunction to prevent the use of those goods. This applies even if the infringement was inadvertent. And again, the exact wording of clauses listing exclusions of liability and limits on liability must be checked. The most common are:

1. exclusion of liability of the supplier for losses that are peculiar to the purchaser e.g. if the impact of the suppliers default upon the purchaser is different from that upon other purchasers,
2. circumstances which are outside the control of all the parties e.g. fire, strikes, flood,
3. exclusion of suppliers liabilities where the event could have been avoided if the purchaser had followed the suppliers advice or instructions.

Where the purchaser has commissioned a bespoke system, the copyright of the programs remains with the author unless there is any express contractual provision to the contrary. The purchaser will also need to make sure that suitable maintenance services will be provided (see above) along with adequate support should any changes have to be made to bespoke programs. In the latter case, the purchaser should insist that a clause be included in the contract to the effect that the source code of bespoke programs be accessible to the purchaser if the original supplier ceases to trade.

Breaches of contract fall into two categories. Breach of condition is where a key element of the contract has been breached; examples are serious defects in the quality or suitability of software, supply of software or hardware that does not meet the specifications laid down in the contract. Under these circumstances, the offended party is entitled to regard the contract as being wholly at an end and to claim damages. Breach of warranty occurs when a minor element of the contract has been breached, for example an isolated failure in the supply of a service, or non-availability of an online database for a period of time would fall into this category. In these cases the offended party must continue to comply with the terms of the contract if they wish to claim damages.

Approval of Telecommunications Equipment

More and more information professionals are becoming involved in the evaluation and purchase of equipment. While the purchase of telephone sets, telex and facsimile equipment is often handled centrally within the organization, the selection of equipment used primarily by the information unit may well be left to the discretion of say, the information manager. Such a purchase is carried out in isolation from the rest of the company, but failure to observe approval regulations can adversely affect the whole organization. The risk is increased in units regarded as 'information centres' and where assessment of novel technology, for example fax or telex boards and packages for personal computers, is carried out. It is easy to forget that telecommunications equipment such as these must be BABT approved in the same way as telephone sets.

Until the British Telecommunications Act of 1981, the supply of telecommunications equipment in the UK had effectively been a monopoly. Today, any manufacturer can sell equipment for connection to the public network provided that it conforms to agreed standards. The Act of 1981 set up an independent telecommunications safety standards board which under the Telecommunications Act of 1984 became the British Approvals Board for Telecommunications, or BABT.

As well as setting the standards for equipment - telephone sets, fax, telex, fax and telex boards for personal computers, modems etc., - BABT oversees the approval procedure. The purpose of introducing the procedure is twofold: first, to ensure the physical safety of the user; second, it is essential that the public network (and that includes the Mercury Communications network as well as that of British Telecom) is protected. Some equipment produces signals which interfere with those used by British Telecom for the control of data flow and the operation of exchanges. Problems are most likely to arise when modems manufactured in the US, and which use Bell tones are connected to UK and European networks. The carrier signals and frequencies used in the USA for data transmitted at 300 and 1200 baud are different from those defined by the CCITT. Apart from the fact that one system will fail to recognize the signals generated by the other, some of the tones can discrupt the working of the carrier network.

BABT approved equipment carries a green circle while a red triangle denotes non-approval. All telecommunications equipment sold in the UK must be endorsed with one or the other. It is not illegal, possess or use non-approved sets. If the equipment is to be used solely on a private internal system, approval is not necessary; but as soon as an external connection to a public network is made, the consequences to a business of using non-approved equipment are potentially serious.

If discovered, the user is asked to remove the apparatus from the network. Persistent offenders may suffer total disconnection from the public network, with the result that they are prevented from using even approved equipment. Reconnection is at the discretion of British Telecom and in the meantime all business communications are halted.

Health and Safety

Information technology in the office environment is covered by health and safety regulations in the same way as other office equipment and furniture. The most obvious hazard is the mass of cabling and wiring that interconnects terminals and peripherals, which all too often is left trailing across floors for people to trip over. Of more widespread concern have been the reports that computers, specifically VDUs, present a serious health hazard to the workers that use them. In many cases, the illnesses that have been reported have been found to be caused by poor job design, inappropriate working practices, and badly designed working areas. The topics is discussed in more detail in the Chapter 9, 'Introducing and using IT'.

Legislation has been introduced in some areas of the USA in an attempt to reduce the incidence of these illnesses, whether they be related to the equipment itself or to job stress. One resolution, commonly known as the 'Suffolk Law', applies to employees operating VDUs for 26 or more hours a week. It requires that operators have a minimum 15 minute break every three hours, that these breaks be part of the working day, and that the employer must provide eye care benefits.

In the UK, the British Standards Institute (BSI) is preparing a standard for VDUs to try and eliminate problems caused by badly designed equipment. The BSI is currently assessing feedback from manufacturers, employers, users and unions. Even if a BSI standard is agreed, it will not be compulsory and the debate on the passible effects of VDUs on health will not doubt continue.

Product Liability

In 1985 the EEC Council published a directive on product liability stating that all member states were to implement national laws which were to the effect that irrespective of fault, producers shall be liable for damage caused by a defect in their products. In the UK, this led to the introduction of the Consumer Protection Act 1987. There has been much discussion about whether software is a product or a service. A guideline from the Department of Trade and Industry has said that: 'Computer software is often supplied as an intrinsic part of a product and in some cases can cause personal injury... Liability in such cases is imposed on the producer of the product. The New York Bar Association also deliberated on the matter in connection with its own liability was, and concluded that software should be deemed to be goods. In theory therefore, if an individual suffers physical injury as a result of a defect in the software, the producer could be liable. Nevertheless, licensees and commissioners of software are advised to remain vigilant over the scope of exclusion clauses in their contracts.

The legislation covers physical injury to an individual which has been caused by a defect in the product. Producers are not liable under the act for loss or damage to the product itself, or for damage to property. Neither does the act cover financial loss incurred by a business using faulty or incorrect software. Purchasers who find themselves in this situation still have to prove negligent manufacture.

A major loophole in the legislation is the state-of-the-art defence. This was included in the EEC directive as an option, each country being left to decide whether or not to include it in their own national legislation. Under the defence, the producer is not liable if he can prove that the state of scientific and technical knowledge at the time of production was such that he could not have been expected to discover or be aware of the fault. The defence is included in the UK act.

In the USA several liability cases, some involving expert systems, are pending. In one, a software bug in a computerized radiation therapy machine is thought to have caused the deaths of two patients. As to where expert systems fit into product liability is an uncertain in the USA as in the rest of the world. While the federal government is enacting regulations to control their use, many organizations are implementing their own checks and guidelines.

Legal doubts over expert systems resulted in commercial realization of systems, some of them up to 17 years in development, being seriously delayed. The Brooking Institute reported that product liability cases increased eight fold from 1974 to 1986, one reason being the increase in number of lawyers specializing in computer related issues. As to who is ultimately responsible for any damages resulting from the use of an expert system, this is still open to question; possibilities range from the user of to the programmer, from the supplier of the end product to the expert who provided the knowledge in the first place, and even the producers of expert system shells are vulnerable if the structure of the shell is found to be flawed.

Conservation and Legal Acceptability of Electronic Documents

Many libraries and information departments are faced with the problem of how best to store their records, journals, books etc. Increasing pressures from within the organization to reduce the amount of costly office space taken up by archives and information sources means that alternative forms of storage have to be investigated. There are minimum retention times for most 'office' documentation which will influence the decision as to which medium will be the most appropriate, but in some cases the law may require that original hard copy be lept thus obviating the need for any decision to the made at all. For example the US Food and Drug Administration requires pharmaceutical companies to retain for two years, the original patient record forms which were used to provide data for product licence applications.

If alternative forms of storage are permissible, there are several media from which the choice can be made: microfilm, magnetic tape, magnetic discs, optical discs. While for most day to day purposes any one of these could provide an acceptable means of storage, the legal acceptability of information reproduced from electronic form must be considered. In general documents stored on magnetic media are not admissible as evidence in a court of law. The opportunity for unauthorized alteration, whether it be accidental or intentional, is far too great. Ideally, the original documents should be presented, but microfilm documents are acceptable if adequate care has been taken in ensuring that each page can be readily identified and that certain procedures for filming have been followed. The existence of an audit trail is all important and must show the chronological sequence of documents relating to a specific case or transaction, and how and when changes to papers, contracts, ledges etc., were made. In all cases where documents in a form other than paper are involved, an expert witness is usually called to give evidence concerning the reliability and accuracy of the storage medium in question.

If large-scale conversion of documents into microfilm or electronic form is required, then procedures are necessary so that the authenticity of the record can be verified. This includes some means of identifying the author and producer of the document; the date; and the version. The last is particularly important for documents that are likely to be altered several times or amended on a regular basis. Careful checking of OCR processed images is just as important as verification of information entered via the keyboard. Some means of confirming that pages in particular sequence are indeed in the correct order, and that they do belong to the document in question are also essential. Checks must be carried at all stages of the process and records kept confirming that the procedures have been carried out.

From the legal point of view WORM discs would seem to be a reasonable alternative to microfilm, since although the user can write data to the disc he or she is restricted to a once only write. It is not possible to subsequently alter or erase the data, a feature which allows an audit trial to be maintained.

Reviewed the capabilities and limitations of the various media for permanent storage of information and the storage conditions necessary to ensure longevity.

Conventional black and white microfilm, which consists of silver halide particles suspended in gelatin, has a theoretical lifetime of more than 500 years if wet processed according to ANSI standards and stored under proper conditions (maximum relative humidity of 30% and a temperature of 15°C. The silver halide 'original' should be kept in a safe and secure store and copies made for everyday working use. Even if stored in apparently ideal conditions, it is recommended that the film be inspected every six years for signs of degradation. Diazo, vesicular and thermally processed silver film (TPS) are unsuitable for permanent storage but adequate for working copies. TPS is used in the production of COM and although it has been estimated that it should retain its integrity for bout 100 years if kept cool and dark, it is advisable to generate wet processed silver halids for ling-term archival purposes..

The shelf life of magnetic tape depends on the method of manufacture and although some may be stable for up to 20 years, many are designed for short-term high-level performance. There is also the problem of 'future readability', formats used in producing and reading the tapes may change if a new system is installed, and format conversion will have to be carried out on all archived material if it is to continue to serve any useful purpose. On average the obsolescence cycle for computer magnetic storage devices is considered to be ten years. Calmes advises against the use of magnetic discs for long-term storage, the main disadvantages being that degradation of data can occur as a result of head crashes and wear, the lack of standards for recording data and its system dependence.

Optical digital discs are an emerging technology and very little is known about their ageing characteristics. There is as yet no archival standard and not enough is known about the physical and chemical characteristics of the medium to enable anyone to specify ideal storage conditions. In theory, optical discs, should have a shelf life of between 10 and 30 years, a time span which is acceptable for most office documentation. Few manufacturers however are prepared to commit themselves beyond five year guarantees and many only give a three year guarantee. Recently there has been controversy over the results of accelerated ageing tests carried out on CD-ROMs which showed that some could start to deteriorate after two to three years. It is now believed that the cause of the degradation in many instances was the corrosive printing inks used by some manufacturers.

Despite the potential drawbacks, a number of companies have decided to go ahead with large scale storage of documents using optical disc technology. Pfizer, the pharmaceutical company, has opted for a central text database system to support research and development, regulatory affairs etc. and the Patent and Trademarks Office have been developing optical disc storage systems. Insurance companies in the USA also seriously considering transferring documents from microfiche to optical discs.

Hendley (1987) has discussed the practical pros and cons of the image processing systems available and made the point that there are no universal standards for electronic image processing. With microfilm, all that is needed is a magnifier and the document can be read directly from the medium. If the image has been stored in electronic form, the system has to be given the size of the origin document, how it was scanned, compressed and encoded before a facsimile of the original document can be generated. This can vary from one manufacturer to another. The ISO's Office Document Architecture standards which includes Office Document Interchange is still in its draft stages and different suppliers tend to use different formats. So for the time being, an organization has to standardize on one manufacturer's system if documents are to be transferred from office to office.

The transmission of documents and contracts sent *via* electronic mail also poses some interesting legal questions. As was mentioned earlier, common law in the UK requires that, wherever possible, original documents and not copies are produced in evidence. Nevertheless, courts may accept fax, electronic mail etc., if expert witnesses provide sufficient evidence concerning the reliability of the hardware, software and operational procedures. But not all are impressed and Newman quotes: 'As one of the many who has received computerised bills and dunning letters for accounts long since paid, I am not prepared to accept the product of a computer as Holy Writ.'

A more important issue is where and when an electronic mail contract comes into force; at present only post and telex have been adequately covered by law. Conventional telex messages are not always treated in the same way as posted documents but at least their status in law is, for the most part, clear and established. However the use of telex services provided as part of an electronic mailbox system is less clearcut. With post and conventional telex systems, delivery is from one identifiable, fixed, geographical location to another. This is not the case with a computer based massaging system. Newman gives the example of an offeror being in New York when he reads an acceptance mailed to his London mailbox. 'Is the contract made in London or New York? The answer is important since it determines which countries' laws apply in the event of a dispute.

An additional consideration is that one may want to confirm the identity of the sender and recipient. Conventional telex machines add answer back codes to a message which identify at least the location of the machines if not the person to whom it is eventually delivered. Similarly, many fax machines can now confirm the telephone number of the recipient and check whether the document has been delivered intact. In the USA, confidence in fax transmission has grown to the extent that mail order firms are now accepting purchase orders and some banks cash transactions by fax. With CBMS, however, there is no confirmation that the intended recipient has received the message, that there has not been corruption of any part of the document *en route,* or that the document has reached the intended destination.

9

Introducing and Using Information Technology

Introduction

In this chapter we will attempt to cover a very large and important area; the ways in which new information technologies are introduced and used. From a very large amount of literature, we will attempt to select those points which are of most direct relevance to information professionals.

We make no distinction, of the most part, between information technology in the information services themselves, and the wider organization. This is for two reasons. First, because the implications of IT, and the means by which it is introduced and used, are essentially the same in either case; second, because we will argue that information professionals can have an important role to play in the introduction and management of IT on a wider scale than in the provision of their own particular services.

For convenience, we will use the term 'organization' throughout this chapter, to mean whatever unit, of whatever size, and whether complete in itself or part of a larger whole, which the technology is serving. This could be the totality of a company, government department, university, etc. It could also be a department or section within a larger setting, if it can be considered separately as regards introduction and use of IT.

Again for convenience, we distinguish in the arrangement of sub-sections between 'planning', 'evaluating', 'introducing', and 'using' IT. In fact, these aspects are closely interlinked, and we have tried to indicate the overlaps in the appropriate places. It is important to the success of the implementation and use of the new technologies within information services that there should be some overall strategy to relate these aspects. For example, in the office automation context, considers six overlapping phases:

* diagnosis
* design
* development
* transition
* implementation
* adaption

There are other equivalent categorizations, some of which are mentioned below, and it is of no value to argue which is 'correct' or 'best'; the important point to note is that there are distinct phases or aspects, but that these overlap and interact, and cannot be considered in isolation.

Two useful sources for further detail of the whole of the process covered in this chapter are the books by. Although written from the respective viewpoints of librarians and office administrators, they are of relevance to an IT user.

Planning for IT

Successful planning for the introduction of IT is an art being learned slowly. The single most important principle behind it, is the realization that IT systems cannot, for the most part, be introduced piecemeal, or in isolation, if the organization is to reap the full benefits. There must be an explicit consideration of the effect of the new technologies on information processing, in the broadest sense, in the organization as a whole. Also, there must be a specific recognition of the potential for interaction and integration between IT systems.

The driving force for the introduction of IT should be some clear need within the organization, related to its true objectives; a 'business need'. This should then be translated into the requirements of those who will use the systems. It is important to try to avoid, as much as possible, the 'technology push' rationale for the introduction of IT. Allowing oneself to be driven by technology leads to introduction of new systems for the wrong reasons: because the technology exists; because it is new and exciting, because everyone is using it' because no-one else is using it yet, and we can be the 'first on the block'; etc. There may be valid reasons for evaluating novel systems, particularly in an R & D environment, but they will be exception, rather than the rule.

Do We Need IT at All?

One of the most important duties of those who have to plan for the introduction of IT is to decide when it should not be introduced. This is not as ridiculous as it may sound. There are many functions within an organization which should not be automated, for a variety of reasons: because it would be impossible; because it would reduce efficiency; because it would be prohibitively expensive; because it would be highly unpopular; etc. Alternatively, a partial automation may be appropriate:

> Automation is not a panacea. Manual systems may be so efficient that they would not be improved by computerization, or to change to a mechanized system may not be cost-effective. It is also often the case that inefficient manual systems can be improved by simple changes in procedures rather than the more drastic and possibly expensive option of automation.

IT planners have a duty to look at all aspects of their organization, with a view to assessing the desirability of introducing new technology, but they must *never* adopt the attitude that a decision not to automate, is, in some way, a reflection on their ability. Their primary responsibility is to their organization, and its members, and not to technology, and their task is to introduce IT *where it is appropriate,* and not wherever it can be forced in.

IT planners, than, must have a sufficient knowledge of their organization, and its aims, and a sensitivity of the needs of its staff, to be able to assess the appropriateness of IT in any part of its work. This will be done largely informally, as part of a continuous monitoring of the organization's operations, and it is to be hoped that most areas where IT introduction would not be beneficial will be quietly identified, and left severely alone.

Once a department or function emerges as a candidate for

introduction, or upgrading, of IT facilities, it must not be taken for granted that this will occur. There must be a 'feasibility study', which must be entirely open, in the sense that there must be freedom to decide that the proposed implementation is not possible, or not desirable, without loss of face on anyone's part. It is this cheerful acceptance of a negative finding which distinguishes the feasibility study from the evaluations to be described later. The nature and complexity of the feasibility study will depend greatly on the scope and size of the area under consideration; there will certainly be some element of cost-benefit analysis included, as well as a thorough examination of user requirements.

Mention of cost benefit brings us to the vexed question of the justification of IT systems, a topic which is inextricably mixed, in practice if not in theory, with planning and evaluation. We will not deal with it as a separate topic, in any degree of detail, but some general remarks must be made.

Justification of IT implementation, particularly in cost terms, is a very difficult task, and one which often appears to be disregarded, in favour of an assumption that automation must somehow be, self-evidently, a 'good thing' in its own right. Gives a clear discussion of the problems, in the light of various justification philosophies, proposes some solutions, and gives a 'justification checklist' for office systems. It is, more often than not, virtually impossible to demonstrate realistic and unambiguous financial advantages stemming from IT. Justification must therefore be multifaceted, and many of the factors involved may not be quantifiable; it must include consideration of the role of the IT systems in the organization's life, and their contributions to its objectives.

Seeing the Whole Picture

As we said earlier, a piecemeal introduction of IT systems in isolation is a recipe for inefficiency and user dissatisfaction. The planners must endeavour to see the 'whole picture'; the place for the proposed new systems in totality. This will primarily involve looking at organizational structure and function, and the work carried out by the users. It must also include considerations of job and task design, and of the location and environmental implications; those things which are usually combined under the heading of 'human factors' (as indeed we have done in this chapter), but which are actually integral to the whole planning and implementation process. So far as possible, the planners must attempt to identify what interactions will occur between apparently separate IT systems, and what possibilities there may be for integration. Even more difficult, they must try to consider the unexpected effects, perhaps side-effects, of the introduction of new systems, which may be beneficial or otherwise.

It is clear that most of this sort of planning is entirely divorced from the details of the technologies which may be applied; those considerations come at a much later stage. This initial planning is much more involved with studies of organizational structure, information flows and communication pathways, and user behaviour. The techniques which will be useful are derived from the 'user studies' area of the social, management and information sciences.

The extent of such studies must be tailored to the scale and significance of the technology change proposed. One would not undertake a full-scale information audit, or user study to purchase a new model of microcomputer. On the other hand, given the all-pervasive influence of the new technology, it is certain that many more problems have been caused, and resources wasted, by inadequate study of these factors than the other way around. Effort expended by IT planners in studies of their organizations and users is always going to be well spent.

Policy Guidelines

There are a number of considerations which must be included right from the start in planning for a new IT implementation. Some of these will be decided on each occasion; others will be laid down as standard policy, and will be followed in each case.

One principal consideration is the general IT policy of the organization; if it does not have one explicitly stated, it should do. This will include factors such as what function IT will play in the overall life of the organization; how integral is to the organization's objectives? Does the organization have a clear policy to keep up with technological development; is IT seen as a strategic tool? Is it the intention to be at the forefront of IT applications, or is it the policy to wait until a technology is well established before making use of it? If there is not clear statement on such matters, those who plan for introduction of technology cannot be blamed if they are at times out of step with the organization's requirements.

There may also be a policy on equipment purchase: to purchase everything from a single major supplier; or to insist that all systems should meet certain standards of compatibility. Are users entirely free to choose their own hardware or software; able to select from a list of 'approved' products; or entirely constrained to the one favoured product for each purpose?

There will certainly be some policy on how systems are acquired. Does the organization have the staff available to undertake development inhouse, and when would this be considered desirable? Is the policy to buy standard software packages and use them as they are, or is there a commitment to customization where necessary, using inhouse staff or consultants?

One of the most important roles for IT planners is to see that these factors are decided upon, and clearly stated: otherwise a degree of chaos (and uncreative chaos at that) is the most likely result. With such policies clearly set out, removing much uncertainty from an area bedevilled by a surfeit of possibilities, it is a much more straightforward task to consider the best way of implementing any particular system, within the overall guidelines.

Do It in the Right Order

There is a clear order in which the implementation of new IT systems would always be planned in an ideal world, and which should be followed as closely as possible in the real one.

First, some organizational need should be identified: to allow research staff better access to external information; to see that relevant financial data gets more quickly to those who need it; to ensure that internally generated competitor intelligence does not get lost; etc.

Second, this general need is translated into more specific user requirements; all scientists should have access to all internal data, including chemical structure searching, from their laboratories; all managers will have access to central and local budgetary data, with tools to analyse it; all competitor intelligence reports must be held in a consistent form, and be generally accessible; etc.

Third, the nature of the solution will be specified. Usually, the *software* will be specified first, rather than hardware, since it is a straightforward transition from a knowledge of the user requirements to a specification of the sort of software system which would meet them. The choice of software determines what the system look like to, and what it does for, the user; in a very real sense it is the system, and it must be considered first. The choice of appropriate hardware can then be made. Going the other way, selecting some suitable looking hardware, and then seeing what can be run on it, is a recipe for dissatisfied users, and waste of resources. Even when it seems that the considerations are purely those of hardware ('we must get more disc space'; 'do we go for a network, or a multi-user system?'), the crucial thing to bear in mind is what will this hardware do for the user; this means what software will run on it, and how efficiently. 'Software first' must be the rule in planning for IT.

This is not, to say that those people involved in planning for the introduction of new technology should not keep a close eye on the capabilities of new hardware developments; it is essential that they should do so. But this must always be in the context of what the hardware will do for the users, and the organization, and this mean what software it will run. It is true that the boundaries between hardware, software and firmware are not as rigid as they were, but this does not negate the general principle.

Avoiding the Main Drawbacks

The introduction of some aspect of the new technologies is all too often a painful experience for all concerned, leading, at least for a time, to lowered efficiency and morale. Apart from a relatively few cases of simple technical incompetence, typically less than 10% in the case of office automation this is usually due primarily to one or more of five failings in the planning (and subsequent implementation) of an IT system:

1. failure to involve adequately the ultimate users of the system,
2. failure to assess the true needs which the system is to meet,
3. failure to appreciate the complexity of the situation into which

the technology is introduced,
4. unwarranted optimism abut the potential of the technology,
5. failure to allow sufficient flexibility for future developments.

These are all inter-related to some extent. The effective introduction of IT is largely a matter of avoiding these problems.

The first point is perhaps the most crucial and the most misunderstood. We are, hopefully, getting away from the 'bad old days', when the new technologies were dumped, sometimes almost literally, on their users by management, with a minimum of consultation. It has become clear to all but the most recalcitrant of managements that people will accept it much more readily if they feel they have some control over it. Most commonly, this is done by letting staff have some choice of alternative equipment - allowing word-processing operators to choose their terminal type, for example - which is certainly better than nothing. This does not, however, really address the central issue; that the users generally know a great deal about the way a job is actually done, as opposed to the way in which manages and system designers believe it should be done. This user knowledge includes things best described as 'tricks of the trade', and in particular the use of unofficial ways of doing things, and informal communication networks. If these are ignored in the process of implementing new technologies, the result may be that the new system will be ignored or bypassed or that it will be used reluctantly and inefficiently.

Unfortunately, it is often easier to preach the virtues of involving the users, rather than actually doing it. It is, for example, little use asking the secretaries which word processing package they would like, if none of them have ever used any such software. Similarly, it is not very productive to rely on users for advice as to how an existing system may be improved; what one will get is ideas for simple incremental improvements, with a few totally unfeasible wishful ideas thrown in for luck. It is in fact, very difficult to make realistic suggestions for major improvements, unless one is knowledgeable about the state of the technology, and it is unfair to expect users to do so.

Getting users involved in planning for new IT systems, and in smooth implementation, is a very specific skill, which is only being learnt slowly, over ten years since the introduction of the microcomputer, which was supposed to 'humanize' technology at a stroke. Essentially, it involves a sensitivity to the true complexities of the users' work patterns, and an ability to match their requirements to the new technologies, rather than to force the users into a pre-set mould of a new system.

The second point, the failure to assess the true needs which the system is to meet, is also closely related. The danger is that a new IT system will be introduced with objectives which are much too narrowly defined and, to compound the error, defined in technical terms, rather than related to the objectives of the organization. To take a trivial example, an information service might introduce online searching in order to 'do more quickly those searches which we currently do in printed indexes'. This is not an unworthy objective, and will certainly be met. But if it is left at that, the many other opportunities offered by online will not be considered, at least at first; the opportunities to do different and more complicated searchers, to search a wider range of resources, to integrate internal and external databases by downloading, etc. It is also true to say that these opportunities might not have been seen, if the users, i.e. the searchers, had simply been asked how their drudgery in printed indexes could be averted. The true objective in introducing powerful online resources has to be something like; 'to improve the provision of external information to the user community' this leads to a realization that much more can be done with the system than just make existing activities more efficient. It must at all times be the overall organizational objectives, the 'business needs', which should be the explicit driving force for IT introduction. IF the objectives are muddled, or just patently wrong, then it is hardly surprising if things go wrong in the implementation.

We have already referred to the background of the third major failing; the failure to appreciate the complexity of the situation into which the technology is introduced. Communications patterns are complicated enough in any organization, and the introduction of the new technologies further complicates the situation, by providing entirely new ways of doing things, and entirely new communication paths and networks. Indeed, as we shall see in the next chapter, the introduction of IT on a wide scale can greatly affect the structure of the organization itself. There is therefore virtually no chance that any significant technological innovation can be introduced as an isolated entity, complete in itself. It will almost certainly interact with other parts of the organization, and with other technological innovations. Failure to allow for this at the outset may result in dire consequences for the effective use of the new system, or in the worst case, for the smooth running of that part of the organization. The library/information community (specifically US academic librarians) has been particularly slow to appreciate this significance of change; what attention has been focused on it has been devoted to the organizational consequences of introducing, for example, library automation, with little thought given to the human consequences.

It is useful to distinguish three kinds of change which may be brought about by the new technology. The first is deliberate organizational change; restructuring of departments, and changes in numbers and duties of staff. This sort of change does not happen rapidly, on the whole, and may require long and difficult negotiations. The second is unintentional changes, as job content, grading structures, salary-patterns, etc. have to be modified to reflect the *de facto* situation, brought about by technical change. This process takes even longer, since it does not begin to take effect until after implementation. The third is delayed organizational change, caused by the slow discovery on the part of the users that the IT systems afford them new possibilities in the way in which they can carry out their work, and that rearrangement of the organizational structure will support these. Experience shows that most changes in the wake of IT introduction are not planned, and do not happen rapidly; rather they are the result of a long evolutionary process.

The fourth potential problem is unwarranted optimism about the potential of the technology. Unfortunately, the claims made by suppliers of equipment and systems, and the prophecies of some of the more optimistic IT 'gurus', are not always well-rooted in reality. We would venture to suggest that virtually no-one who has had much experience of the implementation of IT systems is without their own stories of this nature: the compatible equipment that was not compatible; the communicating terminal that did not communicate; the 'fully-tested' software that could not have been tested; etc. The most cynical response is to insist on seeing, and using, every facility of every component of a system, before believing in its existence, let alone efficiency. Certainly, hard-headed realism must be the order of the day, and claims as to what will be possible, in general and in particular, in the future must be taken with several grains of salt.

The fifth problem, failure to allow sufficient flexibility for future developments, is in many ways least forgivable, and the most often committed. Given the pace of technological advance (notwithstanding the cynical clauses of the last paragraph), and especially the trends towards integration of functions and convergence of applications, anything which tends to lock uses of IT systems into reliance on particular suppliers, hardware, or even technologies, may be a recipe for future problems. So far as is possible, flexibility has to be built into whatever system is planned in as many guises as possible. That means flexibility to:

* upgrade
* network
* decentralize
* change supplier
* change technology (e.g. from magnetic to optical storage) etc.

Technological trends (e.g. standardization, open architectures, upward compatibilities, modularity) are helping this process to some extent. Those who plan for the introduction of IT can respond in two ways. First, to ensure that it is organizational requirements and user needs which predominate in planning, and not technical factors. Second, to design for flexibility from the start, as much as is possible; for example, by using modular, rather than monolithic, systems, thus allowing of easy replacement and addition, as with for example, the library housekeepers systems described in Chapter 4. In fairness however, we should note that there is a great attraction, in a practical situation, for resolving, or at least minimizing, problems of compatibility, standardization and integration by sticking with a single supplier—no-one, as they say, was ever sacked for buying IBM. But, one must have confidence that your developing needs, and your chosen supplier's developing technology will match; that the suppliers will stay in business; etc.

A slight variant on this five-way analysis of problems, identifying three factors acting as breaks on progress in implementing office technology: the 'hard-sell' *equivalent to point 4 above); the 'straight-jacket' (equivalent to point 5), and the 'self-fulfilling prophecy' (equivalent to point 3).

There is now sufficient experience and knowledge relating to IT introduction to ensure that these problems are avoided. Unfortunately, it seems that many people, and organizations, are destined to have to learn by hard experience some of these lessons.

The IT Planning Team

The nature of the team responsible for planning for the introduction of new technology will depend crucially on the nature of the organization in which it operates. In many cases, in small organizations or in individual departments within a lager organization, it may seem a misnomer to use the word 'team' at all, since this task will be left to an individual, not necessarily devoted full-time to this work.

Nonetheless, we think that it is valid to use the term 'team' even here, to emphasize that a *mix* of skills is always required for planning the implementation and use of IT. The lone individual, no matter how well qualified, will be very well advised to seek assistance and advice from others, from both within and without the organisation.

We have tried to emphasize throughout this section that the most important qualities in successful planning for IT are a thorough knowledge of the organization and its aims, and a sensitivity to the needs of its users. Technical know-how comes very much in second place; plainly IT cannot be planned for in total ignorance of its nature, but all that is really necessary is a *broad appreciation* of its capabilities, rather than detailed technical knowledge. This specialist know-how will be brought to bear, on demand, in the later stages of the planning process, and in evaluation and implementation. Thus, if only one person is to be directly responsible for IT planning, it is preferable that they should not be an IT specialist; certainly not someone from a data processing background. Similarly, if the organization is large enough to warrant a team devoted to this purpose, it shouldn't consist entirely of IT gurus, and preferably should not be headed by such an individual. Some of the problems which have resulted from IT development, in the office automation context, being administered solely by computing departments (systems not serving user needs), by office services groups (too narrow a focus with no integration of systems), or by end-user departments (duplication of effort, with systems often failing to work at all).

What is required is a mix of technical skills and knowledge of the technologies, with a knowledge of the organization and its staff, the information and communication flows, and the management consequences. If there is no possibility of having a team large enough to encompass all these skills, then there must be a small 'core' of individuals, not necessarily technical experts, but with a strong user-orientation, able to call on technical knowledge as required, from inside the organization or from outside. These individuals may come from a variety of backgrounds, such as:

* general management
* computing/data processing
* information services
* office administration, etc.

Given a good general awareness of the technologies, the main requirements are for organizational knowledge and appreciation of user needs. There are good reasons for suggesting that many information professionals would fill this role very well.

For example, advocates a tripartite alliance for the planning and building of corporate information systems: between end users (specifying the required inputs and outputs), datas-processing specialists (providing the computing infrastructure and central software), and information specialists (linking the two). The particular relevant skills of the latter she sees as:

* broad knowledge of the business
* familiarity with user needs
* appreciation of the advantages and limitations of IT
* understanding of information flow
* expertise in information storage and retrieval

On the smaller scale, the staff of information services will certainly be responsible for planning for the introduction of IT within their own area, with assistance as necessary from computing specialists. This should be the ideal opportunity to demonstrate to the rest of the organization how this task should be accomplished, and thereby to show the value of the skills of the information professional in this capacity. On the whole, we believe that this does, to some extent, happen; but that too often there is inadequate and ineffective communication of the successes outside the information community. Perhaps this is a reflection of our profession's lack of talent for realistic self promotion.

Many commentators have made the point that the eventual success of the planning and implementation of IT systems within an organization is closely related with the seniority of those in charge of the planning function. In business/industrial settings, it is generally thought desirable to have someone at board level directly responsible for these activities. This serves three purposes:

* It indicates to the organization as a whole that this is something which is taken very seriously.
* It ensures that adequate resources will be made available.
* It brings, most importantly, the planning of IT systems into the main thrust of the organization's activities, at a strategic level.

Even with a large team available, there are strong reasons for advocating the use of outside expertise, consultants, in the planning process (without a large team of varied skills, this is an essential). They can bring a much wider experience of the ways in which IT can be, used, and can help the team to break out of 'straight-jacketed' thinking, based on detailed knowledge of their own organization. Hopefully, the consultants will also have seen most of the worst mistakes being made, and will be able to help in avoiding their repetition.

Evaluating and Choosing IT

The process of evaluating and choosing IT systems and equipment can be fraught with difficulty. This is due to a number of factors:

* the speed of developments
* the complexity of the application areas
* the trend to integration, and convergence, implying that there may be several different ways of achieving the same objective
* the problems of distinguishing between fact and fantasy in the claims of suppliers

* the difficulty of assessing which aspects of technology are meeting real user needs, etc.

Much has been written on this topic, and this section can only attempt to distil some of the more important points. In the reference section, we include some of the more useful and relevant items from a vast literature.

The fundamental requisite for any proper evaluation is an adequate assessment of real user needs, as noted in the previous section. There is then the problem of mapping this onto the suppliers' offerings, so as to choose between them, assuming that some at least are adequate. There are a number of ways of doing this, ranging from the highly formalized decision analyses, appropriate to major purchases within large organizations, to totally informal ways of acquiring small bits of equipment; the latter amount to little more than recommendations for impulse purchases.

On serious danger, which has been encountered by more purchasers of IT systems than would readily admit it, is the temptation to believe that, because the product under consideration is relatively cheap, it is more cost-effective to buy it than to evaluate it. Nothing could be farther from the truth. The true costs come, not in the purchase price, but in the effort expended in implementing and trying to use a system. Quite commonly, it is the cheapest items, particularly to software, which waste most staff time; in implementing the product, in making it work properly, and (too often) in trying to find something useful to do with it. Every acquisition, even of something given free of charge, should be carefully considered, weighing up its potential value against the time which must be taken to try it out.

It is also important to realize that there may well not be a single option which is 'best' on all possible counts; compromises and trade-offs must be made. This may sound obvious, but it is surprising how often people seeking to choose a new system, especially if they are doing so for the first time, waste a great deal of effort in seeking the chimera of the 'ideal' system, rather than identifying one which does what is wanted perfectly adequately. Similarly, given the rapid rate of change and improvement in IT systems and equipment, there is a great temptation to wait just a short while longer, to get the benefit of the new features. This is, of course, a fruitless course, for the new features are immediately succeeded by yet more promises of things to come, and the 'ideal' system recedes into the distance, never quite to hand. In some areas of IT, such as computerized modelling systems using the latest hardware, as well as software, the speed of development is such that it is no exaggeration to say that any system purchased will be obsolete by the time it is delivered. The situation is not so dramatic with the sort of systems likely to be used by information services, but is not really so different. The only defence is to keep in mind constantly that one is not acquiring a status symbol, but a tool to do a defined job; the requirements of the users must also be kept in mind.

Puts the situation bluntly, suggesting that in choosing IT systems one must:

> not worry about what is in store next month or next year. You probably cannot, or need not, wait for these new products. Ideally, you should be looking at the products available today... As long as you select the most suitable software which matches your requirements on mainline, industry-standard equipment, from a reputable supplier, then you will have done all you can to protect yourself against the future.

While this attitude can be taken, too far, if it lead to a disinclination to think about likely future trends and products, there can be no doubt that it has much to commend it.

Any and every IT product should therefore be evaluated in some way before it is brought inhouse. It is highly desirable that there should be a formal *and* informal aspect of every evaluation. The formal aspect ensures that no obvious single factor is overlooked; the informal guards against misinterpretation of the overall picture in a plethora of details.

Formal evaluation will be carried out in a variety of different ways, according to the procedures of the purchasing organization, and the cost of the product.

Describes in details the sort of process which would be gone through in most cases for a 'big' purchase; she writes in the specific context of choice of a library automation system, but the same procedures could be applied to any IT system. Considering library/information systems considering office automation, give slightly different viewpoints on what is basically the same process. This approach assumes that a single system, quite probably including both hardware and software, is to be purchased from a single supplier. The main steps are given below.

1. Choose project Personnel

There are a number of options in choosing a team to select (and subsequently implement) a new system.

For a major purchase, especially if none of the staff of the organization have experience of the type of system being considered, it is advisable to use an independent consultant in some capacity: to suggest a range of possible products: to provide aspects unfamiliar to the organization's staff; to check the list of requirements to ensure that nothing has been overlooked; to provide insight based on experience with similar projects in other organizations; etc. It is probably *not* advisable to give total responsibility for choice of system to a consultant, a popular option, particularly in the USA in the past. The choice of a major new system is of such significance for the staff who will operate it that they must be fully involved in, and ultimately responsible for the process. The value of the independent consultant is in providing an objective and detached view of the situation, and in bringing experience from similar projects in other organizations. In particular, the consultant can help too ensure that the choice of new system is not to constrained by the expectations of the staff of the organization, which will usually be greatly influenced be existing systems and procedures. Without the 'outsider' viewpoint, it may be difficult to envisage anything more than an incremental improvement of the *status quo*.

Clearly, there must be someone from within the organization who will have overall charge of the project to choose, and subsequently implement, the new system. For a small purchase, or for that matter a larger purchase within a small organization, this person may well have to undertake all the work personally. In a larger-scale setting, for example the choice of a database or library automation product to serve a larger user community, there will usually be a team appointed to oversee the process, with a team leader, often termed 'project director'. It is desirable that this person should be as senior as possible, and it is also a good idea to choose someone representing the users of the system, rather than a technical expert. This latter may be a counsel of perfection, since it is often taken for granted that a computer specialist is the only appropriate person to choose IT systems. This all too often, results in technical criteria assuming an overwhelming importance, at the expense of user-oriented factors of equal, or greater, significance in the actual use of the system.

In the case of a system which is to be operated primarily by the information services staff, or maintained by them on behalf of their users, it is obviously appropriate that someone from this area should be the project director. More generally, information professionals can be particularly well-suited to this role in the introduction of IT into the organization as a whole, because of their knowledge of the technologies and of user requirements.

Although it is often best to allow a single individual to carry out the evaluation process, seeking advice from internal and external experts as needed, the choice of a major system may require the setting up of a 'steering committee', headed by the project director. It is easy to be cynical about committees, as devices to ensure confusion and time wasting, but in this context a steering committee can be a valuable means of ensuring that all viewpoints, both technical and user, are represented.

For a particular complex evaluation, perhaps choosing an all-embracing system such as office automation, for a multi-site organization, the steering committee structure may need to be correspondingly complex. For example, there may need to be a 'management committee' to define policy, separate from a 'working group' or 'task force' which deals with the technical factors. In general, such complicated structures are a recipe for inefficiency, if not disaster, and they are best avoided, if local politics will permit. The simplest committee structure which allows full involvement of the users of the system is undoubtedly the best, and if this can be organized on an informal basis, then so much the better.

As with much else, the necessary management structures will be crucially dependent on the nature of the organization itself; bureaucratic organizations require bureaucratic evaluation procedures. It may be also necessary, for example, at some stage to specifically involve trade unions or staff associations, for projects which will have significant effects on working patterns.

2. Define Requirements

Once a decision has been taken that a system is to be acquired, the first essential is to carefully draw up a full list of requirements; easier said than done. This, often known loosely as 'functional specification', is formally termed a 'specification of operational requirements (O/R)', and is defined as:

The statement issued to suppliers giving details of a project against which they are invited to submit proposals. It is an important document which must enable the supplier to determine whether or not he should invest effort in competing for the business.

There are a number of formal guidelines for specifying O/Rs; in the UK, for example, the CCTA has a formal procedure, which is mandatory for UK government departments and recommended for universities. However, formal procedures of this kind are complex an time consuming, and inappropriate for 'small' purchases (although they may be required, even here, by the purchasing policies of an organization).

Even if there is no necessity to go through such a major procedures, it is an excellent discipline to prepare a formal O/R document for an IT acquisition. The process sharpens appreciation of the real needs (which often start out embarrassingly vague), and conveys them very clearly to the supplier. Production of this formal document may also save time in the long run, in helping to plan the evaluation, and (perhaps) draw up a contract subsequently.

The O/R document must, naturally, specify the full range of facilities to be provided by the system, clearly distinguishing between those which are genuinely essential and any which are merely desirable. In its fullest form, it will go beyond this, to specify such things as: relevant background information about the purchasing organization; the environment in which the system will operate; any standards or protocols which must be met; the size of the system, and his likely growth: a timetable for implementation; any special constraints; etc. The O/R speciates the requirements; it *does not* suggest solutions (this is the suppliers' job, nor does it specify the requirements in terms of specific equipment of systems.

Since it may not be entirely clear what is feasible or realistic, especially if some novel or unusual features is being sought, the formal O/R may be preceded by a 'request for information (RFI)', also known as a 'prequalifier'. This is a brief statement of requirements, sent to suppliers with a request for an indication of whether what is being requested is feasible, and at what rough cost. On the basis of replicas received, the full O/R can be drawn up.

3. Identify Possible Suppliers

Before anything further can be done, a list of potential suppliers must be drawn up. In some circumstances this will not be difficult, because the suppliers of particular sorts of systems will be well known to the purchasers. In information services, there are only a very small number of suppliers of specialized systems for applications such as library automation, or chemical structure databases, and user departments who have been involved in the area for some time will be very familiar with them.

It may be however, that the situation is otherwise: that what is being acquired is a much more general-purpose product, a microcomputer, for example; or that it is a product in an area new to the purchaser, for example, an information department looking, for the first time, at electronic mail; or simply that the purchasers want to ensure that over-familiarity does not cause them to overlook something. In any of these cases, the purchasers will have to be more systematic in identifying suppliers. There are a variety of useful sources for doing this, for example:

* personal recommendation from colleagues,
* lists of suppliers maintained by professional and trade organizations,
* directories and yearbooks,
* articles and advertisements in the professional press,
* attendance at exhibitions,
* use of consultants.

There are usually centres of expertise in one's own country which can give advice, since availability of IT systems differs very widely across national boundaries. In the UK, for instance, useful organizations include the National Computer Centre (NCC), the Library and Information Technology, Centre, the Business Equipment and Information Technology Association, Aslib and the Institute of Information Scientists.

It may be worth mentioning exhibitions in particular. At one time, a purchaser could cheerfully assume that attendance at one or two of the major computing exhibitions each year would give a complete view of all important products. This is no longer the case; suppliers are becoming increasingly unwilling to attend the wide variety of exhibitions which now take place, and their lack of enthusiasm is matched by that of users, increasingly disenchanted with the 'general' exhibition. It is often the case that one exhibition gains the status of 'the place to go', and others tend to lose importance. The exhibition associated with the International Online Information Meeting, held in London in December, gained this status during the 1980s, for the whole spectrum of IT systems relevant to information services. It is worthwhile identifying and attending major exhibitions of this sort; alternatively there are an increasing range of closely targeted exhibitions for particular applications.

Personal recommendation is a particularly good source of information on suppliers (as much for those who are *not* favoured as those who are). It may have the drawback of focusing attention on a small group of 'trendy' suppliers, and it is wise to use some of the other methods to ensure that worthwhile sources are not overlooked.

It is very important to get a "feel' for the reliability of suppliers; not just the likelihood that they will be in business to maintain your system next year, important though this is, but how efficient their support facilities are. Also it is important to consider the 'empathy' factor: how receptive the suppliers are to suggestions and requests, and how well they understand the requirements of particular types of customer. These factors are difficult to assess from technical literature, and similar bald facts, and can best be appreciated from personal contact with their staff, and from an assessment of the views of their existing customers who are in a similar situation to yourself.

4. Request and Assess Proposals

Once a list of suitable suppliers has been drawn up, the O/R document should be sent to them; technically this is known as a "request for a proposal (RFP)'. Deal with this aspect at some length. The suppliers will respond with a detailed description of the system which they would propose to supply, its performance, and some indication of cost. Undoubtedly, there would be some discussion between purchasers and suppliers prior to the formal reply; usually a meeting between the purchaser and each of the suppliers. There should also be the chance for the purchasers to see a demonstration of the system, if they have not already done so.

The suppliers' replies will then be considered, and some, no doubt, eliminated at once. It is highly desirable that no more than three possibilities should be taken through to the next, evaluation, stage, otherwise the task will become immense.

5. Evaluate in Detail

The evaluation procedure now aims to enable a decision to be made between a small number of competing systems, or possibly to decide whether just one contender will be suitable. All systems which reach this stage will look reasonable in outline on paper, and the evaluation must therefore look at practicalities in detail.

There is no real substitute for looking at the system working, in one's own environment, and with one's own data. This may well be possible, with the supplier providing either access to the full system for a specified period of time, or access to a restricted 'demonstration' version. Failing that, then demonstrations must be provided at the supplier's site, on data as similar as possible to the purchaser's own, and with members of the purchasing organization, representing all classes of potential user, having the opportunity to use the system freely over a considerable period of time. The standard 'marketing' demonstration will not do at all.

There is of course, a risk associated with the 'ideal' situation of the system being available inhouse for a lengthy trial period: the users may be unwilling to give it back! This is particularly so if any amount of 'real' data has been entered into the system. It those users who try it out like it, particularly if they have no experience of similar systems (if, for example, they are using an interactive retrieval system for the first time), it may be very difficult to continue any sort of objective evaluation. Suppliers are well aware of this effect, and their willingness to supply a system for inhouse evaluation may not be due to simple altruism.

There is also the contrary risk that teething troubles, or unpopular 'consented' factors in a system, may alienate users very rapidly, and unreasonably. The evaluators should make sure that such trials are conducted in a carefully controlled way, without allowing unlimited access to all potential users, and should ensure that judgements are not unduly influenced, one way or the other, by initial experience of one system.

If at all possible, the purchasers will arrange to visit a similar organization to see the system at work. Suppliers will usually be keen to arrange this, and if they are not it does not bode well. It is a good idea to try to visit a variety of other users, and not absolutely rely on those recommended by the suppliers, who will obviously point potential purchasers in the direction of their most satisfied customers. If there is a user group for the system, a good sign in itself, this will be a source of valuable feedback.

This is also the time for extensive technical discussions with the supplier, ensuring that there are no misunderstandings about the capabilities of the system, and its potential for upgrading. There may also be some negotiations about the price of the system, as there is usually a degree of flexibility in major IT purchases.

It is important that there should be a very fully set out 'checklist' of points to be considered, based on the specification of requirements, and that full written records of the evaluations should be kept. Some form of scoring system, or other decision analysis techniques, will also probably be used. Not only will this satisfy the purchasing organization's requirements, if a good deal of money is to be spent, but it ensures that all aspects are given consistent consideration. It is all too easy to find the members of the evaluation team 'fixating' on small aspects of the systems under test, and losing the perspective of the broader picture.

All the above assumes that what is being considered is a 'standard' system, already working in other organizations. It is possible that consideration may be given to adopting a brand-new system, perhaps one on 'beta-test' (i.e. in operational use for the first time). This is only likely to occur if the purchasing organization already has considerable experience with IT systems so that the supplier feels they are a suitable test site. In this case, it can be an exciting experience, giving the opportunity to make use of some state-of-the-art technology, and arguably, get ahead of one's competitors. It can also be a quite harrowing experience, with normal work entirely disrupted, while problems with the systems are sorted out. Being among the first users of a new system is not to be recommended to anyone without extensive expertise in the area, nor to anyone who likes a quiet life.

6. Proceed to Contract

Once the evaluation is completed, a full report will be written, and a decision made on the choice of system. Once this is settled, a contract must be decided with the supplier. This may not be entirely straightforward, in the case of a major and complex system. An intermediate stage is often the writing of a 'memorandum of agreement', or 'memorandum of understanding'. This is a document, signed by both supplier and purchaser, and usually having some legal status, which is aimed at clarifying any and all ambiguities which may be present in the purchaser's O/R document and the supplier's proposal, to remove any misunderstandings which may occur in the drawing up of the contract. The process of drawing up this document may well provoke much discussion, and may cause the suppliers to make extensive changes to their proposals.

When this degree of understanding is reached, the next stage may be a formal invitation to tender, as required by the procedures of the purchasing organization. Once this hurdle is passed, the contract may be drawn up. Contracts for IT systems are complicated, and not to be dealt with lightly by the inexperienced refers to the frequency of legal proceedings between suppliers of library automation systems and their purchasers in the USA, an admittedly litigatious society, as an example of the problems which may arise. It is usual for contracts for major systems to include specification of factors such as maintenance and upgrading, as well as the specification of the system to be installed. Of course, the precise nature of the contract will depend upon the laws of each country: for example, gives useful information and examples relating to the UK.

Finally, it is normal for there to be 'acceptance trials' after installation of a major system, and for these to be specified in the contract. These may include the use of a set of standard tests, such as the system reliability test (requiring that the system operates at a specified level of effectiveness for a specified period of time), the functional validity test (assessing that each and every function of the system performs are required), and the full-load performance test (evaluating the performance of the system under simulated 'peak' conditions).

We have dealt in some detail the this formal and complicated procedure for the choice of a major IT system, albeit with equipment and/or software coming from a single supplier, to show something of the nature of the 'large-scale' end of faith spectrum of the implementation of new technology, and to explain some of the jargon (O/Rs, RFPs, etc.) which may be unfamiliar. Needless to say, most evaluations of IT, especially by and for information services, do not require this sort of procedure (although it is surprising how often it is required, unnecessarily, by organizational procedures, which do not distinguish between a microcomputer and a multi-site office automation system). Describes, with detailed examples of documentation (specifications, proposals, etc.) a variant of this procedure for purchasing a smaller product: a stand-alone word-processing system.

In the case of purchase of a single, relatively small, item of hardware or software, the full procedure described above would be a gross overkill, if only because there is little scope for negotiation with suppliers. The products are available for sale as they stand, and the purchaser must simply choose between them. Nonetheless, something of the same procedure should always be gone through, in an appropriately simplified form, to avoid buying something which will immediately prove valueless, or, much worse, prove valueless only after the expenditure of considerable time and effort.

The first step, choosing project personnel, will not have

the same meaning as for the 'big' purchase, but it is still important that the right people make the choice. This, in practice, means the people who will use the system, with input from someone who appreciates its technical feasibility. This seems obvious, but it is depressing to reflect how often choices are made by people who have neither qualification; typically a departmental manager.

Defining requirements is a vital step, which should *never* be forgotten. If the requirements are really simple and obvious, then it will not take long to specify them (and perhaps realize, particularly when colleagues compare notes, that it is not quite so simple).

Identifying possible suppliers here means identifying the products as well. Much the same techniques will be sued as on the large scale; the 'comparative review' type of article in professional magazines is particularly useful in identifying suitable pieces of hardware and software. Personal recommendation is at least as useful as with the 'big system'.

Requesting and assessing proposals probably has no meaning here, other than asking the salesman in the computer store what is on special offer. Evaluating in detail is rarely possible prior to purchase, although 'demonstration' versions of relatively cheap software systems are increasingly available and most widely-used products can be seen at exhibitions.

Contracts do not have quite the same significance as on the larger scale, although it is very important to check exactly what degree of backup and support you are getting. If a department, or even an individual, is going to be dependent on a piece of hardware or software, no matter if it was cheaply bought, then maintenance and general support are as important as for a large system.

Some of the same general principles, then, are applicable to the choice and evaluation of IT systems and equipment on both large and small scales. The distinction is that, with cheap single purchases, one may be forced into the position of having to do the real evaluation, in one's own real-life situation, *after* making the purchase. The best way of minimizing the risk of making a complete mistake is to use, appropriately modified and scaled down, techniques recommended for 'big-system' evaluation: the checklist and, if appropriate, some, scoring system.

The checklist is the fundamental tool for any systematic formal evaluation of alternatives, and should *always* be used in choosing IT products. It should specify any and all factors to be considered in choosing a system, and is best drawn up by more than one person, to ensure that nothing is missed, and that there is no ambiguity in the points listed. An extensive and detailed checklist for the selection of business computer systems; though not applicable in its entirely to systems for information services, it gives a valuable starting point. O'Rourke (1987) exemplifies the use of a checklist for selection of an online public access catalogue system for a library.

Some form of scoring, if only a series of ticks and crosses, will be used with the checklist. There are, of course, may weighting or scoring systems, of varying degrees of complexity, which may be adopted; the purchasing organization many well have its own favourite which must be used on all occasions. One examples is decision analysis, in which each requirement on the checklist is given a numeric score reflecting its perceived importance, and each contending system is scored on how well it fulfils that requirement; a little arithmetic gives an 'objective' (or at least explicable) ranking of the alternatives. An alternative, very similar in principle, is the Otis decision make and there are numerous others exemplify the use of such a decision aid in choosing a library automation system.

We have seen how the 'formal' procedure for acquiring a 'big' IT system can be scaled-down and modified to suit the needs of a smaller purchase. We should also note that this procedure would not be strictly applicable at the other end of the scale; a large and complex system, with items of hardware and software; and possibly also telecommunications, coming from a variety of suppliers. The same general ideas would however apply, though in the much more complex situation which always applies when the offerings of different suppliers have to be fitted together. Such implementation projects must be dealt with according to the requirements of each individual case they are certainly not for the inexperienced.

The discussion above assumes that packaged systems will be bought 'whole' from suppliers. The procedure does not differ that much if the system is to be written entirely, or partly inhouse or written on demand for specific requirements, or extensively customized. There will almost certainly be a comparison between a system of this sort and a packaged equivalent, unless the requirements are so unusual that no 'off-the-peg' product exists. The specification of requirements, and so on, must be carried out with equal care, and the only significant difference is that negotiations will be carried out inhouse rather than externally (which does not necessarily mean than they will be any less difficult!)

These, then, are the general principles which should be followed in the choice of any IT product; naturally, as we have tried to point out throughout, the procedures will be adapted to suit the nature and scale of the choice to be made.

These are, of course, *formal* procedures, based on the analytical breakdown of the decision into requirements on a checklist, financial limits, etc. To counterbalance this, we must recognize the need for a complementary *informal* evaluation.

Informal evaluation is a means of ensuring that no major mistakes are made as a result of relying on formal procedures ; it is by no means unknown for a formal decision analysis to come to a conclusion agreed by all participants to be nonsensical, yet difficult to amend within the formal structure. The informal approach, entirely qualitative and holistic, gets away from the analytical detail of most formal schemes, and asks 'is this really sensible? Does it fit in with the real needs of our particular users?. Essentially, an informal evaluation looks at the overall characteristics of the IT system and of the purchasing organization, and asks 'are we compatible?'. (The analogy of a marriage, if one thinks of a piece of software which will be at the core of the organization's, or department's, activities, is not ridiculous).

Techniques to be used could include:

* asking whether any similar organizations use the product, and how - if not, why not?
* involving the staff who would use the product, in picturing how it would be used in 'real-life'; this could even go so far as role-play.
* using simulations, or 'gedanken' experiments, to envisage the produce in use.

In short, informal evaluations accept that IT products and user organizations and departments alike have 'personalities';

aspects which it is difficult to capture in formal evaluation schemes, but which must match. Software systems, in particular, have their own 'feel', which can make all the difference between successful acceptance or not. Also, it is important to feel that one can happily do business with the supplier, if it is a major purchase and there will be some degree of relationship over a period; this is another aspect which is difficult to capture formally.

The successful evaluation and choice of IT systems and equipment, to summarize, depends on an appropriate combination of formal and informal evaluation methods, applied within a general framework which ensures that no significant factors are overlooked. It is also crucially dependent on the involvement of both users and technical experts in the decision.

This section has been largely, and unavoidably, couched in rather general terms. There are number of interesting and specific examples of system evaluation, of especial relevance to information services, reported in the literature: for example, information retrieval packages for the special library end-user literature searching aids, and library circulation systems.

Introducing IT Systems

After the planning, and the evaluations come, perhaps the most fraught of all the stages in the implementation of information technology; the actual introduction of the system for real. Again there are many horror stories from the past, but a sufficient body of knowledge and experience for the worst effects to be avoided in the future.

It is worth pointing out one, perhaps inconvenient, fact, which may appear rather obvious, but is often forgotten in practice. The success of the introduction of any IT system will depend largely on the quality of the planning and evaluation which has preceded it. No matter what care is devoted to the actual process of introduction, if the wrong application is being automated, or the wrong system has been chosen, then the results cannot be other than unfortunate. There has been a rather unfortunate tendency, in past years, to concentrate overmuch on the implementation phase, at the expense of the earlier stages. While this is obviously preferable to giving little thought to implementation, it is not a healthy balance.

We must also bear in mind that the process of implementation, as with planning and evaluation, will depend very much on the nature and scale of the application. While it is possible to derive neat categories, we might usefully think of the scale of implementation as ranging from *small* (a stand-alone micro database system), through *medium* (a shared word-processing system for a small organization. There is also the question of the *complexity* of the system being introduced. This will depend on such things as:

* the functionality of the system (i.e. how many different things it does)
* the number of different kinds of users, with different requirements
* the degree of interaction with others systems
* the extent to which a system is networked, rather than stand-alone etc.

The nature of what the new system replaces is also relevant. It may:

* replace an existing automated system
* replace a manual system
* introduce some entirely new function
* integrate a number of previously separate functions (automated or manual)

All other things being equal, the degree of complexity will increase gong down this list.

Crudely speaking, it is the degree of complexity, rather than anything else, which determines the degree of difficulty likely to be experienced in the evaluation. Scale is not such a problem: replacing all of the microcomputers in every office of a large national, or multinational, organization with another make is certainly a large-scale problem. However, it need cause no greater problems of implementation, other than sheer logistics, than doing the same thing in a single department. Once the problems of such a transfer are solved for one group of workers, they are quite probably solved for all.

The major problems of implementation arise when the new system alters work practices, interferes with existing information flows and communication patterns, and, in short, requires people to start doing entirely new things, or old things in an entirely new way. One may, of course, expect technical problems, but they are as nothing to the problems associated with the interference with the work patterns of the (quite probably unwilling) uses. Hence the emphasis on user needs and requirements in planning and evaluating, and hence the need for a 'user-centre' approach to the introduction of information technology, which we will consider later.

Procedures for Implementation

There are essentially three ways of implementing any new system, certainly including IT systems, assuming that they replace, to some extent at least, some system or procedure already in place. If this is not the case, that is the system aims at fulfilling some totally new function, with nothing corresponding to it in place already, then implementation is an uncomplicated matter, in theory at least, of starting from scratch. This would be the case in an entirely new information service, or when an entirely new function was being undertaken, but these are rare events. Much more commonly, the new system replaces, or complements, what is there already, and the implementors must choose between one of the three options. These are:

* an 'all-at-once' changeover
* 'parallel system' operation
* 'gradual' changeover

The first of these, the all-at-once changeover, sees the old system terminated, and the new system introduced, at one time. The clear advantages are that the benefits of the new system are realized immediately, there is a minimal period of disruption as the changeover takes place, and there is no necessity to incur the costs of running two systems simultaneously. There is also a pleasing air of efficient decisiveness about this arrangement. However, these advantages may well be outweighed by the effects of the suddenness of the change, which may not give the system user sufficient time to adapt; the resulting disruption may be severe. Also, if any problems arise with the new system, which will have effectively no backup, their effects on the operations which the system supports, and on the morale of the users, can be drastic. This is therefore, a rather dangerous option, particularly for large systems with many users, or systems crucial to the work of an organization.

The second, 'parallel', option involves running both old and new systems side by side for a sufficient period to deal with teething troubles in the new system, and prove its effectiveness. This incurs obvious costs, and potential user frustration, if they are required, for example, to enter the same information into the two systems; it may also lead to confusion and error, because of the possibility of mixing up the two systems, especially if they appear very similar. On the other hand, this is a very robust solution, retaining the backup security of the old system until the new one is fully proved. This 'proving' is, in turn, made easier by the potential for direct comparison and cross checking between the two systems. If problems are found in the new system, they can be corrected without too much disruption.

The third 'gradual, option uses a phased process of replacement of the old system by the new. This can be accomplished in various ways. If both the systems are modular, then they can be changed over piecemeal; gives the modular, then they can be changed over piecemeal; gives the example of a modular library automation system, with initial introduction, or replacement, of the cataloguing module initially, followed later by acquisitions, etc. This may work well, or may be problematic, depending on how tightly the modules integrate together. Alternatively, within a large organization, the new system may be implemented in one part of the organization at a time; perhaps in one department or branch.

The 'gradual' strategy is very flexible and has to be adapted to the needs of the local situation. It has clear advantages in that the users of the system can be given ample time to adjust to the new procedures, and it minimizes the chances of major problems occurring with the system as a whole. Against these must be set equally clear disadvantages. The overall implementation process may be very slow, delaying the time when full advantage is reaped from the new system. There may be problems in dealing with outside suppliers in terms of specifying contractual terms, for an implementation of this sort. Finally, there may be a sense of confusion and 'disorientation' among the users, if they are in a long-lasting situation of being 'between' two systems. This will require careful attention on the part of the implementors. On the whole, this type of implementation is likely to be best suited to large-scale and complex systems.

It is worth mentioning one particular form of gradual implementation; the *'pilot project'*. This involves the implementation of a system, probably in prototype, form, in a small part of the organization, a department or branch. Here it is tested user reaction noted, and improvements made where necessary; ultimately it is accepted, and implemented throughout the organization, or rejected. Pilot projects are generally recommended enthusiastically, as the first step of large-scale IT implementation. However, it is fair to point out that they have been criticized, especially in the context of office automation implementation, as indicating a lack of commitment to the new system, which has on occasions proved fatal. Pilots are therefore best regarded as part of the implementators' weaponry for complex systems in large organizations, to be used with care where appropriate.

On the whole, it seems that the progression from 'all-at-once' to 'gradual' implementation should be followed as the system to be implemented grows more complicated, and the number of users involved increases. The 'parallel' style of implementation has a lot of recommend it, in many circumstances; certainly, an 'all-at-once' procedure should be regarded rather dubiously, except for simple stand-alone systems. The 'gradual' style of implementation tend to fit well into a flexible 'user-centred' strategy, discussed below.

User-Centred Approaches to IT Implementation

We mentioned above the rationale for a 'user-centred' approach to the introduction of IT systems. Of course, even the most traditional data processing style methods of system design have 'identification of user requirements' as a first stage: but this frequently implies an attempt to squeeze user needs into a predetermined mould, the parameters of which will be determined by the technical concepts currently in vogue. The need for a more flexible and open approach has been discussed frequently, and put into practice much less often, during the 1980s. For example, make a favourable contrast between an 'organization and end-user centred approach' with 'task and technology centred' and 'technology-led muddling-through' approaches. The later two strategies are characterized respectively by tightly prescribed planning objectives, central coordination and control, and obsession with a 'clean design', in the first case, and by a fascination with technology itself, and the expectation that it can be 'injected' into existing organizational arrangements, in the second. Similarly contrasts the user-driven/participative approach with technology-driven and '*status-quo*' strategies.

The clearest formulation of the user-centred approach, and one particularly well suited to the information services context, comes from the Human Sciences and Advanced Technology (HUSAT) Research Group, at Loughborough University in the UK . We will use this as our basis for more detailed consideration of user-centred strategies.

The HUSAT adoption of the user-centred design philosophy stems from a realization that the conventional approach to system design was failing hopelessly in providing adequate information systems. Essentially this process involves asking the users of a system what is required, and then having it implemented by the computer specialists (systems analysts, programmes, etc.). This has the major disadvantage that the users' requirements may never be captured adequately, due to the many possibilities for misunderstanding, and lack of adequate specification of all factors, in this linear design process. Furthermore, even if the system as produced is exactly as required, it may prove difficult and costly to modify it, even for minor changes in user needs. The result has been a generation of systems which were never quite what was needed, and the 'software backlog', mentioned in an earlier chapter.

The clear solution is to involve the users much more directly in the design process, but this in itself has several drawbacks. It is usually very difficult for users to specify exactly what they want, from a new system which they may find problems in envisaging; many requirements only become clear when a version of the system can be used 'for real'. Users therefore tend to specify their requirements in terms of approaches with which they are already familiar, and are particularly unlikely to think (unprompted) of restructuring their working methods. Also, and inevitably, it is impossible to predict what changes may be required even a short time into the future; to respond to changing work demands, or just changing user preferences. This means that a simple involvement of users within the framework of a conventional design progress is unlikely to be productive.

In general, some limitations of a total reliance on user consultation should be recognized. Some of the best concepts for level and effective systems come from sheer intuition on the part of designers, or from extrapolation from other systems, not closely analogous in apparent function. The designers cannot abrogate responsibility for the whole design and implementation, or this aspect will very probably be lost by default. Also, there may be considerable problems if there is a very diverse user group, from which it is difficult even to select 'representative' classes of user; this would be the case with a public-access information system. This would also require the application of trained intuition on the part of the system specialists. These are not arguments against the user-centred concept; rather arguments against an uncritical reliance on the views of the user, unbalanced by the expertise of the information and computing professionals.

We should also be brutally honest, and admit that users, like anyone else, can at times be unimaginative, obtuse, obstructive, and plain bloody-minded. Coping with, and still leaving everyone basically happy, calls for excellent interpersonal skills on the part of the system designers, as well as the single-mindedness to get things done regardless. Adopting a user-centred philosophy is in no way a soft option.

The HUSAT user-centred design physiology is centred around the idea of deliberately allowing for inevitable change. Successful system implementation is a process of technical, human, and organizational change. We need a user-centred strategy for shaping the system to the needs of the users and the organisation'. Its central tenet is that a system will be usable when, and only when, its construction has taken full account of the needs and characteristics of its users.

The concept of 'usability', in this context, has three components. First, there is the idea of *task match*'; the extent to which the system does what the users want, in the way in which they want it. There must be an emphasis on flexibility, to suit the individual user, on adaptability, to allow the system to meet future unforeseen needs, and on an 'evolutionary' capacity, to allow new facilities to be added, links to be made to other systems, etc.

Second, there is a 'user match'; the system must adapt itself to the users' way of working, rather than the other way around. This implies that it must match the existing capacities and skills of users, without requiring excessive training and modification of work styles. Also the ergonomic aspects must be acceptable to the users (this point will be considered later), as must the cognitive aspects of the system interface. This last point means simply that the terminology and symbols used by the system should be those which are familiar to the users; there should be no barrier of 'computerese' to be overcome.

Third, there must be an easy means for users to become familiar with the system; to receive help and explanation as required, and to learn more about the features and capabilities of the system. Conventionally, this would have been done by the provision of documentation and training courses, but this kind of support is of little use to the occasional, inexperienced, resentful, or downright frightened user. For a system to be regarded as genuinely 'usable', according to the HUSAT philosophy, it must contain within itself the means of supporting its users with explanation, help, and learning, at the time, and in the ways, that they are most needed. This will include such factors as: tailoring of responses to the level of expertise to each user; 'transparency', i.e. hiding of details of system operation, when that is appropriate; giving full information on the system's operation when *that* is appropriate (e.g. in the explanation facilities of expert systems); 'navigation' facilities around complex systems, so that users know what the are doing, where they have been, and where they are going to; etc. This is a practical implementation of the concept of 'software ergonomics', to be discussed later.

This user-centred approach can, and should, be brought to bear at all stages of the introduction and use of IT systems; not only at the stage of implementation, which we are particularly considering here, but at the preceding stage of choice and evaluation, and subsequently, in a process of organizational learning and evolution, which we shall consider later.

The key to the approach is, of course, user participation. There is no fixed 'recipe' for its application; rather it comprises a collection of techniques, to be used in different conditions, according to circumstances. This approach is made possibly by a variety of technical developments which allow continual revision and adaptation of system specification. These were discussed in an earlier chapter, and include such things as:

* very cheap processing power, and relatively cheap 'standard' software, so that solutions may be tried out and discarded without prohibitive cost,
* increased flexibility and adaptability, so that systems can be more easily customized or 'bolted together',
* increased compatibility, so that products from different suppliers can be combined in 'pick and mix' combinations, to suit particular needs,
* improved prototyping tools such as fourth-generation languages, application generators, etc., so that trial systems can be put together quickly and cheaply.

Even with the adoption of these technical tools, it would be entirely possible to design a system in the 'old' way: choose, or design, the best technical solution, make the hardware and software work correctly, train the users, and start operations. Much of the benefit is, however, lost, if this is done. Two vital components of the user-centred approach are missing: genuinely *participative procedures,* and a consideration of *'socio-technical' systems options.*

Participations of users must be planned carefully. Ideally one would involve all users in the development of their systems, but this is usually impractical. An alternative is the selection of a group of representative users, but this is also proclamatic, as there are many different interests among the user community, and it may not be realistic to try to find a cohesive working party to reflect a common view, if the system being implemented is a large one, affecting much of an organization's life. It is preferable to try to set up a flexible arrangement of small groups, reflecting reasonably homogeneous user interests. This will help to ensure that all important aspects of design and implementation are considered, but that there is no attempt to impose an inappropriate standardization. It can also assist representatives to remain in close touch with their colleagues, rather than to begin to see themselves as a part of the 'systems team'; this can be a real danger, and may result in an ineffective representation of user needs.

It is important to decide at the outset of IT implementation just how much participation is really required and intended, remembering that, 'one can participate in planning in several ways. Very often, participation means that the potential users listen while specialists tell them what they have planned'.

'Socio-technical' factors are in many ways more important to the users, or non-users, of information systems than strictly technical ones. The latter includes speed of response, storage capacities, ease of use, quality of documentation, etc., are important, and will be seen as such by the thinking user. However, they can appear minor, when compared with such questions as how the new system will affect the nature of the work to be done, the jobs which will be changed (or cease to exist), the structure of the organization, questions of seniority and reporting, etc.

Most people accept that technical systems have organizational repercussions. What is not so widely recognized is that different systems of the same type or different ways of organizing and running systems have very different organizational repercussions. There are many different ways of implementing information technology and the danger is that the debate will be about technical options and not socio-technical options.

The result may be that organizational change consequent upon IT introduction will be entirely unplanned, or, at best, the result of a 'fire-fighting' style of reactive management.

The solution is an acceptance of these social factors as being at least as important as technical parameters, for a system which is to be widely used. Topics such as nature and distribution of work (and especially who is responsible for what tasks at a local level), access to the system (which can have important consequences for information flow and control within the organization), and personnel matters in every sense (including such things as the effect of changing work patterns on career progression), must receive the same careful and participative consideration as any of the technical factors.

In addition to 'learning', in its various guises, users will also need direct help on specific problems, as well as general information, which can be loosely categorized as IT appreciation'. It will be clear that 'user support' requires a number of levels and approaches, and indeed a wide variety of ways of providing it are available.

At the initial stages of implementation, when the system is little more than a gleam in its designers' eyes, a primary need is a means of communicating to users some of the practical realities of what may seem rather abstract and remote. Besides the obvious means of descriptions, oral and written, of what the new system will be like, it is of great benefit if *demonstrations* can be arranged, even if only of part of the total system, or of a similar, though not identical, system. Naturally, it is highly important that such demonstrations are successful and impressive, and anyone who has arranged such things knows very well that the chances of a demonstration of any IT system passing off without trouble are inversely proportional to the importance of the occasion. It is obviously vital to prepare carefully beforehand, and ideally to have something like a video available, in case of real disaster. *Visits* to other sites, or other organizations, where the chosen system, or one very like it, is already in operation, are very worthwhile: although those arranging the visit must ensure that the important points are not masked by differences in procedures or style between the two sites. *Pilot studies,* where the new system is installed 'for real' within one part of the organization, are in many ways the best way of providing an initial orientation and appreciation for the remainder of the users.

It is also worth paying attention, in the pre-implementation phase, to the needs of staff who may have a very real anxiety about the use of IT in any form. This can be overcome to a limited extent by oral and written explanation; a major need is for practical 'hands-on' experience in a 'low-risk' setting. Recommends the 'playroom' approach, which offers the opportunity to try out a variety of simple IT systems, not necessarily related to the system about to be introduced, so that users without experience in IT can build up their confidence in their own time and in their own way. No doubt the necessity for such ploys will diminish, as the general population becomes more IT-literate, but this may be a longer process than some pundits would have us believe.

Training is obviously of great importance, and must be provided in a variety of forms. Perhaps not surprisingly, it is very commonly regarded as inadequate, at least in the context of office technology. Most obviously, it can come from various sources; from inhouse trainers, either from training department, if one exists, or from the computing/information departments; from an external training organization, from the suppliers of the system; etc. There is also the option of using computer-based training modules, now increasingly available, and provided as standard with many software packages; though this should be seen as a compliment, rather than an alternative, to 'people-based' training. In most cases a mix will be chosen, appropriate to the needs of the situation (and the money available, for bought-in training of a high standard is not cheap). It is highly desirable that the staff responsible for the implementation take some part in training, as a way of strengthening their links with the users.

The most obvious form of training is the formal course in the detailed operation of the system, and this will be appropriate for those users who will make extensive use of the system. 'Basic' courses should be available for those who will use it less frequently, or who will use only some of its options. It is also very important, and difficult, to provide appropriate 'appreciation' courses for those who will be affected by the system, but will not be principal users; difficult, not only because of the need to pitch the material at the right level, but because of the difficulty of persuading busy people to take time to learn about something which may seem very peripheral to them peripheral to them.

This kind of appreciation course overlaps to some extent with another user support function; *publicity*. This is, of course, quite vital, since people in ignorance of the capabilities, or even the existence, of a system will hardly be able to use it effectively. In principle, everyone should be informed of everything to do with systems about to be implemented; in practice, it will require considerable sensitivity to decide who is told what, and when. As with all other promotional activities, all available means should be tried, to get the message across. If the new IT systems are being implemented by, or for, the information services, then this will fit naturally into their promotion of their own services, the important of which is increasingly stressed.

Documentation is another aspect of user support, whose importance cannot be overemphasised. Again it comes in various forms, both paper and electronic and ranging from the fully-blown technical manual, through the detailed user guide, to short notes and instructions for the occasional user. Documentation, of some sort, will usually be supplied with all purchased software, but its quality will be very variable, especially, though not exclusively, for cheaper packages. It is often cynically said that the quality of software documentation can be well judged by the industry which now exists to produce books on the use of standard programs and packages, particularly those which have a wide business use, such as integrated packages, word-processing systems, and database systems.

There are two other important aspect of this 'user-centred' implementation philosophy. The need for the support of the users during the implementation phase, particularly support for their learning about the potential of new systems, will be discussed in the next section. The longer term effects of the newly implemented systems on the organization, and ways to deal with it, which terms 'organizational learning and evolution' will be considered in the section on using and managing IT.

Although we have discussed the HUSAT model in some detail, as being a particular good exemplar of a user-centred approach to system implementation, it is by no means the only example. For example, has done a great deal of work on participative approaches to the design and introduction of IT systems. Other examples of participative and user-centred approaches, with some of their problems. The participative approach, in fact, can be seen as part of a broader set of newer, 'unconventional' approaches to system development and implementation.

In the context of the introduction of office automation systems, describes a 'soft', or qualitative, approach to project development, which has much in common with the user-centred approaches. It is intended for situations in which there may be unclear, or even conflicting, objectives in a confused problem area, where effectiveness of solution is at least as important as efficiency, and where 'mechanistic', quantitative, solutions are inappropriate. This is to contrast with a traditional 'hard' systems design philosophy, where clearly defined objectives are to be met by the introduction of systems, whose success can be judged in quantitative, usually cost-effectiveness, terms. The introduction of many IT systems, particularly as they affect professional workers, clearly fall into this 'soft' area, and this alternative approach to implementation is highly appropriate.

As with several other techniques or approaches, which have been mentioned, we do not propose that a user-centred approach can be adopted wholesale as a panacea for removing all problems in the introduction of information technology, either into the information services themselves, or into the wider organization. Indeed, the approach is not intended to be used in this way; it is rather a set of techniques and ideas, to be selected according to each particular situation. Used in this way, we believe that this approach can be particularly fruitful in helping the implementation of IT systems, on whatever scale, to be both painless and productive.

User Support During Implementation

Support of the users of a new system throughout its implementation phase is vital, since it is the success, or otherwise, of the implementation which will, to a large extent, colour the users' view of the system throughout its lifetime. This is not to decry the importance of continuing user support at all stages of a system's development; but the initial stages of the introduction of new technology are undeniably crucial.

It is wrong to think, as IT specialists often do, that user support is synonymous with the provision of technical knowledge about the operation of systems.

* anxiety reduction
* evaluation of indirect consequences
* contribution to design
* assessment of benefits
* `development of operational knowledge
* development of technical skill
* specification of future needs

User support, then, has several aspects. A magic component in assisting users in a learning process, or rather processes. The acquisition, and retention, of skills necessary to operate the new systems in important, as is the overcoming of the mystique of computer systems, which has proved slower to dissipate than many would have believed possible in the allegedly electronic age, and still leads to uncertainty and anxiety in many (reluctant) users, at varying levels of seniority. This may require a very gentle and 'risk-free' introduction to IT in general. Going beyond the straightforward details of system operation, the users will need help to see how the systems matches the individual tasks which they undertake. This leads them to begin to rethink their work patterns, in the wake of the changes brought about by IT, and to see the possibilities for new ways of doing things. Furthermore, if the users are to play a significant part in the design of new systems, as we have argued should be the case, then there must be opportunities for learning in more general terms about alternatives and their consequences, and about the possibilities offered by IT in general.

In fairness, it should be said that many of the suppliers of larger, specialist software systems, such as text retrieval and library automation packages, produce excellent documentation. Nonetheless, the purchaser may often feel the need to produce something themselves for their own users, either to make up for the deficiencies of the supplier's documentation, or to complement it by providing user guides specifically geared for inhouse use. It is important to note the distinction between documentation aimed at the operators of a system, and that directed at its users; sometimes this distinction will be clear-cut, but often it will not. Consider, for example, a large multi-user database or text retrieval system. There will certainly be system documentation for the computer staff who must implement and maintain the system. There will also be documentation for those who create and search the files on it; but these may range from information specialists, whose full-time job is database maintenance, to the occasional user of a general purpose file, a library catalogue, for example. Clearly there are some very different needs here. The situation is, of course, entirely different with a single-user microcomputer program; the user here is just the user! Even so, if a program of this sort is widely used within an organization, it may be desirable to produce documentation which avoids the 'computerese', with which many microcomputer software manuals are afflicted (though there are an increasing number of exemplary exceptions).

There are then a wide variety of needs for documentation of different kinds, and a variety of sources from which it may be obtained. Apart from the system suppliers, and commercially published guides which may be available for very widely-used systems, the basic options are to write the documentation inhouse, or to commission a professional writer to do it. Although some of the arguments in favour of inhouse support staff undertaking training also apply to the writing of documentation, particularly locally-focused user guides, there is a good deal to be said for taking advantage of professional expertise, since the writing of effective documentation is not a trivial matter.

As well as technical system manuals, and user guides of varying degrees of detail, there are other pieces of documentation which may be needed with a large system; describes some of them, in the context of library automation systems. They include:

* *Policy Manual.* This deals with the policies and guidelines which dictate action, rather than specifying details; in the library automation context, this could include such things as the rights of various categories of borrowers.
* *Procedures Manual.* This describes in detail the steps involved in carrying out each, and every, activity which these system permits. There may be 'quick reference' versions detailing the most common tasks, and the manual for a large system may be divided into sections describing self-contained aspects; cataloguing, circulation, etc., for example.
* *Training Manual.* This describes the training, of whatever sort, available for the system, to ensure consistency.
* *Forms Manual.* This describes and exemplifies all of the forms used in the system; this generally implies printed forms, but could also be used for screen forms for electronic transactions.

Plainly, this degree of thoroughness in documentation will be required only in the larger and more complex of systems, but nonetheless it is an indication of the effort which will be required in producing and maintaining adequate documentation for any system. The process of documentation, as with other forms of user support, is not restricted to the implementation phase, but is of continuing vital importance, throughout the life of the system.

Undoubtedly the most important part of any programme of user support during system implementation is the provision of appropriate *support staff*. Defines such a person well: 'someone... who is close to the users, knows the system, knows the users' problems and tasks, and is quickly and easily available to them'.

Many information professionals would like to think that this was an accurate description of them, and indeed, if we add the qualifications that support staff must be good communicators and should be credible to, and respected by, the system users, it is not difficult to see why support for IT introduction should form a natural progression from information service provision.

User support staff will certainly take some part in all of the activities noted above, and in addition will deal with immediate support problems, by being available to deal with enquiries and problems, perhaps on a 'hotline' service in a large organization, and generally providing a focus for help and advice. There may, in a larger organization, be a sufficient number of such staff for them to each take on a group of users on for whom they are responsible. It may be found worthwhile to involve some user representatives, with a particular interest in, and commitment to, the implementation, as 'local experts', or 'gatekeepers', liaising between the main body of the users and the support staff; on the other hand, this may lengthen the chain of communication too much and it should be not assumed to be a good idea in all circumstances.

This role for a group of support staff is very reminiscent of the concept of the *information centre,* in the computing sense, an idea which became popular during the early 1980s, largely as a response to the rapid and chaotic growth of microcomputer systems and software. The information centre staff, generally in large organizations, were responsible for recommending standard software packages to meet user needs, for providing documentation and training, generally from suppliers or commercial sources, for a (generally limited) consultancy and advice role, and sometimes for a limited systems design role, using standard software, and aided by techniques for prototyping and rapid applications generation. The limitations of this idea, in its original form, are increasingly being realized, as a result of the frequent lack of a sufficient identification with user needs, and the limitations of the standard packaged software. There is, however, a close similarity of objective, and to some extent methods, with the user support role being proposed here.

Three basic roles have been recognized for those staff within an organization who have responsibility for helping in the implementation of IT systems, by direct user support. These are *facilitators,* preparing users for change and acting as a link between users and technical experts, *teachers*, training people to sue the system, and *consultants,* problem-solving and troubleshooting. Exactly how the support staff divide their time between these functions, and how each of the activities detailed above (training, documenting, hotline support, etc.) is fitted into the overall support scheme, will depend on the particular situation, and will certainly change over time as the implementation proceeds. The crucial role of these people does not end with a successful implementation, as we will discuss later, in the section on using and managing IT.

Criteria For Successful Implementation

We have spoken above in rather theoretical terms about the ways in which information technology systems should be introduced, and the factors of importance in ensuring success. In order to relate these ideas firmly to reality, it is worthwhile comparing them with some criteria which have been found from experience to make a real difference between success and failure in implementing new systems. Obviously, lists of this kind are not strictly comparable, since they relate to different circumstances, and reflect the views of those who extracted these summarized 'main factors'; nor are they all derived from the kinds of IT implementation of primary relevance to information services. Nonetheless, they do show up some interesting consistencies.

Considers the factors which distinguish successful from unsuccessful implementations of IT on a large scale. Success is characterized by:

* a positive acceptance of change, rather than an attempt to preserve the *status quo;*
* an appreciation of the potential of new technology to change organizational and supervisory structures;
* the active participation of staff, and their trade unions, at all stages;
* committed involvement of key individuals - 'champions of

change' - to promote the implementation, and willing and able to bypass standard procedures;

* provision of good training.

Failure was characterized by:

* failure to adjust organizational arrangements and procedures;
* staff (particularly trade union) concern with changes in conditions of work, rather than content of jobs;
* *de facto* erosion of supervisory roles, without adequate planning.

Quotes examples of the lessons learnt from implementations of office automation systems in large UK organizations. He notes that many of the lessons learnt were, in retrospect, rather obvious, and applicable to any innovation. Among the criteria for success were:

* Start staff working with the new system as soon as possible, and not allowing old systems to continue for any longer than necessary.
* There must be strong commitment from senior management.
* Provide adequate training with facilities such as a specially designed training area.
* Take great care with the choice of supplier, since a mistake here is very difficult to rectify.
* Introduce levels of security, so that everyone has access to as much information as possible, while restricting access to really sensitive information.
* Avoid pilot studies, since they tend to produce a lack of commitment to the new system.
* Ensure that adequate numbers of workstations are available, since demand quickly expands beyond original projections.
* Use information professionals for cost-effective access to external information.

Also draws conclusions from the results of implementations of office automation systems. Among his wishes are :

* Keep sufficiently abreast of new IT developments to understand their potential.
* Plan new systems from the start to allow for integration of new features in the future.
* Involve *all* those affected by the project and its outcome.
* Ensure communication to *all* relevant levels of staff.
* Emphasize training, auditing, and post-project evaluation.
* Consider both effectiveness *and* efficiency of potential solutions.

* Ensure that the project team includes skills from business, information, IT, and the 'soft' approach to information.

Also draws lessons from the 'electronic office' area:

* Communicate to all affected as soon as possible, if only an outline plan, and continue communication throughout the implementation process.
* Build up an expectation and acceptance of change.
* Use pilot studies where possible.
* Identify 'resistors' (individuals and departments who do not want the new system), and give them special treatment.
* Involve the users as soon as possible.
* Adequate training for everyone is essential.
* Communicate the benefits achieved as the implementation progresses, and ensure that everyone knows that they result from the new technology.

Picks out these important points for implementations of library automation systems:

* Appoint a senior person as project head.
* Involve all staff as early as possible.
* Announce the new system formally.
* Be entirely honest and realistic, while emphasizing benefits from new system.
* Regularly report progress.
* Avoid creating an 'elite' group of users of the new system - get everyone involved - give positive support and recognition to those who are particularly supportive to the implementation.
* Emphasize thorough training and documentation.
* Be prepared for setbacks.

Finally, a survey of reactions to the implementation of the OCLS system in US libraries, found among others the following to be associated with good acceptance of the system:

* high degree of participative decision making
* good and frequent training
* good communication, especially early assurances of job security

There are some inevitable inconsistencies; the perceived value of pilot studies, for example. Nevertheless, what comes out strongly is the overall consistency with which the important factors emerge: involving the users in a participative design process; forming an implementation team with an appropriate skills mix, and headed by a senior 'champion'; good communication at all stages; adequate training and documentation; a ready acceptance of, and willingness to plan for, change.

Human Factors

It is purely for reasons of keeping the section headings tidy that we have a section here, headed 'human factors'. For, in truth, the implementation and utilization of information technology is much more about human than technical factors. We hope that this viewpoint is made clear throughout the text. This section serves simply to bring together some of the main points which appear, in various contexts, throughout the rest of the book.

We also hope that it is clear that 'human factors' denote a much wider scope of interest than what is usually meant by 'ergonomics'.

[Human factors] often connotes a rather restricted view of the human being: the view of the machine operator and ergonomic design. These issues *are* important, of course, but more important still are the wider human, organizational and social concerns that provide the context for technological innovation.

We hope that throughout this book we have attempted to retain this broad picture, and have brought this widely-defined human factors concept into all our considerations of how information technology may be operated in, by, and for information services. A useful overview of the same issues, as they arise in implementations of IT in a wider context is given in the volume.

In this section, we will look at three rather specific aspects: job and task design; questions of the physical environment, including ergonomic and health and safety considerations; and 'software ergonomics'. Before going any further, however, we should remind ourselves that many of the ergonomic 'problems of IT' are not to do with IT at all, but to more general problems in the workplace.

The use of VDUs is bringing into the open the fact that many working environments are less than adequate from the point of view of health (in the broadest sense) and that many jobs are not designed at all but rather evolved, often in a haphazard way. So applying ergonomic principles can benefit both VDU and non-VDU users alike.

1. Job and Task Design

These terms describe the considerations which must be given to the effect which the introduction of IT will have on the work of those who use, or are otherwise affected by, the new technology.

'Task design" is the narrower term, referring to the way in which individual operations - checking an entry in a database, issuing a book to a borrower, etc. - are carried out. 'Job design' is broader considering what effect IT will have on the total job; of a cataloguer, an online searcher, etc. Considerations of overall work patterns and of organizational structures are a broader issue and will be covered later.

In terms of task design, IT has two main effects. First, it entirely eliminates some tasks, generally of the highly routine and mechanical sort; typing, sorting and filing cards; retyping, in full, manuscripts with extensive corrections; etc. More commonly, it involves a change in the way many tasks are carried out.

Think of the effect of the introduction of IT on the day-to-day activities of an 'information worker' (in the widest sense), where there is a major move towards handling electronic, rather than paper-based, information. The most immediately obvious effect is that a variety of diverse activities such as: handwriting, typing, using a calculator, extracting and replacing documents from desk drawers and filing cabinets, using the telephone, exchanging opinions and pieces of paper with colleagues, etc. is replaced, to a large extent, by the single activity of looking at a screen and using a keyboard or mouse. No matter that this allows all sorts of different things to be done, such as: electronic filing, accessing databases, creating and editing documents, communicating by electronic mail, teleconferencing, etc. The result is a diminution in the diverse physical activities formerly carried out, and very probably in direct contact with other people as well.

This may very well, though not necessarily, lead to feelings of boredom, frustration, and of pressure, due to a feeling of being 'paced by the machine'. There may also be an impression of a greater impersonality, and lack of appreciation of one's place in the system. When combined with the often less than ideal physical environment, these factors lead to the stress experienced by many clerical and professional workers alike, with the introduction of IT. It has been found, in some large data processing operations, that over 70% of staff suffered from such physical problems as headache, eyestrain, and backache; mostly attributable to poor task design, rather than deficiencies in equipment or environment.

It is of great importance that adequate attention (one is tempted to say that in most organizations any attention at all would be an improvement) should be paid to task design, in order to ensure that the IT systems actually perform to the benefit of their users. While each situation is likely to have its own particular requirements, there are a few general principles which should always be noted.

Perhaps the most important point is the deliberate incorporation of *user control* into all IT-related tasks, since nothing other than this will overcome the feelings of impersonality and being run by the machines. This principle should over-ride all others. It is important, for example, to allow as much *variety, physical movement*, and *personal contact* as possible in the tasks which are undertaken; but these should, at all costs, be left under the control of those affected, and not dictated in detail by management. Similarly, there should be adequate rest periods from VDU work, and the length and frequency of these may well be specified by government legislation, union-employer agreement, or organizational policy; but it is far better to allow those affected to choose for themselves exactly when these breaks will be taken, than to impose something ('five minutes, each hour, on the hour') which may be seen as just another dictatorial imposition, interfering with natural work patterns.

In short, it is important to structure each task, or (better) to allow those who undertake the task to structure it, so as to allow each individual the greatest possible control of work flow and pattern.

These considerations apply particularly to routine work,

but it is important to remember that they are directly relevant to much 'professional' work, and to information professionals as much as any other.

'Job design' involves the considerations of the influence of IT on the total work of an individual, assuming that the most drastic consequence, the total elimination of the job, does not occur. This does not seem likely in the library/information context, with the exception of certain clerical functions, such as filing clerk and copy typist. What is more likely is that certain jobs, entirely based around a single professional skill, will be less in demand in most information services; cataloguers, for example, given the increasing access to centralized catalogue records, or online intermediaries, with the rise of end-user searching. What is required here is training to utilize new systems, and encouragement to move into different, wider, and arguably more interesting roles. Another major factor is likely to be blurring of job boundaries. These aspects are considered in detail, in terms of new roles for information professionals, in Chapter 10.

2. Physical Environment

A great deal has been written about the physical and environmental aspects of the introduction and use of IT, about ergonomic factors and about implications for health and safety. We can do no more here than make references to relevant books and papers. The most useful single source, for IT in the context of information services. These should be consulted for fuller details of what is only mentioned in outline here.

So far as health and safety aspects are concerned, the authorities in each country will have their own legislation, recommendations and standards. Advice and guidance can be obtained from governmental bodies (the Health and Safety Executive in the UK, for example), from employer and trade union organizations, from manufacturers' trade associations (for example, the UK Business Equipment and Information Technology Association), and from professional bodies. It is important that the most up-to-date information and recommendations should be obtained from these sources, and the information given here, or in any of the cited references, is intended only as an introduction to some of the considerations.

Considering the extent of experience and knowledge now available on the physical environment of IT, it is little short of amazing (not to say disgraceful) to see how often it is cheerily ignored, in libraries and information units as much as anywhere else. It was a chastening example to note a speaker at a UK conference in 1987 suggesting that physical planning for IT amounted to making sure that there were enough electric plugs (nor did it help to realize that he was an employee of one of the larger library/information professional associations!).

There are two main aspects to a consideration of the environment effects of IT: its effects on the individual work place, and on the office (or equivalent) environment generally.

The individual workplace, in effect, means the workstation or VDU, and the furniture which supports it. There is now a considerable amount of information on the correct way to install and use VDUs, and we may hope that the 'dump it on the desk and get on with it' philosophy will soon disappear, at least from larger organizations, who should know better. Furniture to support the workstation should be modular, and adaptable both to the size and shape of the individual user, and to the requirements of the task; the extent to which the equipment will be shared by others, the mix of VDU-based and paper-based work, etc.

The VDU has been the source of many of the concerns about IT introduction, both from the health and safety viewpoint. These have included:

* concerns about radiation of various kinds and electrical fields, particularly their possible effects on pregnant women,
* visual problems (eyestrain, headache, etc.), especially after long use,
* musculoskeletal problems (backache, tenosynovitis, etc.), again after long use,
* facial dermatitis,
* psychosomatic problems.

Again, we refer readers to other sources for details, and the latest opinions, However, the general opinion in the late 1980s appears to be that most of these problems are due to factors other than VDU work itself, and can be minimized, or avoided entirely, by careful attention to environmental factors in general, and above all by proper task design, and consideration for the user in the design of systems. Thus, for example, visual problems can be largely avoided by correct lighting conditions and positioning of the VDU, by regular maintenance to ensure that the screen is operating correctly, and by proper task design to ensure regular breaks. Problems are commonly due to inappropriate furniture, to lack of advice to staff on correct posture and positioning of equipment, and by poor task design, which does not allow for breaks and for variation in work, and the opportunity to move around. Due to a combination of strong electrical fields and low humidity, and is readily avoided by creating proper environmental conditions.

Psychological and psychosomatic problems are particularly worrying. They are believed to be caused primarily by changes in the nature of the job (boredom, loss of control of work patterns, fears about job security, etc.), rather than by anything to do with IT equipment. The solution lies in proper task and job design, and in the user-centred approaches discussed earlier. Obviously, whether or not IT is involved in any way, there will be problems if people find that their work provides little job satisfaction, and no opportunity for self development.

Turning to the overall environment, there are number of problems which may be created by IT. These problems (with their most obvious solutions) include:

* *Wiring and Cabling-* IT equipment uses a lot, and the main safety problem of IT is its capacity for causing electrical and fire hazards, as well as tripping unwary users - modern office settings increasingly include 'cable management systems', to tidy it all away,
* *Lighting-* is crucially important, in avoiding visual problems in the use of display screens - a combination of diffuse 'uplighting' with 'spot' lighting is generally best,
* *noise-* is a problem, mainly with the older breeds of printer - until these are phased out, they are best placed in a separate room, or muffled with acoustic hoods,
* (*heat-* is all too readily generated by all IT equipment, and requires efficient temperature control (it is ironic to think that this was, in the past, always provided in the interests of the machines in air-conditioned computer rooms, not so often in the interests of their human operators),
* *humidity-* or rather the lack of it. IT equipment generates very dry air, which can cause health problems - air conditioning,

and humidifiers (or windows which open) will solve the problem. Ionizers are also said to help in some circumstances,

* *static electricity*- is generated by much equipment, and should be controlled by antistatic mats, sprays, etc.

Again fuller details are given in the references scited earlier.

It is important to remember that there will always be some users who have particular problems with IT; those suffering from conditions such as migraine or photosensitive epilepsy, or wearers of certain type of contact lenses or spectacles, may find particular difficulty in lengthy use of VDUs. The worries about effects of VDUs on pregnant women have already been mentioned; the fact that most medical opinion tends to suggest that there is little grounds for concern should not be a cause for dismissing this problem out of hand. It is to be hoped that the attitude of sensitivity to the needs of the individual user, which we tried to emphasize throughout this book is the only realistic basis for a satisfactory use of the new technologies, would be applied in these cases, to ensure that the introduction of new systems does not become a source of misery for such individuals.

In short, we are not suggesting that getting the physical environment of IT right is necessarily a simple matter. However, there is sufficient experience available to ensure that there should be no serious problems, in the great majority of cases. Providing that these are adhered to, the overriding factor in ensuring the acceptability of the new technology is the degree to which the systems help the users in their work, and the degree to which the users control the technology, and not the other way around.

The human being is more than just a biological chip tossed in among the microchips. Humans will still need both privacy and socialization. They will still need a sense of accomplishment, of mastery. They will still tired, be subject to stress, and find that there is only so much attention one human being can allocate to a task. Each human being will still be unique.

3. Software Ergonomics

Regardless of all other factors, the interaction of users with IT systems is through the interface of software; it is this, more than anything else, which determine show the system 'looks and feels' to its users. 'Software ergonomics' is the study of how to make software systems accessible and acceptable to their users. We will not go into detail, since the topic has been covered in detail elsewhere, and many of the points have also been covered in earlier chapters.

It is worth noting explicitly that software ergonomics relates only to the level of user interaction with the system; menus and prompts, WIMP interfaces, online help and explanation; error messages and recovery procedures; etc. It is not generally understood to relate to what the system actually does, or how well it does it. This is, of course, a major limitation; the best designed software, from the ergonomic viewpoint, will not be appreciated in the longer term by its users if it does not do anything very useful.

Most of the concepts of software ergonomics equate roughly to the idea of 'user friendliness', a user quotes graphically a particular piece of software as being 'as user friendly as a cornered rat'). It relates directly to the 'feel' of software, and to usability of a system, both of which we mentioned earlier. The concept is very difficult to define exactly: it has been suggested that user-friendly software should be: 'adaptive, transparent, comprehensible, natural, predictable, responsive, self-explanatory, forgiving, efficient, flexible, and available'.

Software ergonomics is not going to be directly within the control of users, except in the case of systems developed inhouse. Nevertheless, in view of its extreme importance in determining the acceptability of the new technology, it should be a major factor in considering which software to acquire.

4. Conclusions

We have perhaps over-stressed the 'problem' aspect of human factors of IT introduction. It is important, as a counter-balance, to remember that many people actively like working with new technology; some for its own sake, but most, probably, because it can remove routine drudgery, and make jobs more satisfying. Certainly, this should be the case for information professionals, and indeed one study in US special libraries found that staff in that situation suffered few of the problems sometimes associated with the introduction of IT. Provided that the basic 'rules', now becoming well understood, are followed for the proper use of the new technologies, relating both to physical environment and task design, there is no reason why the introduction and use of IT should be a painful experience.

Using and Managing IT

It is only too tempting to imagine that once the new system is set up, and working correctly, then it can be essentially forgotten. This is far from the truth. There are a number of activities which must be undertaken on a continuing basis, if the new technology is to make its full contribution, to the work of its users, and of the organization.

Monitoring and Management of IT

It systems do not operate in a vacuum; they are involved in a changing situation, and in many respects they contribute to that change. It is therefore very important that their performance is constantly monitored; not merely to ensure that nothing goes wrong, but that they are continuing to make an optimum contribution to their users' working lives.

1. Monitoring

When a new system has been implemented, there will be a fairly intensive period of monitoring, auditing, and evaluation, to ensure that it is fulfilling the intentions of its designers. Once this period has ended, and the system is regarded as fully operational, and in routine' use, some degree of monitoring must continue. This may be carried out in many and various ways, according to the nature of the system and the organizational context. This is done in one, or both, of two basic ways. First, there may be a monitoring of system use, provided by the log of the computer system; this will show who uses the system, how frequently, for how long, etc. There may also be built-in routines which enable the system managers to assess what is being done with the system, and with what degree of success, but this is a more difficult process. Second, there may be a direct assessment of user reaction; formally, by surveys interviews, etc., or informally, receiving opinions in general conversation. Obviously, the closer the system operators are to their users, the more chance they will have of getting a realistic picture of how well things are progressing.

It is worth mentioning that it can be quite difficult to assess the use of a distributed, interactive information system, especially if anything beyond the barest statistics of use are required. With centralized information services, such as online searching via an intermediary or a batch computer search, all queries came through the information services. In the case of printed information resources, the users could at least be observed in the library. Neither of these views is available for an interactive system available at the user's workplace. One result of moving to such a system, paradoxically, can be that knowledge of the users' activities immediately becomes more difficult to obtain.

On the other hand, it is very easy, to collect and store various statistics of use and performance from computerized systems; because it is easy, there is a great temptation to do so. Unfortunately, such statistics do not always have very much meaning in showing how and why the system is being used, and, even more significantly, when it is *not*. Collection of system use figures can never be a substitute for detailed, qualitative assessment of user satisfaction.

These concerns apply to a large system, with numerous users. In the case of a small system, used just within the information services, or perhaps by just one person, it would seem impossible that there could be a problem in assessing how the system is performing. This is not absolutely true. Although obvious system faults will be quickly spotted and reported, it is very easy for a small group of users, or even an individual, to fail to make best possible use of the system; perhaps simply because they have not been shown how to use some options. Very commonly, the system will be working perfectly well of the purpose for which it was purchased, but there may be other opportunities of its application which have not occurred to its users. This problem is even more likely to be occurring somewhere in the case of a large system with many users.

The best defence against this problem is to have an individual or group (The users themselves with a system within an information service, or a support group for a larger system) constantly considering the system capabilities, the changing needs of the users, and the way in which this system, or similar ones, are used in other organizations. If this is done thoroughly, there should be no very great shortfall in making best use of the system.

2. Maintenance

System faults will of course occur from time to time in the best regulated environments, and there must be some means for dealing with them. This will largely be a case of seeking specialist outside support, although in the case of software written inhouse the remedy is in the hands of the developers. There will generally be some form of maintenance contract covering hardware; this may be from the manufacturers, from the dealer from whom it was purchased, or from a specialist maintenance company. Contractual arrangements for maintenance differ from country to country, but in general one gets what one pays for. A system which is entirely crucial to the organization's operations will clearly need a maintenance agreement specifying immediate response, perhaps with provision for a replacement machine, if the problem cannot be corrected within a short time. Less crucial systems can get by with more relaxed, and cheaper, maintenance agreements.

Software also gives problems from time to time, and support is usually provided by the supplier; either as part of the initial purchase price, or on an annual maintenance agreement. Naturally, support for very cheap microcomputer software is usually minimal or non-existent.

Undoubtedly the worst situation is when some fault develops in a system, and it is not clear whether the fault lies in hardware or software. The first response of the respective suppliers will be to blame each others' product, and the user will need considerable skills of diplomacy and assertion to sort matters out. If the hardware comes from different manufacturers, or if networks or telecommunications are also involved, the situation verges on the hopeless. It is worthwhile, if at all possible, arranging for a single organization to have charge of the maintenance of such complicated systems; this simplifies matters greatly, and can save the hapless user from much nervous strain.

There may be some temptation for a small organization, or department, to think that maintenance agreements are an unnecessary luxury, more appropriate to larger units. The reverse, if anything, is the case. A large organization will probably have skilled staff, who can attempt many repairs themselves, if unnecessary (though in most cases it is the policy that they should not do so); it will certainly have the financial resources to pay for repairs and replacement when needed (though it will probably consider that an appropriate contract is more prudent). This is not the case for the smaller unit, which may be just as dependent on its IT systems; guaranteed maintenance support, is a must in this situation.

3. Upgrading and replacement

We mentioned above that, such is the rapidity of advance of IT, that a system once installed will quickly become obsolescent. This is just a fact of IT life, and users and operators alike must decide what to do about it.

The most immediate, and inevitable, occurrence will be demands from the users for improvements and modifications to the system. How these are met, if at all, will depend on the nature of the system, and how it was acquired.

If the system has been planned properly, there should be a clear 'upgrade path'. This may cover a variety of possibilities: to move to more powerful hardware - a large computer, or even a different kind, e.g. a minicomputer rather than a micro; to change from a single-user system to multi-user, to link single-user machines together in network, to add a new software module to a system, to integrate two separate functions together, etc. Part of the skill involved in the initial planning process is to anticipate user needs, and to allow for upgrading to meet them.

Perhaps the easiest requirements to satisfy are those which simply involve improved hardware; more processing power, increased storage space, better display, screens, etc. With hardware constantly improving in performance and falling in price, such needs are not usually a great problem. Much more difficult are requirements for small changes in what the system does; not a completely new function (which, paradoxically, may be easier to supply, by purchase of a new package or module), but a relatively minor modification to what exists. If the user has some control over the software, because it has been written inhouse, or is flexible enough to be adapted locally, then all is well. If, on the other hand, modifications have to be made by the supplier, then the situation is not hopeful. There is essentially no chance of getting a modification made to a standard business package to suit individual users. For specialized packages, such as those for library applications, the suppliers may be more willing to consider customization on request, but probably at a considerably price. There are well-attested stories of trivial modifications which cost more than the original purchase price. This is certainly the point at which the attractiveness of the cheap, standard package begins to wane, and the advantages of some degree of inhouse control become clear.

However, the system operators have to retain a sense of proportion. If a package is satisfying 90% of the users 90% of the time, that is probably as much as can be hoped for, and it is not realistic to think of trying to satisfy each and every user request (which may well be contrary to the vehement wishes of someone else). The need is for a sufficient knowledge of, and sensitivity to, user needs to be able to spot those changes which are really important, and to find ways of making those changes.

There will be some changes which will present themselves unasked, in the form of new versions of software. Sometimes these come free of charge, sometimes for a specified price, often as part of a combined upgrading/maintenance contract. It may seem churlish to do anything but accept these thankfully, but some thought is required. If the upgrading amounts to no more than minor 'cosmetic' improvements, and the fixing of faults, then it will of course be implemented. If, however, the suppliers have significantly changed aspects of the software, then it should not be assumed that these changes will suit everyone; it is entirely possible that the best course may be to leave the 'superseded' version of the software in place. The most common reason for this would be that the software had added many more 'features', which did not happen to be required by the users, at the cost of simplicity of operation, which the users valued. To install the new version under these circumstances, simply because it was new, would be simply perverse.

Finally, it has to be remembered that all IT systems have a strictly limited life. A vital part of the management and monitoring of their operation is the consideration, and earliest outline planning, of what will replace them. The earlier this is given consideration, the more likely will be a smooth transition. This means that system designers must keep themselves aware of new developments and trends in IT, which may shape the equipment and systems of a few years hence. This will necessitate being aware of what is happening in the 'frontline' areas of IT research, since technical advances have a way of rapidly affecting even relatively unsophisticated equipment; technologies developed in supercomputers, for example, found their way into desktop business micros in a remarkably few years. On the other hand, as we mentioned earlier, it is only too easy to be put off from developing or acquiring any system at all, by the prospects of what may be available tomorrow. Those involved with IT have to consistently steer their course between the technological of either disregarding, or being paralysed by, the promises of future developments.

Continuing User Support

We propounded earlier the idea that user support, in its various guises, is of vital importance during the implementation of a new information system. It is of no less significance during the lifetime of the particular application of new technology; indeed, a failure to provide continuing support to users will very probably result in systems being used to much less than maximum effect. The general principles of user support remain unchanged from those applicable during the implementation phase and we will not repeat them here. There are, of course, some changes of emphasis.

Training will be needed throughout the life of a system, as new users arrive, and will require essentially the same training as was given in the implementation phase. Other training opportunities will emerge at later stages. These may include: refresher and updating courses, particularly emphasizing any new features of the system; detailed training in particular aspects, for those users who have had only a basic introduction, and 'evangelistic' training, to encourage those who have not used the system.

Documentation also remains important. The 'standard' documentation will remain, modified to reflect changes in the system, and there will be the opportunity to prepare additional guides to features which turn out, with experience, to be either particularly popular, or difficult to use. Again with experience, there will be the chance to reconsider the form of the documentation, to review the relative proportion of printed and electronic documentation, to consider the use of video, etc.

Publicity must be kept up to date, both to inform users about new features in the system, and simply to ensure that existing staff do not forget about it, and newcomers are informed of its existence.

Direct user support will continue, at least for complicated and widely-used systems, though at a lower level than during implementation. Reminds us that no matter how good the quality of the formal support mechanisms (documentation, online aids, etc.), users with problems will always prefer to turn to another human being. The initial 'hand-holding' troubleshooting role will gradually change into that of the consultant/advisor, primarily helping the users to identify new ways of using the system. In particular, the potential for integration with other activities and systems can be explored, and the basic use of the system stabilized. The role of the 'gatekeeper', or 'local expert', from among the users can be re-examined at this stage; it may be thought appropriate to let this role lapse, if it was used in the more frenetic conditions of implementation. Alternatively, with users more comfortable with the system, and with new possibilities emerging for its use, it may be a good time to consider its introduction.

Organizational Learning and Evolution

This concept stems from the HUSAT philosophy, and is really an extension of the continuing user support role, including the explicit recognition of information systems as agents for evolutionary organizational change.

If it is successful [the implementation] does not simply introduce a technical system. It starts a process of individual learning and of organizational learning... Users find new ways of working, have ideas about what else might be advantageous and want new facilities added to the system... Therefore it is necessary, once this process has begun, to provide the facilities to promote continued learning and evolution.

These facilities would include the continuing user support noted above, and the provision of resources to modify the existing systems, and to plan for their replacement. It may also be desirable to have a formal *review body,* a forum at which users and designers/operators can discuss problems with the systems, ideas for improvements, and new user requirements; this may be seen as a successor to the project team, or steering committee, which oversaw the implementation. Whether this degree of formality is necessary depends on the scale and nature of the local situation what will certainly be necessary will be some form of regular audit of system operation, concentrating on its role in the context of a changing organizational structure and changing user needs.

On the Smaller Scale

We have discussed the use and management of IT systems largely in the context of the 'big' system; whether an organizational resource, such as office automation, or a widely-used system within the information services, such as a text retrieval package or library automation system. It would be wrong to think, however, that smaller systems (micro-based, single-user, special purpose, etc.) do not merit the same care in their management. *Taken as a whole,* a number of such systems, within an information service or throughout an organization, have just as much significance, and must be monitored and managed with as much consideration, as the single large system. Indeed, the potential for confusion, duplication and inefficiency (or, to put the best complexion on the matter, for synergy and creative interaction) made likely by the use of a variety of small systems dictates the need for a even closer monitoring of their effects and effectiveness.

Within a small organization, or a small information unit, the relative effect of a single IT system (perhaps a database, or an office management package) on the operations of the unit and its staff can be just as profound as that of the largest multi-site system in a large organization; not only the absolute scale is different. The need for monitoring and management is therefore just as great, although on the smaller scale the techniques will be different, and the personal contact between users and those supporting them will be closer. It will be important in this case to make continuous comparisons with similar organizations, to avoid the common problem of the small, isolated unit; assuming that one's own procedures are the only way of doing things, and that one's own experiences are necessarily universal.

Conclusions

A good deal is now known about the procedures to follow, the things to concentrate on, and the problems to beware of, in the introduction and use of IT. We have tried to outline the most significant of these, emphasizing the value of a flexible user-centred strategy, closely adapted to the needs of a particular situation. We have also tried to show how the success of any implementation of new technology is closely connected with the degree of appreciation and acceptance of the change which it will bring to individual work patterns and organizational structures alike.

Information professionals are well suited to take an important and leading role in the planning, implementation, and continuing development of the new technologies, both in their own services and in their organizations as a whole.

10
Implications for Information Professionals

Introduction

In this chapter, we will discuss the impacts and implications of the introduction and use of new information technologies on the work of what we will choose to call, for want of a better term, 'information professionals.' We note that has suggested that the term, 'has no practical value and, arguably, does more harm than good by encouraging individuals to develop an inflated sense of their own importance.' We will, however, risk his wrath by continuing to use the term, in the belief that our readers will know what we mean. An equivalent, and arguably more appropriate, terminology would be 'information specialists', and we will use the two descriptions more-or-less interchangeably.

In using these terms, we mean to distinguish that group of people *who would regard themselves as primarily involved in information service provision* from the much larger group who could reasonably be designated 'information workers.' The latter, according to some of the more evangelistic exponents of the 'information society' would include virtually all administrative and office workers, teachers, etc., and it would be very difficult to say anything useful about such a diverse group. It seems more straightforward to rely on individuals' perception of their own role and function, rather than any more supposedly 'objective' criteria, in determining where any boundary should be drawn; if you think you are an information professional, you probably are. This highly pragmatic definition is a means of dealing with the blurring of the boundary between the kind of information workers who are our main concern here, and the increasingly large number of those who undertake some information functions, but would not regard themselves as members of an information profession in any real sense. 'Information workers', in our sense, correspond roughly with the 'information manager' groups identified.

We have no intention of being drawn into fruitless debates as to which subgroups of the information communities should be included within the scope of the following discussions. There are very many librarians who would emphatically claim a place within the scope of information specialists, as we have defined it, and doubtless there are others who would not. The same is true of archivists, market research analysts, computer systems designers, museum documentalists, etc. One of the lessons to be learnt from a consideration of the effects of the new technologies is that these tribal divisions, though they still have a value for broad categorization, are becoming largely irrelevant in terms of the activities carried out. Our definitions are loose and pragmatic, and our claim is only that they are useful in limiting the scope of our remarks so that they may have some practical value.

Consideration of the impacts of IT on individual information professionals leads naturally to some thoughts on the changing role of the information services in which they work; this both affects and is affected by the situation of the individual. This discussion of services follows on, to some extent, from the material in Chapter 7, which deals with the impact of IT on some particularly significant activities within information services. It is continued in Chapter 12, in which the role of information technology in the wider organization, and the specific contributions of the information professional and information services are examined.

Is there life after IT?

When we consider the impact of the new technologies on information professionals, and the services or departments in which they work, it seems clear that there are three basic possibilities. First, there may be no significant change whatever. Second, there may be a total disappearance of the information specialist, and information service, as such. Third, there may be significant changes, which nonetheless leave individuals and services recognizable thereafter. We will look at these in turn.

1. Plus ca change

We might expect to be able to dismiss the first supposition out of hand. Surely, all information people and services are using IT by now, and, of necessity, changing and being changed. The situation is in fact not quite so simple as this. For one thing, we have little doubt that it is quite easy to find, small information services, and small sections of larger ones, operating apparently quite happily with no more advanced IT equipment than an electronic typewriter. Indeed, it would take more moral courage than we possess to state categorically that computerization, or equivalent, is a forward step in every case. Thus, despite the indications that the very low-priced business computers, of the type introduced have penetrated many computer-resistant bastions, we believe that a significant number of information professionals and services will eschew any extensive use of IT in the immediate future, and that this fact must be allowed for, and not dismissed.

However, there is rather more to the 'no real change' scenario than this. Very many implementations of IT simply replace one system (manual of simple automated) with another (automated, perhaps more sophisticated), with not much real alteration in what is done, or why. Examples might be: the replacement of an electronic typewriter with a stand-alone word processor; the choice of an automated journals receipt system to supersede a manual equivalent; the adaption of online searching of a computerized database instead of reliance on a printed indeed. Note that any of these things could lead to significant changes in procedures, to integration of functions, and to gains in effectiveness as well as efficiency of service, but that they need not necessarily do so. Thus, new technology can be, and frequently has been, introduced without any real change resulting, in the work of information specialists, and the pattern of information service provision. Makes the point, in the context of the introduction of computerized information handling into UK academic departments, that newly introduced IT systems generally fit initially into the existing work structures and communication patterns, not unlike the telephone and photocopier. (He notes, however, that some degree of change is then likely to take place.

One has to ask, however, how long the 'no real change' scenarios described above can remain valid, in light of current trends in IT. We have already made reference to the flood of simple, cheap, yet effective business microcomputers; and the same point could be made for other types of equipment. Of equal, or greater, significance are the changing communication patterns brought about by developments in technology, the effects of which on some important aspects of information service provision were outlined in Chapter 7. It is hard to avoid the conclusion that those information departments which do not embrace the appropriate aspects of the new technologies will increasingly drop out of the mainstream of communication, and will offer, for the most part, an unacceptably sub-standard service. Please note 'for the most part' every information service will have some aspects of its work which are best left untouched by IT, and a few services will correctly choose to avoid the new technologies, by virtue of a very specialized subject orientation, exceptional user community, peculiar financial o. other circumstances, etc. Similarly, most information specialists will want to leave some part of their working lives untouched by technology. This should not be taken an as invitation to maintain an ignorance of technology; here, as else-where, one needs a good background knowledge before making sensible decisions on what to avoid.

On the whole, 'no real change', in whatever form and for whatever reason, is not a recipe for success in dealing with IT, either at a personal or departmental/service level. Nor is it a realistic expectation, for most cases, most of the time.

2. Doomsday or stagnation

The second possible consequence of the large-scale introduction of IT into an organization's information handling systems could be the elimination of information services; at least as we have known (and loved) them. For UK inform. .on people, at least, this idea is almost synonymous with the 'Doomsday Scenario'. This provocative concept, suggested probably with tongue in cheek, was first delivered in 1976, and subsequently refined, though never repudiated. It arose from an analysis in which technological developments were only one of a number of trends (the others being social, educational, managerial, and economic) which led to propose that 'the days of the information officer and library worker are numbered. The IT components of importance are a general increase in the power of technology, and specifically of systems developed for 'non-professionals', or 'end users'; and 'transparent' systems with improving telecommunications. Sees these trends, combined with the other factors, as leading to the demise of 'traditional' library and information services, and the elimination of the 'intermediary' role. Technology will place full information handling capabilities in the hands of the ultimate users, who will take advantage of decentralized electronic information sources.

IT, enables information to be generated or acquired, stored, retrieved and processed, reformatted and repackaged, and communicated in a decentralized fashion, within and without the organizational boundaries; hence the threat to the 'traditional' information unit, essentially a centralized focus for all these activities. This analysis begs many issues, including those of the control of quality and compatibility of the organization's information resource, but there is a good deal of truth in it.

In common with virtually all those who accept his ideas, does not, in fact, take his 'doomsday' theme so far as to envisage all information professionals being entirely disposed of. Rather he sees a change from information provider, by storing and retrieving information on request, to trainer/advisor to end users. Other roles include: marketing services, and generally promoting the value of information; system design, where the information professional can provide a valuable perspective on user needs; intelligence, involving information analysis, which in turn requires subject specialization, and a sound knowledge of the priorities of the organization. He also foresees an ever-increasing need for information brokerage and consultancy, outside the traditional organizational information department.

It may be suggested that there is not much doom here, and that these are in fact prescriptions for change rather than immolation. Indeed, in as much as the scenario is negative, from the point of view of information professionals, this is enforced by economic and managerial, rather than technological, factors. The exception is the case where a library/information unit, within an organization which was introducing new technology widely, stuck to its 'traditional', and non-technological role. It appears hold out much hope for the survival of such a unit, and neither, we imagine, would anyone else.

Identify a fate somewhat less drastic than total closure for information departments which do not develop and change: stagnation. This is characterized, among other things by several factors:

- There is a lowering of status and importance, as traditional library and information roles are increasingly seen as 'low level' activities.
- The information unit will increasingly be left with the uninteresting work which others do not wish to do, and information professionals will be excluded from decision making on, and implementation of, information policy in general.
- Cost-cutting, and general reduction of support, will begin (or increase).
- The increasing involvement of users in personal information handling of all sorts will have an entirely negative impact on the information unit, rather than providing new opportunities.
- There will be an increasing in ability to recruit high-quality staff, with appropriate qualifications and outlook, leading to a thoroughly vicious circle.

Worries about something rather less drastic than obliteration. Considering the information professions' role in office automation, he fear that 'they will become ever more marginal, as the really essential skills become part of the repertoire of the computer professional, the accountant, the office administrator, and the management services team'. In general, he believes that information services in special libraries and information units in business and industry are under most 'threat' from IT; traditional libraries in the academic and public sectors will survive because they fulfill clear and important needs unchallenged for the foreseeable future by any IT products. This latter view is in contrast to many commentators who believe libraries to be doomed, because of the spread of electronic publishing, the 'death of the book', etc.

Points to studies which suggest that there is a strong correlation between the drastic slimming down, or actual closure, of information units, and a lack of ability on the part of the managers of those units to market themselves effectively; basically a failute of communication. Equally, closures, or less drastic reductions, may well be due to economic factors, or simply irrational or psychotic management, entirely beyond the control of the information staff.

It seems then that there is little prospect that the appropriate introduction of new technology could lead to genuinely dire consequences, on an individual or collective basis, for information professionals, who are prepared to adapt, their roles and work patterns. Doomsday, in its full sense, is reserved for those who try to preserve a traditionalist approach to 'services, in an environment in which the new technologies are appropriate, and will, in any event, be introduced by someone. Stagnation, to some extent, awaits information professionals, singly or collectively, who are unwilling or unable to be flexible enough to take advantage of the opportunities offered by IT.

3. The nature of change

We have tried to show that the introduction of new technologies is not likely to lead to mass extinctions of information staff and services, but neither will a reliance on traditional service patterns, albeit including some IT systems, be an adequate response, save in the most unusual circumstances.

Change is therefore the crucial factor in the introduction of information technology into information services (as indeed it is in virtually all organizational contexts, as we saw in Chapter 9). We cannot claim this as a new discovery, as it has been commented on by many writers, for example: 'The major feature of library automation is continuous change'. 'If there is going to be one constant in the future, it will be change'. 'Change must be the order of the day if the information department is to survive etc.

A word of caution may be in order. Changes in technology, and its applications, do not happen, for the most part, nearly as rapidly as one might think from reading, for example some IT magazines; the sheer inertia of existing work patterns sees to that. As points out, dramatic changes are most likely to be seen in those organizations which have invested a good deal of resources into the new technology, and this is particularly so if there is some centralized strategy for IT introduction. In other cases, change will almost certainly be patchy, and for the most part slow.

Nonetheless, change there must and will, be. But what sort of change? Here, we have to deal with one of the most significant, and perhaps little-appreciated, aspects of the influence of the new technologies on information services. That is the electric, nature of the changes which will have to come about. It is simply no use looking for some simple formula, applicable to all cases ('information departments halved in size, half the staff systems specialists, change over to electronic current awareness....').

There is no such formula.

In the rather wider context of the introduction of IT into the organization as a whole, notes that there are significant differences of opinion in the literature on such apparently fundamental matters as whether IT will:

- centralize or decentralize authority within the organization.
- increase or decrease opportunities for employee participation and involvement,
- increase or limit job satisfaction,
- allow operational staff greater access to information, and thereby power over their work, or increase management control.
- magnify or reduce the role of middle management, or equivalent, in passing information up and down the hierarchy.

Just about the only point on which a clear consensus has emerged is that IT will bring about change in organizational structures. With this background of confusion, we cannot really feel guilty about failing to provide detailed predictions for such microlevel features as the operations of the information services.

It is entirely possible to introduce IT systems and equipment into existing patterns of service. Going on from this, it is equally possible to lay down guidelines, applicable to all circumstances, as to how IT based information services should be implemented and operated. Guidelines of this sort could approximate, at the extreme, the standardized sorts of procedures followed by traditional library/information units, using printed resources.

While such general, and rigid, guidelines can be drawn up, and indeed have been in some circumstances, they are in fact, highly inappropriate to the potential of new technology systems. An important attribute of these systems, as we have tried to emphasize throughout this book, is that, by comparison with manual systems, or with systems based on earlier generations of technology, they provide great flexibility in the ways in which they can be tailored to precise local user needs. This is partly a reflection of their decentralized nature, and partly of the power of manipulation provided by appropriate software. One need only consider the relative flexibility of, for example, a library card catalogue (physically fixed in place, and limited to pre-set access points) with a distributed relational database (sharing neither disadvantage) to get in idea of the flexibility and adaptability conferred by the new technology. This is in effect wasted, if IT systems are fitted permanently into the straighjacket of standardized work patterns and professional activities and roles, mostly designed to operate system of the past decades.

Information technology, appropriately introduced, provides a very rich environment for the generation, acquisition, packaging, and communication of information. If done appropriately and sensitively, this will respond to the nature of the organization, and of the individuals within it, so that it will not be possible to generalize about exactly what is done, and how. This is the central theme of the user-centred design and implementation philosophies, discussed in Chapter 9. Of course, there must be some general guidelines, and indications of good practice (and the converse). But flexibility and adaptability to local conditions will be the primary considerations. This should apply to all aspects of IT introduction and use, but is particularly appropriate for the information services, with their tradition of close knowledge of user needs, and their intermediary function.

Expresses some of the ideas using the analogy of adaption by 'genetic drift': 'adaption, not along expected lines, or on some formula basis, but in an impromptu, unforeseeable, and essentially non-deterministic fashion.'

In other words, there are many ways of introducing new technology in areas of information service, and, providing only that they meet local needs, and are appropriate for local conditions, they are all valid. The process must be one of flexible adaption, taking advantage of the opportunities, given by the new technologies, which present themselves for providing new, and more effective, services. This does not do much for anyone seeking a neat and tidy general description of the role of the new technology in information services, nor of its influence on information professionals. On the other hand, it does provide a direction for the development of information services, and of the role of the information professional, which can take full advantage of the potential of IT.

Changing work patterns

We now look at some of the changes in work patterns which may result from the widespread introduction of the new technologies. If the discussion is rather general, this reflects the impossibility of making precise predictions in a rapidly changing environment, in which there will be a great deal of necessary adaption to local factors. The most that can be done is to indicate some general, and hopefully reliable, directions in which developments will occur.

1. Blurring of job boundaries

There seems to general agreement that one of the most consistent effects on working patterns stemming from the introduction of new information technology will be a blurring of hitherto well-defined job boundaries. Evidence for this comes both from 'theoretical' considerations of the likely effects of IT, and from practical experience. The latter relates mostly to office automation in general administrative setting, but some evidence is merging to suggest that the same consequences will follow with libraries and information units.

'Blurring of job boundaries' is another of the rather general descriptions of the implications of the introduction of IT, and may imply a number of different things. In a library/information context, this could refer to a number of different boundaries: between professional and non-professional; between information professional and end user; between technical and user-support functions; etc.

Why should this be so? It is not immediately obvious that this would be one of the effects of information technology;

indeed, initial introduction of IT is almost invariably done within the context of existing job functions. There are, however, a number of factors which come into play almost at once to begin to alter the status quo, sometimes dramatically, more usually quietly and steadily.

First of all, IT offers opportunities for information handling tasks, in the broadest sense, to be done in quite different ways from previously, with the potential for entirely new systems, services, and communication pathways. This fact has been missed in many cases, when IT was seen as simply making existing procedures more efficient. Second, and of equal significance, IT very often provides the opportunity for several alternative ways of providing services, which otherwise would be much more limited.

Consider, for example, a published abstracting and indexing service. In printed form, an information department has few options: essentially to buy it, singley or multiply, or not, and to decide on whether it is to be primarily a tool for information staff, or is to be promoted to end users. If the service is computerized, the number of options increase dramatically: to continue to acquire the printed form; to search it online, with or without downloading, by information staff or end users; to acquire it inhouse, in magnetic or optical form, centrally or distributed; to take the whole product, or to strip out sections of interest; to leave it as a standalone system, or to integrate it within a wider framework, or to encourage users to take those parts of it which are of relevance to them: etc. The increased flexibility in this example is, in fact, relatively minor, when compared with the introduction of larger IT systems, more far-reaching in scope.

This combination of potential for new ways of doing things, and a sometimes bewildering flexibility of approach, conferred by the new technology is the basis for its blurring effect on traditional job boundaries. To this must be added the extent to which IT enables tasks which were previously the perogative of professions, in this case library/information professionals, to be effectively and efficiently carried out by others. This is promoted by three particular factors of IT:

- Read access to expertise by telecommunications; for example the downloading of bibliographic cataloguing or indexing records, from a central system, means that local expertise is no longer at each site. Similarly, ready availability of communications systems such as electronic mail and teleconferencing means that professional expertise can be spread more thinly.

- Expertise may also be provided locally in the form of expert system software. It is as well not to make too much of this, since the extent to which such systems will ever be effective replacements for experts, rather than aids to them, is open to question. Nonetheless, it is clear that such systems can, and will, help to spread professional expertise.
- Effective IT systems, with powerful hardware and sophisticated software, can provide much simpler access to many information systems. This does not merely mean the avoidance of complicated command languages and interfaces, valuable though this may be, but may also provide a 'transparent' interface, so that the user need not know the intricacies of coding and indexing systems. Examples of these are access to chemical structure searching systems via graphical interfaces, avoiding the need for nomenclatures and notations, and automated means of allowing access to controlled vocabulary databases, without the user needing to know the nature of the thesaurus.

It is important to note that these factors do not in any sense remove the skill or expertise from the whole process. Rather they insert it at a different place in the cycles the cataloguing/indexing expertise is applied once, at the central system, rather than separately in each information unit; the knowledge is encoded once in a expert system, rather than being invoked on each occasion it is needed. Obviously, the farther this sort of trend progresses, the more significant will be the consequences for the number of information professionals occupied in technical duties in individual information departments.

It seems fairly clear that one immediate effect of these factors will be a continued erosion of any clear boundary which still remains between the work of 'information professionals' and others. This is, of course, not really a new departure. Information handling is part of the working life of very many groups of people, and always has been. What is new is the extent to which tasks which had hitherto been thought of as solely the remit of the library/information professional are being placed, through the effects of IT, within the area of competence of the user community (this going far beyond the bounds of 'end user searching'), and of other groups concerned with information handling and processing; data processing departments, office administrators, etc. This is the negative side, which is usually presented, as we have seen earlier, as a threat to 'traditional' information specialists and departments. However, crumbling boundaries can be crossed from both sides, and there are many opportunities for information professionals to become involved in a wider spectrum of activities than heretofore. This is what is sometimes referred to as the 'emerging market' for information workers. Basically the boundaries to be crossed are those between the information department and its user groups (leading to the information analysis or intelligence role), and between the information department and other information handling functions (leading to a systems specialist and information resource management role).

This may lead to changes in the organizational structure, so that there will no longer be an 'information department' as such. (This would do no more than reflect the changes which IT is likely to bring upon organizational structures as a whole. The most likely prospect is that the library/information function will be absorbed, with a greater or less degree of formal restructuring, into a broader grouping, dealing with information services in the widest sense. For example, sees the overlap in commercial organizations between the information unit, computing/data processing, and office services; analogously, in the academic library context, proposes the merging of the library/information functions with computing services and with the educational resources providers. The degree to which the formal structure changes will, of course, depend crucially on the nature of the organization. It is worth noting, however, that most commentators see the influence of IT as tending to break down rigid hierarchical structures, by promoting novel communication patterns, and services, which could not have fitted into existing structures. We may certainly expect to see more flexible, 'network-style', organizations emerging, and the demise of the compartmentalized library/information unit will probably be a consequence of this in many cases.

A second important form of boundary blurring is that which

may occur within the library/information unit itself (or whatever replaces it), between staff at different levels. This matches what has been predicted, and observed, within general administrative, 'office', work. Again, there is a very electric mix in the effects of new technology, but one model which seems of fairly general applicability is described. He considers a hierarchically arranged administrative structure: top, middle and junior management, secretaries, and clerical staff. Information is requested from the top, and passed up form the bottom, with refinement and evaluation at each stage.

IT is first introduced at the lowest, clerical, level, with immediate and predictable results; a much-reduced clerical workforce, with many clerical functions automated. Beyond this, however, the matter gets more complicated. Top management is, on the whole, little affected, operating mostly by personal contact, and reliance on information passed from the lower levels of management. At these levels, the availability of powerful and easy-to-use information systems allow much information collection, coordination, and analysis to be done directly by secretarial staff. The result, according to Hoskins, will be the replacement of the hierarchically defined middle manager-junior manager—secretary ranks, by a large and rather amorphous 'information assistant' group, directly serving top management, and a reduced core of middle managers. There is considerable evidence that this sort of effect is indeed occurring in many organizations.

For example, reviews the effect of IT in changing the role of the secretary, noting that they are in the front line in dealing with the new office technology, with consequent reduction in routine and repetitive tasks. Views however differ as to how much these are being replaced by devolved higher-level, almost junior management tasks, leading to an expanded role, and conversely to what degree 'secretaries simply found themselves with less work to do, and the embarrassment of having to conceal this from their managers'. Notes sadly that the potential for constructive and positive job design was rarely perceived by mangers, though in the few organizations studied in which it was, secretaries gained much higher levels of satisfaction and feelings of 'self-actualization'. Obstacles of changes in role and function are linked much more closely to organizational structures, and to social and 'political' attitudes within the organization's culture, than to technical factors.

While this hierarchical model is not directly applicable to many information units, there may, nonetheless, be a strong analogy. In this case, we would expect to see:

- a greatly reduced number of unskilled clerical staff;
- a greatly expanded group of 'para-professionals' ('information assistants', 'information administrators', 'information coordinators', etc.), undertaking many technical tasks, (i.e. database compilation and validation) with the aid of IT systems;
- a reduced number of professional level staff in technical functions, (e.g. cataloguing, online intermediary), counter-balanced by increased numbers in direct user-support, and in 'new' functions (e.g. systems specialist);
- information service managers adapting to mange this changed form of unit, and a wider scope of services.

There are indications that this may well be the pattern, at least for some units. Indeed, para-professionals became established in US libraries at a relatively early stage, supplanting professional Librarians in such tasks as cataloguing and acquisitions. This trend appears to have caught on more slowly in the UK and continental Europe, although a report on the influence of IT on the information profession in the UK spoke of 'a two-tier profession of information analysts and para-professionals', commented that 'the library profession will need more strategists, fewer middle-ranking professionals, and more technicians or para-professionals'. If this is indeed to be the common pattern, then it will require new initiatives in information service management, especially with respect to career development.

2. Deskilling or enrichment

One of the main concerns voiced about the introduction of new information technologies is the extent to which they will lead to a degree of 'deskilling for those whose jobs are affected. Deskilling generally implies that the use of IT systems removes elements of choice and judgement from a task; the operator must simply follow instructions and setdown procedures. At worst, the automated system will be effectively controlling its human users. The issues are very much the same as those involved in the automation of factory work, removing the skills of the craftman.

Most discussion in this area has related to clerical and secretarial, rather than professional, work, since these are the areas most directly affected by IT to date. The situation is rapidly changing, particularly with the advent of technologies such as expert systems, which explicitly aim to emulate, and under some circumstances to replace, the human expert. Deskilling of the work of the information professional is therefore a topic worth discussing.

First of all, we should note that by no means all commentators view the deskilling issue very gloomily. There is a counterview, which suggests that the main impacts of IT will be to remove the more routine and unstimulating aspects of professional work, so that deskilling would not be a real issue. Further, there is the prospect that, for workers in the secretarial, or para-professional, groups, IT systems could enable an expansion and enriching of job functions. Makes this point strongly for the 'traditional' office secretary role, though pointing out that it is dependent upon changing attitudes towards what is 'appropriate' within the organizational culture. Overall, this viewpoint suggests that the new technologies will lead, if anything, to the opposite of deskilling, on the whole. This is supported by a NEDO study (The Impact of Advanced Information Systems: the Effect on Job Content and Job Boundaries), which found that many more jobs had been enriched by IT than had been deskilled.

In order to get some idea of what this may mean for the information professional, we should remind ourselves of how IT could lead to the deskilling of such work. The three points mentioned in the previous section are relevant: distributed access to expertise via telecommunications; local access to expertise in intelligent systems; simpler access to information systems for the inexpert user. There is no doubt that, if these facilities expand as they are expected to do, and if information unit takes full advantage of them (neither of which are by any means inevitable), then the effect could be considerable. It would imply that the unit was taking advantage of professional expertise remotely, by way of telecommunications links or software, rather than directly in the form of an information professional. We should note that it is entirely the technical aspects which are being affected. Remote access to a cataloguing system can provide a standard catalogue entry, but cannot tailor it to local needs. End-user access can be provided through a 'friendly front-end' system, but this system cannot assess whether the real needs (perhaps unexpressed) of the individual user and of the organization are being addressed.

The use of IT systems does therefore provide some potential for the technical aspects of the work of information professionals to be deskilled, in as much as sophisticated system will be able to provide the same results, in the hands of a para-professional (whose job, it is worth noting, will be considerably enriched). By contrast; there is no possibility of the user-oriented aspects of the information specialist's work being deslikilled; rather the contrary.

On the whole, deskilling will only be a significant problem for those individual professionals who seek to remain inflexibly attached to technical procedures, rather than adopting a wider, and user-oriented, view of their role.

3. The end of the intermediary?

The intermediary role is perhaps the commonest target for all those who foresee great changes for information professionals in the wake of the introduction of IT. Ironically, the intermediary in the sense in which the term is generally used, is largely a product of one of the earliest of the new technologies to make any impact on information work; online searching. Prior to this, the most common role for the information specialist was the provision of an information resource, most commonly a library, albeit with additional materials as required by the nature of the information unit; this resource being available for direct access by its users. To be sure, those special libraries and information units with a more active role carried out searches, current awareness scanning, etc. on behalf of their users; but the division of labour was largely one of convenience and economics. The users were, or at least considered themselves to be, as capable of dealing with printed resources as the information staff.

The intermediary role only became prominent with the

adoption of computer systems for information handling, although initially it was not known by this name. The early computer systems generally batch systems operated inhouse, were sufficiently complex and unreliable as to put off any but the most determined user, and reliance was placed on trained information workers. The advent of online searching should, in principle, have made matters better, by simplifying the process and providing interactive searching. However, the remaining complexities of the many command languages used, combined with the unreliability of the early computer and telecommunications systems, served as a bar to most users, while the very obvious costs of online searching were a powerful argument for restricting use to trained specialists; the intermediaries.

There has been a fairly constant stream of criticism of this role, largely on the grounds that it imposes a barrier between the information and its ultimate user, which is among other things, stifling of creativity. Perhaps, as this is a reflection of the perjorative connotations of the very idea of the 'middleman'; neither creative nor productive. The new IT products now seem to offer a way of circumventing the information intermediary altogether, by allowing access by simple to use 'front-end' systems, with some degree of intelligence, to external databases, or by allowing these database to be brought inhouse, on magnetic or optical storage. Software for searching inhouse database, whatever their provenance, is rapidly improving, to the extent where most users should have no difficulty in carrying out most searches.

So, is the intermediary doomed? The answer is probably yes, if we consider the 'rigid' form of the intermediary; that is an information professional through whom all search requests must be channeled. There may well be some cases where, for reasons of particular organizational needs (finance, security, etc.), the rigid intermediary role will be maintained, though this will probably be against the wishes of most of the users. The benefits of allowing users to take advantage of the ready and direct access of information provided by the new information systems will be too clear-cut to allow the rigid intermediary to survive by default.

However, we should distinguish another creature, whom we will call the 'adaptive' intermediary. This is a less clear-cut role, appropriate to the multifaceted nature of the IT systems with which they must deal. Essentially, the adaptive intermediary aims to fulfill any and all roles necessary for assisting users to make best use of information systems. (This brings to mind the description of the 'library keeper' in the philosophical college proposed, who was also to be 'Apothecary, Druggist, and Keeper of Instruments, Engines, etc.). This could involve using the systems on behalf of the users when it is appropriate to do so: complex searches, time-consuming searches, searches outside the user's normal areas of interest, searches where there is some particular importance in having a comprehensive result (where, for example, there are legal implications), etc. Also, the intermediary, in this sense, might be solely responsible for searching in particularly complex, new, or expensive systems. However, there would not be the restrictive insistence on the use of the intermediary of all searches, which would help to foster a fuller sense of partnership between the information staff and the user communities.

The adaptive intermediary would also take an active part in assisting the users to make best use of the systems available; by obtaining access to systems, evaluating and recommending, training and offering support and advice. 'The adaptive intermediary role coincides to a large degree with the 'facilitator', 'teacher', and consultant' roles in the introduction of IT generally. It also points towards a potential role for the information professional as 'change agent', providing support and assistance at appropriate points in the users' problem solving processes, helping to articulate problems and find solutions, a much-expanded function, but one which is not totally divorced from the 'traditional' intermediary role.

It is important to realize that the intermediary role is not restricted to carrying searches on demand, i.e. being an intermediary between users and information in databases. It is equally relevant to think of information professionals as intermediaries between users and data processing specialists, in the development of corporate information systems. Points out that large organizations had to 'invent' the role of intermediary between users and technical staff in order to support users during the large-scale implementation of the new technologies during the early 1980s. Pointing out that technical skills were not enough, he suggested that such intermediaries needed 'technical knowledge, business knowledge, knowledge about user learning behaviour, interpersonal skills, etc., which all sounds rather familiar. This seems a clear case of the information professions failing to make their case effectively, since goes no to lament the difficulties of training such intermediaries, and of fitting them into the organizational structure.

Even considering just the 'traditional' intermediary role, there seems to us no doubt that the enthusiasm of users for doing all their own searching has been rather overestimated, for instance, finds that while scientists and engineers may be keen to do their own searching, managers would far rather delegate. A commonly found result of end-user training programmes is that, while there may be initial enthusiasm, it is often only a minority of end users who want to continue to carry out all their own searches (at least in bibliographic sources, as distinct from factual or numeric databanks). The majority retain, or revert to, some reliance on an intermediary, perhaps for all searches, perhaps for more complex or time-consuming searching, or where the subject matter is unfamiliar. Even when end-user searching is enthusiastically adopted, it may be accompanied by an increase in use of intermediaries, with a greater total number of searches being done, in a more information-conscious environment.

In short, many, if not most, users in all kinds of organizations will continue to welcome the assistance of an intermediary, at least in some cases. As more and more information becomes available, in a variety of forms and with a variety of access methods, this will probably become more, rather than less, the case. The identification of sources, from the vast range available, is a particularly important role: has the splendid metaphor of information professionals as 'electronic monks', acting as gatekeepers and guides to the universe of knowledge, much as more traditional monks did in medieval times. The adaptive intermediary (monk or non-monk) seems to have a bright future.

4. The decentralizes library?

We use the term 'library', rather than information unit, here, because it is the library which is thought of as the centralized physical information resource. Therefore, it is the library which has been earmarked by some for extinction, in the aftermath of widespread IT introduction.

The reasons are not hard to see. The new technologies offer, in principle, a means of storing vast amounts of information in electronic form, either created directly by electronic publishing, or input on a large scale by technologies such as optical character recognition (OCR). Telecommunications allow this information to be transferred to where it is required, there to be displayed in the most useful form. Describe one vision of the possible consequences; the library as an 'information utility', with powerful communicating workstations at the core of all library services, with transparent access to remotely-stored information, via networks at local, regional, national, and international level. However, it is possible to go even beyond this concept. Since all information in the electronic system can be made available at any point. There will no larger by any need for anything resembling a conventional library; rather the information resource will be entirely decentralized.

This idea fits in rather neatly with the concepts of 'telecommuting' and 'outworking'. Given adequate, telecommunications, there is no reason why information workers, in the broadest sense, should be tied to a physical workplace. Rather they can work at home, or at a convenient neighbourhood centre, acquiring the information they need electronically, by electronic mail, remote database access, etc. This in turn ties in with the idea that, for reasons which are as much economic as technical, some organizations will tend to contract out their service functions, which could include information services, to outside consultancies, rather than retain them as an integral part of the organization.

There has been a good deal of discussion of the opportunities presented, and problems likely to be posed by telecommuting; indeed the cynic might feel that there was a great deal of generalized discussion, with few real examples, particularly involving professional level workers. One of the few such examples is provided by Diana Hill (1988), who describes telecommuting within CPS Professional Services, a business unit within the UK systems house ICL. All CPS's 300 employees (managers, systems analysts, programmers, consultants, and technical authors) are based at home, dispersed throughout the UK. All share the same working patterns, including managers;

this is felt to be a major factor in the success of any telecommuting scheme. It is interesting to note that the home-based work pattern was initially established entirely without IT support, relying on the postal service. Now, heavy reliance is placed on electronic communications (electronic mail, access to remote computers and databases, and above all, a telephone answering machine), in order to maintain productivity. Management of this distributed work group has to apply exacting and precise control, and has to use several means to overcome the isolation felt by staff: newsletters, regular telephone contact and personal meetings, and social events. 'Mentoring' of telecommuters is particularly important, and there is a problem in ensuring that staff working in this way keep skills up-to-date; distance learning facilities, and specially modularized course are provided.

Another interesting example is that of F International, a software service company with over 1000 homeworkers, more than 90% women, and mostly working partly and flexibly, rather than exclusively, from home. Many of the same concerns are voiced as with CPS, particularly the need for adequate training and management control.

Telecommuting is perceived as a great success by both CPS and F International management. Staff can choose their place and hours of work, can avoid career breaks, and can flexibly combine career with other commitments; this leads to a highly motivated and productive workgroup, and avoids losing skilled staff. In principle, these advantages could apply to many organizations, facing skills shortages of professional staff. However, it is clear that many practical problems remain; few organizations, for example, would have the support networks, both electronic and human (service engineers etc.), which ICL had already set up for their customers, and were able to use directly for their telecommuters. Although IT equipment and networks are becoming cheaper and more reliable, there is still a long way to go before all organizations are able to take full advantage of the potential for decentralization. Telecommuting is losing its 'cottage industry' image, but more slowly than might have been expected.

The whole set of ideas outlined above leads to a concept of total decentralization of information resources, for service providers as well as for users. Such a major change in the nature of information services is worth a closer examination. There is a great deal which could be said about these issues, and we can only give them a rather cursory examination here.

First, there are a few inconvenient facts (inconvenient, that is, for those who most enthusiastically propound such notions), which should be mentioned. The first is that, although the 'death of the book' has been regularly pronounced since the 1960s (and, indeed, earlier, if we recall suggestion in 1913 that the invention of the cinema removed the need for books), there is little evidence of its impending demise. On the contrary, the position of print-on-paper seems as strong as ever, in the late 1980s. There is, of course, an ever-increasing amount of information available in electronic form, and electronic publishing is beginning to find its own niche, as a valid form of delivery for some types of information. Nevertheless, the idea that all worthwhile information will shortly be available in computer-readable form is not tenable; the 'electronic library' belongs, for the foreseeable future, in the same never-never land as the 'paperless office'. Commentators such as Christopher Evans (1979), who believed that the 1980s would see the book being 'the long slow slide into oblivion', may have been less dramatically mistaken than those who foresaw a more immediate doom, but even they appear to have underestimated the great ergonomic advantages for print, the associated economic factors, and, above all, the deep attachment which its users have for it. Of course, it is true that the totality of information in some restricted areas—financial and technical, for example—will be available in electronic form, but this is by no means the total electronic panacea preached by some.

Indeed this is arguably a very good thing. Argues cogently that a 'paperless society', however it may be organized, would pose a positive danger to the health of any community which adopted it:

> The advocates of the paperless society...see the need for improved communications, to be sure; but they interpret communications in the narrow sense of 'information transfer', of moving 'bits' from here to there. They look forward to a society in which all knowledge is reduced to information stored in computer files with access to it readily available by on-line consultation at a terminal. Even where this question-and-answer way of life does

> not encompass every human need, the terminal still suffices because it also provides references to articles in journals which in turn are also available on-line. A few odd and doubtless insignificant people may still want to read books, or do what is contemptuously dismissed as 'literary research', and this may in extreme cases require a visit to such libraries as may still exist for the sake of their 'archives.'

Larsen (1988) also criticizes the overenthusiastic adoption of the electronic library idea.

In addition to these questions as to its effect on scholarship and culture, we should not forget that the migration of information from print to electronic media, to whatever extent it occurs, will pose problems for general public access to information; in particular for the developing world, and indeed less advantaged users in the developed countries. We consider this further in the chapter on ethical issues.

It is also generally accepted that display technologies, and software, are not yet adequate for total reliance to be placed on them for information delivery. No doubt high-resolution display screens, of both large and small scale, and software techniques such as hypertext, will improve the situation, but not rapidly enough to bring about the total transformation envisaged.

Nor should we forget that information transfer and communications is very much a social, rather than a purely technological affairs. For example, considers the consequences of this context of library reference services. It is by no means clear that electronic networks will provide an adequate alternative to conventional workplace arrangements, and the slow take-up of working practices based around them seems to bear this out. A point which should not be forgotten, when ideas such as electronic outworking for information professionals are mentioned, is that usually it is the peripheral, rather than the core, activities for an organization which are prime targets for this sort of transformation. A major component of arguments for new roles for information professionals in the IT age is that the information function is very much a core function, and it could be highly counter-productive if the information unit were to be regarded as peripheral, purely because of an over-concentration on the technical possibilities for decentralization.

Of course, we should remember that this question, as all the others in this area, does not have a clear-cut answer for all circumstances, because of the eclectic range of solutions enforced by the nature of the technologies. In the case where an organization, including the main users of its information services, chose to operate in a dispersed fashion, by means of electronic networks, then the information services would no doubt follow suit. More usually, however, information staff will be well advised to seek to retain as close a contact with their users as is possible, and this aim will not generally be helped by electronic decentralization.

In summary, it is certain that there will be a great more information available in electronic form, that this will come from a variety of sources, and that the services which will be provided to make use of it will go far beyond the capabilities of the traditional library/information unit. Similarly, it is certain that some information professionals will take advantage of developed telecommunication facilities to work from home, to work on a contract basis, or in other ways to break from traditional employment patterns. However, this will not have as great an effect on the pattern of information service as some commentators have suggested.

New roles for the information professional

Having examined some of the influences which the introduction of IT may exert on information work, and the changing work patterns which are likely to result, we now look at some of the new roles which may be available for the library/information professional. We emphasize that this is not a complete enumeration of possibilities; nor are each of the roles mentioned uniquely distinct. On the contrary, there is a great variety of alternatives, covering a wide spectrum of interconnected functions. All that we can attempt here is to identify some of the more clearly delineated roles, as examples.

It is also important to realize that these are not functions which are in some ways 'reserved' for the traditionally-qualified information professional; there is bound to be a healthy interchange with people from other backgrounds, both related to subject specialism and to technological knowledge. This is both inevitable and beneficial, and is not to be confused with the practice, now fortunately largely historical, of putting less-than-adequate performers in other functions into the 'quieter' or 'easier' information world. If this was ever justifiable in the past, it is certainly not so with the increasing importance and complexity of the information function.

> The information professions still badly need recruits with qualifications and experience outside the conventional information sphere. This requirement is not at odds with the desire to see libraries and information units run in a professional manner. The earlier criticism over the use of failed technical and computing staff to run libraries still stands. It is not essentially a criticism of their background, more the fact that they have failed . The profession increasingly needs dynamic well-motivated individuals, not those who have failed elsewhere and are looking for somewhere to hide.

If the information professional is to make a success of adaption to some of these new roles, then it will need to attract and retain people of the highest calibre; it is to be hoped that the challenges offered by these new tasks will help this process.

1. User support

The user support function is a combination of several roles, including advisor, facilitator, trainer, and consultant. It also includes many of the functions of the 'adaptive intermediary', discussed earlier.

In many ways this is not truly a new function. 'User education' in libraries, for example, has a long history while librarians and information workers must surely always have been involved with advising their patrons on the best way of finding the information. To a large degree, however, this sort of activity has been 'fitted in', among the information specialist's main work; information provision and intermediary services.

With the growth of electronic information systems, the potential for this 'user-support' role has expanded considerably. For one thing, the diversity and complexity of information resources has greatly increased. At one time, resources in a given subject area would be limited basically to books and journals, plus perhaps other paper resources, such as pamphlets or maps. The users, by and large, knew how to deal with these as well as any information specialist, and all that was necessary was to make the users aware of their existence, and perhaps provide some explanation and assistance with the more complex indexes. There may now be a much wider range of printed resources, plus databases available either on an online host, or on magnetic or optical media for inhouse use. Searching techniques, perhaps involving special purpose hardware or software, and facilities for processing, analysing and displaying results, are correspondingly improved. This embarrassment of riches provides the justification for regarding this as an important future opportunity for information professionals.

The roles envisaged are quite varied: training users to operate systems effectively; writing documentation and user guides (it is often necessary to provide a 'local' guide to a bought-in package, to supplement the supplier's offering); trouble-shooting and problem-solving; acting as a link between users and technical experts; recommending and specifying new systems; bringing new developments to the attention of potential users; advising on optimal solutions to users' information problems (often in the broadest sense). The 'adaptive intermediary' role, mentioned above, is also included, as is its extension, the 'change agent'.

In the strictly computing context, the UK National computer Centre's 1987 survey found the most common end-user support role, with percentage incidence to be as follows :

End-user support role	*Percentage incidence*
Training	87
Hardware/software selection	76
Development of applications	71
Assessing feasibility of user proposals	66
Advisory service	66
Evaluation for new products	58
Data extraction	55
Promoting end-user computing	33
Maintaining applications libraries	25
Newsletter	21

The information professional's role in this sense need not be limited to what are traditionally thought of as 'library-type' systems; i.e. external literature, and to some extent data, and some kinds of internal files. Because of their knowledge both of user needs and of technical factors, information specialists can be well placed to play this kind of role across a much wider spectrum of IT systems, such as office automation. We tried to emphasize in Chapter 9 the extent to which the information professional is well suited for this kind of activity, in the planning team and in the user support function, at all stages of implementation and use.

The skills required for this role will be logical extensions of those traditionally possessed by the information professional, with some new ones grafted on. When considering something like our 'adaptive intermediary', notes the most important skill as:

- basic knowledge of traditional library functions because the essential problems of organization, classification, filing, and retrieval will remain as central matters of concern in any information system.
- general knowledge of the potential uses of the information technologies, both individually and in combination, in order to maximize the benefits for different potential applications, with an emphasis on software systems,
- knowledge of the range of available database for particular types of uses and users, what is in them, how to access them and use them efficiently,
- a degree of knowledge of the specialized fields of information to which clients desire access.

In the context of support for office automation, proposes a rather similar list of components of profes-sional expertise:

- detailed knowledge of the information needs of clients;
- knowledge of data in document record formats; important factors in bibliographic data structures are readily transferable to other kinds of data;
- knowledge of vocabulary control; again what was developed for bibliographic data is much more widely applicable;
- knowledge of external information resources, and of their analysis and repackaging;

- general IT awareness, especially relevant to training.

So the skills and outlook of the information professional are directly applicable to the user support role, along a spectrum from a major concern with traditional information resources (albeit increasingly in electronic form) to an involvement with new technology in contexts far removed from traditional library/ information concerns.

2. Database administrator

It may seem strange to indicate 'database' administrator as a new role for library/information professionals. Have we not been involved with creating and administering databases of various sorts, from the library card catalogue onward, as an integral part of our work?

The rationable for suggesting this as a new role comes from a realization of the significance of the central role played by the database in the IT strategy of an organization. 'Database' here implies the repository of information of immediate significance for the organization's objectives. In technical terms, this almost certainly implies a relational database management system. The data dictionary or data directory which controls this system comprises, in many ways, an information map of the organization, and its administration is a vitally important function.

Database administration, in this sense, relies very much upon the skills traditionally associated with information professionals; understanding of the technology, and appreciation of user needs. There is not, in fact, any real conceptual difference between the data dictionary/directory approach to the organization of information, and many traditional tools, such as thesauri and classifications.

Information professionals are thus well fitted to undertake this sort of work. This argument is made forcefully and discussed.

Although this role may be seen as a 'technical' one, somewhat akin to cataloguing and classifying, which we have argued will diminish in importance with the increasing influence of IT, there are, in fact, significant differences. Database, as understood here, is of such pivotal importance to the organization that information professionals undertaking this role will be occupying a central role within the organization's activities. In many ways, the database administrator function is a step towards information resource management, which will be discussed separately below.

3. Subject specialist/intelligence officer

Subject specialization is hardly a new concept for information professions. In the special library/information unit context, it has a long history, and is generally agreed to be highly advantageous, if not essential. In other library/information settings, subject specialization is not so well established. In academic libraries it is of relatively recent introduction, and there is still controversy as to its value, particularly in view of the 'tension' which can often exist between librarian's subject orientation, and their technical or administrative roles. Makes makes a powerful argument for the increasing importance of subject qualifications in information services of all kinds, with William Melody (1986) emphasizes their importance in matching the increasing degree of specialization in electronic information resources.

Subject specialists, in the traditional library and information sense, use their subject knowledge in order to better carry out traditional functions associated with the information provider and intermediary role; selecting resources, carrying out searches and current awareness, etc. Somewhat beyond this is the 'intelligence' function, a much more active process of information collection, analysis, evaluation, and presentation. Indeed, it was the development of this intelligence function as a response to technical and economic problems facing the UK chemical industry in particular at the time of the 1914-18 War which are generally regarded as a major step towards information services as they are known today. A related idea is that of the 'technical liaison information officer' (TILO), a subject specialist information professional assigned to a particular group of users as an integral part of the team, providing comprehensive information support. The TILO idea has gained and lost popularity with monotonous regularity within industrial information units, perhaps as a result of the same tensions as seen in academic library subject specialism.

It may be surprising to find such a well-established practice being promoted as a 'new role' for information professionals, with the introduction of new technology, but in fact there are good reasons. Foresees a smooth transition from the information function to the intelligence function, driven by the ability of the new technology to provide large amounts of information readily at the analyst's desk. This allows effort to be shifted from the gathering of raw information, since IT systems will allow for effortless storage and retrieval, to its evaluation and analysis. Examples would be 'competitor intelligence', i.e. finding out what the opposition may be up to, and identification of opportunities for one's own organization: new markets, potential new products, licensing opportunities, etc. This is of most obvious relevance to the commercial world, but is by no means restricted to it.

Makes the similar point that the ability of IT systems, specifically online searching, to deliver large amounts of raw information rapidly may cause severe problems of quality of output. The hapless user may simply be deluged with information of undoubted relevance, but doubtful significance or usefulness. Dalton argues that this can be offset by making more use of subject specialists in the information department for evaluation and analysis of information.

It would be as well to be cautious before advocating a subject specialist approach as a panacea for the problems brought about by IT introduction. (Indeed, staff in information departments in settings such as the chemical and pharmaceutical industry, where subject specialization has been for decades, may wonder what all the fuss is about). There are already many people fulfilling the intelligence role (market researchers, analysts, planners, etc.), so that there must be careful thought as to exactly what aspects of this function can best be handled by information professionals, and in what way their existing expertise and viewpoints can most profitably be utilized. With these caveats, however, a deeper involvement with the actual information being handled within information systems, as well as a deepened awareness of the needs of individual users and of the organization, can only help information specialists to take full advantage of new technology.

4. Systems specialist

Plainly, those library/information units with a serious commitment to information technology application will need to make an equivalent commitment to provide the human resources to ensure that they systems are used to the best advantage. A common way of doing this, during the first decade or so of the introduction of IT into information services was the employment of a 'systems specialists' within the information group. This is clearly a potential future role for information professionals, and worth looking at further.

First of all, we must clearly distinguish between two things. First, there is the need to ensure that all staff of the information service are familiar with the IT systems which they may need to use; equally important to ensure that they understand, in a more general way, the advantages and opportunities offered by the new technology, so that they will be able to spot potential improvements. Second, to have a smaller number of staff, perhaps just one, to work full time, or nearly so, on IT applications.

> there is an important role for a few who really appreciate both information and computing, and ... all information scientists will have to be continually aware of the broad potentialities of whatever new technology, comes along. Most of all, they will have to learn to analyse their requirements logically and express them so that others can help them.

Also carefully distinguish these two aspects, in proposing an information research team, within the Glaxo UK information services, exclusively involved in IT applications and development work. This is quite distinct from their proposals for training all staff in IT systems, such as word processing, and in general IT appreciation. The latter should be regarded as a sine qua non for all information professionals in departments which make significant use of IT, but it is not what is meant here by the term 'systems specialist'.

There are undoubtedly excellent opportunities for information professionals, with appropriate qualifications, to take on a systems specialist role. Increasingly, opportunities for employment will occur with consultancies and software houses providing packaged systems for user organizations, as well as that with the user organizations themselves. This reflects the trend towards bought-in packages, rather than DIY software, even in the larger information units: smaller units are unlikely ever to have afforded the 'luxury' of a systems specialist. On the other hand, we are very far from the ideal situation in which an information department can simply acquire information technology equipment and systems and expect them to be installed and operated by staff with no particular expertise. Problems of integration, networking, and conversion of material from one form to another will require expertise within the user organization, and preferably within the information unit itself, for the foreseeable future. Total reliance upon the expertise of the supplier, or consultants, or of colleagues from other departments, is usually a recipe for frustration and inefficiency.

We should note that there has been something of a change in the meaning of the term 'systems specialist', in a library/information unit, over the past few years. Initially it implied someone able to actively deal with technology, at a 'nuts and bolts' level: anything from repairing broken equipment, to writing new computer systems from scratch. While there may well still be a place for this sort of thing, the focus of attention is moving much more towards the specification, evaluation, and selection of equipment and systems. This reflects the trend towards much wider availability of packaged systems and software (databases, library automation packages, etc.), so that rather than developing a system from scratch, perhaps using a programming language, systems specialists over the next few years are more likely to be combining and interfacing packages and hardware to form the optimal solution for their organization's needs. The pace of advance in development and introduction of the new technologies is likely to increase, and in particular the convergence of technologies will produce entirely new forms of system. In order to evaluate these, and to select the most appropriate for the departmental and organizational needs, the information unit must have sufficient expertise available; again complete reliance upon outside sources is undesirable, if the information unit is any position to have expertise available inhouse.

Much will, of course, depend on the relationship between the information unit and other departments involved with IT, particularly the data processing or computing department. Ideally, there should be a synergistic relationship, with the technical knowledge of the computer specialists complementing the user orientation, and wider organizational perspective, of the information specialist. Of course, the real world seldom lives up to ideal expectations, and there may be inadequate support from other departments, or no support at all. In these circumstances, the information department may have to take steps to acquire sufficient technical systems expertise for itself.

These considerations also apply to information professionals employed by software developers and consultancies. Their contribution will generally be to direct and guide the technical expertise of information technologists and software engineers, and to ensure that products are adequate to cope with the richness and subtlety of the real information which they will handle, and to meet the needs of the real users whom they will serve.

It need hardly be said the if the information services function expands to that it is acting, to some degree, as a resource for the whole organization on IT matters, then it is all the more important that a proportion of its staff are genuine systems specialists. In many ways, however, information professionals, because of their appreciation of the nature of the information to be handled, of the needs of the users and of the organization, and of the communication patterns which the new technologies must foster, will be better suited for developing IT on an organization-wide basis, than will the technically-oriented computer professionals. The main requirement is for a good overall knowledge of IT concepts, and of where the relevant technologies are likely to be going, combined with an appreciation of the uses to which they may be put. Information professionals are in a good, perhaps uniquely good, position to fill this role, for the information unit itself, and on a wider scale. The value of their combination of skills in the planning and implementation of IT, and in supporting optimal use of the new technologies, maximizing their value to users and organization alike, has been emphasized in Chapter 9.

We have tried to indicate that the systems specialist role

is of great importance in the future development of information services. It is of vital importance that this role is seen in proper perspective, as a natural extension of past practice. Information professionals must not sacrifice, or play down, their unique expertise and vision, in an attempt to become a second-rate form of computer scientist.

5. Information resource manager

Information resource management (IRM) is a concept which has come very much to the fore during the 1980's particularly in the USA, but also in the UK and in continental Europe. It is also often referred to under the less grandiose terms of 'corporate information management' although this terminology is rather unfortunate, since it carries the implication that IRM concepts only have meaning within large industrial or commercial organizations. Although, for obvious economic reasons, this is the major focus of activity at present, the ideas are certainly of wider applicability and, indeed, largely originated in government bureaucracies.

Essentially, IRM involves a recognition that all information within an organization is to be regarded and managed as a single, integrated, and highly valuable resource. In a commercial setting, information is held to be a strategic weapon in competition, and management of information technology the key to its use. Development of the new information technologies has acted as the primary spur to the formulation of the IRM concept, by providing ready access to a mass of information, but at a high cost, and with the constant threat of duplication and inappropriate and incompatible developments, leading to inefficiency and sometimes downright chaos. IRM can be seen, therefore, basically as an integrating and rationalising force, with the further prospect that it can actively promote the value of information, in the widest sense, in the 'unreached' areas of the organization.

The consequence is that there will have to be individuals, and departments, charged with managing the totality of an organizations's information resource. This would encompass activities and responsibilities currently dealt with by a number of groups: computing and data processing, library and information units, office system managers, etc. gives examples of the changes in organizational structure which could support this. Much has been made by some commentators of the opportunities for information professionals to become involved in this area, as perhaps the only way of breaking out of the mould of 'traditional' library and information functions. Their argument is that IRM, involving as it does the overlap of technology with user requirements, and powered by the recognition of the value of information to its users, and to the organization in general, is a natural development of the skills and outlook of the information professional.

Suggests that this is so, pointing out that information professionals have experience with text-based systems, a general background, a wide knowledge of information sources, and (particularly important) knowledge of user behaviour patterns. He defines the IRM function as resources management plus systems consultancy, analytical current awareness, and identification of sources.

Unfortunately, it sometimes appears that it is much easier to promote the general idea of the metamorphosis of the information professional into the Information Resource Manager (also known as the Chief Information Officer, or any of a multitude of synonyms), than to carry this through in actuality. Certainly, the professional literature to the late 1980s shows little indication that this is a generally successful trend. This may be for many reasons, and it may be simply that more time is needed for the transformation to occur. In giving an account, with a greater degree of practical detail than is usual, of how the information unit may begin to approach problem of involvement of corporate information management, list some of the possible reasons for lack of progress:

- Most information professionals lack ambition to succeed at the highest level, and may even exhibit inertia and lack of belief in themselves.
- Most information professionals are unwilling or unable to contemplate their work as anything other than traditional service provision, and particularly fail to see possibilities for IT applications outside their traditional functions.
- Information professionals are too often content to leave it to others (typically a computing department) to handle problems of information handling in general.

- There is a general lack of appreciation among information professionals of the potential influence of IT on corporate information handling.
- There is a failure to accept that change must be the order of the day if the information department is to survive.

This fairly damning catalogue must ring true for the great majority of cases in which information specialists have considered involvement in IRM issues, and is echoed by other commentators suggests bluntly that the lack of 'business nous and commercial savvy' among information scientists may be a block to upward mobility into IRM.

Speaking particularly of librarians, gives reasons why they may not be able to cope with the consequences of an involvement with advanced technology:

- Librarians may not be ready for the structural changes which may be involved, believing that they should not 'rock the boat' of current smooth operation.
- There may be a fear of loss of functions, status, and jobs, and of the inability of learn new skills.
- They may not really believe that, if they do not adapt, their functions will be taken over by others.
- They may be unable to relinquish some cherished beliefs: that the role of technology is to improve current operations; that para-professionals should not undertake any tasks currently done by professionals; that the intermediary searcher is always better than the end user; etc.

Adds three more factors which hold back the information professional:

- identification with the old-fashioned technology of the book and the library;
- lack of seniority;
- a 'service mentality' leading to hesitancy in taking responsibility for change is organization-wide working practices.

He considers that 'with appropriate changes in training and perception', information professionals can attain the IRM role. Perhaps that is an appropriately optimistic note to end the discussion.

Conclusions

In this chapter, we have tried to assess the influence of the new information technologies on information professionals and on the departments in which they work. If we have failed to provide clear-cut prescriptions, then that reflects the fact that there are none, and if the discussions have seemed, at times, confused, then that too reflects the situation.

Information professionals are faced with continuous change, which cannot fairly be described as a state of transition, since there is no indication that stability will be regained, at least in the near future. The more dire prophecies of the virtual extinction of the information profession are ill-founded, provided that appropriate responses are made. These responses are based on an attitude of flexibility and adaptability, and, in particular, a willingness to adapt to the particular, and changing, needs of the local situation.

New opportunities, and new roles, will present themselves for information professionals, though will in no sense be reserved for them. These will be very varied, reflecting the electricism of the response to IT of different organizations; information specialists will increasingly have to find and develop their own 'niches', appropriate to the situation. These new roles will however largely be grounded in the traditional skills and attitudes of library/information professionals. The result will be a much broader, and perhaps more outward looking, profession, though one still based firmly on principles of technology Although widespread discussion of these opportunities has occurred only recently, as long ago as 1971 was identifying rules for the 'sniffer', or intelligence officer, the 'gate opener', the 'mixer and modeller' of different kinds of information, he 'horizontalist' or 'generalists', etc.

Let us give the last word who sums up the situation very well:

No-one yet knows with any certainty what role the information professional may find in the midst of all the current changes ... At the core of society and industry where there is still a need for the information professional's know-how to handle and trace information. It is a short step from this to helping the lay user in interpreting the implications of the new information technologies. If this type of service function still lies at the heart of our professions, then the wider implications of change must be recognized. Qualified information staff increasingly have a role to play in publicity, computing, education, systems design, marketing, communications, etc. If one single factor characterizes the role of tomorrow's information professionals, it is likely to be variety and the range of opportunities open to them.

11
Education and training

Education and training is an area of IT which is frequently neglected or left to chance. While many organizations are prepared to invest heavily in the technology itself, few have a structured approach in training the users of that technology so that it can be used in the most efficient and effective way. Not only are the people who will be using IT ill prepared, but also those whose responsibility it is to decide on the role of IT in corporate strategy lack appropriate skills.

It is often the case that an initial 'induction' course in how a system fits into the workings of the office or department, and basic instructions which amount to 'press this key and it will do this' is all that an information worker receives. Continuing education designed to meet the specific needs and capabilities of an individual tends to be forgotten and the person is left to their own devices to both assess their training needs and identify means of meeting those requirements.

The reason for this omission in corporate policy is due to several factors: the need for such training is not always self evident to those responsible for staff training; it may be assumed that the term user friendly means that the system will tell the user the next step that is to be taken in any process or operation; and in the case of information professionals it is taken for granted that they already know how to work with the technology, or if they do not that they are able to 'pick it up' as they go along. In this chapter we will look very briefly at the different methods of training available to information professionals. We will also mention some of the additional skills that are of help to the information specialist in coping with their changing role but which are not directly related to information technology.

A knowledge or understanding to IT has become essential if one is to operate an efficient and successful information service. All too often when an organization is pruning its budget it is the library and information functions that come under scrutiny. Staff are either kept at existing levels or reduced, despite the fact that the organization's information requirements may be increasing. In these situations, introducing some form of information technology may be the only way of maintaining a satisfactory service, or even surviving. But information technology in no panacea.

> ...in order to apply the new technology to information management, an understanding of new technologies and those still on the horizontal is required...not at a technical level, but rather at the level of appreciation, involving at least enough knowledge to be able to carry on an intelligent dialogue with those who are technically qualified.

Paradoxically, it is the workers outside of the traditional information environment who today have a better grounding in the basics of information technology and its practical applications. Secretarial courses include modules on word processing, electronic typewriters, how to operate telex and fax machines. At the other end of the scale, there are new courses being offered as part of management studies and in business schools for senior executives and managers. While a number of information specialists do indeed fall into the second category, the aspiring information professional who carries out most of the day to day tasks falls between two stools. Even some library and information schools are failing to rise to the challenge, and has found that: 'Nearly all library schools have wanted to join the "IT bandwagon" but, unfortunately, some have progressed no more than a "bolt-on" approach'.

Even in those schools where information technology forms an integrated part of the course many students subsequently find that it is insufficient in both quantity and breadth. Former students who took part in a study reported suggested that courses should include:

- more online searching

- more practical management administration
- evaluation of software packages
- data protection, copyright law
- continued development of emphasis on applications of new technology

It was also suggested that courses must make students more confident with the new technology. It must be said though, that formal academic courses are improving in this respect albeit in a piecemeal fashion.

An information professional's training does not stop the moment they complete their formal training and enter work, in fact an increasing number are entering the profession from other disciplines without any background in library and information work at all. Even for those who have acquired some knowledge of the technology, advances are occurring at such a rate that it is soon out of date and inadequate, and the need for continuing education becomes necessary. There are several ways in which this can be achieved. Reading the relevant journals and attending exhibitions and meetings will keep one up to date with what is happening on the broader front of technology and explain some of the theory. Putting it into practice is another matter.

There are a number of courses which concentrate on specific topics e.g. desktop publishing, data protection. They can come from various sources: inhouse trainers from training departments or computer/information departments, educational establishments, commercial training organizations, professional associations, and the manufacturers and suppliers of the technology. They can be part or full time requiring attendance outside of the company, but several organizations now offer inhouse training tailored to the company's specific needs.

There is also the option of using computer-based training or computer-aided learning programs, sometimes referred to as CBT or CAL. The simplest of these are the tutorial files included as part of many software packages. They are somewhat general in nature being product based rather than application or' people based but nonetheless give a good grounding in the use of the product. Moving up a step, there are interactive programs which require the student to participate in the learning process by entering commands and data as he or she would then working with the software. Again these tend to be rather general but a number of organizations are collaborating to produce industry or application specific modules.

The most complex, and most expensive, are the systems based on interactive video discs. The methods so far described will run on a personal computer which is probably going to be used anyway for the system being taught. Interactive video discs require, in addition, a laser disc player and associated software. They have the great advantage, though, that they can integrate moving and still pictures, and sound into the basic training program and thus simulate real-life situations to a greater degree. They are of particular benefit when teaching management or sales techniques but have been used to teach everything from how to handle a nuclear power plant disaster to emergency medical care.

An advantage of computer-based training of CBT is the one to one interaction. The trainee can work at his or her own speed, concentrate on those areas that are giving them trouble, and CBT can be used repeatedly for reinforcement. There is an often quoted axiom which states that we recall 25% of what we hear, 45% of what we hear and see, and 70% of what we do. On this basis interactive training should provide the most efficient means of training. It also removes the human element in that human teachers can have good and bad days; computer-based training is at least consistent and ensures that all essential points are covered with each trainee. Furthermore CBT can save companies time and money since their staff can be fitted in between tasks.

There are some drawbacks, one of them being that it does not always get 'fitted in' between tasks. The workload may be such as to make this impossible, and the fact that a person is seen sitting at their terminal running a CBT program may be taken by some to mean that person has not been given enough work! Therefore, if CBT is to form a major part of a training program, management must accept that time must be allocated in *advance* to the activity and that it must take priority over other activities at that time. Another difficulty is that CBT is generally inflexible. It provides oversimplified and sometimes awkward choices that do not take into account an individual's own work style. This is an area where the introduction of expert systems can be of benefit by extending the capabilities of CBT and one into which there is much research at present.

So far the emphasis has been on the technological aspects of an information professionals work, but in many respects an information professional is expected to be a jack of all trades, master of 85% of them and know who is master of the remaining 15%. Brittain (1987) has divided the skills required by information specialists into three groups: primary, secondary and tertiary skills. Primary skills cover statistics, information retrieval, classification, natural language processing, logic and applications programming. Secondary skills include the manipulation, and presentation of information while tertiary group are more concerned with organizational structure and producers. Although they form three distinct groups, the activities are interdependent with information technology being the common thread.

Rather than being just gatherers, classifiers and storers of documents, information professionals have become more concerned with the use and management of the information itself, and with adding value to it. These are all activities which will probably involve the use of technology at some stage. Some respondents made the point that presentation skills can be vital in library and information work, an area not always covered in training.

Once a library's or information unit's customers become aware of the variety and high quality of services that can be provided with the help of IT, they start to use the services more often and may encourage their colleagues to do the same. The information unit is usually expected to cope with the increased demand with existing staffing levels until a case demonstrating the need for extra staff has been made. Good management and organizational skills are essential if one is to first, present one's case effectively and second, survive and remain sane in the meantime. Time management is just one aspect but a vital one. The ability to organize one's activities and administrative tasks, to assess the relative importance of the demands which are placed upon scarce resources, and to prioritize requests for information in the most effective way does have to be learned. Many people acquire it the hard way, though experience, but most management courses now include it as an essential part of the curriculum.

The need for language skills is commonly discounted because it is assumed that any worthwhile references will always be published in an English language publication. This is not so and certainly in business information at least a reading knowledge of one or more foreign languages is desirable. Articles on companies and their activities are published in newspapers, magazines and journals all over the world and will not always be in English. Electronic publishing has made available media which can be searched through online databases, for example the full text of many newspapers in their original language can be accessed online. So not only must the information specialist be able to make sense of a foreign language article, he must also be able to input the correct terms when searching for it.

So how is the information professional to tackle the task of training? The first step is to ascertain what is on offer inhouse in the way of courses, manuals, books, journals, CBT etc. Then one should identify the appropriate professional bodies of which one can become a member. These may be for computer or information professionals in all industries or industry specific. Many run courses, exhibitions and conferences of their own, as well as being able to offer advice on career development and other courses, both part and full-time. Journals are an important way of keeping up to date on theory and practice, and many carry information and advertisements on courses, exhibitions, meetings etc. Towards the end of the book, we have given a listing of relevant organizations, and sources of information for keeping up to date, both of which we hope will prove helpful.

12

The Effect of Information Technology on the Organization

We have already discussed the implications of IT for individuals as regards career development and prospects, and the effect that technology can have on their day-to-day activities. In this chapter we will be considering the broader issues of the effect of IT on organizations as a whole.

There is no question that IT is having a considerable impact on working patterns of both individuals and organizations, and that indirectly it can bring about changes in organizational structure. There is the direct influence of technology on how workers tackle individual tasks; an obvious example in information work is the use of online databases in place of manual searching of printed indexes. Word processors have become so common that in some organizations executives are now expected to type their own memos and letters using their desktop personal computer. This is an innovation that not all welcome as they may have lost the services of a secretary as a result; for many a secretary is more of a status symbol than anything else and the loss seen almost as a form of demotion or failure within the organization.

Information technology can lead to changes in organizational structure—in some cases the company organization undergoes a complete metamorphosis—as a result of changes in procedures, systems, re-allocation of responsibilities, and even culminating in a complete change of corporate personality.

There is less agreement, however concerning the exact nature of the changes and the manner in which they happen or are implemented. Summarized very neatly the conflicting conclusions reached by different authors:

(a) IT will centralise/decentralise authority within the organization;

(b) IT will allow operational staff greater access to 'management information:, or it will atrengthen management control over the flow of information;

(c) IT will magnify/reduce the role of middle management as summarisers and filters of information up and down the hierarchical pyramid;

(d) IT will increase/limit opportunities for employee participation and involvement;

(e) IT will change/freeze existing organisational structures;

(f) IT will limit/increase job satisfaction;

(g) IT consumes capital/puts capital to work.

What is certain is that office work as a whole will undergo prodigious and continual change. Information technology can indeed overcome hierarchical boundaries by encouraging a more 'chatty atmosphere' and a freer flow of information through electronic mail, teleconferencing, networked databases. Introverted individuals are less inhibited in contributing ideas and opinions via an impersonal medium such as the computer than in face to face confrontations. On the negative side some users become addicted to the system and are forever accessing their mailboxes for messages, or they get 'message phobia' and ignore their mailboxes completely.

It is often said that companies must embrace new technology if they are to achieve or maintain a competitive advantage in the market place. 'Competitive edge' is difficult to assess both qualitatively and quantitatively, and the evidence for and against is inconclusive. One cannot deny, though, that some companies have had to embrace the new technology just to survive. The adoption of EDI (electronic data interchange) is a prime example, and in this case not only is technology affecting an individual organization, it is altering the way whole industry sectors operate. Many industries e.g. car manufacturers will not deal with suppliers who do not use EDI for exchanging formal documents such as orders and invoices.

EDI has brought about many changes in the way that

companies monitor and control their activities. Its advantages include reduced order time, improved supplier performance, reduced transmission errors, closer links with and greater control over suppliers, all of which enables a manufacturer to reduce his inventory and introduce 'just-in-time' manufacture. This in turn reduces purchasing and administration costs.

At a more local level, information departments and libraries cannot afford to think of themselves as islands and independent units but must become aware that their role within the organization must change if they are to survive, something that many have failed to realize. As we mentioned earlier, there is likely to be a blurring of job boundaries as more people within the organization become 'information processors' in the widest sense. The traditional information providers will have to learn to adopt a higher profile, and to market and demonstrate the effectiveness and value of their services. There is too much preoccupation with the 'threat' of end-user searching, and not enough appreciation of other developments which have a greater potential for affecting the status and very existence of central information and library units.

End-user searching

It has been suggested that end-user searching will eventually become commonplace but the literature fails to confirm that this is a universal trend. Many customers of information units are reluctant, for a variety of reasons to carry out their own searches but others are keen to do so and can be present in sufficient numbers so as to free the information professional for other functions within the organization. Rather than feeling threatened the information professional should look upon it as an opportunity to develop new services, and to take on new roles such as those of trainer and consultant. Information units are ideally placed and their staff expertly qualified to act as a centre of coordination and advice, but it is worrying that according to one survey many librarians are not involved in new developments within the organization and that they remain unconcerned that that is the case.

End-user searching does not mean the end of the information specialist's role in online searching. End users tend to be adept at searching one or two databases which, inevitably, are not appropriate for every enquiry. On these occasions the enquirer will need advice on what other systems are available and on the searching techniques that should be adopted to retrieve the information. And then a specialist will always have to be on hand to deal with problems with start ups, PSS error messages, breakdowns, unexpected responses from the host etc.

Searches for information may be unknowingly repeated, so the information unit should act as coordinators of information activities within the organization and encourage users to check with them before embarking on work. This gives the unit the opportunity to set up a skills and knowledge 'database' so that people with the relevant expertise can be brought together to work on a particular problem. The result is more cost effective for the company, and unnecessary duplication of work and expenditure is avoided.

There are a variety of reasons why some end users are loath to perform their own searches. There is the time taken to learn log-on procedures and how to prepare search strategies, and even a reluctance to read user manuals. In many instances this is because of time constraints; end users refer to online systems when they have the least amount of time to contend with such matters 'I need the information for a meeting in half an hour', is a common remark accompanying a request for information. There are, though systems now available that overcome many of these barriers. Log-on procedures can be automated so that the user need press only one or two keys to be online; and there are front end interfaces which help the user set up the search strategies and choose the most appropriate database.

There remain other objections though. Managers are sometimes reluctant to allow free access to online systems because they fear an increase in costs. End users may consider that information retrieval is not their job, an opinion held even by experienced information handlers such as journalists, city analysts and management consultants whose job entails almost continual data gathering and manipulation. They maintain that that is why a librarian or information scientist has been employed, and that their own time is best spent analysing and manipulating the data that has been retrieved for them.

Many managers and executives find themselves already

overloaded with information and have no desire to increase their workload further, but it is also inefficient utilization of manpower resources to have, for example, the managing director carrying out online searches. The role of the information officer here is perceived as being a sifter and organizer of information, as someone who removes extraneous and irrelevant information, and who puts the information back into context and into a readable form.

Finally, many people are still reluctant to use electronic equipment; one merchant bank's users referred to terminals as 'the magic machine'. Thus the dream of organizations becoming populated with end users of external online databases is unlikely to become a total reality. The development and use of internal databases containing processed and evaluated information, is a more likely scenario, especially with local area networks making access to data easier.

Dissemination of information within networks

The installation of local area networks is seen, not just as a means of sharing hardware and software resources, but also as a method of gathering and distributing information within the whole organization. The information unit as the traditional providers of data should logically be in the ideal position to coordinate such a project. Having identified the corporate strategy and decided how information services can contribute to achieving the corporate goals, the unit should have the necessary expertise to implement the new style of services. Information services are moving away from the role of mere guardians of books and journals; they must adapt to supplying information, experience and knowledge in other forms and via alternative media. That is not to say that the 'paperless' office is anywhere near to becoming a reality. On the contrary, study by found that the volume of paper being handled by organizations is rising by 25% per year.

Corporate intelligence networks are a means of gathering and disseminating widely dispersed intelligence. They give access to individual expertise and provide a way of pooling intelligence acquired by a variety of individuals during the course of their job e.g. competitor information obtained by sales representatives while out in the field. Intelligence networks involve people not normally accustomed to collecting data or inputting it in a structured way. It can be difficult maintaining the initial enthusiasm and momentum, unless there is continual encouragement from professional staff and the project has the support of management in all departments. In order to be successful there must be coordination to assign responsibilities for particular types of information, rationalization to minimize duplication of effort, and procedures to ensure compatibility of all information within the network.

While the collection of information for intelligence networks ultimately falls upon the few who have the will and the ability to process the data in a reliable and consistent way, access to the system will usually be by all levels of staff. The availability of company internal databases via networks to managers should, in theory, improve performance by making up-to-data information more readily available. But the network needs to be able to support a wide range of abilities and aptitudes for IT. Decision support systems (DSS) facilitate access to and assist in the manipulation of data into an appropriate form.

Many DSS are based on expert systems; there are products now on the market which interface with other types of software such as spreadheets and DBMS. Thus it is possible to set up separate databanks and databases using the software most appropriate for the type of data, which can, with the help of the expert system, be interrogated by users of the network via a single series of commands and menus. While it is important to take into account staff who are infrequent users or less able to cope with electronic information, those who are perfectly at ease with the new media must not be neglected. Menus which guide the searcher through the system step by step may be helpful to the novice, but can be irritating to the experienced user. An easy means of bypassing the 'help' is therefore essential.

The introduction of new services means greater interaction between the information specialist and all levels of the organization especially senior management. This requires a high level of interpersonal skills and confidence on the part of the information professional if the information centre is to achieve and maintain a high profile within the organization. This of course means that there will be more interaction with other disciplines, and may necessitate training in areas other than those normally considered as part of an information professional's continuing education programme.

Teleconferencing

We now go on to look at a form of technology called teleconferencing that is used by a small number of organizations but which in its potential effect on work patterns is second only to telecommuting. Teleconferencing is a generic term covering many technologies and distinct systems which enable geographically separated groups of people to exchange information by electronic means. There are three forms of teleconferencing: computer conferencing; audio conferencing and video conferencing.

Computer conferencing is an extension of electronic mail where several individuals are able to access and input comments and information into a communal mailbox. Its advocates do not see it as a replacement for face to face discussions which are part of the of the decision making process, but rather as means of eliminating many of the intermediary meetings that take place in order to exchange information. A communications consultant, lists four major advantages to computer conferencing:

- A record is automatically made of every comment that is made, so that a check can be made in the event of any subsequent misunderstanding.
- Participants do not have to spend time travelling.
- Several conversations can be handled at one session which is not possible when talking in person.
- People who may normally by inhibited by heated face to face discussions, or reluctant to communicate across hierarchical boundaries, are able to contribute as much as a more extrovert personality.

The disadvantages are:

- The lack of non-verbal clues (body language) makes it hard to assess the degree of genuine acceptance, or rejection, of a proposal or piece of information.
- The absence of verbal clues such as sighs, raised voice, etc. make assessment of true feeling difficult.
- Humour is difficult to convey and looses much of its effect if it has to be annotated with a phrase indicating that a joke was intended.

Audio and video conferencing have been slow to gain acceptance. This is understandable in the case of video conferencing because, until recent technological advances became more widely available, it was not a venture that was economically viable for many potential users. Audio conferencing allows several geographically separated groups of people to converse with each other over the telephone. Video conferencing as its name implies, allows pictures to be sent as well. This was rarely considered as a serious option until recently when a combination of high capacity lines, data compression techniques and new coding methods were developed.

Audio conferencing is much easier to set up on an ad hoc basis and can be very useful if one needs to gather together people scattered around the country for an urgent meeting. It has been successfully used by the pharmaceutical industry as a way of discussing the progress of multicentre clinical trials with doctors, without having to gather them together in one place. Video conferencing, because of the type of equipment involved requires more preplanning. Several attempts at introducing it have failed not solely because of user resistance to something new, but because it was used in the wrong situation or in an inappropriate way. Some organizations have attempted to replace their annual company conferences with a form of video conferencing, the intention being to reduce expenditure on travel, hotel bills etc. In many cases it was a failure because the main benefit of many of these events is not the training, which the organizers purport to be the main reason for holding the meeting, but the increased motivation which results from getting together on an information basis with other members of the company.

In those situations where education and training has been its sole purpose, it has sometimes failed because what has been presented to the scattered groups of people has been in effect, a series of televised lectures. It has only been accepted, when a totally new approach to presenting material to the audience has been implemented. Describes how video conferencing was introduced as a means of teaching groups of medical students scattered across London in the various colleges of University of London. The lecturer has to take on more of the role of a television director, combining shots of slides, overhead projections and exhibits with the 'straight' camera shots of himself presenting the information. As users become more adept in the new techniques and the number of organizations able to give advice and training on the subject increases, it is likely to become a more popular means of communication.

Telecommuting

Telecommuting, also known as remote working, homeworking or outworking, is a natural progression from teleconferencing. Employees stay at home to do their work and remain in contact with the office or clients via a terminal and telephone line. The concept of homeworking is not new; sales representatives have always fitted into this category but it is only comparatively recently that other groups of employees have been given the opportunity to work from home. A few work at home in order to complete a report or project: others have abandoned altogether the daily trek into the office. A survey carried out by the Henley Centre for Forecasting suggests that in the UK more than four million people will be working from home by 1995.

Some companies' implementation of telecommuting have been a resounding success while others have had such disastrous results that law suits have been brought against them by their employees. In most of the examples reported in the literature, the telecommuters remain as employee of their organization. In two cases though, they have in effect become self employed and worked on a freelance basis. One project was a failute with many of the telecommuters eventually taking the 'employer' to court. The second was a success, which was due to the fact that the participants were highly motivated and entrepreneurial in spirit, and advice was given by their former employer on setting up and running a business.

Proponents see telecommuting as an opportunity to increase productivity while offering greater job flexibility. Detractors of the system liken it to an 'electronic sweatshop'. Homeworkers may be more vulnerable to low pay, poor working conditions and unemployment. While this is unlikely to be a problem for top-level professionals, it could be a real concern for those involved in routine functions such as transaction processing. So far, though, homeworkers are generally better educated and qualified than the general workforce, and less prone to the electronic sweatshop conditions.

On the technical side many companies have found that it is vital that appropriate equipment such as high baud rate modems and leased lines to the central computer are installed in the homes, the emphasis being placed on high speed, reliable telecommunications.

For employers there are several advantages to telecommuting.

- increased worker productivity due to there being fewar distractions at home than in the office, although this may not apply to workers with children at home,
- expansion of the labour pool geographically,
- reduced costs and overheads as less office space is required.

For employees there is the prospect of greater flexibility and convenience since they are able to fit the work in around family and home commitments.

However there are problems if face-to-face interaction is important in a job, and in these situations it may be necessary for the employees to spend some time at home and some at work. Standardized work such as transaction processing is ideal for telecommuters but some have expressed concern that this could lead to a devaluation of the jobs associated with telecommuting and the establishment of a lower paid workface. Certainly there are opportunities for employers to shop around. In Scandinavia, tele-cottages were originally introduced in remote communities to provide access to information technology together with training, and to create employment in rural areas.

The tele-cottage project has developed to the stage where its participants can now offer their services to small and large enterprises across Scandinavia. It is a scheme that is potentially open to abuse as the homeworkers are more likely to be exploited as a result of their isolation. However, great care has been taken to ensure that the employees receive just wages and that their rights are not infriged upon.

As illustrated by the pilot studies described by Benham (1988) the social and psychological effects on the workforce must be given as much consideration as the technical aspects of implementing telecommuting. In those companies where it has been a success, special efforts have been made to prevent feelings of isolation developing by establishing support groups, and also to ensure that the telecommuters are treated in the same way as 'office' employees. For example no distinction is made in terms of benefits, salary or career paths. Even sales reps, who are commonly thought of as being independent and highly self motivated, can feel isolated.

13

Transmission Systems and Multimedia

Data Transmission

Analogue and digital data were discussed in chapter 2. The transmission of digital data has a number of advantages. For example, each amplifier in the succession of amplifiers needed to boost analogue signals generates additive 'noise'. Not only can digital impulses be noiselessly boosted by regeneration, they are also in a form which may directly stored, processed, etc., by a digital computer.

Was among the first to utilize these advantages. In this he specified a transmission method called Pulse Code Modulation in great detail—a system still in wide use today. In PCM circuits a smooth analogue waveform is sampled by an electronic device at fixed intervals to determine its height. The numerical value of each step corresponds to the value of the analogue waveform at that instant. This value is transmitted as binary code—thus if there are, say, 16 steps, each step may be represented by a 4-bit code ($\log_2 16 = 4$). If the waveform samples, now represented as values, are taken, say, 10 times per second, 104-bit codes, that is 40 bits per second, will be transmitted. During conversion, the level of the analogue signal may be measured with sufficient accuracy at the sampling instant by comparing its value with a staircase waveform containing steps of known values. There have to be enough steps for the digitized representation of the waveform to be good enough for a particular application: 256 different levels is usually considered sufficient for most purposes.

Thus if the level of the analogue waveform corresponds at the sampling instant to, say, step 102 in the staircase waveform, that number must be transmitted.

Data transmission speed constraints

Multimedia information in image, sound, and other formats is described by a large number of bits. When it is electrically communicated, the bandwidth of the telecommunication channel must be wide enough to transports it at an acceptable transmission rate, even when efficient data compressions is used. The cost or unavailability of suitable links is a severe constraint.

If an 'on-off' pulse representing a symbol, signalling element, or bit, is transmitted once per second, the signalling rate is said to be one baud. The greater the number of steps or levels per baud, the larger the number of bits per second transmitted: 256 steps (8 bits) is sufficient to make the 'staircase' waveform described in the preceding section closely resemble the shape of the original waveform. It is also necessary to ensure that a waveform sample is taken often enough to describe the levels of its highest frequency component. Made the remarkable discovery as far back as 1928 that all the information in a smoothly changing analogue waveform can be extracted by measuring its value at least twice per cycle of the highest frequency component. For instance, if you want to digitize a PAL television waveform, you must sample its highest frequency component at least twice per cycle and transmit its digital value at that rate.

The great benefit of digitization, whether for data transmission or computer processing, is partially offset by the disadvantage that the band-width required for a communication channel satisfactorily to 'transport' the burst of pulses, representing values at each sampling instant is about ten times more than the bandwidth required to transport the analogue signal representing the same data. If the signalling rate (frequency) is increased, a wider bandwidth may be required so there is an incentive to transmit as many bits per signalling element as possible.

It would appear that to send large volumes of data through a narrow band channel it is only necessary to make each baud represent a large number of bits without increasing the baud rate.

But if a signal being sent at the maximum permitted level is increasingly subdivided to provide more levels, eventually the small level changes will be comparable to the level of channel noise impulses. The receiver will then provide erroneous information, being unable to distinguish between signals and noise.

C is the maximum theoretical rate for data transmission through any channel—a target rate which may be approached by a highly efficient system but never reached. Since speeds and costs are the most important factors in today's telecommunication networks such a yardstick is extremely valuable. This equation was one of the major findings as described in his famous paper:

The maximum rate that information may be sent through a noisy band-limitated communication channel using ideal coding, expressed as the channel's 'information capacity', C, is:

$$C = 2W \log_2 n\,(S+N) - 2W \log_2 nN$$

$$= W \log_2 (1+S/N) \text{ bits per second}$$

where C = channel 'information capacity'
S = average signal power
N = average gaussian noise power

In practice a variety of methods which are much more ingenious than the simple method of 'voltage level coding' are used to add data without increasing the signalling rate. The phrase 'ideal coding' means that the rate C can never be reached, but recent development in codes approaching the 'ideal' have enabled speeds to be increased considerably.

The problems of transmitting multimedia picture constrained by channel bandwidth will be evident by considering the data volumes which might need to be transmitted, as shown in Table 2.2 in chapter 2. The top four rows of the last three columns show the Mbit totals for CRT 'picture frames' at 1, 8, and 24 bits per pixel. Table 2.3 shows that the volume of data contained within most multimedia pictures lies within this range—from the 512 × 342 screenful of the early Apple machines, through television frame screens to the Nokia monitor.

For a monitor like the Flanders, 24-bit per pixel operation is unlikely. But the Nokia monitor requires 200 Mhz bandwidth digital/analogue convertors and driving channels when the signal has been decompressed to be applied to the tube.

If a user wants to transmit pictures for full-screen reproduction somewhere within the range covered by Tables 2.2 or 2.3, the additional factors to be considered are the availability and cost of a channel with a given bandwidth, the compression ratio, the acceptable response time, and the correct synchronization. Consider, for instance, the transmission of 46 Mbits—the data volume representing a 1600 × 1200 24-bit colour picture corresponding to the screen capacity of the Nokia monitor. The result of transmitting and displaying these data at 24-bit per pixel (Table 13.1) display on the Nokia would be a picture of excellent quality and colour. The quality after, say, 20:1 compression/decompression equivalent to sending only about 2.3 Mbits, depends on the method used but it would still be good.

Table 13.1 Transmission times for a 1600 × 1200 24-bit picture

Speed	*Channel Type of line*	*Duration including 20% OH* *Uncompressed*	*Compressed* 20: 1
64 kbps	ISDN B	12 mins	36 secs
128 Kbps	2 ×ISDN B	6 mins	18 secs
1 Mbps	leased	46 secs	2.3 secs
25 Mbps	leased	1.8 secs	0.09 secs

The bandwidth for occasionally or routinely transmitting data for such pictures depends on today's availability of the ISDN between stations, or on the economics of renting special lines, or using a suitable network. Transmitting at, say, 25 Mbps or more would be feasible for organizations sending large numbers of multimedia pages or pictures. There are a few practical examples today such as station-to-station satellite or wideband cable press links. The transmission speeds required over future super-highways for services such as Video on Demand are another matter. An idea of the possible compromises suitable for managing the delivery of this type of data is provided in the VOD section of chapter 2.

Modems

The part of a telecommunications system which an average user is most likely to meet is a modem. A modem will usually be within he user's premises or attached to or within a multimedia computer. Signalling at either end of a telecoms channel is performed by modems (MODulator DEModulators), which exchange data in a form suitable for transmission in the channel. The modems are connected to machines—data terminals, computers, workstations, fax machines, videotex terminals, etc., which generate and receive signals in machine format. The modem converts machine format signals to channel format signals or channel format signals to machine format signals.

Data signalling may be carried out on the Public Switched Telephone Network (PSTN). In the UK the cost of a 'data call' is the same as the cost of a voice telephone call according to the duration, distance, and time of day. On a data network, such as PSS, the connection to a 'node' or interconnection point, will normally be made via a PSTN or special analogue line.

A modem is usually packaged in a box with front panel controls and plug and socket connections, or it may be constructed on a board to be plugged into a socket within a microcomputer, in which case control and indicating functions will be displayed on the scree. The modem-computer and computer-telecoms channel connection normally handle data serially.

The advent of liberalization of privatization brought with it the removal of the PTT's modem monopoly in many countries. The modem market became highly competitive so there is now a very large choice and modems are available for a wide range of speeds. At one time it was thought that the PSTN could be used at speeds up to 2400 bps. Faster modems were available for better, more expensive, analogue leased lines. However, the size of the market has prompted some ingenious ways of getting the most value out of PSTN signalling using modems working at speeds thought to be impossible a few years ago.

The simplest type of modem—is a small box connected to a terminal with a cable, and to the telephone line via the telephone handset which is inserted into a shaped receptacle on the Coupler. The receptacle contains a microphone to pick up incoming telephone line tones from the earphone fitted within the handset; the tones are converted into digital signals. Outgoing digital signals from the terminal are converted into tones fed into a small loudspeaker picked up by the microphone in the telephone handset. The use of Acoustic Couplers has declined because of their susceptibility to acoustic noise, the now widespread use of plug-and-socket telephone connections, and the arrival of cheap directly connected modems.

Modems on a plug-in board to be used in a PC slot are convenient and popular. Standard modem circuits are available on chips and a modem board usually contains two or three chips with a few separate components also mounted on the board. Alternatively, modems are supplied in freestanding boxes with cable/plug-and-socket connections.

Modems usually conform to 'V series' CCITT Standards so that any pair of modems having the same V number should work together. Performance advances include higher speeds (over the PSTN in particular), compression, error correction, and lower prices. Higher speeds are mainly achieved by data compression and working at more bits per baud; susceptibility to noise increases accordingly. Error correction reduces the effects of noise. Compression enables more data per bit to be transported.

A form of compression was introduced by who noted the size of the stocks of letters and hence their frequency of occurrence, when visiting a local printing house. He designed the Morse code accordingly with E as ".", and Q as "– –. – ". This general principle is still used, but the modern equivalent in 'run length coding', where long strings of binary noughts and ones are represented by short codes.

Added improvements and the necessary complexity are enabled by cheap storage and processing power. In the BTLZ method, frequently occurring character strings are stored as a dictionary of short, fixed-length codewords. When a listed string recurs, a short codeword is automatically substituted for it.

Most error-detecting/correcting systems are based on the automatic addition of extra bits to a block of a given number of data bits at the transmitter to enable a checking procedure to be carried out at the receiver. A repeat of erroneous blocks is automatically demanded. In some modems the quality of the line is monitored and blocks of characters are retransmitted if erroneous.

Current modem developments have been towards new compression systems, sophisticated modulation schemes with more bits per symbol, improved methods of error correction, and the addition of functions such as telephone answering machine control. The complexity required for these functions is embodied in mass-produced chips so prices have not increased much. Modem chip sets are now available to provide a wide range of performance alternatives and different functions. Slightly increased prices have been accompanied by far higher speeds so transmission time costs have dropped substantially.

The most recently introduced type of modem—to the CCITT V34 recommendation—first checks the characteristics of the channel and chooses the most suitable carrier frequency—the optimum centre frequency that will support the maximum number of symbols. A good example of a V34 modem is the Hayes Optima priced at 579. It enables files of facsimile data to be sent from a PC to a fax machine. It includes a 16 Kbyte data dictionary for short code look-ups to increase transmission speeds.

Video data transmission

In order not to make existing black an white receivers obsolete when colour TV was introduced, it had to be possible for a B&W receiver to provide B&W pictures from colour transmissions. A rather complicated arrangement was devised whereby chrominance (colour hue and saturation) data providing the extra information about colour for the new receivers would be included. These data would be discarded by B&W receivers. Chrominance data are sandwiched between luminance (brightness) data elements so the new transmissions occupy a transmitted frequency band no wider than before.

The Nyquist sampling rate still applies to the digitization of television signals without loss of information, and needs to be considered in conjunction with the 1986 CCIR recommendation 601. The recommendation attempts to provide some common ground for 625 line/50Hz (PAL) and 525 line/60 Hz (NTSC) systems.

TV signal sampling is specified as '4:2:2', meaning that digitization is carried out by using 4-bit luminance sampling done at 13.5 MHz, plus two 2-bit colour-difference samples each done at 6.75 MHz. Thus the transmission rate for the 8 bit total without information loss will be:

$$(13.5+6.75+6.75) \times 8 = 216 \text{ Mbps}$$

One way of achieving modest compression is by sampling at lower rates than those just specified, using data interpolation methods for the partial restoration of missing data, and including comb-filtering in the processing circuits to removing 'aliasing' (distortion) effects produced in the process.

The above considerations are likely to be the starting point for the various compression systems used in multimedia systems, such as those described in chapter 3 under 'video'. More information about compression is provided in chapter 3.

For HDTV the bit rate using similar sampling methods would be over 2 Gbps—i.e. 20 times greater than PAL bit rates—requiring a far greater channel bandwidth than is needed for the current PAL service. For digital PAL or HDTV, special coding techniques could reduce these rates substantially—perhaps down to 70 Mbps for HDTV.

Local Loop Alternatives : Fibre

The wires between telephone exchanges and homes are a narrow-band bottleneck limiting the flow of information to ISDN rates, assuming a home can afford ISDN. How long will it take before something better and cheaper arrives? When it does, will unlimited information arrive for home users?

Perhaps fibre will be the medium of the future. Fibre might be the solution to a major end-to-end wideband connection. The 'fibreoptics to the home' idea has been in the air for many years. Think it will remain there. 'Substantial penetration will not occur for at least twenty years', he believes. Others disagree. KMI, a US forecasting company, think that 'Europe's fiber-in-the-loop market will skyrocket from its current 60M level to 4 billion in eight years' (Photonics Spectra, February 1993).

Several recent media events are likely to hasten the arrival of information into the home although little is discussed about demand and costs. Speculation about wide bandwidth via fibre into the home has been rife for years but not much has happened recently to raise hopes in Europe.

In July 1991 a major study in the EC's RACE programme concluded that fibre to the home should be delayed until costs fall or until the volume of telecommuting or HDTV sufficiently increases the justification for it. The study concluded that a fibre shared between 32 subscribers would cost ECU 1200 per subscriber-30 per cent more than copper. The cost would increase to ECU 2000 shared among 8 subscribers, and ECU 2500 for fibres for individual homes. Much of the cost lie in the associated electro-optical components, which can only be reduced by quantity production.

An alternative technology is being developed by Ionica, which received its licence in February 1993—a consequence of UK deregulation policy. It proposed launching a service competing with Mercury and BT, bypassing the local loop with a home-to-exchange wireless connection. It hopes to offer equal service at lower cost.

In the United States, methods of overcoming the local loop problem—called 'bypassing'—have developed into an industry. Fibre may still be a possibility thanks to further deregulation which took place in July 1992 allowing the Bell companies to provide means for subscriber selection of video programmes.

Cable-TV is transported mainly by coaxial cable carrying 155 channels of 6 MHz analogue television. All of the Bell companies are testing new systems in conjunction with cable companies. Estimates for the cost of installing fibre nationally have been up to 400 billion. Bell companies have made a substantial investment in deregulated British cable companies.

In 1991, suggested that ADSL technology should be feasible. Since then it has progressed to the trials stage. ADSL is discussed in the 'Methods of transmission' section which follows. With regard to information to be delivered by ADSL the Bell researchers suggest that authors would be expected to index articles and users would submit interest profiles for matching against their needs. Unfortunately, say the researchers, 'the current state of the authoring art for multimedia is inadequate .... authoring of an article frequently requires the services of a programmer and several weeks of effort', They express the hope that it will improve. Interaction must be simple and 'it must be possible to economically deliver information.'

Telecommunication channels for wideband multimedia data

The advent of sideband nationwide networks running at speeds of up to per second or more will eventually reduce the telecoms bottleneck—a bottleneck created because existing networks, representing an enormous amount of invested capital, have been pressed into service for transmitting data at speeds for which they were not designed. In the UK, the ISDN provides relatively fast data delivery; the purpose-designed Super JANET nationwide inter-university wideband network capable of running at speeds of over 600 Megabits/second started operating in 1993.

From the Bellcore Laboratories, discuss problems of sending large files over networks and concludes that 'very little effort has been made. To examine the network aspects of hypermedia applications'. After providing some tables showing the order of magnitude of P-objects'—that is, a range of items from magazine articles to motion video frames—concludes that large amounts of information would be delivered unnecessarily. Fast, unpredictable shift in end-user requests for service would be very hard to fulfil.

It is worthwhile quoting another conclusions, although they are already well known, namely that studies show that for response time, toleration of delays depends on how the user perceives the communication. If the user expects the system to be of a type that has no internal complexity (one which responds to stimulation without going through computational states) then the response time expected is in the order of 0.2 seconds.

Transmission protocols and standards are a very important part of attempting to ensure that multimedia data may be exchanged and reproduced by a receiving machine exactly as intended by the sender regardless of the machines being used or the route taken by the data. This subjects is discussed in chapter 9.

Methods of transmission STM

Synchronous Transfer Mode (STM) is a method which is widely used for wideband signal transmission. It is gradually being replaced by more efficient methods. The signalling elements used in STM wideband transmission are 'framed' by timing impulses from which terminals can also derive their synchronization. The supposedly synchronous bit rates are not in fact exactly synchronous and have to be brought into synchronism by bit stuffing, or 'plesiochronous' methods. Dummy bits have to be added in order to make up elements of the right length to ensure synchronization. STM is associated with Synchronous. Time Division Multiplexing (STDM), where signalling elements from multiple sources are accommodated in a single circuit by being allocated specific time slots in the multiplexed stream from each data source. STDM is inefficient for sources which send data intermittently because some time slots will then be unoccupied. STM is likely to introduce delays into transmissions caused by error correcting or other procedures.

Packet Switching: ATM

Circuit switching means that users are interconnected by a channel—for example, a telephone line—via conventional switches which make the user-line-user connections. It is a physical path set up for the duration of the call for the sole benefit of its users.

In Packet Switching (PS), switches of the kind that are easily visualized are not used. Messages are split into a number of packets and are dispatched from a network node independently through any available network path. Upon arrival at the node to which the addressee is connected, the packets are assembled into the original sequence and presented to the addressee as a complete message. The net effect is that the same amount of data is transported over a network of much smaller capacity than is possible in a circuit-switched network. Computer-controlled store and forward nodes ensure efficient error-free transmission. Nodes are usually interconnected by at least two telecom channels.

A gap in PS transmission may be relatively short—for example, a gap during a telephone conversation—but it is immediately occupied by as many packets from other users as there are time slots during that gap. Consequently the data occupancy of the network is considerably higher than in a circuit-switched network where a fixed channel is available even when it is empty of data for most of the time.

PS includes other advantages such as error correction and multiple-route availability—if one route fails, another is instantly available.

The Asynchronous Transfer Mode (ATM) protocol has been agreed between the CCITT and ANSI for future wideband networks. ATM is not based on element timing so it does away with the STM system's synchronizing problems. Error correction, which causes delays, is not needed. ATM embodies the advantages of both circuit switching and packet switching. This makes it attractive for network providers and users.

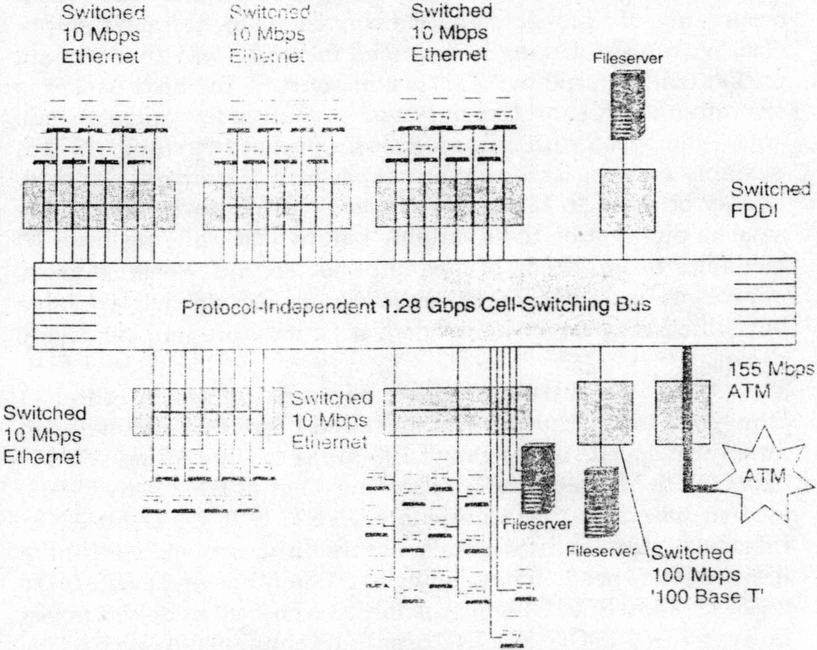

Fig. 13.1 The LANNET ATM switched hub
Source: LANNET

So-called 'ATM switches' as very important. They do not consist of contacts or semiconductor on-off switches. An ATM switch would be interposed between a LAN and, say another LAN, each LAN being configured as a 'hub' serving a number of workstations. Instead of the workstations being connected directly to the LAN, where intercommunications are restricted because of shared bandwidth, each workstation has a line direct to a switch port in the hub, capable of full bandwidth rates regardless of the other LAN traffic. A large hub by LANNET is shown in Figure 13.1. The controlling ATM switch runs at 1.28 Gbps, permitting up to 128 stations to communicate, each running at 10 Mbps as if they were connected to a line capable of that rate, regardless of the traffic from other stations.

A problem with Packet Switching is that it may increase the length of an already long message, say in videoconferencing or multimedia, to an unacceptable length because of the random occurrence of time-slots and waiting times for the next empty slot. With ATM, timing is arranged in such a way that when a packet (called a cell in ATM) is transmitted, the next packet is sent after a very short time interval—usually a few microseconds long—compared with milliseconds for packet switching. ATM is 'scalable' because its format is independent of transmission rate. It may be used in LANs, WANs, etc., at whatever data rates may be dictated by the available bandwidth, ranging from 10 megabits to hundreds of megabits per second. Because users pay only for cells dispatched, not for bandwidth which is available but which may never be needed, it is versatile and relatively cheap.

ATM transmission speed depends on the method of transport, for instance a system called Fibre Channel will run at several speeds in the range 100 Mbps to 1600 Mbps. ATM is expected to be used in a Synchronous Digital Hierarchy (SDH) system based on the American SONET. SONET is an ANSI interface standard for synchronous data transmission at a hierarchy of speeds commencing at 51.84 Mbps and going up to 2488.32 Mbps. SONET will probably also be used as the transport layer in the B-ISDN. SONET uses SDH channels to carry ATM-based data—which embodies the several advantages discussed above, replacing the existing Synchronous Transfer Mode (STM) system used in trunk network. SDH is controlled by accurately synchronized timing impulses and is based on multiples of the CCITT-recommended bit rate of 2.048 Mbps ('Megabits') in Europe and on 1.544 Mbps ('1.5 Megabits') in the US.SDH will be based on a 'harmonized' 155.52 Mbps. A SONET frame carrying ATM-based structures consists an 'overhead' section, and a data load section within which the ATM-based data is carried. User network interfaces are provided for data running at 155 Mbps or 622 Mbps (approx.) or faster, over SONET fibreotic channels.

ADSL

Asymmetric Digital Subscriber Line (ADSL) is a new method devised to transmit data between the local public telephone exchange and a subscriber over an existing twisted pair telephone cable. The rate can be 2 Megabits per second or more for over 90 per cent of the 'local loop' in the UK. A page of text produced on a word processing machine is coded as about 6000 Mbytes or 48 Kbits, so 42 pages per second could be transmitted at this rate, compared with about 1.35 pages/second over a 64 Kbps ISDN channel. A 16 Mbyte high-resolution colour picture compressed by an attainable 10:1 would take about 6 seconds by ADSL.

ADSL was proposed by the Bell research workers. It has since been tested and an international standard is in the process of being agreed. A telephone twisted pair designed for speech in the frequency range 400 to 2800 Hz should support a bit rate of up to some tens of kilobits per second (assuming 'ideal coding') according to criteria for channel capacity, so how can an ADSL bit rate of 2 Mbps be accommodated?

The answer is by 'automatic equalization' and special coding. The frequency response is flattened by filters to compensate for the enormous high-frequency loss, and 'ideal coding', or something approaching it, is achieved by dividing the channel into numerous sub-channels, each automatically accommodating as many bits as noise allows in that channel. The complex circuits needed are once again enabled by the astonishing advances in microelectronics.

ADSL was tested by BT on the lines of 60 of its employees and is now being tried out on 2500 members of the general public. Oracle software will be provide for BT to test interactive TV over copper phone lines in Colchester using up to a 200:1 compression ratio. A massively parallel computer and server will be installed at the local telephone exchange—but what will be the cost of ADSL coding and decoding at the exchange and at a subscriber's premises? More information is awaited.

Networks
Introduction

A telecommunications network consists of communicating devices, such as terminals, an intercommunicating medium, such as cable, and a means of establishing communicating paths through the media. Networks cater for the need of people with information-intensive occupations, mainly in the business area; they are steadily increasing in importance for multimedia data transmission and may culminate in the widely publicized 'Information Superhighway'—the last network to be discussed in this chapter.

A Managed Network is a network directed and maintained by a telecoms organization on behalf of a client. A Metropolitan Area Network (MAN) is a 'Super LAN' fibrotic ring operating at 150 Mbps or more over an area of about 50 m. More efficient within-site, short-distance private networks designed for data exchange between terminals and computers called Local Area Networks (LANs) are now widely used.

LANs (described below) set up in different parts of the same site may be interconnected, so a station on one site may exchange messages with a station on another. A LAN group on one site may be connected to a LAN group on a distant site by a suitable link able to convey messages satisfactorily over long distances. The arrangement is then called a Wide Area Network (WAN)—a label also applied to almost any type of long-distance network.

MANs and LANs do not usually use switches to make fixed connections between stations for the duration of a message; instead, messages passing along the network contain address headers which are recognized by the addressed station, which then captures the message.

Specialized types of network have been developed in the last fifteen years, although WANs, based on lines leased from the telecoms authority, came into use earlier. The main driving forces have been the arrival of compact, powerful, cheap technology and the need for business 'communications.' Telephone systems used to be run by a public authority, except in the United States. After arguments about the virtues of state-run monopolies versus privately owned networks, the latter have steadily gained ground. However, the rate of change has been slow.

Vested interests have frustrated the efforts of the European Commission, who believe that some kind of unified European system is essential. In many other parts of the world, safe, phlegmatic state-controlled monopolies are still preferred. The upheavals and uncertainties following a change to private operations are unwelcome.

Private telephone networks consist of an internal exchange for interconnecting telephones within one site, and lines leased from the authority to interconnect exchanges on different sites. This arrangement has become used for data transmission, perhaps based on a Private Automatic Branch Exchange (PABX). More recently still, Metropolitan Area Networks (MANs) have been developed to convey messages over intermediate distances—for example, between LANs linked to other LANs in the same city. A major objective in these various types of network is first, to make the system transparent to the user. This means that a user sends a message to another, unaware of the complexity of the intervening media and of the routing procedure. A second objective, particularly important when one user communicates with another in a different organization, say overseas, using equipment and networks supplied by a different manufacturer, is that in spite of these differences, messages may be satisfactorily exchanged. The objective of the international OSI standardization effort, described in chapter 9, is an attempt to make this possible.

The phrase 'Enterprise Network' describes a network providing access to all kinds of information via an organization's all-pervading network. For large organizations this means the provision of LANs on different sites in the same or in different countries interconnected by a Wide Area Network. According to a KPMG report: 'although 50% of IT investment goes on the desktop, less than 5% of the top 1000 UK companies have achieved complete integration of their computing environments'.

LANs have been widely adopted in libraries. There will be a LAN in the British Library's new building for about 1300 users costing about 1.5 million including the cost of the fibreotic backbone. It will include twisted pair spurs for LANs, and netware will be used.

So-called distributed computing, meaning decentralizing by using networked computers, is now widely used. Taking account of this trend, new generation operating systems will include networking facilities which previously were only supplied as separate packages. Windows for Workgroup (WFW) is a self-explanatory title of a networking application which will be incorporated in Microsoft's 32-bit Chicago, otherwise known as Windows 95, and Daytona, a 1995 successor to Windows NT.

The commercial linkup between Novell and Microsoft has prompted Chicago's easy access to Netware. According to Udell (1994), Chicago 'enjoys access to WFW, NT, and Netware resources, including redirected drives, printers, and file-based and client-server network applications.' Chicago and Daytona can run NETBIOS networking using TCP/IP protocols.

Microsoft is also working on software called Dynamic Host Configuration Protocol (DHCP) to overcome the network address problem for people who want to plug in a portable at different times and at different locations. Running with a server, it maintains a collection of addresses allocated to users as they appear, usually for a limited period of time. With DHCP and the Windows Internet Naming Service (WINS), another new development, it will be much easier for machines running them to communicate over Internet using the TCP/IP protocols.

IBM has also launched a new 32-bit operating systems called OS/2 Warp which will work with 4 Mbytes of memory—smaller than is needed for Windows 95. It includes built-in arrangements for Internet communications. OS/2 Warp is priced at a low 70 and is aimed to increase the 6 million customers for existing OS/2 software as against the 60 million users claimed for Windows.

Local Area Networks (LANs)

In a LAN a cable spur from the network connects to an adaptor card plugged into a computer. The card contains the necessary intermediate components which handle 'driver' software—that is, software designed to communicate with the network being used. Widely separated LANs may be interconnected by leased lines such as those available in the UK from BT, Mercury, and Cable companies in the US a T1 1.544 Mbps link is often used.

The major types of LAN protocols are Contention and Token Ring. The first Contention LAN, called ALOHA, was developed at the University of Hawaii around 1972. Ethernet, developed by Robert Metcalfe at the Xerox Palo Alto laboratories in the mid–1970s, became a leader. It was first used for interconnecting Alto computers—precursors of the Xerox Star from which was descended. The Ethernet Contention system uses Carrier Sense Multiple Access with Collision Detection (CSMA/CD). All stations listen and wait to transmit a packet message addressed to another station when the cable is clear. In the event of two stations transmitting at once, one or other jams the network, waits for a period of time of random length, and then tries again.

Token Ring or 'Token Passing' systems were developed at the University of California at Irvine and at Cambridge University. Empty data packets circulate and a station wanting to transmit detects a 'token' empty packet, enters an address, and adds a frame consisting of a header followed by a message of up to 4500 bytes. The station empties the packet when it next comes round. All stations examine all packets, accepting only those addressed to them.

Low and medium speed wireless LANs get rid of the cabling problem and enable workstations to be easily sited in the most convenient positions. Radio LANs may require a licence and are liable to interference, but are better for the higher speeds. Infrared LANs are less expensive, but are obstructed by line-of-sight obstacles.

There used to be considerable controversy about the merits and capacity of competitive LANs and they were classified according to topology or protocol. Now that data rates have become faster they tend to be divided according to speed—low/medium: 10-20 Mbps; high: 50-150 Mbps; supercomputer: 800 Mbps (proposed), and Ultragigabit (proposed): 100-10,000 Mbps.

As speeds have increased there has been a strong trend towards the use of fibrotic interconnecting cable. A Standard for FDDI, the Fibre Distributed Data Interface—was agreed in 1990 (see chapter 9) FDDI stations use cheap Light Emitting Diodes (LEDs) for the transmitting element and PIN Field Effect Transistors (PINFETs) for reception. An FDDI network consists of two contra-rotating rings for increased reliability.

LAN networking, or any kind of networking for that matter, introduces several new considerations. A fairly heavy memory overhead is added to participating micros and, unless they are sufficiently powerful, operations are likely to be slow. For accessing databases outside the networks a shared gateway is required with enough ports to provide adequate service per user, assuming that only some fraction of users will require simultaneous service.

Apple has its own protocol called Appletalk for intercommunication over a LAN. Each computer on an Appletalk network is allocated a network number. Appletalk consists of three elements—the Link Access Protocol which controls the mechanics of the CSMA/CD network, the Datagram Delivery Protocol which manages the communications between stations, and the Appletalk Transaction Protocol which controls the dialogue—for instance, a file transfer request—between Appletalk stations. Appletalk runs on an Ethernet CSMA/CD network or on Token Ring. Novell and 3 Comprovide compatible networking systems so that Macs can be used as workstations and share data with PCs, Unix, DEC, and IBM minis/mainframes.

The most popular data rate for Lans is nominally 10 Mbits per second, but the rate decreases appreciably when a number of users are exchanging data—the bandwidth is shared by the users. LANs work perfectly well in most cases when short bursts of data, such as electronic mail messages; are being exchanged. However, the maximum speed for LANs are on the increase and existing LAN users do not have to change the cabling or the software to use them. These faster systems, which run nominally at 100 Mbytes per second, are more expensive than ordinary LANs but much less expensive than FDDI optical networks.

LAN operating systems

IBMs NETBIOS was the first network operating system and was designed primarily to enable DOS-based PCs connected to a relatively small LAN to access printers or file servers. Two types of operating system dominate the market—Novell, who recently bought in to Digital Research for 72 million, are alleged to have 75 percent of it with its Netware operating system-version 4.1 was introduced in December 1994.

Most operating systems run on a server and arrange for users to access network resources in such a way that the access mechanism is 'transparent'. It appears to the user, working on his own application with his own computer operating system such as MS-DOS, OS/2, etc., that he or she is accessing files, databases, etc., in his or her own machine.

Operating systems are able to connect to equipment on the network made by various manufacturers using various protocols as they are added to the network, and support the major transmission standards such as Ethernet and Token Ring. A user is able to do much more than simply exchange files. Traditional 3270 terminal emulation and basic file transfer are replaced by arrangements where the mainframe looks after the corporate database, and networked workstations provide user-friendly information presentation.

When users try to access the same file, all users except one are locked out until any changes made by that user are completed. In the case of shared access to a database, special arrangements need to be made if lockouts are not seriously to slow down access. Methods include locking out an individual record basis, read locks for queries and write locks when the database is being updated, or better still, lockouts on a row-by-row basis. Such arrangements require database reorganization—for instance, the database and the database management software reside in a server, while each PC contains a database user interface.

Peer-to-peer LAN operating systems are widely used for implementing these facilities. Reviews four such operating systems where users can share each other's files. They all use DOS to access files on the hard disk of a server but this is expected to move on to improved arrangements with Windows 95, OS/2, and others. Consider that of the four systems tested—Artisoft's LANtastic 6.0. Microsoft's Windows for Workgroups 3.11, Novell's Personal Netware 1.2, and Performance Technology's Power LAN 3.11, LANtastic (119 per node) is the best. A LANtastic server requires memory of 45 Kbytes per client, runs a cache, and will support an unlimited number of nodes. It includes various security precautions, E-mail, and fax software.

The Integrated Services Digital Network (ISDN)

The CCITT's definition of ISDN is 'a network evolved from the telephony network that provides end to end digital connectivity to support a wide range of services, including voice and non-voice, to which users have access via a limited set of standard multipurpose interfaces.' It is a digital transmission system able to handle digitized voice and data on an 'end-to-end' (subscriber-to-subscriber) basis. Preliminary world standards were set in 1984. It took until 1992 for its slow development to lead to many applications, controlled as it is by the policy of the PTTs, not by market demand.

The public ISDN network represents a transformation in stages of the telephone system into a wider bandwidth data network, where the data may be speech, text, graphics, halftone or colour images, or motion video. Several of the world's major PTTs are in the process of converting the telephone system into a subscriber-to-subscriber ISDN data system without interrupting existing facilities.

The Plain Old Switched Telephone System (POTS) is by far the most universally available communication channel into homes and businesses. The frequency band of POTS is just about wide enough to transport data up to 140 Kilobits second (Kbps)—the speed specified for the ISDN primary data rate. A 64 Kbps circuit may be used for either digitized speech or data. A typical domestic terminal consists of a PC with special plug-in card or a purpose-designed terminal which will use one circuit, and a digital telephone which will use the other. Two subscribers can talk to each other and at the same time exchange diagrams, illustrations, etc., between their terminals, the necessary control signals being exchanged over the signalling circuit. ISDN subscriber options are as follows:

- Basic rate access: 2 64Kbps 'B' channels for data or voice, and a 'D' signalling channel. Typically one B channel would be used for digitized voice and the other for data.
- Primary rate access: 30 B + 1 D channel (Europe), 23 B + 1 D channel (US). Typically for the connection of Private Automatic Branch Exchanges (PABX) for integrated digital access.

The ISDN, if used at the 2 × B channel = 128 Kbps data rate, could deliver quite a good picture in about 36 seconds. If

30 ×B channels are made wholly available for multimedia, the transmission rate would be about 2 Mbps, reducing picture delivery time to less than 2 seconds. Transmission duration could be decreased in both cases by data compression. Thus 40:1 compression for a 2 × B channel would enable a picture to be delivered in less than one second which would be acceptable for many applications.

A number of different devices are available for ISDN ranging in cost in the UK between about 500 and 500. Some come as cards enabling a PC to be used for ISDN work; others are in self-contained boxes.

Diverse opinions are expressed about the ISDN. Inoue from NTT thinks that 'ISDN will be an indispensable means to business activities in the 1990s' and Temime from France Telecom forecast that 'half of all French companies will have an ISDN PABX by 1995.' Commenting about the ambivalence of phone companies, considers that 'connectivity is simply not there', while editor of Telecommunications magazine, thinks that 'many countries are simply disinterested, despite useful initiatives'.

The ISDN may be too slow for effective multimedia communication, but in a recent report believe that even its much faster proposed successor will be a non-starter. They say: 'B-ISDN is dead' and 'Perpetuating it for a new technology is a gave mistake.... ATM is the only technology which supports real-time voice and video'. Forecast success for 'ATM-based B-ISDN', but as ATM is not mentioned in the rest of the article, this is rather confusing.

There is a severe 'critical mass' problem which inhibits the widespread adoption by business users, the information-conscious section of the public or by the public at large, of any new 'information network' which somehow has to get itself into a 'take-off' situation.

The critical mass has long been surpassed by the telephone system, where the number of telephone subscribers far exceeds the number needed to encourage new subscribers to join. Potential subscribers know that they will be able to talk to a significant fraction of the world's population should they install a telephone.

The ISDN is ultimately supposed to become a national

and international network. The general opinion of non-PTT commentators seems to be that it has been developed too slowly, that little attempt has been made to market it, and that its supposed virtue are inadequate and may be overtaken by other schemes able to work at the higher speeds called for today.

However, a CEC-sponsored users' forum, which first met in September 1990 in Brussels, appears to have got off the ground. The ISDN cannot live without users. 'Until the equipment suppliers and public network operators that have driven ISDN developments for the last two decade realise this and ensure an adequate role for users in standards, applications, and tariff definition, the market uncertaintly that has dogged ISDN will not end', says a commentator.

The next stage—the Broadband ISDN—was confidently forecast in the United States. 'I expect to be economic on a parity basis probably around late 1993'. In reality it seems as if the ISDN may arrive in the late 1990s if it is not overtaken by something better, and the Broadband ISDN early in the next century. The B-ISDN will require a much larger investment than the ISDN. It is expected to provide integration of multiple electronic media which will allow for the full range of communication capabilities ranging from telemetry and voice at the low end to HDTV at the upper end, stimulating the extensive use of high-resolution image communications and high-speed data exchange between computers. The most likely protocol will be ATM. The B-ISDN will probably require interconnection via a Network Node Interface (NNI) to a SONET-type monomode fibrotic network with special switching. Subscriber rates will start at 155 Mbits per second. The availability of such speeds depends on the time it will take for the existing narrow-band copper subscriber loops to be replaced by fibrotic or other wideband transmission links.

The Internet

Introduction

The Internet is a large network formed of interconnected networks in the United States some time after Scott's demise, and later extended to other countries. The World Wide Web is a bit tangled, but, so far as I am aware, no deception is intended.

As the Internet is becoming so widely used for transporting multimedia data, some basic information about access, services, and functions is provided here. Many books have been published about it. Information about getting connected and access is given. In-depth information about Internet's TCP/IP protocol and its relationship to the OSI protocol is provided. Care is necessary in choosing the right book; it may well be already out of date.

In 1969 Internet's precursor ARPAnet (Department of Defense Advanced Research Projects Agency network) was designed for communicating information about military research and for withstanding damage from an enemy; it used multiply connected pathways. Later it connected to NSFNET, funded by the National Science Foundation, in order to interconnect academic researchers via five large computer centres. NSF sponsored the development of the Transmission Protocol/ Internet Protocol (TCP/IP)—a communication protocol enabling message to be understood by different kinds of interconnected machines. Internet's wide usage has made TCP/IP a very widely used protocol at the expense of OSI, a more systematic attempt to create an internationally agreed Standards model. Internet became used for commercial purposes as an extension of its use by the research departments of corporations under the general agreement of use for research and educational purposes. The academic/military research requirement has become steadily more relaxed and many other kinds of users are now connected to it.

Several other large networks, built for different purposes, are also connected to Internet to form an enormous intercommunication highway. These include the National Research and Education Network (NREN) established by Act of Congress in 1991, SuperJANET, the UK academic network developed from JANET (Joint Academic Network), and the European EUnet network. In due course the OCLC network and Performance Systems International (PSI) cable TV network will probably be connected as well. Internet provides access to thousands of databases and intercommunication for millions of people the world over.

Schwartz (1993) reports that by using a research algorithm called NETFIND he can search domains, such as departments within a company containing 5.5 million people who have electronic mail addresses. Examples domains include over 3000 educational and nearly 1000 commercial domains in the US, 836 domains in Germany, 360 in the UK, 184 in France, 18 in Iceland, and 1 in Antarctica. The total number of different countries on the Internet system at the time of writing is 53. It was suggested in a late 1994 news items that there were 20 million Internet users and that the growth rate was 10 per cent per month at that time.

Gates (1993) divides Internet activities into three phrases—the research phase up to the mid—1980s, the academic club phase (mid-1980s to early 1990s), and the communicating phase (early 1990s onwards). The fourth phase is approaching—the process of making the Internet self-supporting has started. A principle funding agency, the National Science Foundation, is moving its support from the Internet to the experimental very high speed Backbone Network Service (vBNS), which will be used for research purposes. The objectives is to develop a network able to run at 155 Mbps, and ultimately up to 622 Mbps.

The main Internal backbone (NSFNET), operated as a non-profit service since 1990, was sold to America Online in 1993 with maintenance by MCI, Sprint, and others. Accordingly 'The Internet will go where private money sends it'.

Services

Introduction

As at September 1993, described a number of Resource Discovery Services'. A selection is shown here.

- WAIS
  (Thinking Machines, Apple, KPMG, Wide Area Information Service Project). WAIS provides access to over 300 databases.
- ARCHIE
  A system developed by McGill University which runs database servers and interfaces to other systems. It offers access to over 2 million files and 3500 software packages accessed from 47 countries about 50,000 times per day.
- PROSPERO
  A system of Internet director registrations with their contents, run with the aid of 50 servers, and with clients from 10,000 systems in 30 countries.
- WORLDWIDE WEB (WWW)
  A system for full text document searches using hyperlinks to

interconnect documents. Developed at CERN.

- INDIE

  (Distributed Index) developed at the University of Southern California which enables users to search all participating databases.
- GOPHER

  Developed at the University of Minnesota, Gopher contains indexes to documents accessible via Internet held by university, government and corporate organizations.
- MOSAIC

  A collection of Web browser client software versions for a number of different computers, so that a user may connect to a Web server for browsing purposes.

There are many others. Some say that it is easy to become 'hooked' on Internet, but others find that some searches may take a very long time. Client-server operations will work with a range of popular operating systems such as MS DOS, OS/2, Unix, Apple Mac, and others. Client users are presented with menus showing the availability of 'nodes'—documents or items containing chemical, 'mathematical, or other data collections. Nodes are sometimes arranged hierarchically.

Offers services to Internet clients by connecting them to a server—that is, a computer controlling a large volume of stored data of various types such as text, images, sound, etc. The Protocol is a method for retrieving the attributes of a node rather than its contents. An attribute contains information about the Node such as a particular aspect of it, like TIFF data, or an abstract of its contents. Servers are very widely available.

But the World Wide Web (WWW) is the service mainly responsible for the recent rapid growth in the numbers of hosts and users. A major feature of it is the improvement in search facilities since searching was done using.

Subsequently, search software was introduced by a humorist who called it VERONICA, meaning Very Easy Rodent Oriented Netwide Index to Computerized Archives. After these various attempts to make searching and retrieval easier in a rapidly growing system, the people at CERN, the research establishment in Geneva, decided that something better was needed. A client-server system, HTML, with hyperlinks was introduced, as described below.

A useful information source Internet services and Standards is provided.

Access

Discusses three ways of accessing the Internet:

- Gateway access
  Accessing via another network to which your computer is connected. The network/Internet gateway may limit activities.
- Remote terminal access
  Access using a PC connected to an Internet host via a modem. The host will be running e-mail, Gopher, etc.
- Full access
  Via a PC which is an actual Internet node, using for instance Serial Line Internet Protocol (SLIP) or Point to Point Protocol (PPP).

Considers that there are two major reasons for using Internet—for electronic mail or as a subscriber to a general facilities gateway. In the UK. offers electronic mail at 12 per month minimum fee with connect rates, at 16p per minute during peak hours. Compulink Information Exchange (CIX) provides full access at 3.60/hour poeak rate. Access to BRS, and other databases is available, assuming prior arrangements with suppliers.

Most information about the Internet assumes that a PC will be used as the access machine. Some useful information for Apple users is provided. He points out that there are 35,000 servers on the Web and claims that 100 new sites are added every day. Consider that WWW is 'the information vehicle of the decade'. The way a user obtains access to the Internet in the UK is typical and is described here: user may connect a personal computer to an Internet provider who is operating a log-on, sometimes called a shell, account with an access provider. The simplest connection is machine-modem-dial-up telephone line using SLIP (Serial Line Internet Protocol) or a later version of it PPP (Point to Point Protocol). Data generated by the machine or received from the provider will be in packets managed by the Internet Protocol (IP), which assembles machine data into packets and dissembles packets from the Internet into machine readable data. Other ways of connecting include the ISDN, X25 (see Glossary) if an intermediate packet-switched network is being used, or leased line if heavy usage is expected.

Access providers usually provide not just one POP (Point Of access Point) at some central point, but several around the country. This enables a user to select the nearest POP for connection in order to minimize telecom fees: In major countries the collection of POPs operated by a number of access providers enables most people to find one which is close to their address.

Browsers and search tools

A server may by browsed by any user who has the associated client browser program. For example, to connect to a World Wide Web server the server's address should be prefixed with the letters HTTP (Hyper Text Transfer Protocol). This negotiates admission for the browser and initiates the use of HTTP for message control. Browsers usually contain search tools, which range from the crude to the moderately effective. The tools enable a user to search the material which is available to that browser. Searching for information from a well-organized information database is an unequal struggle, which was the founding problem of Information Science (see 'Indexing' in chapter 4). Searching the Internet adds further dimensions and greater difficulties which, by and large, remain to be tackled.

Because of the specific problems of searching rather than browsing, the former is described below in a separate section.

The World Wide Web

The WWW is the Internet service mainly responsible for the recent rapid growth in the numbers of hosts and users. In some useful information provided for Apple users, points out that there are 35,000 servers on the Web and claims that 100 new sites are added every day. Consider that WWW is 'the information vehicle of the decade'. A good information source for Internet Services and Standards.

An Englishman working at the CERN Physics Laboratory, development Web protocols Hypertext Mark-up Language (HTML) and the Hypertext Transport Protocol (HTTP).

HTML is like a simplified form of the Standard General Mark-up Language (SGML) used for defining the format of technical documents and manuals. HTML includes the interlinking ('hyperlinks') of separate but related items as used in the original Apple HyperCard software. HTTP moves data quickly from point to point using Internet's TCP/IP transmission protocol. HTML includes the Internet's name of a server and the name of the file on it holding data hyperlinked to the source document. Provides an example describing a video clip in a remote computer using a string of symbols called the clip's Universal Resource Locator (URL):

Click < A HREE = "http://www.noware.com intmovie.mpeg">
for an interesting move.</A>

"www.noware.com" is the address of a computer containing a file called "intmovie.mpeg", "impeg" meaning that the file is mpeg-Compressed. A Web browser on a user's client computer which has downloaded a document containing this URL will contain he phrase 'click for an interesting movie.' When this phrase is pointed to with a mouse and clicked, a copy of the video clip will be transferred from the server to the client machine and the file can be viewed as long as the client computer contains the appropriate decompression software.

The Web is arranged in client-server form. The server stores data, and provided a client computer contains compatible browser software, server data may be read on the client via the network. Web servers store documents containing pointers linking an object in a document (e.g. a word or phrase) to other documents on the same or a different server. HTML enables pointers to be inserted and HTTP handles the linkage mechanism. Hopefully the association between the source object and the destination object will reveal another relevant document, or a relevant part of it.

The Hyper-G browser 'supports tools for structuring, maintaining, and serving heterogeneous data. It guarantees automatic hyperlink consistency, and supports hyperlinks among multimedia documents, full-text retrieval, and a Unix-like security system.' Hyperlinks are indicated in a document as 'anchor' items—for instance, a highlighted word. Hyper-G will also support anchors in graphics, sounds, 3D objects, Postscript documents, or video clips. The author of a document must indicate which items within his or her material should be designated hyperlink anchors—for instance, a word might be highlighted. The anchor may indicate a hyperlink connection to a relevant part of the same document, a different document on the same site, or a document on another site. The author becomes involved in a kind of indexing operation. The effectiveness of information retrieval by searching carried out by hopping from and anchor to other documents and, in turn, from those documents to further documents, depends on an author's earlier activity as an 'indexer'. As just mentioned, the existence of such connection is at the discretion of authors.

A cross-platform language called Java was developed by Sun Computers in 1995. If an HTML tag called an <applet> is used on a page being run on a HotJava browser, the referenced URL is read and some byte code is transferred to the client page. A Java virtual machine (a small package of software associated with the user machine operating system) will execute an application at that position on the page. For example, a weather applet devised by Sun has its own URL. When a HotJava browser comes across a page containing that applet, it reads the URL, transfers a weather map on the page, and provides for an interactive application—if the mouse is moved on to a city and clicked, the current temperature, wind speed, and humidity of that city appear at the top of the screen. Note that this idea greatly increases the information content of a page, with more information being released when a user interacts with it.

Java is an object-oriented programming language which will run on any machine provided that it contains a Java virtual machine compatible with its own operating system. Major Web browsers are available in alternative forms for major machines, and the latest versions of them will adopt Java. In December 1995 announced that they would adopt Java tools for applications. IBM will be using Java to enable objects to be sent to and retrieved from client machines.

Setting up your own service on WWW

If you wish to set up a Web site, space may be rented on an access provider's computer, or your own site with its server may be connected to an access provider company via a dedicated line of adequate capacity. Server software may be downloaded from the Edinburgh or other Web sites. Your site needs to be named and registered with the CERN laboratory and major search engines. Pages of text need to be converted into HTML form. Creating and maintaining a Web site is a job for professionals. Most people will access the Web via a dial-up telephone line to the computer of an access company or by hiring a dedicated line according to how much they want to use it.

If most of the people for whom you wish to set up a service are already Internet users, setting up your own service with the Web for interconnections may be a net benefit. Required frequency of use will determine one major component of the cost, ranging from hiring space on the computer of an access company using dial-up access to leasing a dedicated line.

The other major cost is organizing your data into a suitable format and ensuring that your service enables others to find the information they want easily when they use it. If advantage is to be taken of hypertext links enabling a user to hop from one place to another, then you will need to know about HTML described above. The right person to set up a service is a librarian or information scientist who knows how organize a search and retrieval system.

No doubt many people set up a service because they cannot resist the new toy or because of the keeping-up-with-the-Joneses syndrome, with the value of rapid communication and the ability to change it on a daily basis as a secondary consideration. But unless the service is easy to use and accommodates information that users need, the novelty will wear off and so will usage.

Searching and data delivery

To quote one librarian: 'Finding what you want may be difficult. Internet is like a library where all the books are piled on the floor in disorganised heaps with no organisation or indexing....except that lots of little gnomes throw the books around so they're never in the same place next day.' If there are 4 million hosts—and no centrally organized method for finding one wanted item out of, say, at least 100 million in total, it is hardly surprising that finding what you want is a difficult, sometimes impossibly difficult, task.

The scale of the Internet and the fact that it was developed without plans for searching has prompted the development of several 'search engine' facilities associated with browsers as shown in Table 8.2. ARCHIE, Gopher and VERONICA (Very

Easy Rodent Oriented Netwide Index to Computerized Archives) were followed by the WWW containing hyperlinks which act as a search aid. Hyperlinks are used in search engines developed for use with the Web such as Web Crawler and Lycos. Other newer search tools include Yahoo and IBM's QBIC search system (see chapter 10). QBIC enables searching for images by colour, texture, pattern, or shape, or combinations thereof. Shape questions may be devised like 'Are there any pictures of red cars with six wheels?'

In addition to search tool effectiveness a user must consider the volume of information available to a browser's search tool (see Table 8.2).

Table 8.2 Browsers and searchable documents

Tool name	Number of documents
Lycos	11M
Excite	1.5M
Open Text	1M
Infoseek Net Search	1M
Web Crawler	250,00
Yahoo	85,000
Galaxy	55,000

Yahoo (Yet Another Hierarchical Officious Oracle) was reintroduced in July 1995 following a survey of 67,000 users students at Standford University. Later they formed a business, earning revenue by advertising, and maintaining and improving the system. This browser is exceptional because it includes a search screen showing fourteen major subject categories in hierarchies, each with up to nine sub-categories, for example:

Regional
US states
Idaho
Boise
Education
Colleges
Biose State University
Departments and programs
History of Western civilization

Hyperlinks are included at all levels. Yahoo's entries are found by starting at its home page; searches may include Boolean AND and OR logic. Yahoo searching is believed to be at present the only system providing facilities based on library practices. Yahoo grew rapidly during 1995 but its weakness at present is it that it contains a relatively small number of searchable documents.

The impression may be given that indexing and searching are a simple business. In an article entitled 'Web Search', under the heading 'Basic Indexing', talks about WAIS: 'Once you've got the index built it's a snap to connect Web clients to it.' The essence of the system—the indexing arrangements themselves—is not discussed.

Describes several search engines, Lycos in particular, showing a search using the phrase 'Turning machine'. Lycos uses 'a probabilistic technique to skip from server to server catching URL's'. The results are not described in enough detail to assess the effectiveness of the search.

Mention the Web's 'free-wheeling....largely uncommercial nature .... analogous with a library where all the books have been donated by patrons and placed randomly on the shelves'. The authors describe a search using the Web Crawler Indeed 'covering more than 50,000 documents on 9,000 servers ....constituting a credible test site for assessing the utility of network discovery tools as foraging facilitators'. Using the phrase 'citation analysis' for searching, they consider the results to be 'strikingly idiosyncratic'. With the exception of the first hit, 'it is not at all clear how any of the others might relate, directly or tangentially, to the topic of "citation analysis."

Lists URLs for a number of medical servers and comments on Web search engines, which she considers 'offer high returns in the quantity of resources yet low discrimination in terms of the relevance and quality of information delivered .... traversing links can be time consuming and sometimes fruitless'. She goes on to describe several organizations which are currently assessing the usefulness of Web sites. A new service called OMNI will provide UK access to high quality biomedical resources that the filtered, evaluated, described, and classified.'

Internet files, containing diverse unstructured texts covering all aspects of human endeavour (of which science forms a small part) have become searchable during only about the last three years. Moreover, the Internet was evolved from a system for academic information exchange rather like a glorified bulletin board. Its files were not designed to be readily searchable, although the Yahoo browser/searcher mentioned above should help.

This situation may be compared with systems for the online searching of databases covering the scientific literature. In the three hundred and thirty years which have elapsed since the Journal des Scavans [sic] and Philosophical Transactions were first published, numerous databases and methods of retrieving information from a structured scientific literature have been developed for searching thousands of scholarly journals. Searches for scientific information are still usually carried out by intermediaries but the ubiquity of the Internet encourages the efforts of naive users to search it. The Web has acquired a bad name, reflecting poor search results obtained by over-expectant searchers. It would seem to be even more necessary, whenever possible, to get an experienced searcher to search the Internet on your behalf. You may want to enjoy the serendipity, if not the noise, or a searcher may not be available. In these cases be prepared to spend a very long time doing it yourself while your telecom charges mount up. The amount of traffic and the size of the files being moved may exceed the network's ability to transport data within a reasonable period of time—a symptom of the Web's growth rate. The Web's servers and its client browsers can handle bit-intensive multimedia. When network use increases unaccompanied by an appropriate increase in channel bandwidth, it takes longer to transport a file. Things will get worse before they get better.

An experienced Internet user, has described frustration caused by network limitations:

> I have given up using ftp after mid morning because the transfer rates that I achieve are impossibly slow, simply because of the number of users on the networks. Add to that the videoconferencing and broadcast systems that can now be used over the Internet, and you will end up with a network that is next to useless for communications and information retrieval.

Throwing a question at the system without regard to necessary preliminaries is more likely to generate frustration than answers. It will pay off to find out more about sites likely to contain information of the kind which is required. Start with a known URL if possible. Using Hyperlinks in a search tool such as the Web Crawler may produce some results. Choose local sites containing indexed information which will not include the delays inherent in using remotely stored files or search engines. Accumulate search notes during every search for future use. There is a huge amount of literature about the Internet but not much about effective search procedures. Some work needs to be done on how specific items of information may be located and retrieved from the huge volume stored on Web servers without consuming large amounts of time.

Workstations in the computer department at the University of Southampton are on the university's network, itself connected to the Internet via Super JANET. At 14.30 UK time I asked a user to retrieve a picture using the World Wide Web. He was unfamiliar with the availability of picture files and eventually found a database about the Vatican library which contained pictures and retrieved a picture of unknown resolution and colour fidelity. After 10 minutes a small part of it had been scanned out at the top of the screen. It was going to take perhaps an hour to be delivered but we did not wait. The user said that the net slowed down considerably during peak periods, but allowing for that it was obvious that the delivery period for a picture file over the connection route picked up on this occasion was unacceptably slow although compression/decompression was being used.

The Internet: commercial activity, payments, security

Expansion of business applications on the Internet is restricted by security considerations. Many people seem more relaxed about security than they used to be—for example, they will quote their credit card number over the telephone. Compuserve's 'UK shopping centre', in association with Interflora, and others, arranges payment by asking customers to key in their credit card number.

Evidently this procedure is considered to be unsatisfactory. Visa and Mastercard, with their partners Microsoft and Netscape respectively, tried to arrange better security, but in late 1995 they announced that they had failed to reach an agreement. A group of 65 banks, companies, and government agencies called the Financial Services Technology Consortium (FSTC) is now trying to establish a standard for electronic commerce.

Academic researchers have a natural bias to the open exchange of information; for business, however, secure communications is a basic requirement. Also no business is going to make a serious commitment to the Web, possibly risking its commercial future, unless it has confidence—and ideally, some say, in the Web standardisation process.

(Dettmer 1996)

A new business organization has been formed called the World Wide Web Consortium (W3C). As at October 1995 there were 50 US members, 37 European, and 8 Asian. Secure communications and other Web issues are being worked on.

Internet is an 'electronic toolbox of business functions'. File Transfer Protocol may be used for 'fast easy and cheap office-to-office file sharing'. A UK manager is quoted as saying that the Internet is heavily used for communicating with the head office in the States.

However, two UK companies, Forrester Research and Phonelink report a very different picture from their surveys. Barriers include lack of widespread reliable network access, low access speed, and lack of security. Only 27 per cent of 211 executives surveyed said that it contributed to their business. 'The undoubted potential of the Internet has not yet been matched by its ability to deliver practical business benefits'.

By contrast, reports that the chairman of the FCC believes that computer networks are the single biggest factor behind restoring productivity in the United States economy. Referring to the Internet in particular, he think that

> the government should intervene as little as possible except to ensure competition ... competition will sort out such issues as how much bandwidth should every home, what sort of interfaces customers prefer, and the content that should be drawn down different pipes.

Security is unimportant for Internet academic communications, but that is not the case for the large amount of business and commercial data now passing round it. Security may be obtained with routers and 'firewalls'. Firewalls include the use of secure application gateways requiring user identification and password; packet filters allowing only specified access and capable of coping with certain security flaws may also be used.

Payment for Internet services is an interesting topic. People who think that the Internet is free are mistaken. Some costs, such as network costs, can be hidden from users because their employer pays for them.

Those who cannot afford to wait for the half hour which it may take to carry out a search during busy hours may have to turn to changed services. Unisys has started to charge licensing frees for certain compression algorithms; consequently Compuserve will probably start charging for programs which use that algorithm.

Security is important in financial transactions involving, for instance, payment mechanisms for goods in home shopping, and those which need personal or business privacy. A big effort is in progress to perfect secure electronic payment systems and they are gradually being introduced. Reviews the requirements and options available for making secure payment. He concludes that interest is growing rapidly and a number of trials are in progress, particularly by suppliers of Web software.

Pipex, one of the largest Internet service providers in Europe, was testing its newly installed security system in May 1995. It will provide a service for the end-to-end encryption of credit card details with authentication and clearing for cards used by home shoppers.

Netscape started a new service at the end of 1995 using a Secure Sockets Layer (SSL) for its Netscape Navigator Browser. When they are connected to a Netsite Web server all data exchanges are encrypted (see the superhighway section at the end of this chapter). A key in the corner of the screen shows that data are being transferred securely; a broken key indicates that SSL is not being used. Otherwise a user will not know whether or not a transmission is secure.

For organizations using Internet as an inter-site network, as US company, Raptor, will set up the sites as a virtual private network with message authentication, encryption, and access rules. In June 1995 IBM announced that it would now provide connection-secure Web browsers and servers for its OS/2 and Aix-based systems. It also offered Secure Hypertext Transfer Protocol (S-HTTP) and SSL. IBM's secure browser called the Web Explorer for OS/2 provides drag and drop and graphic streaming facilities.

In a Byte review Singleton (1995) mentions two secure electronic payment systems to be introduced by Visa/Microsoft and Master Cards/Netscape. Singleton also describes six different existing commercial secure electronic payment systems. In June 1995, First Data, the largest company processing bank cards in the UK, merged with the First Financial Management Corporation which owns a subsidiary called Nabanco dealing with card settlements. Nabanco will be using a secure payments system developed by Microsoft for its proposed new network, a deal between Microsoft and Intuit for a similar purpose having been called off. Sun is also considering a secure payments system. Large companies are taking a growing interest in secure payment systems for networks. Their use in financial transactions looks like becoming the norm before long.

The Internet: making telephone calls

Internet phoneware software can be purchased from several vendors.

When a call comes in, a tone sounds on the user's computer; the user then clicks on an icon contained in the phone software and this displays the caller's name.

The quality of speech depends on the type of compression used, the speed of the modem, the sampling rate, and certain other matters. At 9.6 Kbps the quality is poor; at 28.8 Kbps it should be satisfactory. If the machine is not connected to the Internet at the time, the caller is informed. If the recipient accepts the call, it is routed to the other party via each party's connection to their local Internet service provider. The phone software vendor will operate directory services of various kinds, accessible through the vendor's directory server. Directories will probably be regularly updated. You can download a directory and edit it to provide your own telephone book.

The Internet : broadcasting (sound)

Points out that 'becoming an audio broadcaster on the Internet requires far less sophisticated and less costly hardware' than is required for multimedia or video activities. Organizations like ABC and others are already providing news broadcasts. The World Radio Network repeats its short-wave broadcasts over the Internet using a 45 bps line to connect its server to the M-bone. Browsers will soon be expected to support Multipurpose Internet Mail Extensions (MIME), which include the provision for handling audio streams.

The Internet and multimedia

Since 1991, traffic running at 45 Mbps has become possible at 16 major sites on the NSFnet part of Internet. The use of cable-TV as a wideband network connected to Internet was scheduled to be introduced during 1994. The idea is to connect organizations using 10 Mbps Ethernet to a 100 Mbps Metropolitan Area Network (MAN), itself connected to Internet via Performance Systems International (PSI) cable-TV channels.

The possible exchange of multimedia data over the Internet is discussed. Worthington consider that USENET, which offers network news, is a good source of information about images. There are also some actual image files available such as weather maps, geological survey pictures, and satellite images, to be retrieved from the TELNET archieves; or, using a special File Transfer Protocol (Ftp), from various other sources. A version of FTP called Anonymous FTP does not require a user ID or password for publicly available files. You may use your e-mail address as a password. A huge volume of data exists on these files.

E-mail over the Internet is now used by many organizations. With low cost and fast delivery it is believed to account for much of the Internet's traffic. At present security is inadequate unless special measures are taken. Internet e-mail suffers from the usual e-mail problems.

- Uncertainly whether the message has reached its destination
- Uncertainly about delivery if addressed to an organization rather than an individual
- Doubts about compatibility if spreadsheets or other documents types are e-mailed

- Doubts about recipient's ability to decompress if compression is used
- Lack of sophistication of people using the system.
- Clogging up systems with junke e-mail
- Necessity to take special security measures

'Telecommunications administrations are willing to provide new interactive services' but they do not cite any evidence for that claim. Instead they discuss the need to standarzie elements of 'Multimedia and hypermedia information retrieval services' and Audio-visual Interactive Services (AVI) in particular. Discuss the requirement for standardization in terms of 'scriptware' considered 'as a view on a set of objects assembled for a particular usage'.

The progress of these idea within the CCITT and ISO committees mentioned will show whether such work is too far ahead of the market and whether attention will be concentrated on real needs. For general communication over Internet between any two users, the maximum bandwidth, and so telecoms speed, is that of the link in the chain with the narrowest, bandwidth. In practice this is about 128 Kbps, meaning that such a link could carry data at about 5 Mbps if compressed by 40 to 1. This is satisfactory for many data types but is inadequate for television and multimedia.

The Internet problems

Traffic problems on the Internet have been described by : 300,000 files, many of megabyte size, were downloaded from a NASA server during one week in July 1994. In a peak hour 6000 requests were handled. The possibility of having to close down the service was considered.

The Internet needs better addressing facilities. They will be incorporated in a new version of its TCP/IP protocol to be called IPng or IPv6. The draft protocol calls for a 16-byte address field—more comparable with the OSI 20 bytes field. Its present field can contain only 4 bytes. Sooner or later Internet will be improved, presumably by installing adapters, wretches, routers, and hubs so that versions of Fast Ethernet may be used.

Acceptable quality for digital television services, the basis for public entertainment, is hard to specify. At present the 128 Kbps M-Bone limits quality to small frames in a window recurring at from one to four frames per second. But 5 Mbps data compressed by 40:1 are 129 Kbps—a quality adequate for some purposes. It seems likely that a 200:1 ratio will become usable without too much loss of data enabling to be transmitted at 25 Mbps—well well short of good full-screen motion-picture reproduction.

The Internet protocol TCP/IP is also a constraint for some applications, particularly entertainment. But for many purposes, relatively poor-quality low-cost Internet videoconferencing may be preferred to a more expensive, specially leased wideband line. A distance learning project at a US naval school and an underwater science scheme developed, using Internet as a videoconferencing link, have been described with enthusiasm.

A lawyer, for drawing attention to regulation on the Internet. 'Most of the media's concerns,' he says, 'have been with hyping on-line shopping and video on demand rather than discussing the necessary liberties and legal frameworks for cyberspace.' Murray also raises the well-known argument about whether information providers should behave like common carriers who accept responsibility for the delivery of a message but not its contents. Siegal complains that the Internet is not a good medium for commerce, but at the same time aroused controversy by advertising on the Internet the fact that her law company would help people to enter a US immigration lottery. It turned out that the company was 'charging 95 to submit a name and address to the Immigration Service whereas anyone could do it simply by mailing a postcard to the local Us consulate.'

Can't see how freedom to advertise on the Internet can be easily restricted: 'all data looks the same'. He asks how a node can be expected to differentiate between data packets originating from 'Siegel's advertising mill' and advertising coming from an anonymous mail server in Finland.

It is difficult to find out about the usefulness of Internet for particular requirements because there is no consensus. In the heading of an article, the author says that 'Bringing the Internet to today's business environment is crucial for companies keen to exploit the opportunities for economy and better customer service'. The article extols the virtues of Lotus Internotes and the Electronic Embassy for providing information about foreign embassy services on the WWW.

But according to the Aslib (London) publication IT Link, the World Wide Web seems to be 'stuck in a rut producing a plethora of rather pointless self-publicity material for individuals and institutions, together with some interesting, but hardly useful, multimedia tasters.' Blakeman, also writing in IT Link, says that she is beginning to wonder 'if it is worth all the hassle.' These words come at the end of article which starts with 'If anyone tells you that surfing the Net is a piece of cake, point them in my direction and I will convince them of the error in their ways.' She particularly recommends something called Netdial, which provides connection to five different services and provides a log of your activities. The trouble is that to find Netdial, Blakeman must first type 'ftp.sunet.se/pub/pc/windows/winsock-indstate/netdial/nd250s.zip'.

Other Networks

The JANET and Super JANET networks

The Joint Academic Network (JANET), an X25 packet-switched network interconnecting several major Packet Switching Exchanges in the UK, is in turn connected to a number of universities and research establishments X25 is the CCIT recommendation for the interface between asynchronous Data Terminal Equipment (DTE), and the point of entry to a packet-switched network (Data Circuit terminating Equipment (DCE)). The JANET network has been upgraded to work at 2 Megabits per second (Mbps) over most of its links. JANET was established by the Computer Board in 1984. By 1990 over 130 institutions were connected to it. JANET is connected to Internet, using the TCP/IP protocol. JANET users are not charged, but the suppliers of some services may charge. A project called Super JANET was first discussed in 1989 and in 1992 British Telecom was awarded a contract for 18 million to provide and operate this new fibre-optic network working at up to 622 Mbps. The operation is breaking new ground, and may encounter fewer regulatory constraints since it is a 'private' system not publicly available and so not subject to regulation politics. When the project started in 1993 it ran at 34Mbps, with six sites interconnected.

Super JANET uses Switched multimegabit Data Service (SMDS) under its immediate future telecoms regime until it changes to Asynchronous Transfer Mode (ATM) protocol. SMDS is a 'bandwidth on demand' system enabling what amounts to 'closed user group' transactions to be processed. The network will also incorporate a billing system so that, if necessary, charges may be made for services. SMDS is a 'cell based' not a 'packet based' system (Cawkell 1993b), so picture data are transmitted as a virtually continuous data stream to arrive in one piece. Under SMDS, 'user channels' may, in effect, be set up between a terminal on a network and the server at the database end. It will appear to the users as if he has a dedicated line to the database.

'Intelligent' Networks (IN)

This term, coined by the Bell Organisation, implies that a range of easily selectable services will be available over a network. The network may include the provision of a Private Virtual Network, that is, a switched network of the type normally only available in private line system, but whose costs are closer to the costs of a public network. Such a network would include the facilities of an ISDN network, with enhancements. The phrase has come into use to imply certain facilities which are expected to evolve with these networks. Networks will embody the necessary circuits and software needed to control and deliver the kinds of services permitted by the much wider bandwidth.

Central databases will control a wide range of network services such as billing and credit card payments. When a customer initiates a toll-free or credit card call, it will be intercepted and managed by the signalling network, which directs it to a centralized database. The database handles the call and returns it through the network to the appropriate switch for completion. The network provides 'intelligence' centralized in databases and its features are no longer solely dependent on resident network hardware and software.

Abernethy and Munday (1995) make several points:

- It may take a considerable time to install switch-based new services.
- A key requirement is to separate basic functions such as path switching, from the software controlling new advanced features.
- The requirements for the rapid introduction of new services

are driving developments.

- Reliance on switch manufacturers for new services needs to be reduced.
- The ability to offer integrated service packages must be improved.

'Intelligent Peripherals' which would provide additional functions needed could be:

- Special voice announcements
- Synthesized voice or speech recognition
- Audio conference bridging
- Information distribution bridging
- Protocol conversion
- Text-to-speech synthesis

They remark on the importance of IN Standards (see chapter 9). Their comments fall short of the comments quoted earlier, about the expected benefits of intelligent Networks. In an articleabout future possibilities rather then current Standards, three kinds of network, are envisaged: interactive cable-TV networks, packet data networks, and multimedia networks. 'The suppliers of multimedia services information will become utilities.'

'Information appliances' will plug into utilities as today's domestic appliances plug into the gas, communications, or electricity utilities.

'Intelligent Agent' is a phrase gaining ground to describe a chore executed by software embodying artificial intelligence functions. Both IBM and AT&T are reported to be developing networks with agents. An agent stands in for a subscriber as a proxy.

According to IBM's Alter Ego, for example, will undertake an instruction such as: 'If I get mail from the CEO, page me. If I get any faxes from Finland, forward them to my hotel in Orlando; send all other mail to Murray.'

Personal Communication Networks (PCN)

PCN is intended to provide communications over a wide area. Accordingly the access network of fixed radio stations are placed in cells in a similar manner to existing cellular radio systems.

A new generation of cordless telephones called CT2 was developed in the UK and later the idea spread to the United

States, where there were a large number of applications to the FCC for licences. A user would be connected to the public network via antennae (aerials) along major highways and his portable radio-telephone, providing wireless access to the PSTN.

Later, introduced a third-generation system called CT3 which included two-way calling. In 1991 a UK licensee called United estimated that there were nearly 8 million households as potential users, and trials indicated that there could be 1.8 million households who would actually use the system.

The Digital European Cordless Telecommunications (DECT) system is a development of CT2 able to run on the ISDN and working in the 1880-1900 MHz band. The DECT standard was finalized by ETSI in July 1992. Each European country which is a member of the EC must make the frequency band 1880 to 1900 MHz available for DECT systems. These could include business or residential applications, mobile radio or personal communication services.

GSM 900 is a complete network system for a Pan European Digital Cellular network operating on a 890-915 MHz band uplink, and 935-960 MHz downlink. The appropriate Standards for GSM were approved by ETSI in 1990 and incorporated in the DCS 1800 Standard. The Standard provided various options and design alternatives.

Personal Communication Networks will fit in somewhere between Mobile Cellular Radio and Telepoint. Telepoint's success will be badly affected unless it is well established before PCN arrives. In fact PCN appears to be a much improved Telepoint. The system will be quite similar to Mobile Cellular—radio handsets, base stations in cells, and network accessing and interconnecting services. The range of the pocket-size radio handsets will be shorter so there will be more cells—perhaps including individual short-range cells covering a household or a farm. Personal Communication Networks progressed from idea to development work to service licensing in a remarkable short time. In January 1990, the UK department of Trade and Industry (DTI) awarded PCN licences to Mercury/Motorola/Telefonica, British Aerospace/Matra/Millicom/Pacific Telesis/Sony, and United formed by STC/US West/Thorn EMI/DBP Telekon.

PCN users will carry cheap portable radio telephones communicating via the PCN base-stations. However, the companies just mentioned reconsidered their positions because of slow take-off. The technology has not yet been fully worked out—but that does not deter the forecasters. It has been estimated that the European market will be worth 635 million by 1996, with the UK taking 43 per cent, France 11 per cent, Germany 8 per cent, and others 38 per cent.

Cable-TV networks

Cable-TV networks are the odd man out in the categories of network here described because they were originally developed for one purpose only—the distribution of television data to viewers who were outside the range of television broadcast stations. Later they became the means of providing a large choice of stations regardless of geographical location, from a single multi-channel cable-TV connection.

In the United States, satellite links with the necessary bandwidth for interconnecting widely spaced centres of population with local cable TV centres became available in the late 1970s. First Amendment considerations restricted such systems until the Nixon administration reversed the Johnson decision by introducing an 'open skies' policy. Plurality of choice then removed the end for FCC regulation. By 1982 there were estimated to be 25 million subscribers in the US, but today about 65 per cent of all US homes are connected.

In Belgium over 80 per cent of homes are connected while in the UK the number is about 600,000 connected, although growth is rapid.

The case for considering cable-TV for multimedia transmission in the United States is twofold. First, it is second only to the telephone network as a ubiquitous telecoms media, and second, being designed for television signals, it is wideband.

The performance of cable systems depends on layouts. With 'tree and branch' the main supply line splits off to separate cables for delivery to households, where a desired channel is selected. With 'star' networks—an arrangement amenable to interactive two-way services—cables radiate out to local distribution boxes from which channels are switched into the cable for each household as controlled by the cable operator according to the customer's subscription schedule.

Most cable-TV network systems in the US provide a choice

of 110 channels, each occupying a band 6 MHz within a cable with a 54-750 MHz bandwidth.

The American Television & Communications Corporation (ATC)—a cable company with 4 million subscribers—has provided some information about its technology, particularly in regard to the feasibility of wiring homes with fibre. ATC are running fibrepotic cable from the head-end at the cable control centre along the existing coaxial cable ducts to distant network nodes, the coax having been disconnected. The existing coax from nodes to subscribers completes the network. Consequently the noise generated by, and the power supply and maintenance required by, the amplifiers at intervals along the disconnected coax are no longer a matter of concern. ATC consider this evolutionary 'fiber backbone' approach and the introduction of other necessarily gradual pay-as-you-go measures to be appropriate because 'the enormous investment in completely new plant necessitated by a radical change to new architecture would be highly imprudent unless set-off by huge new revenue streams.'

The implication is that all-fibre systems are going to be slow in arriving in the US and even slower in other countries.

Figure 8.2 (after Large 1995) shows how the frequency spectrum in a cable for supplying 500 homes in a US systems for new markets might be used. The arrangement would provide 62 channels of analogue and HDTV video, and 330 switched digitally compressed program channels shared with others. The 'upstream' spectrum is reserved for signals originated by users.

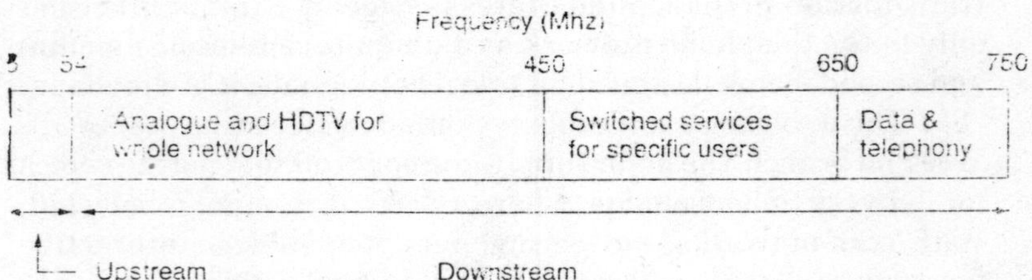

Fig. 13.2

Such a cable with this bandwidth in a modern system would consist of a fibre 'backbone' from the head end to a local node with coaxial cable from that point to each of 500 households.

A Video Dial Tone network (Dixit 1995) is a relatively new idea for organizing a joint wideband cable-telephone system for VOD and interactive TV services. It provides equal access for multimedia providers and dial-up services for users. Audio, video, and data streams are multiplexed into each 6 MHz channel. Control and management functions and signalling are handled by a separate network which connects to users and providers. The arrangement allows for any number of servers from different information providers to be connected to users for 'near VOD' services for movies with a maximum waiting-to-start time of 15 minutes for any movie selected. ATM switching is used to switch movies from one channel to another.

According to the Oracle company has already supplied a storage unit to one of its customers with a capacity approaching one terabyte. A future requirement for a library holding the world's estimated 65,000 films compressed to 1.5 Gbytes per film would be for 95 Tbytes of storage.

Synchronization and timing

Review some of the problems that may arise in synchronizing sound to video. The authors describe the SMPTE time code described below and the Vertical Interval Time Code (VITC), recordable within the vertical interval between video frames. The authors emphasize the importance and difficulties of synchronizing sound when video compression and non-interlaced frames are used.

Continuous synchronization refers to lip sync, music-video sync, etc. Event driven synchronization may be fixed by a user, or by the reaching of a particular point in a presentation. Both types are particularly important in distributed multimedia applications where a number of computers are interconnected by one or more networks and may be accessing different information sources. The most obvious multimedia requirement for synchronization is 'lip sync'—audible speech correctly synchronized with visible lip movements. Another is the need to synchronize audio clips with video clips during an authoring/editing session. Yet another occurs during the transmission of data of different kinds of aremote location via networks using different protocols. The transmission needs to appear to be 'seamless' and synchronized.

In a presentation to be recorded on, say, videotape, a passage of music or speech must start and end at the same instant as the related sequence of video frames, and remain in synchronism for its duration. Presentation software incorporating a 'time line' or 'construction window', makes the editing process easier. Editing is carried out on either MIDI data or a sound waveform (see chapter 6, pp. 157-9). In Premiere, for instance, a video clip and the audio data which were recorded with it are locked in synchronism. However, you may want to accompany a motion video clip with background music recorded separately. In this case the video clip, represented by an icon, is dragged on to the video track on the time line and the first frame of it is displayed; the named sound recording, represented as a 'forzen waveform', is dragged on to the audio time line and positioned to correspond to the starting point of the video frame. When recorded for presentation, the music will be heard at the right time to accompany the video.

A way of dealing with synchronization more precisely is to use the Society of Motion Picture and Televisions Engineers (SMPTE) time code—widely adopted for audio and video synchronization purposes; it may be used for finding a particular video recording. Each frame in a TV programme can be individually identified and located by the SMPTE hours/minutes/seconds/frame code. For example 01:18:39:3 means 1 hour: 18 minutes: 39 minutes: 3. For videotape these data are recorded as an 80-bit word on every frame by a time code generator in a process called striping. The code is recorded in the vertical blanking interval and is then known as the vertical interval time code.

For other media it may be recorded on a track such as an audio track, and is then known as linear time code. Time codes are written on to tape by some camcorders, or may be recorded using a Time Code Recorder. For sound a similar technique is available called the MIDI time clock, which send MIDI time code (MTC) down the MIDI cable connection.

For serious work, machines are available, such as the Timecode Machine from Opcode, which enables MIDI data to be timed with the SMPTE time code and synchronized with SMPTE-encoded video frames.

Alternatively, a general way of implementing sound/visual sync is to arrange for a visual cue to pick up the appropriate instant on the music track by aligning the audio track with the visual cue—for instance, a video frame. The alignment of visual to audio is done against the displayed MIDI time code track.

Distribution and synchronization in multimedia networks

Requirements for multicast networks capable of transporting multimedia data are of particular interest because such networks will be required for the Information Superhighway, assuming that the ideas of its more ambitious supporters come to fruition.

For example, discuss service control and management of a broadband network conveying information from a large number of third-party interactive and distribution services. A consortium called TINA-C of about 40 telecoms companies is attempting to define an information networking architecture for the purpose.

Parts of a distributed system which may cause transmissions to become asynchronous are discussed see Figure 8.3. points out that the end-to-end delays in multiple data streams include skew (difference in presentation time between supposedly synchronized objects), jitter, utilization (for example, duplication or dropping of video frames), and speed differences.

The proposed method for eliminating asynchrony consists of introducing controlled buffer storage large enough to smooth out the maximum end-to-end or latency delays. Extra delay is introduced by controlling the rate at which a bufer releases data in order to bring about synchronization.

Synchronizing sound and vision with the aid of authoring software for a presentation was described in chapter 6. The process of actually ensuring that it is done effectively has not been very well covered in the literature. Synchronizing in distributed multimedia network systems—an essential requirement for the Information Superhighway—is still being researched.

Most people working in this field consider that users will demand a certain Quality of Service (QOS), mainly in regard to delay-sensitive data and freedom from errors. Because of the different kinds of errors and timing in different kinds of data, for instance, between video and audio, the usual way of dealing with the problem is to separate data into different major categories and arrange to control them separately to bring about synchronizations.

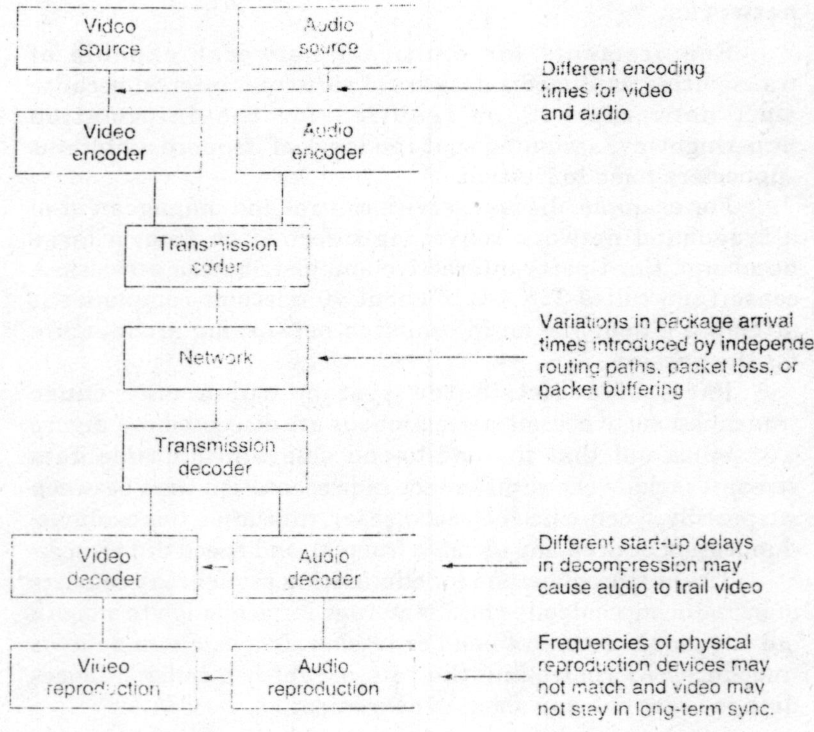

Fig. 13.3 Causes of asynchrony in a distributed multimedia system
Source: alter Fuhrt (1994)

Aspects of the problem confined to a database system rather than to those introduced by networked transmission are considered by saiedian and Awad (1993). The database is imagined to be divided into media-specific sections such as voice database, visual database, etc. Each section has its Media Specific Synchronizer (MSS), with all MSSs controlled by a Global Sync Manager (GSM) which receives messages from the Database Management System (DBMS). When a user sends in a request, the DBMS sends it to the GSM, which breaks it down into parts to be sent to a media-specific section and to provide processing information regarding start, pause, resume, etc. For example, if a user viewing already delivered video requests it to stop, the GSS ensures that associated voice or music also stops.

Networks may be of the 'one-to-many' or 'many-to-many' types, but a large public system is likely to be of the 'several-to-many' type. Propose a large public system to serve the area in southern California and include a description of a proposed synchronizing technique. The scheme consists of a number of information providers connected to a hub operated by a metropolitan areas provider such as pacific Bell. The hub contains a server with numerous disks, distribution being controlled by an ATM switch. The metropolitan hub connects to a number of smaller huns, each with an ATM switch, which handle local requirements such as the university library, the La jolla residential area, etc. The authors provide an unrealistically small example of a 100-client system in a residential neighbourhood capable of supplying a service of 100 video programmes, each one hour long. The suggested storage requirement for MPEG-2 compressed data to be delivered at 4 Mbps is $4 \times 100 \times 60 \times 60/8 = 180$ Gbytes.

To carry the data for switching and assuming that nearly all the data are downstream, the switch needs to handle 100 clients all looking at different programmes, so its maximum requirement is data handling at 400 Mbps. Note that the scheme provides only one type of service for only 100 users. If the service managed 1000 users, the switch's capacity would have to be 4 G bytes.

The authors point out that while intermedia synchronization is important 'synchronisation is mainly an inter-media requirement... playback of higher level components of a document may be temporally related as in sequential or partially overlapped playback of two video programmes on a personal channel'.

The proposed technique is to deal with sync hierarchically in three levels—'strands', 'rope', and 'chains', where a strand handles audio and video stored on different disks in the same server, ropes tie strands together, and chains tie ropes. The procedure is complex: For continuity-guaranteed serving of multiple clients, storage servers employ the optimal Quality Proportional Multi-Client Servicing (QPMS) algorithm' developed for HDTV multi-user storage. Rope control involves 'relative time stamps' in each strand.

Also discuss one-to-many multimedia distributed systems, providing as examples ' remote visualisation, distributed simultations, media storage services, and on-demand multimedia services such as accessing CATV or an on-line video rental store across a network' Moreover, they say that research issues must be solved 'before we can realize large-scale dissemination services across a high-speed Wide Area Network' (my italics).

> A multimedia dissemination service must provide service to a large number of subscribers at the same time. Because end-to-end delays and loss characteristics of the WAN differ vastly at recipients dispersed across it, the problem of meeting QOS requirements at a large number of receivers is much harder.

Their proposed remedy is a system called quality Management Transport protocol (QMTP), which 'uses a combination of rate-based flow control, redundant transmissions, and occasional feedback message (Negative ACKs) to deliver QOS within an acceptable range at each recipient'.

Address a further complication in their paper about user interactivity in distributed multimedia systems. Their proposed Timed interaction Policy Server (TIPS) system is about teleconferencing and computer Supported Cooperative Work (CSCW) where synchronization during interaction between each teleconferencing group is needed. 'Interaction in terms of a working application is often an error prone and labour intensive task .... Minor changes to the intended structure can require a major rewrite of the application,' say the authors. Their proposal is to separate the synchronization structure from the rest of the application. Each application has its own 'TIPS service agent' containing a description of application events in a formal language. This is regarded as the defined local 'policy' for that application. Each service agent communicates with the service agents of other applications in order to effect synchronization .

Network management

Network management usually means the inclusion of the necessary monitoring facilities to enable faults to be diagnosed and reliability maintained. It can also mean controlling other machines or facilities on the network from a 'host' machine for 'one-to-many (or vice versa) sessions such as teacher control of machines in a class of pupils.

The most well-known management system is the Simple Network Management Protocol (SNMP) developed for the real world of TCP/IP networks. OSI people are beavering away at the OSI-compatible equivalent CMIP (common Management Information Protocol) but it will be a long time a-coming. At least 30 different SNMP software packages are available. Each arranges for a dedicated machine, which must include a good GUI (Graphics User Interface), nominated the 'Network Management platform;

The software arranges for data like network topography, traffic levels, errors, faults, etc. to be displayed. The human manager can customize display modules to include, for instance a building plan showing wiring and stations.

Applied Telecommunications

Library networks

A 'library network' often means a library resource-sharing co-operative, not necessarily a number of libraries connected to a computer network. Library networks in the general sense have been functioning for many years simply because few libraries can supply the needs of clients from their own stocks and it makes sense for several smaller libraries to make their combined stocks available to all their clients.

Computers were adopted by library networks to make their task easier and in due course enabled other resource to be shared as well as book or serial stocks. A small network, NELINET, was operating between five New England university libraries in 1968. Requests to computers in a central office were made from terminals in outlying libraries for catalogue card production, book labels, etc.

The Library of Congress has been a library-system leader in the US, but its activities were matched by the Ohie College Library Center, which became the Online Computer Library Center (OCLC Inc.) and aggressively introduced several innovations, Another leader in the US was Research Libraries Information Network (RLIN). Both these organizations have been active in developing library systems and networks.

The US National Science Foundation is considering the promotion of multimedia libraries for supporting research, education, and commerce, together with a 'libraries without walls' project for an online system of at least 100 million items including books, maps, cartoons, photographs, etc. This scheme may be related to the distributed Internet digital library, which is, or will be, available via World Wide Web. It is a project sponsored by ARPA and devised by a consortium called CNRI composed of MIT and the University of California.

The UK JANET network described earlier is used by libraries mainly for calling up someone else's Online Public Access Catalogue (about 50 OPACs are connected), for document requests via the British Library's ARTtel service, or for connecting to the International Packet Switched Service (IPSS) and accessing online database. UK library networking is becoming widely used, encouraged by the UK Office for Library Networking at the University of Bath.

The British Library operates a CD-ROM network for the benefit of clients using its Science Reference and Information Services. A total of 28 CD-ROM products may be accessed from nine workstations. The system uses CD Net with the disks held in 3 Novell Netware 3.11 file servers each containing 28 drives, so there is plenty of room for expansion. Any user may search any disk with very little delay due to disk-to-to disk transfers.

The arrival of computer-based integrated library system encouraged the use of within-site LANs for sharing various resources, and the use of LANs in a small number of libraries in the UK and US was reported. See also CD-ROM networks in this chapter. Other applications include the support by a large public library of its services at its branches, the provision of special software access for clients, and arrangements for access to a catalogue from networked microcomputers.

Virtual Private Networks

A Virtual Private Network (VPN) appears to be the brainchild of the US Sprint Communications company, which runs a long-distance fibrotic network in the USA. They have teamed up with Cable & Wireless, owners of the North Pacific and PTAT Atlantic cables, to offer a 64 Kbps ISDN-like service, aimed at multinationals. One-stop billing and integration with private networks will be included, and users will appear to be using their own international network.

Many businesses already have extensive private networks. The requirement of a Virtual Private Network is to obtain at least the facilities currently obtained by using leased lines but at a lower cost. A VPN includes dynamic bandwidth allocation purchased on a 'pay as you use' basis as an alternative to paying for dedicated lines which are only occasionally used full capacity.

CD-ROM networks

Heavy usage of several CD-ROMs in one location can be managed by buying extra drives and subscribing to several copies of the same CD-ROM. In 1998, by which time LANs, particularly in libraries, had become commonly used, the idea of enabling several users to access one or more drives using LAN interconnection was introduced. Either PCs or Apple Machines may be used for CD-ROM networking.

Most of the information which follows applies to PCs, an application which is not as easy as networking with Macs. For Macs on an Appleshare network the CD-ROM drivers are installed in the 'server folder and CD-ROM players on the network become available to all users. The following list explains some of the acronyms and jargon in use in this field

- BIOS
  Basic Input/Output System. Software designed for IBM PCs and stored in ROM for controlling input/output functions and screen data.
- CD-ROM driver
  A software package which enables a computer to control an

attached CD-ROM drive.

- MSCDEX(MS dos CD rom Extension)
  An MS-DOS extension enabling a CD-ROM disk to be accessed like a hard disk, overcoming the inability of DOS recognize a disk capacity exceeding 32 Mbytes. MSCDEX redirect Bios CD-ROM read or write requests to itself.
- NETBIOS (Network Basic Input/Output System)
  A PC telecom protocol/interface for connecting IBM PCs PS/2s and compatibles to each other via a LAN. It establishes a communication session between named stations. It was the first network operating system and was designed primarily to enable DOS-based PCs connected to a relatively small LAN to access print or file servers.
- NLM
  Network loadable module. Software used when a network does not have a CD-ROM file-server installed. One module per installed CD-ROM drive is included in the network file server.
- Pre-to-peer operation
  Access to a CD-ROM drive attached to a particular computer by another similar computers on the network using inter-computer commands.
- Pre-casching
  Writing a CD-ROM on to a hard disk of equivalent capacity so that a computer can access and transfer data at hard disk speeds which are much faster than CD-ROM access and transfer speeds.
- SCSI
  Small Computer System Interface.
- Server
  A dedicated server (file-server) is a fast microcomputer with large memory capacity connected to a network acting as the controller of a CD-ROM drive or drives for the use of network clients using their own machines.

With reference to the server - the last item in the list above - a shared resource of this kind is likely to be less costly than the possession of comparable facilities by individual users. A non-dedicated file-server is a lower cost alternative where a workstation acts as a server as well as functioning as a user's workstation. If the file-server PC is sufficiently powerful, number of users can access it at the same time with some degradation of performance. For example, in throughput tests of a Storage. Dimensions Filemaster II machine, the speed degradation when there were 4 users instead of 1 was 41 percent.

The Filemaster II contains a 33 MHz processor and 4 Mbytes of memory with cache and two 150 Mbyte disks.

Opti-Net file-server software was one of the first for CD-ROM control. It enables up to 100 users to control up to 32 drives. Describes how it was used with six workstation accessing 16 drives. Describe a networking system using software and a 486 micro computer as a file-server.

Organized a client-server network capable of managing up to 2000 workstations connected to a TCP/IP 2 Mbps fibrotic network. Users may search all servers and will be supplied with data from whichever server is running the disk containing the required data. Inter-campus operation can be provided using Internet with TCP/IP protocol as if it was a WAN.

A comprehensive CD-ROM networking system enabling up to 100 users to access any number of servers on a network is described specification. They offer two types of network called Ultra*Net and Ultra *Net NT. Both are designed for DOS-based networks but Ultra*Net NT includes several improvements including Internet-compatible protocols for searching Internet-connected players by arrangement with their owners/publishers. They recommend the Toshiba 4101 dual-speed or the 3501 quad-speed player for SCSI MPC computers.

Ultra*Net includes the means of pre-caching the contents of a CD-ROM on to a 9 Gbyte hard disk. The disk will hold up to about twenty titles from nominally 640 CDs depending on contents and compression method adopted. To the user, the disk will appear to be a normal CD-player except that it will be much faster. Fenwood claim an improvement of between 2 and 5 times for a single user, but for five or more users performing different searches a performance improvement of up to 200 times is claimed. Up to eight 9-Gbyte drives can be accessed via their servers.

Provide installation training, and support. Complete system range from server. 7 players, and licence at a total cost of 7405, to their most comprehensive server, with 4 quad-speed players, two 9 Gbyte drives and a licence for an unlimited number of users at 24,000. The server in the large system includes a pentium processor with 32 Mbytes of RAM and a one-Gbyte hard disk.

In February 1995 the British Library announced that it

had been using a CD-ROM network in its Science Reference and information Service at Aldwych and Holoborn, London, since August 1994, as explained earlier.

Other network applications

Covers a number of aspects of multimedia networking in. She makes a number of points with educational application in mind:

- Multimedia makes heavy demands on storage and transmission.
- Predictable transmission according to the application is needed.
- Data compression reduces demands usually at the expense of some loss of detail.
- Methods of access and interconnections have important consequences.
- Costs of transmission will determine the pace of networked applications.
- Standards for networking are essential.

In addition to numerous military application, much of the activity in this rapidly growing field is centred on medical imaging, museums, art galleries, and photographic achieves. This area is covered in chapter 14.

High-regulation 2560×2048 8-bit (=42 Mbits) radiographs viewed on the UCLA medical network are displayed on Megascan 300 dots per inch monitors. Bits are delivered to the CRT at 8 Mbytes/secon is considered necessary in the supply network so that a radiograph that has been called up will appear in two seconds. UCLA found that a 1000 Mbps network from Ultra Net met their requirements for many simultaneous wideband imaging processes.

The Information Superhighway

Introduction

If the ISDN is too slow and its implementation is lethargic, and if fibre may not be arriving yet, why is there new optimism about the nationwide delivery of multimedia entertainment and other programmes? It seems that a complex combination of cables/Internet, deregulation Politics, or new methods of overcoming the constrains of the local loop could enable online wideband communication to arrive sooner than expected. Extra-ordinarily sophisticated low-cost chip-based high-speed processing has become available to distribute and select data.

The 'arrival' of an Information Superhighway (IS) could mean usage by 5 percent or 25 per cent of major organisations or by some percentage of the whole population. The phrase 'universal wideband service' which is being discussed, of course means availability to the whole population. The idea has not always met with approval.

Since half of American adults are illiterate [if that for the US it applies equally well to Europe] it would be far more logical to give people subsidies for newspaper and magazine purchase and keep the public libraries open longer than to subsidise superhighway development; nothing is more misguided or misleading than to suggest that access to it is somehow central to determining wealth or poverty in the information age.

The increasing disparity between the 'information rich and the information poor' introduces another discussion. Considers the global distribution of wealth and network density. The figures (1990 data, from a world bank report) in Table 13.3 speak for themselves. Table 13.4 shows the number of Internet hosts per selected country in 1992- by 1996 the number will have doubled (at least). Jacobson quotes the remarks made by the Tanzanian prime minister at an international telecommunications conference. It is insensitive to talk about new broadband and mobile networks that would provide multiple new services to wealthy countries when 25% of the world's population lacks access to an adequate basic telephone and millions have never used one.' 'Have-not' considerations may be 'insensitive' but they have not reduced expansionist talk at current telecoms conferences. Suggests no remedies.

Table 13.3 Development indicators

		Country income levels		
Low	Middle	High	US	
Population (in millions)	2948	1104	830	249
GNP per capita	350	2220	19,950	21,790

Table 13.4 internet hosts per country

Country	Hosts
United States	591,049
Australia	43,262
Germany	42,486
Canada	37,021
UK	32,843
Sweden	20,321
Netherlands	20,225
France	18,508
Italy	7458
Portugal	1291
Mexico	776
Chile	146
Tunisia	25
India	6
Thailand	1

Yet another objection to the IS is lodged. He thinks that the Information Superhighway is nothing less than an 'environmental menace. The coming information superhighway portends 'an environmental disaster of the first magnitude. Because people will be able to live and work in rural America and having open space round your house is equated with a high standard of living, dream homes with several acres of land 'will require the destruction of forests and open land across the country'. An apartment building with 200 families will become 200 five-acre homes occupying 1000 acres. The best and the brightest will leave the urban blights' and blight, for instance, that little gem of a state'. Since 1950, population has increased by 50 per cent. Its few suburban areas are 'chock full of expatriates from nearby metropolitan areas.

To return to the question of network capacity: there is no data speed limitation problems with cable, which was designed to transport television signals. The speed of any route through the Internet network available to the average user depends on the speed of its weaker link - about 128 Kbps.

The ultimate objective of the IS is to provide a global universal telecommunication network to deliver entertainment and information. It is potentially one of the most important developments in telecom services ever considered.

Regulation

The United State

General regulatory conditions in the US are gradually relaxed. The FCC has removed restrictions stopping local telephone operators from offering home entertainment over their networks. Bell Atlantic is reported as being almost ready to provide such services .

In spite of the relaxation, a recognized authority working at Columbia University, Introduces a telling discussion . He states that because of the inadequacy of public finance, regulations must be arranged to stimulate private investment. The business objective is high profits and competitive advantage, but existing regulations are designed to limit earnings and market power and 'represent a formidable roadblock to increased private investment '. Argues that flawed regulation may not slow down the development of the IS, if the government does not over-regulate and so discourage the entry of new players into the market. Herein lies the most pitiful irony of the situation. The most fundamental drivers of private market investment incentives are exactly the opposite of what government authorities are prepared to adopt. He recommends doing it the old-fashioned way' by removing market entry restrictions, profits, and operational scope.

Existing regulation are an example of the politics of 'turf regulation. The turf in a given region is allocated to monopoly providers of cable- TV. Telephone, broadcast, and often newspapers (in the US). Significant cross-market ownership is not authorized to any extent. Investment in public networks outside the established core is stagnate in spite of industry buzzwords like 'seamless nationwide' 'high speed digital' and 'information superhighway' meanwhile, a cornucopia of alternatives is filling market niches. They include private satellite systems, cellular networks, wireless' cable, packet data radio, etc.

Consider that the argument for a best case return on capital indicates that for every 1000 invested per subscriber for access purposes, 14 of additional revenue per month per household would be required for capital recovery over a 10-year discounted payback period at a 12 per cent return rate. Most types of service require considerably more than a 1000 investment. Consequently, unless an integrated network operator is allowed to freely pursue all revenue opportunities... it is very difficult to justify mass deployment of the new broadband to the home technology'. Finally:

> Nowhere in the most basic of economic principle is it clear that two or more local media monopolies is better than one ... the choice fro a broadband infrastructure network may be one provider or none .... Why would policy makers want to prevent companies from investing to modernize parts of the infrastructure, like household lines, that everyone wants to use but no one company can afford to build on its own ?

The year 1934 was a milestone for telecommunications in the United States. In that year the Telecommunications Act became law: it has survived with some amendments ever since. The Act brought in a supervisory agency for regulation, the Federal Communications Commission (FCC). ARPANET, the Defence Department's Advanced Research Projects Network, which developed into the Internet, was founded in 1969.

In the late 1980s several computer companies formed the computer System Policy project to consider their options. In 1990 the High performance Computing Bill was introduced, directing the National Science Foundation (NSF) to develop the National Research and Education Network (NREN) and to provide 400 million to develop a 3 gigabit/ second network. The High performance Computing and communications initiative, covering advanced systems, technology and resources, became an Act in 1992, authorizing the extension of Internet by connecting the NREN network to it. A National Competitiveness Act covering an information superhighway infrastructure was proposed.

In mid-1993 an example was set by the White House and other agencies. They initiated a public information service by enabling certain files to be accessed via internet, issuing e-mail addresses for the purpose. Drily comment: 'In view of the recognised differences between the UK and US government cultures of access to information there is little for the UK public compare with the White Hose information dissemination initiative'. In September 1993 the Clinton administration published a nine-point agenda to encourage the construction of the highway. This White House agenda aimed to ensure that it would be available to all at affordable prices. Al Gore, the Vice-president, said that the federal government would act as a catalyst for a National Information Infrastructure (NII) to be built by the private sector. According to one observer:

> The NII is imagined to consist of a network of competing networks made seamless and transparent by government standards and operated and maintained by government standards and operated and maintained by private industry. This competitive marketplace will benefit consumers small and large by yielding better services at lower prices. The phone companies can compete and win in that environment and so can the cable companies, wireless companies, long distance providers, and many others who have the know-how to give consumers what they want.

Subsequently Gore broadened the concept to a Global International infrastructure in the hope that all governments would join in. The message was reinforced at the end of the year with the announcement of a 'Telecom Summit' in early 1995 and promised legislation to open markets. We must 'work toward our goal of connecting every classroom, library, hospital and clinic to the NII by the year 2000', said Gore.

A far-reaching attempt was made in late 1994 to introduce a Bill to amend part of the 1934 Communications Act which would drastically alter the tights of communications companies. Telephone companies would be allowed to enter cable-TV and would probably be allowed to enter into manufacturing, electronic publishing, and security services as well. Cable-TV would be allowed to provide phone services. Having passed the House of Representatives, the bill, sponsored, was blocked when it reached the Senate. It was thought to provide too many advantages for the Bell companies. Meanwhile, the FCC authorized the first video dialtone service for New Jersey Bell to supply service to homes in Dover Township. New Jersey.

A major change in regulatory conditions in the United States finally occurred when signed the Telecommunications Act on 8 February 1996. Summarizes the major issues being discussed at the end of 1995 when two different version of the Act were passed by the House and the Senate followed by attempts to draft a single compromise version. The major issue were:

- Allowing competitive entry into the local telephone market.
- Removing the remaining restrictions on the Belcos except for rights of competitors to use their transmission facilities.
- Allowing telephone companies to provide video programmes to subscribers in their area.

The imminence of the Bill prompted a merger between which would have been worth $ 25 billion. In spite of the passing of the Bill early in 1996, these two companies changed their plans and now intend to launch a long-distance telephone venture.

Cable-TV plus Internet already have a customer-base large enough for multimedia entertainment/information service viability. The cable-TV operator Telecommunications Inc. Denver, alone has 10 million subscribers out of an estimated US total of over 50 million. However, the technical problems of the cable to Internet interconnection, and Internet's bandwidth limitations must first be solved.

Europe and the Union

In Europe about 30 million homes are connected to cable but connections are patchy. Germany has about 13 million subscribers. It is not clear whether these figures refer to 'homes passed' by cable, households actually connected, or the total number of viewers in connected households. However, this is a fairly large base from which something like a superhighway might emerge.

Thinks that 'Conflicts of interest paralyse the decision-making process or spin it out to such extremes that European markets, industries, and institutions often give the impression of unchangeable, immovable objects in a highly fluid world. A lot of chat and no action turns information highways into information hypeways'. The commission of the European

Communities has had an uphill struggle against vested interests when trying to establish some kind of unified European telecoms system. It decreed an open market for certain services by the end of 1989 and free competition for terminal purchases by 1990. In July 1990 'framework directives' for competitive services were proposed, backed by the force of Article 90 of the Treaty of Rome. They 'would herald the dawn of a new era', said the commissioners. If not by 1992, then perhaps by 1995, they would 'open up unlimited opportunities for the telecommunications industry, for business users and for the individual consumer'. In April 1993 the EC ministers voted with 'Decisive indecision' (in the words of the journal Telecommunications) to delay full liberalization of public for Growth, followed by plans submitted in June 1994 by Commissioner Bangemann to liberalize telecoms by 1998.

It is believed that the Commission may attempt to break up media monopolies by introducing new publishing and broadcasting to guarantee pluralism.

The current progress of European telecoms in regard to coping with the success of the Internet, and the merits of OSI and TCP/IP protocol Standards are discussed under 'Protocols and Standards controversy' later in this chapter.

Japan

In 1985 the NTT monopoly became a private company and the market was opened to competition. A number of international, national long-distance and local, and mobile services soon became established. NTT plans to make its backbone trunk a terabit fibrotic highway with loops round Tokyo for through traffic. It already provides ISDN services and plans to start installing broadband ISDN with ATM protocols in 1996 using optical fibre in local loops. Toda (1993) from NTT describes the company's telecom plans in some detain and suggests that entertainment, business, conference, health care, library, education, and other services are likely to be expanded.

The UK

UK cable received considerable government publicity in the long-forgotten days of 1982 when it was thought that all technology was a Good Thing. Development was slow, but in

1990 26 new cable franchises were offered to bidders and government policy was changed, lifting the ban on foreign ownership. US telephone companies, unable to enter the cable business under existing regulations in their own country, invested heavily in UK cable, believing that this was the way to enter the UK telephone business. Additional franchises have increased the total of homes passed to at least 9 million, but only about 600,000 households are actually connected. However, there were 50,000 new connections in the last two months of 1993 so growth is rapid, about half of all the subscribers have also opted for cable-telephone services. There is no apparent difference between a cable telephone and a conventional telephone call. Your telephone number is allocated at a BT exchange.

The Department of Trade and Industry (DTI) 1987 broadband highway report contained a classic bureaucratic killer phrase: 'We did not presume to consult potential users' and 'technology continues to advance very rapidly. The UK might end up by locking itself into a sub-optimal technical infrastructure.' This excuse for doing nothing is, of course applicable to new technology at all times.

A 1994 report (Anon. 1994b) from the same department came to exactly the opposite conclusion. The UK has 'an opportunity to develop a communications infrastructure that is at least as good as any in the world. It is an opportunity that the UK cannot afford to lose', it said.

On 22 November 1994 , the government decided not to lift the 'entertainment' ban on BT, imposed earlier to encourage cable start-ups. BT's plans to spend 15 billion on fibrotic cabling have also been abandoned. Reguly (1996) quotes a broadcasting research group who say: 'One has to look at cable as the channel tunnel project of the TV industry. The payoff might not come until the next millennium.

American investment in the US cable network is declining and 'Since cable companies (in the UK) have no earnings, pay no dividends, are less than halfway through a 12 billion construction programme, and are pioneers in a new industry, the City has had a difficult time valuing them.' Only one in five of the 6 million homes passed by cable subscribe: 'There is talk that some American and Canadian groups have read the riot act to their cable subsidiaries in Britain.' Reguly, quoting David Miller of General Cable, says:

> In the coming years they will try to introduce VOD, home shopping and banking... but there's a good chance this extra effort won't give the cable industry star status - BSkyB is getting bigger, a fifth terrestrial channel is coming and so is digital terrestrial TV.

In October 1994 the DTI reached a telecommunications agreement with the United State in order to encourage competition with existing carriers in transatlantic services, and to allow other organizations to lease lines to interconnect the telephone networks of the two countries.

The BBC intends to install up to seven compressed 5Mbps PAL digital TV channels on a single satellite transponder. It is currently considering whether it should use the potential of this new digital TV system to offer more than conventional entertainment services. It could become a lumbering but formidable provider. Its erstwhile Deputy Director of Engineering wrote the standard 650- page work about Digital Television (Sandbank 1990). The digital TV timetable is supposed to be: services in the US to start during 1995, finalization of a European Standard at the end of 1996, and the first European services to be launched in 1997 on channel 35. European progress crucially depends on completing the Standards on time. The BBC will also be starting up twelve national digital audio broadcasting services with the assumption that the majority of listeners will be using portable and mobile receivers.

At the Science policy Research Unit, University of Sussex, UK, covers similar deregulatory topics for the UK as Egan did for the United State (p. 233). His advice is a little different. Instead of allowing private industry full rein, he advocates redressing imbalances in network access: 'Regulation in the name of public services is not only possible; it will be essential in the future... regulation, imperfect as it is, will play a crucial role in monitoring and guiding decisions by the players in the market. ' 'Network openness' is the key factor. The terms for network interconnection- so that new entries can gain access to the networks with the consequent access to businesses and households-are critical. They depend on the degree to which the IDO will unbundle and provide access to service functions and on an agreement for reasonable charges for the use of the IDO's network by new entries. He considers two possibilities - separate the global and domestic.

Services of the IDO: the domestic off shoot would then negotiate connections between the global IDO and new entries. Alternatively, use accounting mechanisms to achieve network openness.

An organizational environment is needed for an ongoing debate about changing technology and markets. Regulatory activity should be directed towards a minimum set of essential and manageable tasks.

Copyright

In the peggy case in the assumption that a film distributor can exploit a film by 'all means known or hereafter devised' may have to be changed. In the case brought about by a video re-recording of Lee's earlier recording of Lady and the Tramp without permission, a court ruled that video could not have been anticipated at the time of first recording. There are some unique aspects of copyright in the United States when the Fairness Doctrine occasionally overrides the. Third Amendment, as discussed.

The anxieties of publishers and recording companies, art galleries and museums with regard to infringements of their copyrights could be reduced if they grasped the opportunities for promoting their holdings and their revenue-earning possibilities for promoting their holdings and their revenue-earning possibilities. Obtaining tights can be extremely difficult for potential developers unless the collecting societies respond to new needs and find mechanisms for licensing an adequate volume of material, says Nicholas Hgham, a London solicitor. If they do not do so, then the voices of those who already call for compulsory licensing, or for an emasculation of rights of copyright into a mere right to economic compensation for the use of a work, will be increasingly heard.'

Competition, demand, and company shakeouts

The progress of technology is far easier to forecast than its social effects. The behaviour of people when confronted with a digital information superhighway is uncertain. What information will customers perceive to be of value and what will they be prepared to pay for it ? We know that certain kinds of information delivered without delay are considered to be valuable. Information concerning the money market, and the rate at which it is update, are a rare example where value may be assessed. Other occupational information has often not survived the test of profitability in the marketplace. The idea of trying to establish a monetary value for information has almost been abandoned (Repo 1998).

The probability of success for a profitable consumer information service is hard to predict. For example, what would a consumer be prepared to pay for the convenience of a Video on Demand Service and associated costs in competition with a video hire service currently charging about 1 per day.

The players in multimedia markets feel that if you want to succeed on a future information superhighway you need to be master of the technology, telecoms, and information content; if you own a big network you must have some material to send along it. The hardware people see the benefit of owning a complementary company to supply the 'software'. Copyright is not viewed as a serious problem. If you want a chunk of material, you set up some kind of joint operation. The early battles between VHS and Sony's Betamax recording systems might have gone Sony's way if VHS had not been able to supply a volume of VHS consumer tapes. Sony soon recovered and was one of the first companies to purse this policy.

The race started in earnest in the 1990s. 'No set of companies ever changed so much, so fast'- and they were triggered by a single event. In August 1993 A court in Virginia ruled that bell Atlantic could operate a cable-TV net work. The eight Bell telephone companies, spun off when AT&T was broken up in 1984, were prevented from such operations until then by the 1984 Cable Act. In November 1992 chairman, had predicted that by 2001 the global megamedia industry would be worth 3.5 trillion - i.e. 3.5 million dollars. Following the court decision a deal was agreed between John Malone, Chief Executive officer (CEO) of and Ray Smith, chairman of Bell Atlantic, the second largest of the eight Belco telephone companies, spun off when AT&T was broken up. They agreed to merge their two companies in order to deliver interactive 500-cahnnel TV and two-way video communications. The other filed similar suits in their regional territories and embarked on various other manoeuvres.

The Atlantic Bell-TCI deal fizzled out later for various reasons but that did not affect the general momentum. Southwestern Bell took over two cable networks and paid 650 million for them. 'Many executives in both industries saw the beauty of combining rather than battling,' observes Maney. This deal was immediately followed by another - US West (another Belco) offered 2.5 billion for 25 per cent of the time Warnner cable system. It would, Florida.

Book is about the 'key players' who are trying to control the industry. 'This gives you a picture of the leaders of the companies because strong leadership and vision seem to be keys to success in megamedia.' He thinks that Wall Streets focus on the next quarter, and success as judged by the price of a company's stock is inadequate. 'My focus is overwhelmingly on U.S. companies. The reason is that the United States, in general is far ahead of the rest of the world in megamedia. Sony owns Columbia/Tristar, which has a library of 3400 films and 25,000 TV episodes, Disney and TCI have an agreement for a new compressed digital-cable TV channel called Starz, running until 2004 for access to Disney movies, and IBM and Sears offer the Prodigy home shopping service. Disney's pairs theme-park may be a doubtful investment but Aladdin has earned 440 million so far and revenues from The Lion king will probably exceed it. Disney is the biggest movie producer, making about 60 films every year; it is planning to build 500 stores world-wide selling Disney character branded goods. If Disney was taken over it would cost the acquirer about 3.5 billion, says Maney.

Two Important factors not mentioned by Maney contribute to the potential success of megamedia in the United State. In past years the US Department of Defense has been a huge customer for IT products and the US government has provide a mammoth network, the Internet- a superhighway precursor - for nothing. Much will be learned from its inadequacies.

At that time he pointed out that US industry produced more than twice the goods and services of Europe, including the UK. He noted that American society gambles much more money on human intelligence than it wastes on gadgets.

The Personalities of CEOs provide one viewpoint, but their permanence and the effects produced by their successors are unknown. Doubtless the CEOs of Xerox, which failed to capitalize on inventions from its PARC labs, Commodore with its pioneering but unsuccessful Amiga machine, and nearly 20 per cent of installed micorcomputers in Europe at one time. Inmos are examples of companies which seemed destined for success had something to say about operations of these kinds:

> Leaders in revolutionary times tend to have uncertain careers. Some fail because they are too slow to embrace revolution's possibilities and promises. Some fail because they cannot mange expectations. Some succeed either through a mixture of luck, energy and ability, or because they know how to make the many facets of inertia and change work together to their advantage, having the position, resources and commitment to make this happen.

Takeovers and mergers continued after the period covered by Maney. In 1995 MCI Communications and the News Corporations, chaired by Rupert Murdoch, agreed a 2.4 billion deal; their first project would be an electronic newspaper. MCI owns Internet MCI, which provides services such as electronics shopping, while the News Corporation runs Delphi Internet Services.

Discusses 'Gilder's Law' which postulates that the price of a service, product, or idea decreases by 30 per cent time that production doubles. The extraordinary success of Netscape is a case in point. Netscape was valued at 2.8 billion when it came to the market in August 1995, 16 months after it was founded. It introduced Netscape 1.1 with HMTL before it was agreed as Standard, did deals with Macromedia, Adobe, and sum (Java), and very rapidly established itself as a major force on the Internet, believing that in due course it would be in a position to take advantage of a huge expansion in interactive multimedia operations.

It looks as if the will follow the trend in the trend in the media merger and takeovers. Broadcasting Bill, referred to in the regulation section in this chapter, is accelerating the progress.

The Merger of United News & Media, a vintage slow moving newspaper company, and MAI, an aggressive television and financial services group, is expected to be the first of many such deals in Britain...the age of the media conglomerate is here.

UN&M own the Daily Express and the *Sunday Express* while MAI's major interest are in Meridian, Anglia and the new Channel 5 television. The value of the merged company is nearly 3 billion . The merger took place in April 1996.

AR&T is planning to build a business in the UK worth 1 billion within five years provided that OFTEL relaxes its regulatory conditions. In particular AT&T wants OFTEL to guarantee that customers could change their telephone company without changing their telephone number, and without adding an additional code in front of it, AT&T, having itself been split in 1984, is planning to split itself into three parts by the end of 1996.

It is as well to bear in mind some remarks made about the information superhighway; they are equally applicable to multimedia/megamedia. He says:

> We have never been very good at predicting the future use of technology, even when we have had some success in predicting technology changes themselves. We may, by now, have a shrewd idea about some of he new tools that will be available to us, but we should be very wary indeed about assuming we know how they will make their impact.

We know that we will have much more powerful and cheaper computing ....we know too that we can bank on having a lot more communications capacity- and that an unstoppable combination of technological progress and political liberalisation will ensure lower prices, [but] we really should have learned by now that the availability of tautologies is only one surprisingly small factor in a range of influences that determine social and behavioural change.

The conclusions reached following a survey in Europe are listed in a CEC 1993 report. They are rather mundane. Residential needs are reported as first, access to quickly changing information such as news, stock prices, and the weather, already adequately supplied by existing media. A second need is transactional support for home banking, travel reservation, and teleshopping, Nothing is said about new forms of entertainment.

The CCTA suggests that the government might use an information superhighway for:

- Tax, social security, vehicle registration, and other official correspondence;
- Information such as school prospectuses, job vacancies, etc;
- Electronic mail;
- Appointment booking - e.g. at hospitals.

Changes in lifestyle spending are slow- leisure spending in the UK has remained at about 8 per cent of GDP for some years, and TV viewing has stayed at about 26 hours per week since 1985 - this is one aspect of use which needs close attention. Set-top box information/entertainment providers will need to obtain a larger slice of a cake which remains about the same size.

The development of set-top TV media selection superboxes

A 'First generation' set-top box manages the decoding of incoming data from a media channel and reconstructs it in a format for human assimilation - for example, as a television programme to be viewed on the associated TV receiver. It also enables the user to request information - for example, the title of a film to be viewed on the receiver.

For the developed information superhighway a second or third generation' 'superbox' may have to accept data from one or more channel types - for instance, cable, broadcast television, satellite, ratio link, mobile station, telephone line, etc,- and may also have to be able to send information, such as a tape recording from a camcorder, to another subscriber.

The first stage in this process is likely to be a box capable of receiving data from one channel type, decoding and reconstructing it, and also capable of sending user's instructions for a selected programme. The ubiquitous TV set, acting as the man-machine interface, will be surmounted by a set-top box. The viewer will choose information to come back down the line to be displayed and printed as required. The information which the system handles may arrive via one of the numerous channels just listed. Several questions need resolving. Is there a channel/ service leader which will become dominant? Will all providers supply information using their own channels? Will they interconnect or combine to share a single channel in some way? The form of the superbox will presumably be dictated by the type of the dominant channel- or will it be required to handle several different types of channel? The success of a channel will depend on the faith and finance of its owner, the date by which it becomes widely available, and the perceived success of its services.

ATM switches are of special importance for superboxes. Various types are becoming available. In this application they are used for a different reason from methods describe earlier in this chapter. The switch multiplexes a number of channels, and switches at a bit rate of at least n times the bit links to set-top boxes in homes are each to receive a 2 Mbps service from a central point via an ATM switch, the switch must run at least 200 Mbps.

Superboxes are being developed. For example, Compression Labs are reported to be supplying Bell Atlantic with an ADSL (discussed earlier) or fibre system capable of showing MPEG compressed movies with a good quality 720×480 display. Movies, health care, education, and children's shows are said to be available. Microware's OS/9 operating system and MPEG compression/decompression will be used.

See chapter 9 covering the question of Standards which are currently being discussed in the United States.

The development of at least two types of box is well advanced in the UK-designed to make use of the potential of their owners' channels-for BT it is the public telephone network, and for the Cambridge Cable consortium the cable-TV network.

Most of the telephone network in the UK. In 1990 it carried out trials with fibrotic lines to households at for multi-channel TV, access to a videodisk library, and teleworking. The trials ended in 1992. In November 1994, BT dropped its plan for a 15 billion fibre information superhighway after the government refused to lift the ban on BT's entry into TV broad-casting.

BT will make the most of the enormous investment in the 'copper loop', which provides it with an entry to business and homes. Regulatory legislation does not appear to prevent it from offering services such as VOD. It started trials in the spring of 1994 although OFTEL warned it in November 1994 that a full system must be consistent with UK policy. The trials are mainly based on DMT ADSL (Discrete Multitone Asymmetric Digital Subscriber Loop), in which the maximum bit rate of the PSTN, nominally about 140 Kbps, is extended by equalization and the selective use of frequency bands within the channel, to up to about 2 Mbps.'Asymmetric' means that the return path from a subscriber works at the lower rate of 64 Kbps. Acceptable television pictures from, say, an 80 Mbps service, compressed by 40:1, could be delivered and viewed over such a system. In those trials, supplying about 2000 households in Colchester, Essex, BT is using material from the Sears group and W.H. Smith for home shopping, Thomas Cook for holidays and travel, the BBC, Carlton, Kingfisher, Granada, and Pearson for TV programmes, sport from BSkyB, and music from BMG Video, EMI, Polygram, Sony, and Warner. A massively parallel computer with an Oracle media server and nCube software is used at the head end. Set-top boxes supplied by Apples by consist of LC475 machines with MPEG decompression and Quicktime, receiving data at 2Mbps. Viewers' requests, sent at the 64 Kbps rate, are received at a central point via an ATM switch.

A different approach is being used in a trial started in 1994 by a group composed of Olivetti, Online Media, Acorn, Cambridge Cable, ATM Ltd, Anglia Television, and BNR (Europe), a subsidiary of Northern Telecom. An interactive set-top box will handle bidirectional ATM MPEG-1 composed television data running at 2 Mbps. The superbox is based on Acorn's 32-bit ARM610 chip, a version of the Advanced RISC machine's chip designed by ARM, an Acorn Computer subsidiary, being manufactured by Texas Instruments, VLSI Technology, and others. The chip's speed is claimed to be 140 Mips/Watt (a measure of integer processing performance) compared with the latest Apple/IBM power processors rated at 35 Mips/Watt-far slower at a given power dissipation. The ATM network associated with the superbox has been described. Each component such as a camera, audio system, display, etc. is treated as an 'ATM direct' module controlled by an ARM RISC processor, each module being directly connected to the network. The network will convey 'many streams of multimedia data, perhaps thousands, which are active simultaneously'.

In November 1994 I was informed that this superbox should be available next year at about 300 giving plenty of room for reduction if mass-production is put in hand. Will the general public be able to cope with the potentially much more complex set-top box interface? That depends whether system designers make time to try it out on average members of the public before releasing it.

Protocols and Standards controversy

A protocol is a set of rules governing the exchange of data. A controversy has developed which could seriously upset the idea of a global information superhighway, so it is a matter of some importance. In the protocols of interest here, OSI (an internationally agreed protocol supported by the EC), and TCP/IP (of American origin) control the several functions requiring attention when two terminals intercommunicate over a network. Separate rules are applied to each function. The rules enable all kinds of incompatible network, equipment, software and interface functions to work together in order to present information on a recipient's terminal in exactly the way that the sender intended.

The EC introduced a series of standardization measures in the period 1977 to 1989. In 1990 the European standards Organisations had at least 3000 items, worked on by 250 technical committees, which they were required to digest by January 1993. They would then have to be agreed, tested, and eventually incorporated into products- a far distant prospect. However, the idea that the European Committee for Standards (CEN), on which US interests were not represented, could become adjudicators of the IT industry in Europe...had the American manufacturers up in arms'. Most of the new Standards would be accommodated within the European-supported OSI-conscious. The Department of Defence published the GOSIP report specifying that US telecomes products should support OSI. Meanwhile, the Internet, using TCP/IP, was growing and TCP/IP had becomes virtually the *de facto* protocol. Recognizing the inevitable, in 1994 the Federal Internetworking Requirements Panel (FIRP) proposed a change in the GOSIP policy, relaxing its OSI preference and recommending that TCP/IP should receive equal support.

The way in which the TCP/IP protocol handles the *en route* functions differs from the way OSI and its family of Standards are carefully considered and agreed. You can not rush the careful attention and inter-country agreement which must be given to processes intended to endure. TCP/IP protocols were developed by a single organization - ARPA - for a single country - the United States. The ARPA control software became TCP/IP in the early 1980s. Both the popular and erudite literature about OSI and TCP/IP present pictures of two protocols influenced by nationalistic, general complexity and state of implementation, point, depending on the source of the literature and the author's prejudices.

In September 1994 an EC paper pointed out that the Internet has 2 million hosts in the US and nearly a million elsewhere. EUnet GB is the largest European commercial provider operating in 25 countries. The paper continued with a discussion of Internet problems and opportunities.

In December 1994 the EC launched its Information Society Project Office to 'help promote international cooperation by aiming to build a global information infrastructure', among other objectives. It also issued a proposal to 'lift restrictions on the use of cable TV network for the carriage of all liberalised telecommunications services'.

A 'working Paper' was published by the Directorate General Research of the European Parliament, presumably in anticipation of the February 1995 DG7 conference in Brussels. Apparently an 'official' document, it carries a disclaimer saying that the opinions expressed are 'not in any way those of the European Parliament'. It calls for action by the European Union and quotes an article from *Le Monde Diplomatique* entitled 'Qui tirera profit des autoroutes de I' information?' in support of a 'What's to be done about Internet?' The paper, translated from the French, was published ostensibly to discuss Standards. Internet's TCP/IP protocol is 'an essentially monocultural model', whereas OSI is 'polyculturally inspired', says the paper. A quotation from *Le Monde Diplomatique* is used to support criticism of Internet: 'The concerns of the public are being disdainfully disregard as greater support is given to the objectives of the giant cable, telephone and leisure companies.' The paper concludes that 'a specifically European Internet' should be developed 'as a support for the Standards chosen by the Europeans'. It says:

> By allowing the other side to choose the playing field the European Union is obliged to leave everything to their initiative, to move forward at the pace they impose, to

play on unequal terms, and ultimately to retreat on other fronts.

Having discussed the merits of OSI standards versus Internet's TCP/IP protocol, the paper continues:

> By forcing the market to give up the immediate advantage of marketing the first available standard instead of collecting information about existing standards and the structure of potential demand, the political authority has the possibility of increasing the probability that the final choice will be a more sophisticated standard offering better prospects.

.... [The EU should] develop a specifically European Internet as a support for the standards chosen by the European, both for equipment and for services (applications) and by means of tax incentives.

The probability that the EU could introduce measure to successfully defeat seems remote. This phrase comes from Servan-Schreiber's book describing what he considered to be the decline of Europe in the face of an American economic invasion. It inspired presented to the President of France, which prompted substantial changes in French policy.

In market forces versus governmental action contests, market forces usually win. The lessons of history are clear. The need for standardized protocols cannot be denied but if you are successful (e.g Japanese group 3 fax, and IBM's SNA) you can get in well ahead of the competition. Your equipment generates a *de facto* standard. The official Standard which arrives five years later-a typical time lag-may well be different from your system but it not concern you. Your updated system is still better than your competitor's which conforms to the new Standard, probably already out of date. OSI versus TCP/IP is a somewhat similar higher level contest.

Summit-type conferences are now commonplace. *The Times, in* reporting such a conference in its 30 March 1995 issue, said on its front page that you can tell one by the presence of 'Marble, plate glass, Mercedes Benzes, Royalty, men with walkie-talkies, and women in hats'. If this conference marked a turning point it would 'only be for the quails' in the lunch provided.

It is hard to tell whether the G7 Information Society

meeting in Brussels on 24-26 February 1995 will have been a turning point or not. The speeches made by the dignitaries reported are the usual expressions of hope, with the possible exception of some remarks made by Klaus Hansch, President of the European Parliament. Hansch said that information exchange should be 'on the basis of fair exchange and reciprocity'. 'For similar reasons of equity the Union support the nation of international Standards laid down by International Standards Organisation should apply universally.' These Standards are those embraced by the OSI model, not TCP/IP.

If a confrontation develops, the supporters of one side or the other might back down. Alternatively, both side might be obstinate and there will be some kind of face-saving fudge. Alternatively again, bridging of some kind might be introduced to make interconnection simple; this seems rather unlikely because the necessary gateway would be inconvenient, complex, and expensive.

Security

Good security practice must be applied in a variety of ways wherever confidential information is handled. The aspect of interest here is the security of the contents of a message during transmission. A message is a series of symbols representing text, graphics, sound, picture, etc. A code is the substitution of codewords for plain language, while the two major types of cipher - transposition and substitution - are operations on individual characters. Ciphers and cryptography (from the Greek kryptos, hidden, and graphein, to write) are used to prepare secret messages.

One of the weakest parts of any telecommunication system is the area through which messages are passed outside the control of the sending and receiving stations. They may then be monitored by third parties; their contents should remain secure if the messages are enciphered. Describes several methods suitable for networks such as the Internet, and presumably for an information highway, by controlling access to routers - a key unit which allocates routes which are controlled by data contained in a message. A scheme called the Terminal Access Controller Access System (TACAS) protocol provided by Cisco Systems, is also described. It controls servers to which authorized users have access. Ajluni goes on to describe the DES and PKA systems (see below). The design background to such systems is discussed in a more advanced article. A brief description of the background to enciphering methods is provided below.

A great deal of effort was devoted to devising supposedly secure encryption systems for messages transmitted by radio during the Second World War and at least as much effort to breaking them. The first, and possibly the biggest, code-breaking effort was made by the Government Code and Cypher School (GC&CS) at Bletchley Park.

An early system which endured was the 'one-time pad', invented by G.Vernam in 1917. As used in the war, a one-time pad contained lines of columnized randomly generated decimal numbers held by message sender and recipient. The letters of a message to be sent were first encoded into numbers, using a simple substitution code. The sender subtracted each number, without borrowing , from a one-time pad number, starting at a particular columns and line on a particular page, and the result was transmitted. The message contained a group - the 'key' - at the beginning telling the addressee where to start on his pad. The recipient, starting at the place indicated by the sender on his copy of the same one-time pad, subtracted each received number from his one-time pad number without borrowing, thereby deciphering the message, and then changed the numbers back to the original letters, using the same substitution code as that used by the sender. Provided each new message was enciphered using a part of the pad never used previously, the method was perfectly secure.

This system is clumsy when a very large number of users is involved. The major alternative wartime system was for all users to have a machine containing rotating wheels. An input character produces an output character according to the positions of the wheels, which determine the path taken by an electric current. One or more wheels rotate by one position each time an input character is typed. The greater the number of wheels and the number of positions that can be produced. Only if the positions of each of the identical wheels in a receiving machine are the same as those in the sending machine during the transmission of a message can the identity of each character be determined by the receiver. The 'key' is the starting position of each wheel. This was the basis of the 'Type X' and 'Enigma' machines. Unlike a one-time pad was used once only, messages could not be read without key and pads. The machine method was thought to be almost as good and much more convenient; the number of alternative output characters that the same input character could generate was so enormous that it was believed that it was impossible to read a message enciphered with a machine without the key. However, GC&CS did develop a method for reading messages enciphered with the Enigma machine.

The DES (Data Encryption Standard), RSA (invented by Rivest, Shalimir, and Adelman), which is somewhat simpler to manage, and PKA (Public Key Algorithm) are probably the best known method of encryption used to today.

The DES specifies an enciphering for the high-speed processing of data by computer hardware. A 56-bit key is used for multiple permutations of blocks of plain text composed of 65 bits inclusive of 8 errordetection bits. To decipher, it is only necessary to apply the same algorithm to an enciphered block using the same key. Everyone knows the algorithm but only the sender and receiver know the selected key.

RSA, based on factorizing large prime numbers, uses a 512-bit key, making it slow, although less slow than it may appear because of the development of fast, dedicated processing chips it is considered secure because it would take a 1000mips (millions of instructions per second) machine running for 2000 years to break it.

The PKA, however, embodies an additional factor to nullify the possible effect of the security risk inherent in the DES; with DES, information about keys could be intercepted *en route* to perhaps many correspondents. PKA uses two separate keys - a public enciphering key and a different secret deciphering key. The inverse of the enciphering functional cannot be derived even if the enciphering functions are known.

Netscape uses a 128-bit key for RSA encryption in the US. In August 1995 its RSA 40-bit encryption key, uses abroad, was broken by French students using two supercomputers with 120 workstations. The version of RSA called RSA-129 was also broken in 1995 after an even larger effort.

The distribution of information about PKA keys to the message recipient is not necessary because of the so-called 'trap-door' method of using oneway enciphering and inverse functions. The PKA also embodies a signature to authenticate the sender as actually being the person he is purporting to be.

In a method invented recently by Robert Mathews, the inconvenience of distributing keys to intended message recipients in advance is overcome. It includes a device which causes the same set of random numbers always to be generated by a particular triggering number. Actually the system as just described could not work because a truly random number list cannot be repeated. In fact the numbers are 'pseudo-random numbers when triggered by the same triggering number. Each set of pseudo-random numbers generated by a different triggering number is sufficiently different from all other sets to make cipher-breaking almost impossible.

The only way to determine the randomness, and hence the indecipherability of a message using a particular system design,.is to subject messages to 'merciless attacks' using the armoury of known cipher-breaking techniques to see if the system can resist them.

A different solution is needed for the case when a large computer, connected to a communication network, contains files of different security classifications, and it is desired to make the installation available to a number of people who themselves are within different security categories. Machines can embody a security 'kernel' or interface between the operating system - that is, specialized software controlling computer functions - and the hardware. The function of the kernel is to cheek the access rights of each user to any information-containing system element. It may, of course, be necessary to encrypt data flowing through the network as well.

Hackers have successfully broken in to supposedly secure systems and have received a great deal of publicity. The wide use of the Internet and the need to make many types of message secure demands that users can send them knowing that they cannot be read by a hacker. The arrival of an information superhighway conveying a greater number of message for a large number of different purposes makes message security essential.

Benefits and growth

In discussing the arrival of digital television, believe 'it can only be understood in the widest possible context, if at all ....we can only speculate about some of the possibilities.... many issues remain questions'. These remarks occur in a section of his article entitled 'Some imponderables and creative hurdles'. Although this part of his article is about the board imponderables in digital television, I am giving list the new title of 'Evolutionary uncertainties affecting an information superhighway'. This title describes its contents equally well. A formidable list of questions is provided by the author.

1. How will computer architectures, operating systems, and databases change to encompass digital video?
2. Will advanced services such as HDTV, interactivity, and home information systems becomes commercial as the result of entertainment processors in every home?
3. Will digital video mature to become a software utility? What new algorithms will become part of the repertoire ?
4. How will entertainment, information access, and home-office needs be satisfied by a customized integration of different of different video, networking, and service modules ?
5. How will the competition in the local distribution of video emerge ?

   Telephone, satellite, cable, terrestrial broadcast, and package media may compete, combine, or divide distribution among them based on content. What impact will this have on the emergence of technology ?
6. How will the diverse needs of commercial users merge with entertainment ?
7. When will content-based browsing, filtering, and assembly of multimedia databases become practical ?

❑ ❑ ❑

Index

C

J

K

L

Q

R

U

V

***